Thomas More's Trial by Jury

Thomas More's Trial by Jury

A Procedural and Legal Review
with a Collection of Documents

Edited by

Henry Ansgar Kelly, Louis W. Karlin,
and Gerard B. Wegemer

THE BOYDELL PRESS

© Contributors 2011

All Rights Reserved. Except as permitted under current legislation no part of this work may be photocopied, stored in a retrieval system, published, performed in public, adapted, broadcast, transmitted, recorded or reproduced in any form or by any means, without the prior permission of the copyright owner

First published 2011
The Boydell Press, Woodbridge
Paperback edition 2013

Transferred to digital printing

ISBN 978 1 84383 629 2 hardback
ISBN 978 1 84383 873 9 paperback

The Boydell Press is an imprint of Boydell & Brewer Ltd
PO Box 9, Woodbridge, Suffolk IP12 3DF, UK
and of Boydell & Brewer Inc.
668 Mt Hope Avenue, Rochester, NY 14620–2731, USA
website: www.boydellandbrewer.com

A catalogue record for this book is available
from the British Library

The publisher has no responsibility for the continued existence or accuracy of URLs for external or third-party internet websites referred to in this book, and does not guarantee that any content on such websites is, or will remain, accurate or appropriate.

This publication is printed on acid-free paper

Contents

List of Contributors	ix
Preface	xi
Thomas More in History	xi
The Background to the Trial	xiv
The Trial	xv
Abbreviations	xviii
Chronology	xix
1 A Procedural Review of Thomas More's Trial	**1**
Henry Ansgar Kelly	
Introduction	1
The Official Records of the Trial	3
The Indictment	6
The Conduct of the Trial	16
The First Part of the Accusation: Silence	18
The Second and Third Parts: Collusion with Fisher	31
The Last Part of the Indictment: More's Alleged Statement to Richard Rich	35
The Jury's Verdict	38
Post-Verdict Events: Alternative Versions	41
Jury System vs. Inquisitorial System	46
Conclusion	48
2 Natural Law and the Trial of Thomas More	**53**
R. H. Helmholz	
Introduction	53
The Right to Silence	56
The Necessity of Proof	59
The Rights of Conscience	63
The Invalidity of the Henrician Statute	66
Conclusion	69
3 A Guide to Thomas More's Trial for Modern Lawyers	**71**
Louis W. Karlin and David R. Oakley	
Introduction	71
Jurisdiction	72
Substantive Law of Treason and More's Defenses	73
Arrest and Detention	78
Grand Jury/Indictment	79

Arraignment/Plea	81
Role of Petty Jury	82
Role of Judges	84
Trial Rights and Practice	85
Post-Trial Rights and Practice	89
More's Initial Refusal of the Oath of Succession and His Final Argument at Trial	90

4 Thomas More's Three Prison Letters Reporting on His Interrogations — 94
Elizabeth McCutcheon

Overview	94
Letter of *c.* April 17, 1534	97
Letter of May 2 or 3, 1535	100
Letter of June 3, 1535	102
Recapitulation	106
Appendix: Interrogations of Thomas More between April 13, 1534 and June 14, 1535	109

5 Judicial Commentary on Thomas More's Trial — 111

Preliminary Comment	111
Michael Tugendhat	
Round Table	119
Edith Jones, Sidney Fitzwater, Jennie Latta, Michael Tugendhat	

Appendix 1: Documents — 137

1	Act of Recognizing Henry VIII as Supreme Head of the Church in England (Nov.–Dec. 1534)	137
2	Act of Treasons (Nov.–Dec. 1534)	138
3	Trial of Charterhouse Priors Houghton, Webster, and Lawrence and the Bridgettine Monk Reynolds, April 23–29, 1535 (Bag of Secrets)	140
4	More's Letter of May 2/3, 1535	142
5	Tower Interrogation of More, June 3, 1535	145
6	More's Letter of June 3, 1535	145
7	Trial of Charterhouse Monks Middlemore, Exmew, and Newdigate, June 1–11, 1535 (Bag of Secrets)	148
8	Interrogations of Tower Servants, June 7–11, 1535	150
9	Richard Rich's Report on Thomas More, June 12, 1535	157
10	Tower Interrogation of Fisher, June 12, 1535	159
11	Tower Interrogations of Fisher and More, June 14, 1535	163
12	Trial of Bishop Fisher, June 1–17, 1535 (Bag of Secrets)	165
13	Cromwell's Rembrances, *c.* June 18, 1535	167
14	Henry VIII's Order to Publicize the Guilt of Fisher and More, June 25, 1535	169
15	More's Trial, June 26–July 1, 1535 (Bag of Secrets)	172
16	More's Indictment	175
17	Guildhall Report	186
18	Spelman's Report	195
19	Pole's Account	196

20 Roper's Account   203
Appendix 2: Thomas More's Trial: Docudrama   210
Bibliography   223
Index   233

Contributors

Sidney Fitzwater, JD (Baylor), is Chief Judge of the United States District Court of the North District of Texas, and serves as Chair of the Advisory Committee on Evidence Rules of the Judicial Conference of the United States. He was appointed a United States District Judge in 1986 and served as a state judge from 1982 to 1986.

R. H. Helmholz is Ruth Wyatt Rosenson Distinguished Service Professor of Law at the University of Chicago. His publications include *Canon Law and the Law of England* (1987), *Roman Canon Law in Reformation England* (1990), *The Oxford History of the Laws of England*, vol. 1: *The Canon Law and Ecclesiastical Jurisdiction from 597 to the 1640s* (2004), and, with others, *The Privilege Against Self-Incrimination* (1997).

Edith Hollan Jones, JD (Texas), is Chief Judge of the United States Fifth Circuit Court of Appeals. She was appointed a Federal Judge to that court in 1985 and has served as Chief Judge since 2006.

Louis W. Karlin, JD (UCLA), Fellow of the Center for Thomas More Studies, University of Dallas, is Research Attorney for the California Court of Appeal, Second District, in Los Angeles, and author of papers on Thomas More's *History of Richard III*, *Dialogue Concerning Heresies*, and *The Life of John Pico*.

Henry Ansgar Kelly is past Director of the Center for Medieval and Renaissance Studies at the University of California, Los Angeles (UCLA), and currently Editor of the Center's journal, *Viator*. Among his writings are *The Matrimonial Trials of Henry VIII* (1976), *Inquisitions and Other Trials Procedures in the Medieval West* (2001), "Thomas More on Inquisitorial Due Process" (2008), and *Law and Religion in Chaucer's England* (2010).

Jennie D. Latta, JD (Memphis), is Bankruptcy Judge in the Western District of Tennessee and author of publications on property and bankruptcy laws. She was appointed a Federal Judge of that court in 1987. She is also a doctoral candidate in philosophy at the University of Memphis.

Elizabeth McCutcheon is Professor Emerita and retired Chair of Graduate Studies at the University of Hawaii, and past President of Amici Thomae Mori and Editor of *Moreana*. She is author of *Sir Nicholas Bacon's Great House Sententiae: The Latin Text along with the First English Translation* (1977), *My Dear Peter: The Ars Poetica and Hermeneutics of More's Utopia* (1983), and "More's Rhetoric" in *The Cambridge Companion to Thomas More* (2011).

David R. Oakley, JD (Georgetown), Partner, Anderl and Oakley, PC (Princeton, NJ and Perth Amboy, NJ) specializes in the area of criminal defense. He is a Fellow of the Center for Thomas More Studies at the University of Dallas.

Sir Michael Tugendhat, QC, Judge of the High Court, Queen's Bench Division, is author of publications on data protection and libel law and, with Iain Christie, of *The Law of Privacy and the Media* (2002, 2010).

Gerard B. Wegemer is Professor of English and Director of the Center for Thomas More Studies at the University of Dallas, and author of *Thomas More: A Portrait of Courage* (1995), *Thomas More on Statesmanship* (1996), *Young Thomas More and the Arts of Liberty* (2011), and co-editor of *A Thomas More Source Book* (2004).

Preface

Thomas More in History

Thomas More is one of the most famous persons in history. His life spanned the last part of the fifteenth century and the first part of the sixteenth century. Just as the best-known figures of the fifteenth century are undoubtedly Joan of Arc and Christopher Columbus, as was asserted by the Devil's Advocate at the opening of Joan's canonization trial in 1892,[1] it could be argued that More ranks as one of the most familiar historical persons of the first half of the sixteenth century, along with Martin Luther and Henry VIII. Henry VIII and Thomas More joined together at first to oppose Luther and what they perceived as heresies in his writings, but they would later come to a parting of minds. They differed less on doctrine and faith than on Church law and discipline, with More considering Henry not a heretic but rather a schismatic, an advocate of caesaro-papism, "the supremacy of the civil power in the control of ecclesiastical affairs."[2]

But More is perhaps the most elusive of these five persons, despite the many biographies and studies about him and his accomplishments and his eventual downfall at the hands of his king, his one-time friend and enemy at the end, Henry VIII.

Until fairly recently, More was undoubtedly most familiar as the cheerful humanist whose fanciful *Utopia* caught the imagination of the whole world of his time and has retained its fascination to this day, along with the adjective that memorializes it, "utopian." For a long time he was admired on all sides, and especially since the midpoints of the twentieth century, as the protagonist of Robert Bolt's *A Man for All Seasons* (the play of 1960 and film of 1966).[3] At the time of the celebration of the 500th anniversary of More's birth in 1977, the historian Hugh Trevor-Roper summed up this positive view when he said that More is "the first great Englishman whom we feel that we know, the most saintly of humanists, the most human of saints, the universal man of our cool northern renaissance."[4]

---

[1] H. A. Kelly, "Joan of Arc's Last Trial: The Attack of the Devil's Advocates," in *Fresh Verdicts on Joan of Arc*, ed. Bonnie Wheeler and Charles T. Wood (New York, 1996), pp. 205–38, at 208.
[2] Rightly pointed out by Seymour Baker House, "More, Sir Thomas," *ODNB*, section on "Opposition to the Royal Divorce."
[3] Robert Bolt, *A Man for All Seasons: A Play in Two Acts* (London, 1960). Bolt wrote the screenplay for the Columbia Pictures film, which was directed by Fred Zinnemann.
[4] Reported by R. W. Apple, Jr, "Gallery in London Presents an Exhibition for All Seasons," *New York Times*, December 4, 1977, as having been spoken "a few days ago." Trever-Roper's comment is cited by Marvin O'Connell, "A Man for All Seasons: An Historian's Demur," *Catholic Dossier* 8 no. 2 (March–April 2002), 16–19.

But in more recent times, the tide seems to have turned against More in many quarters, especially with regard to his approval of the death penalty for convicted heretics.[5] Even in earlier decades More had his critics. Herschel Baker, professor of English at Harvard, during a course he was teaching in 1962 on "Religious Backgrounds on Sixteenth-Century Literature," commented that if he had been on Thomas More's canonization panel he would have voted against bestowing the honor upon him, since More was a successful politician, a status incompatible with sanctity.[6]

More's beatification (the first step towards canonization) took place in 1886, along with 53 other Englishmen, including Bishop John Fisher and the seven monks convicted of the same offense.[7] All were declared martyrs, meaning that they did not have to pass muster on the outstanding holiness of their lives; it was sufficient that they could be shown to have died for the Catholic faith. The most celebrated of all devil's advocates, Cardinal Prospero Lambertini, who later became Pope Benedict XIV (1740–58), gave the example of Mary Queen of Scots as a perfect example of someone who could easily be declared a martyr because of her motivations at her death and the motivations of those who tried her and executed her.[8] In the *Roman Martyrology*, however, More is lauded not only as a martyr for his fidelity to the Catholic faith, after having been imprisoned for resisting King Henry's repudiation of his marriage and the primacy of the pope, but also as a family man of the most upright life and as head of his country's legislature.[9]

---

[5] As House says ("More, Sir Thomas"), "No other aspect of More's life has engendered greater controversy than his persecution of heretics. Critics argue that as one of Europe's leading intellectuals, and one with particularly strong humanist leanings, More should have rejected capital punishment of heretics. His supporters point out that he was a product of his times, and that those men he most admired (including Bishop Fisher, also martyred by Henry VIII) lamented but accepted as necessary the practice of executing heretics." A recent popular novel, *Wolf Hall*, by Hilary Mantel (London, 2009), which has as its protagonist a sensitive and thoughtful Thomas Cromwell, presents More as dour and humorless, a torturer of heresy suspects, who gets his comeuppance when he is condemned to death and executed.
[6] Testimony of H. A. Kelly, present in class.
[7] F. G. Holweck, *A Biographical Dictionary of the Saints* (St Louis, MO, 1924), p. 979.
[8] Benedict XIV, *Opus de servorum Dei beatificatione et beatorum canonizatione*, 7 vols (Prato, 1839–42), 3:119 (3.13.10). For the trial of Mary Queen of Scots and her execution under Queen Elizabeth (1586–87), see Jayne Elizabeth Lewis, *The Trial of Mary Queen of Scots: A Brief History with Document* (Boston, 1999).
[9] *Martyrologium Romanum*, new edition (Vatican City, 2001, rev. 2004), entry of June 22 (p. 348): "Sanctorum Ioannis Fisher, episcopi, et Thomae More, martyrum, qui, cum Henrico regi Octavo in controversia de eius matrimonio repudiando et de Romani Pontificis primatu restitissent, in Turrem Londonii in Anglia trusi sunt. Ioannes Fisher, episcopus Roffensis, vir eruditione et dignitate vitae clarissimus, hac die iussu ipsius Regis ante carcerem decollatus est; Thomas More vero, paterfamilias vita integerrimus et praeses coetus moderatorum nationis, propter fidelitatem erga Ecclesiam catholicam servatam, sexta die Iulii cum venerabili antistite martyrio coniunctus est" ("The feast of Saints John Fisher, bishop, and Thomas More, martyrs, who, when they resisted King Henry VIII in the controversy concerning the repudiation of his marriage and the primacy of the Roman Pontiff, were thrust into the Tower of London in England. John Fisher, Bishop of Rochester, a man famous for his learning and dignity, was beheaded this day before the prison by order of the said king, while Thomas More, the head of a family, most upright in his life, and leader of the body of legislators of his nation, because he remained faithful to the Catholic Church, was joined in martyrdom with the venerable prelate on the sixth day of July"). In the previous edition, ed. Cuthbert John and Anthony

In contrast, Joan of Arc, although she too was condemned to death in a trial organized by the English government, but in an ecclesiastical court, was not declared a martyr when she was beatified in 1909, but only a holy virgin (if she were a man, she would have been called a confessor), even though her trial and condemnation were later repudiated and overturned by a papal commission. In such a case, when the candidate for sainthood was not classed as a martyr, it was necessary to prove, in a lengthy trial before the cardinals in Rome, that she or he had lived a life of heroic virtue. The entry in the *Roman Martyrology* says of Joan only that she fought bravely for her country and was condemned to be burned to death by her enemies in an iniquitous trial.[10]

We note that there is no reference in the *Martyrology* citation for More to any iniquity in the trial that convicted him, but there are many interesting similarities between his trial and that of Joan, even though Joan was prosecuted under the inquisitorial process, a procedure employed as well in English Church courts, including the Legatine trial of 1529,[11] whereas More was tried under the jury system of English common law. More had defended the fairness of the inquisitorial system as employed by English bishops against heresy suspects in his controversy with Christopher St German in 1533, in his *Apology* and *Debellation*.[12] But in the case of Joan of Arc, contrary to the requirements of Church law, Joan's judge, Bishop Pierre Cauchon (who was receiving a *per diem* stipend from the English) followed the abusive practices of many Continental heresy-inquisitors: he did not charge her with specific crimes committed in the past, but only with statements she made during a month of enforced interrogation.[13] Similarly, the charges against More were compiled from statements he allegedly made – and failed to make – during his time in prison.

Recently, Bishop Cauchon has found a defender for the validity of the procedures he used in prosecuting Joan,[14] and the trial of More has also found cham-

---

Ward (Rome, 1998), the entry for More, under July 6, reads: "Londini, in Anglia, sancti Thomae More, regni Cancellarii, qui, pro fide catholica ac beati Petri primatu, jubente Henrico Octavo rege, decollatus est" ("At London, in England, [the feast] of Thomas More, Chancellor of the realm, who was beheaded by order of King Henry VIII for the Catholic faith and the primacy of St Peter") (p. 162).

[10] *Martyrologium Romanum*, p. 312 (May 30): "Rothomagi in Normannia Galliae, sanctae Ioannae d'Arc, virginis, puellae Aurelianensis nuncupatae, quae, cum fortiter pro patria dimicasset, tandem, in hostium potestatem tradita, iniquo iudicio condemnata est et igne cremata" ("At Rouen in Normandy in France, the feast of St Joan of Arc, virgin, called the Maid of Orleans, who, after fighting valiantly for her country, was at last betrayed into the power of the enemy and in a wicked tribunal condemned and burned").

[11] Inquisitorial procedure was used not only in the Legatine trial of the marriage of Henry VIII and Catherine of Aragon, but also in the trials conducted by Archbishop Cranmer for the annulment of Henry's marriage to Catherine in 1533, and for the annulment of his marriage to Anne Boleyn in May 1536 (conducted simultaneously with her treason trial), less than a year after the treason trials of Fisher and More. See H. A. Kelly, *The Matrimonial Trials of Henry VIII* (Stanford, CA, 1976).

[12] H. A. Kelly, "Thomas More on Inquisitorial Due Process," *English Historical Review* 123 (2008), 847–94.

[13] H. A. Kelly, "The Right to Remain Silent: Before and After Joan of Arc," *Speculum* 68 (1993), repr. in *Inquisitions* as ch. 3, pp. 992–1026; idem, "Saint Joan and Confession: Internal and External Forum," in *Joan of Arc and Spirituality*, ed. Ann W. Astell and Bonnie Wheeler (New York, 2003), pp. 60–84.

[14] Daniel Hobbins, *The Trial of Joan of Arc* (Cambridge, MA, 2005), Introduction, pp. 1–32. I am

pions as well as denigrators. It is the purpose of this volume to review the known facts and reports about his prosecution, and to offer new "positions" and conclusions.

The Background to the Trial

Thomas More, the son of a prominent judge, Sir John More, was unusual in receiving both a humanist and a legal education. He became a member of Parliament in 1504 and undersheriff of London in 1510. He early attracted the attention and friendship of the young Henry VIII, who was still only 17 when he became king in 1509, shortly before he married Catherine of Aragon, his brother's widow. More was named master of requests and a privy councillor in 1518, and was knighted in 1521. On the recommendation of the chancellor, Cardinal Wolsey, More became speaker of the House of Commons in 1523.

Henry began to press for an annulment of his marriage to Catherine of Aragon in 1527, and when the trial of the matter in 1529 by the papal legates Cardinal Wolsey and Cardinal Campeggio was suspended and advoked to Rome, Wolsey was removed from his office as chancellor of the realm. Henry offered the position to More, who accepted it only on condition that he would not be required to support the annulment initiative. This initiative soon fell under the direction of Thomas Cromwell, Wolsey's former assistant, and one prominent aspect of the campaign was to assert English royal control, as opposed to papal control, over local ecclesiastical matters. Early in 1531, the clergy of the Province of Canterbury were coerced into agreeing to call Henry the Supreme Head of the Church in England, "as far as the law of Christ allowed." When the clergy further yielded their independence to the king in 1532, More resigned as chancellor.

In 1534, Parliament passed the Act of Succession, requiring subjects when asked to confirm by oath their agreement to the right of the offspring of Henry and Anne Boleyn to succeed to the throne. More refused to take the oath that was presented to him, presumably because it included approval of the annulment of the marriage of Henry and Catherine, and he was imprisoned, in anticipation of being tried and convicted of violating the statute. The stipulated crime for refusing the oath, however, was not treason, which carried a death penalty, but rather the lesser offense of misprision of treason, which carried the penalty of life in prison (More however was never tried for this crime).

Towards the end of the same year, 1534, Parliament passed three more statutes that would affect More, one convicting him of misprision by attainder, another recognizing Henry as Supreme Head of the Church in England, and the third declaring it treason to oppose any royal title by word or deed. It is important to note that, even though the penalty for infringing the third statute was the hanging, drawing, and quartering imposed upon persons convicted of treason, this statute (the Act of Treasons), unlike the Act of Succession with its mandatory oath, carried no requirement to give a positive affirmation on any subject.

---

preparing a response, "Questions of Due Process in the Trial of Joan of Arc," in a volume of studies of famous trials.

The two latter statutes came into effect on February 1, 1535, and in the next months a total of nine persons were tried, convicted, and executed for opposing the king's new title: three Carthusian priors and a Bridgettine monk in April, three Carthusian monks in early June, Bishop Fisher in mid-June, and More at the end of June, with conviction on July 1 and execution on July 6 (like Fisher and More, the six Carthusians and the Bridgettine monks have been canonized). All of these trials will be reviewed below.

The Trial

The trial in which More was convicted of treason was long denounced as a typical political miscarriage of justice, with participants simply doing the bidding of the reigning tyrant. But in comparatively recent times, specifically since 1964, the trial has been taken seriously as a carefully prepared and executed judicial process in which the judges were amenable to reasonable arguments. We, however, have reasons to disagree with this consensus, and wish to open the case for reassessment. To that end we have assembled together all of the surviving testimonies to the trial for a re-examination.

The official records of the trial, contained in the "Bag of Secrets," are quite meager. There is the text of the commission of oyer and terminer appointed on June 26, 1535, to try Thomas More for treason, and the bill of indictment produced by the commissioners, together with the report that it was found to be a true bill by a grand jury, and the further report that More was charged with the listed crimes, to which he pleaded not guilty, but then was found guilty by a petty jury. No account is to be found here of the actual conduct of the trial. The most important item is the indictment, from which we can tell exactly what More was charged with.

He was charged with violating a combination of two of the statutes that had been passed by Parliament in the previous November–December (1534). As noted above, the first statute acknowledged the king and his successors to be Supreme Head of the Church in England, and the second statute declared that anyone who maliciously wished by words or writing "or by craft attempted" to do any harm against the king or queen, "or to deprive them of the dignity, title, or name of their royal estates," would be guilty of high treason. The indictment, however, leaves out the qualification about words or writing or craft. It accuses More of violating the statute in three ways: first, by maliciously remaining silent when questioned about the king's title of supremacy; second, by maliciously conspiring with Bishop John Fisher to deprive the king of this title; and third, by maliciously asserting to Solicitor General Richard Rich that Parliament did not have the right to declare the king Supreme Head of the English Church.

There are two main accounts of what went on at the trial. One is by an eyewitness, whose report was quickly disseminated abroad, especially in a French version known today as the *Paris News Letter*. The original account was in Latin, and it is best preserved in a Guildhall manuscript (**Doc. 17**). The second main account was by More's son-in-law William Roper, written 20 years after the event, on the basis of what certain persons who attended the trial recounted to him.

There is this major, crucial difference between the two accounts: the Guildhall version reports that only three charges were levied against More, namely, malicious silence and two instances of malicious conspiracy with Fisher, and it was on the basis of these three charges that the jury found him guilty. Roper's account, on the contrary, makes it appear that there was only the single charge of making an assertion to Richard Rich impugning the royal supremacy.

The consensus resolution (spearheaded by Professor J. Duncan M. Derrett) between the two accounts is that More's objections against the parts of the indictment were sustained by the judges, and that these charges were dismissed; and, as a consequence, More pleaded not guilty only to the last part, dealing with Richard Rich. However, apart from the fact that there is nothing at all to suggest that the judges responded favorably to any of More's arguments, and the unlikelihood that these judges, some of whom had undoubtedly helped to construct the case against More, would so easily have dropped most of it, there are positive reasons to doubt this analysis of events, which will be set forth in the procedural analysis by Henry Ansgar Kelly, in which it is concluded that More was charged and convicted on the whole indictment.

Prominent among the reasons for this conclusion are the accounts of the trial given by Henry VIII's cousin, Reginald Pole (who would go on to become a cardinal and Archbishop of Canterbury in Queen Mary's reign), based on an eyewitness report, and the account given by one of the judges at the trial, Sir John Spelman.

As is well known to historians and laymen alike, notably from Bolt's *A Man for All Seasons*, the final charge relied upon the testimony of Richard Rich, which was denounced by More as perjured. We will show that there are extant two accounts of More's conversation with Rich, one in the report that Rich made, which formed the basis of the indictment charge, and the other as reported by Roper. We conclude that Roper's account is More's version of the exchange, in which he denied that Parliament had the power to make a person pope, whereas by Rich's account, followed by the indictment, More denied Parliament the power to make Henry Head of the English Church.

As for what happened after the verdict was announced, we have three different accounts. According to the eyewitness account represented in the Guildhall Report, More revealed his real opinion concerning the Statutes upon which he had been convicted and sentenced to death, in order to exonerate his conscience. According to Pole's account, however, More had refrained from giving his opinion about the law declaring the king Supreme Head of the English Church in order not to harm his defense. But once he was found guilty, he spoke out in order to prevent Englishmen from accepting, out of ignorance or imprudence, what he now termed was a pestiferous statute that was inimical to them. Finally, according to the Roper account, More acted on his earlier promise to speak against the indictment after an adverse verdict came in, but before the sentence of death was imposed. According to this report, More spoke in order to void the indictment, on the grounds that the Statute was contrary to the laws of the Church as a whole, and also contrary to Magna Carta and the laws of England.

The consensus view, following Derrett, is that the Roper account is the most accurate, showing that More was making a standard motion to overturn the verdict. There is, however, no evidence that such a motion was ever used in criminal cases in the sixteenth century.

The question of whether the judges should have accepted More's alleged motion has been considered the only legal difficulty raised by the trial, but we have isolated what we consider to be a more important question: whether the judges treated More fairly and according to law in not accepting his contention that he did not fall under the Treasons Statute. More argued, first, that he did nothing by spoken or written word or by deed to impugn the king's title, and specifically, that his silence, or refusal to speak on the subject, should be not construed as opposition but, if anything, as affirmation; and, secondly, that he did nothing out of malice, which was a necessary condition for incurring the statutory censure.

These points will be discussed not only in the procedural review below, where the parallel proceedings against Bishop Fisher will also be discussed, and in R. H. Helmholz's discussion of natural-law principles and requirements, but also in the review of major legal issues by Louis Karlin and David Oakley, which will focus on a comparison between sixteenth-century and modern law, and in the discussion in chapter 5 by Justice Michael Tudendhat and in the round table participated in by him and Judges Edith Jones, Sidney Fitzwater, and Jennie Latta at a conference on More's trial held at the University of Dallas, November 7, 2008. Elizabeth McCutcheon's essay deals with the interrogations of More in the Tower, which formed the main basis of the charges against him.

All of these discussions are keyed to the pertinent documents here included, which are re-edited and, where appropriate, provided with English translations, with the expectation that the presentation of these sources together will help to put the trial events into perspective. In this way we hope that greater justice will be done to the facts and meaning of the facts of More's trial than has been done in the past.

In an appendix, we present a docudrama or dramatic reading of More's trial, based on the reports of the Guildhall witness, Spelman, Pole, and Roper, to suggest a plausible, though obviously conjectural, sequence of the events of the process that ended in the conviction and execution of Sir Thomas More.

Henry Ansgar Kelly
Louis W. Karlin
Gerard B. Wegemer
July 1, 2011

Abbreviations

CJC	*Corpus Juris Canonici.* 3 vols. Rome, 1582. Available online at http://digital.library.ucla.edu/canonlaw
Correspondence	*The Correspondence of Sir Thomas More.* Ed. Elizabeth Frances Rogers. Princeton, NJ, 1947
CW	*Complete Works of St Thomas More.* 15 vols. New Haven, CT, 1963–97
DNB	*Dictionary of National Biography.* 22 vols. London, 1908–9
Last Letters	*The Last Letters of Thomas More.* Ed. Alvaro de Silva. Grand Rapids, MI, 2000
LP	*Letters and Papers, Foreign and Domestic, of the Reign of Henry VIII.* 23 vols. in 38. Vols. 1–4 ed. J. S. Brewer; vols. 5–13 ed. James Gairdner; vols. 14–21 ed. James Gairdner and R. H. Brodie. Emended repr. Vaduz, 1965
MED	*Middle English Dictionary.* 17 vols. Ann Arbor, MI, 1952–2001
OED	*Oxford English Dictionary.* 20 vols. 2nd edn. Oxford, 1989. 3rd edn, online (in progress)
ODNB	*Oxford Dictionary of National Biography.* 60 vols. Oxford, 2004
PRO	Public Record Office (in The National Archives, Kew)

Chronology

March 26, 1534: Act of Succession (25 H8 c. 22), effective May 1, 1534, penalty of high treason for maliciously writing or acting against it, misprision of treason for maliciously talking against it, and misprision of treason for obstinately refusing an oath to support the Act

April 13, 1534: An oath of succession is put to More at Lambeth Palace, which he refuses

April 17, 1534: More imprisoned in the Tower for his refusal

November–December, 1534

    Act recognizing the king as Supreme Head of the Church in England (26 H8 c. 1) (**Doc. 1**)

    Act giving the text of the required oath of succession (26 H8 c. 2)

    Act making it high treason to maliciously deprive the king and Queen of the dignity, title, or name of their royal estates, by word or deed; effective February 1, 1535 (26 H8 c. 13) (**Doc. 2**)

    Act of attainder against Bishop Fisher and others, convicting them of misprision of treason for refusing the oath of succession (26 H8 c. 22)

    Act of attainder against Thomas More, convicting him of misprision of treason for refusing the oath of succession. (26 H8 c. 23)

April 23–29, 1535: Trial of three Carthusian priors and one Bridgettine monk (**Doc. 3**)

April 30 (Friday), 1535: More interrogated by Cromwell, Hales, Rich, Bedill, and Tregonwell (dated by More, **Doc. 4**, §2; dated May 7 in the indictment, **Doc. 16**, §4)

May 2–3, 1535: More's letter to Margaret (**Doc. 4**)

May 12, 1535: More writes to John Fisher; see indictment §5

May 26, 1535: More writes to John Fisher; see indictment §6

June 1–11, 1535: Trial of Carthusian monks (**Doc. 7**)

June 1–17, 1535: Trial of Bishop Fisher (**Doc. 12**)

June 3, 1535: More and Fisher interrogated separately; see indictment §§7, 9; **Docs 5 and 6**

June 12, 1535: Richard Rich's disputed conversation with More; see indictment §11; **Doc. 9**

June 14, 1535: More interrogated again (**Doc. 11**)

June 18, 1535: The Carthusian monks hanged

c. June 19, 1535: Cromwell's remembrances concerning Fisher and More; **Doc. 13**

June 22, 1535: Bishop John Fisher beheaded

June 26, 1535: Commission of oyer and terminer concerning More (**Doc. 15**)

June 28, 1535: Grand jury meets, accepts indictment (**Doc. 15**)

July 1, 1535: More charged and found guilty (**Docs. 15–20**)

July 6, 1535: More's execution by beheading (**Doc. 17**, §15)

1

A Procedural Review of Thomas More's Trial

Henry Ansgar Kelly

Introduction

From the very beginning the trial of Thomas More, like that of Queen Anne Boleyn, was widely condemned as a travesty of justice, and this characterization lasted into the twentieth century; it was a kangaroo court organized by the unscrupulous secretary of the tyrant Henry VIII, Thomas Cromwell.

It cannot be denied that the king considered the outcome of the trial to be a foregone conclusion. As James Gairdner, in calendaring the state papers of Henry VIII's reign, pointed out long ago, the king issued a circular letter on June 25, 1535 ordering the treasons of Bishop John Fisher and Sir Thomas More to be set forth to the people. This was after Fisher had been convicted and executed, but before More had gone to trial.[1] But in comparatively recent times the trial has been taken seriously as a carefully conducted judicial process that holds up well under modern legal scrutiny.

This revisionist view of More's trial was chiefly the achievement of J. Duncan M. Derrett in the assessment that he published in 1964 in the *English Historical Review*, "The Trial of Sir Thomas More," which he brought out in a slightly revised form in 1977.[2] Derrett is Emeritus Professor of Oriental Laws at the University of London, where he taught Hindu law from 1949 to 1982. In the year following his essay on More's trial, his inaugural professorial lecture was titled, "An Oriental Lawyer Looks at the Trial of Jesus and the Doctrine of the Redemption."[3] But the study of early English law was also well within his scholarly purview. His essay on the trial and many of his other writings show

---

[1] Gairdner, *LP* 8, January–July 1535 (1885), Preface, p. xxxix; cited also by T. E. Bridgett, *Life and Writings of Blessed Thomas More, Lord Chancellor of England and Martyr under Henry VIII* (London, 1904), p. 425. For the entire circular letter in question, see **Doc. 14**.

[2] J. Duncan M. Derrett, "The Trial of Sir Thomas More," in *Essential Articles for the Study of Thomas More*, ed. R. S. Sylvester and G. P. Marc'hadour (Hamden, CT, 1977), pp. 55–78, 591–6, revised from its original form in the *English Historical Review* 79 (1964), 449–77.

[3] J. Duncan M. Derrett, *An Oriental Lawyer Looks at the Trial of Jesus and the Doctrine of the Redemption: An Inaugural Lecture Delivered on 21 October 1965* (London, 1966).

that he is an expert Latinist and highly trained in the history of English law.[4] In 1960, four years before his *EHR* article, he published a very valuable edition of what he established as the earliest eyewitness account of More's trial, which I will refer to, in modified form, as the Guildhall Report, edited and translated in the Documents below.[5]

Derrett's reconstruction of the More trial has been taken as definitive ever since it first appeared, as witnessed, for example, by the Tudor historians Sir Geoffrey Elton[6] and John Guy.[7] His main conclusions have also been supported by the pre-eminent historian of English law for this period, Sir John Baker, first in the introduction to his 1977–78 edition of the law reports of Sir John Spelman (one of More's judges), and more recently, in 2003, in his volume in *The Oxford History of the Laws of England*.[8]

However, I believe that there is room for serious discussion and reconsideration at every step of the trial, and one of Derrett's main conclusions, that most of the charges against More were dropped, is especially dubious. On this point,

---

[4] Derrett was a scholar in classics of Jesus College, Oxford (1940–42, 1945–47). He took an MA from Oxford and a PhD from London, and qualified as a barrister-at-law.

[5] J. Duncan M. Derrett, "Neglected Versions of the Contemporary Account of the Trial of Sir Thomas More," *Bulletin of the Institute of Historical Research* 33 (1960), 202–23,at pp. 214–23. For my edition of the Guildhall Report see **Doc. 17**. Derrett also edits here the *Paris News Letter*'s French text, which he shows to be a translation of the original Latin text.

Another very important article of Derrett's on the trial is "The 'New' Document on Thomas More's Trial," *Moreana* 3 (June 1964), 5–19, with comments of E. E. Reynolds, pp. 20–2. Other pertinent essays by Derrett are: "Thomas More and the Legislation of the Corporation of London," *The Guildhall Miscellany* 2.5 (1963), 175–80, repr. in *Essential Articles*, ed. Sylvester and Marc'hadour, pp. 49–54, 589–91; "More's Conveyance of His Lands and the Law of 'Fraud,'" *Moreana* 5 (Feb. 1965), 19–26; "More's Attainder and Dame Alice's Predicament," *Moreana* 6 (May 1965), 9–26; "Sir Thomas More and the Nun of Kent," *Moreana* 15–16 (Sept.-Nov. 1967), 267–84; "*Juramentum in Legem*: St Thomas More's Crisis of Conscience and the 'Good Roman,'" *The Downside Review* 91 (1973), 111–16; "The Affairs of Richard Hunne and Friar Standish," Appendix B in Thomas More, *The Apology*, ed. J. B. Trapp, *CW*, 9: 215–46; "More's Silence and His Trial," *Moreana* 87–8 (Nov. 1985), 25–7. His latest article on More is, "More and How to Choose a Wife," *Moreana* 168–70 (Dec. 2006, March–June 2007), 222–4.

[6] G. R. Elton, *Policy and Police* (Cambridge, 1972), p. 409: "More faced the court on July 1st, in one of the famous trial scenes of history. Famous indeed, but only recently correctly interpreted. Mr Derrett's reconstruction has produced as accurate an account as we are ever likely to have, and the detail of events is best read in his paper." Elton's own account of the trial is on pp. 409–17.

[7] John Guy, *Thomas More* (London, 2000), p. 205 n. 5: "On all procedural and legal matters concerning More's trial, I have followed Derrett, whose article is considered definitive." Guy covers the trial in chapter 10, "Whose Conscience?" (pp. 186–208). See also his account of the trial in *A Daughter's Love: Thomas and Margaret More* (London, 2008), pp. 257–63.

[8] *The Reports of Sir John Spelman*, ed. J. H. Baker, 2 vols, Selden Society 93–4 (London, 1977–78), Introduction, 2:23–396, at pp. 139–40; *The Oxford History of the Laws of England*, vol. 6: *1483–1558* (Oxford, 2003), pp. 417–18. Derrett's conclusions are also accepted by Hubertus Schulte Herbrüggen, "The Process Against Sir Thomas More," *Law Quarterly Review* 99 (1983), 113–36, esp. pp. 129–30 (he cites only the 1964 version of Derrett's article, p. 113 n. 1). Schulte Herbrüggen gives a good review of the sources and early reports of the trial on pp. 114–17.

at least, I find earlier accounts to be more plausible, culminating in the book-length study of E. E. Reynolds, which was also published in 1964.[9]

My mode of proceeding will be to set out and comment upon all aspects of the trial from the beginning to the end, raising whatever questions seem called for. In the interests of historical authenticity, I will be on the alert for anachronistic legal terminology in previous accounts. A chief guide to vocabulary usages of the time will be the Parliamentary statutes.[10]

The Official Records of the Trial

The surviving records of Thomas More's trial, as found in the "Bag of Secrets" (*Baga de Secretis*), are calendared by James Gairdner in the *Letters and Papers of Henry VIII*,[11] and can be summed up thus:

1 Saturday, June 26, 1535: Appointment of a special commission of oyer and terminer for Middlesex County. On the same day, the new commissioners order the sheriff of Middlesex to bring the grand jury before them in Westminster Hall on Monday, June 28.
2 Monday, June 28: The grand jury appears and finds the bill of indictment against Sir Thomas More to be a true bill.
3 Wednesday, June 30: The commissioners order the constable of the Tower, Sir William Kingston, to bring Sir Thomas More before them on Thursday, July 1.
4 Thursday, July 1: Sir Thomas is brought to the commission by Sir Edmund Walsingham, lieutenant of the constable; he pleads not guilty. The commissioners order the sheriff to present a petty jury that very day. He does so, and Sir Thomas is again summoned. The jury returns a verdict of guilty. Judgment is given as usual for high treason, that is, execution at Tyburn.

The commissioners consisted of twelve councillors and a "quorum" of seven justices.[12] The councillors were named in this order:

1 Sir Thomas Audley, chancellor
2 Thomas (Howard), duke of Norfolk (Anne's uncle)
3 Charles (Brandon), duke of Suffolk (married to Henry VIII's sister)
4 Henry (Clifford), earl of Cumberland
5 Thomas (Boleyn), earl of Wiltshire (Anne's father)

---

[9] E. E. Reynolds, *The Trial of St Thomas More* (Montreal, 1964). The Italian translation, *Il processo di Tommaso Moro* (Rome, 1985), contains updated notes by the translator, Marialisa Bertagnoni. Guy, *Daughter's Love*, goes so far as to count the alleged dismissal of charges "the first of two electric moments, since the professional judges upheld his plea in law" (p. 260).
[10] *The Statutes of the Realm*, 12 vols (London, 1810–28, repr. 1963, 1993).
[11] *LP* 8, no. 974, pp. 384–6 (**Doc. 15**).
[12] For an analysis, see Schulte Herbrüggen, "The Process," p. 129.

6   George (Hastings), earl of Huntingdon (father-in-law of Reginald Pole's nieces)[13]
7   Henry (Pole), lord (baron) Montague (brother of Reginald Pole)
8   George Boleyn, lord (viscount) Rochford (Anne's brother)
9   Andrew, lord Windsor (keeper of the Great Wardrobe)
10 Thomas Cromwell, secretary
11 Sir William FitzWilliam (treasurer of the household)
12 Sir William Paulet (comptroller of the household)

The justices were:
1   Sir John FitzJames (chief justice of the King's Bench)
2   Sir John Baldwin (chief justice of Common Pleas)
3   Sir Richard Lister (baron of the Exchequer)
4   Sir John Porte (justice of the King's Bench)
5   Sir John Spelman (justice of the King's Bench)
6   Sir Walter Luke (justice of the King's Bench)
7   Sir Anthony FitzHerbert (justice of Common Pleas)

The same justices had served on the commissions of April 23 (three Carthusian priors and the Bridgettine monk, Richard Reynolds) and June 1 (John Fisher and three Carthusians monks, Humphrey Middlemore, William Exmew, and Sebastian Newdigate).[14] The same was true of some of the councillors: Rochford, Montague, and Cromwell were on the April 23 panel, and Audley, Norfolk, Cumberland, Wiltshire, and Cromwell were on the other. There is, however, no indication in any of our records that Cromwell took an active role in More's actual trial, contrary to Robert Bolt's play, but according to the Bag of Secrets he was present; only Pole's brother Montagne and treasurer FitzWilliam were missing from the bench (**Doc. 15**).

Quite clearly, the sheriff had already gathered candidates for a grand jury when the order came down to him on Saturday. When the jurors appeared on Monday, they were shown the indictment that had already been drawn up, doubtless by Cromwell, whose practice it was in cases of treason prosecution to compose the interrogatories to be put to the suspects beforehand, and then, in due course, to draft the indictments.[15] In this case, we know that he had consulted with the some of the judges before they were named to the commission, since on a page of his "remembrances," or memos for his next visit to the

---

[13] See the entry on Hastings by Claire Cross in the *ODNB*: in 1531 he negotiated the marriage of his eldest son, Francis, to Catherine, eldest daughter and co-heir of Henry Pole, Lord Montague (Reginald's brother), and later obtained Montague's other daughter, Winifred, as wife for one of his younger sons, Thomas.

[14] *LP* 8, no. 609.i (p. 229) (**Doc. 3**); no. 886.i (p. 350) (**Doc. 7**). Two other justices of Common Pleas were included as well in these commissions: Sir Thomas Inglefield and Sir William Shelley. Shelley had served as undersheriff with More, and had been reported to the Council for his opposition to heretical books, "and for the Lent assize of 1535 he was transferred to the home circuit under the watchful eye of his junior, the attorney-general Christopher Hales ... Shelley was dropped from the summer assize of 1535, when the judges were given specific instructions to publicize the supreme headship and the exemplary executions of Fisher and More; he was not commissioned again for almost a decade" (Christopher Whittick, *ODNB*, s.v. Shelley).

[15] John G. Bellamy, *The Tudor Law of Treason* (London, 1979), p. 145.

court, one note reads, "Item to know his [the king's] pleasure touching Maister More"; and to this Cromwell has added, in his own hand: "and to declare the oppynyon of the Jugges theron, & what shalbe the kynge plesure."[16]

The date of this entry, including Cromwell's addition, and of the whole page has been inferred from two other memos further down on the page:

> Item when maister Fissher shall go to execucion with also the other.
> Item what shalbe done farther touching maister More.[17]

In the first, "the other" has been taken to refer to More, meaning that, since the page must be dated to some time before Fisher's execution on June 22, More's conviction was a foregone conclusion already at this point. I, however, believe that this is unlikely, since the next memo is an inquiry about further plans concerning More. I suggest that readers have been thrown off by thinking that "other" must be singular, whereas it could be either singular or plural.[18] If the plural is intended here, it refers in all probability to the three Carthusian monks (Middlemore, Exmew, and Newdigate) who were convicted by the same commission that convicted Fisher (they were found guilty and sentenced on June 11 and Fisher on June 17). If so, since they were not executed until June 19, the page of memos must have been written before that date, and More's fate was still awaiting the king's pleasure.[19]

On the occasion of the presentation of the indictment to the grand jury, the commissioners were represented only by the seven justices on the panel. It was their function to explain the indictment to the jurors, and introduce any witnesses that they wished to support it. Undoubtedly, the jurors simply stamped the ready-made indictment with their approval at the end of a probably very brief session. As usual, no records survive of the grand jury proceedings, and doubtless none were made, since secrecy was the regular rule for the process.[20]

---

[16] J. B. Trapp and Hubertus Schulte Herbrüggen, *"The King's Good Servant": Sir Thomas More, 1477/8–1535* (London, 1977), p. 126, with a photograph of the manuscript front page (bottom part cut off) on the inside front cover (**Doc. 13**). The page is headed "Remembraunces at my next goyng to the Courte." See also David Starkey (guest curator), *Henry VIII: Man and Monarch*, ed. Susan Doran (London, 2009), item 157 (picture of the full top page), p. 159, with description by John Guy, "What to Do about Sir Thomas More?" Guy says of it: "Written out by a clerk, but corrected in Cromwell's own hand, the text relates to a meeting between Cromwell and Henry at Windsor, where the court had moved on 12 June." Gairdner, *LP* 8, no. 892 (p. 353) dates the sheet simply "June" (of 1535).

[17] The next memo is on another subject ("Item touching the conclusion for my lord of Suffolke"), but the following one returns to Fisher: "Item to send vnto the king by Raffe the behauiour of Maister Fissher."

[18] See *OED* s.v. "other" B.4.a for plural examples (e.g., Shakespeare, *Midsummer Night's Dream* 4.1.65: "awaking when the other do").

[19] We need not conclude that the memos were written after Fisher's conviction on June 17; they may have been written earlier, on the assumption that the bishop's fate was a foregone conclusion. If so, then the memo about reporting Fisher's behavior to the King (see n. 17) would most likely refer to an account of his trial.

[20] I refer to the explanation given, for a slightly later period, by J. H. Baker, "Criminal Courts and Procedure at Common Law, 1550–1800" (1977), as reprinted in his collection of essays, *The*

As for the petty jury, the sheriff must have had them at the ready, too. In the similar orders for juries for the trial of Middlemore, Exmew, and Newdigate on June 11 and for Bishop Fisher on June 17, it was specified that the jurors were to be from among "the inhabitants of the Tower."[21] In other words, there was to be no searching at large for candidates.

But before the jurors were summoned on the Thursday, More himself was stood before the commissioners to have the entire indictment presented to him. According to later procedure, at least, as stated by Sir John Baker, "it was necessary that the Indictment itself be in Latin [interpreting a Statute of 1362, and citing cases of 1607 and 1618], but the prisoner was not entitled to have it read in Latin [case of 1661], unless he could assign some error in law upon hearing it [so Matthew Hale, c. 1676]."[22] But we may consider it likely that the whole indictment was read to More in its original Latin.

According to Derrett's interpretation, More's objections against the first three-fourths of the indictment were sustained by the commissioners, and those parts of the indictment were dismissed; and as a consequence he pleaded not guilty only to the last part, dealing with Richard Rich. If so, only this last part of the full indictment would have been explained to the petty jury, and they would have found him guilty only of making a treasonous assertion to Rich. However, I will suggest reasons to doubt this analysis of events.

In a standard criminal trial, More would have been entitled to 20 peremptory challenges to the prospective jurors, but there is nothing in the reports to indicate that he made any objection at all; and, according to Baker, it is questionable whether such challenges were allowed at all in cases of treason.[23]

The Indictment

Contents of the indictment

The Latin indictment against Sir Thomas More, which was found to be a true bill by the grand jury and which was revealed to him in its entirety only as he stood trial on July 1, 1535, before the commission of oyer and terminer, consisted of a range of charges, which were divided into four "articles" by Elsie

---

Legal Profession and the Common Law (London, 1986), pp. 259–301. On pp. 281–2, he explains the routine for indictments at assizes or sessions: clerks prepare the bills of indictment, and prosecutors take them into the grand jury room, along with prosecution witnesses.

[21] LP 8, no. 886 v, vii (p. 350) (**Docs. 7, 11**). The names of More's jurors are given by R. W. Chambers in his notes to *Harpsfield's Life of More*, ed. Elsie Vaughan Hitchcock, Early English Text Society original series 186 (London, 1932), pp. 349–50 (see **Doc. 15**). Guy, *Daughter's Love*, characterizes five of them thus: "Sir Thomas Palmer, Henry's favorite dicing partner; Sir Thomas Spert, the Clerk Comptroller of the Royal Navy; Gregory Lovell and Geoffrey Chamber, both minor courtiers; and, most disconcertingly, his old enemy John Parnell, the fast-talking Lutheran and vintner to the Boleyns who had tried to have him impeached" (p. 259). Chambers considers the identification of the juror Parnell with the Parnell who accused More of bribery (Harpsfield, pp. 153–4) only possible, not probable, let alone certain.

[22] Baker, "Criminal Courts," pp. 282–3.

[23] Baker, *Spelman's Reports*, 2:108 and n. 10. Before 1530, the number of challenges allowed was 35.

Vaughan Hitchcock in 1932,[24] and her divisions were accepted by E. E. Reynolds in 1964, but designated as "counts."[25] Derrett, also in 1964, likewise distinguishes four "counts," but his divisions are different from those of Hitchcock and Reynolds. I will avoid the term "count," since it seems at this time to have still referred only to the expanded complaint made in court by a plaintiff in a civil suit: it is his "recounting" (in French, *conte*, story; in Latin, *narratio*).[26] This point is made by Geoffrey Parmiter, who observes that the term was not used for indictments until the seventeenth century.[27] As for the term "charge," in the sense of "accusation," it was already in use, though no one was yet speaking of "charges" in the plural. In the Guildhall Report, More refers to the individual accusations against him not only as "parts," but also as "heads" or "chapters" (*capita*) and "articles," standard terms for charges in ecclesiastical trials.

I have chosen to divide the indictment into twelve sections, which are given in full, in Latin with English translations, among the Documents below.[28] Here is my summary:

§1 Grand jurors of Middlesex County on June 28, 1535 present as follows:
§2 Since, by the Act of Supremacy, 26 H8 (1534) c. 1,[29] the king was accepted as Supreme Head of the Church in England;
§3 And since, by the Act of Treasons, 26 H8 (1534) c. 13,[30] it was made high treason to deprive the king of his titles,
§4 Nevertheless, Thomas More on May 7, 1535,[31] seduced by diabolical instigation, maliciously attempted to deprive King Henry of his title of Supreme Head when, before Thomas Cromwell and others, upon being asked whether he approved of the king as Supreme Head, he maliciously remained silent and refused to give a direct answer.
§5 On May 12, More maliciously wrote to Bishop John Fisher, consenting to Fisher's denial of the supremacy, telling him of his own silence, and calling the act a two-edged sword.
§6 On May 26, More wrote again to Fisher, warning him not to use these words, lest there appear to be a confederacy between them.
§7 On June 3, Fisher remained silent on the question and called the act a two-edged sword.
§8 On June 3, More maliciously persevered in his silence.

---

[24] "Sir Thomas More's Indictment," ed. Elsie Vaughan Hitchcock, in *Harpsfield's Life of More*, pp. 267–76.
[25] Reynolds, *Trial of St Thomas More*, pp. 65–9.
[26] J. H. Baker, *An Introduction to English Legal History*, 4th edn (London, 2002), p. 76.
[27] Geoffrey de C. Parmiter, "The Indictment of St Thomas More," *The Downside Review* 75 (1957), 149–66 at p. 158; idem, "Tudor Indictments, Illustrated by the Indictment of St Thomas More," *Recusant History* 6 (1961–62), 141–56 at p. 147. In the latter article, Parmiter holds that the indictment listed multiple facts but charged only one crime, denial of the supremacy. But it seems clear that he was being charged with committing that crime multiple times.
[28] See Doc. 16 for the compete indictment,
[29] For the text of the Act of Supremacy, see Doc. 1.
[30] For the Act of Treasons, see Doc. 2.
[31] This interrogation actually took place on Friday, April 30, according to More's letter of May 2–3 (Doc. 4, §2).

§9 Also on June 3, More likewise called the act a two-edged sword.

§10 In order to conceal their treason, More and Fisher burned each letter as soon as it had been read.

§11 On June 12, More told Richard Rich that subjects could not be obligated by an act of Parliament making the king Supreme Head.

§12 "And thus the aforesaid jurors say that the aforesaid Thomas More falsely, traitorously, and maliciously by craft schemed, contrived, practiced, and attempted to deprive" the king of his title of Supreme Head.[32]

(Let me note here that, though there are two acts, or statutes, at issue, it is usual to speak of violating "the act" or "the statute," in the singular, referring, of course, to the second, the Act of Treasons.)

To Sir John Spelman, one of the justices on the commission, this presentment boiled down to two charges:

1 abetting Fisher's treason (cf. §§5–7, 9–10);
2 attempting to deprive the king of his title (cf. §§4, 8, 11–12).

Specifically, Spelman says that More was arraigned for treason as aider-counselor-abettor to Fisher and also because, falsely-maliciously-traitorously desiring-willing-scheming, he contrived-practiced-attempted to deprive the king of his dignity-name-title of Supreme Head on earth of the Church of England.[33] In his use of synonymous triplets Spelman rivals the indenture-style rhetoric of the indictment.

Now let us consider the impressions left by witnesses of the trial. In a report of the trial that was made to Reginald Pole, to judge by Pole's account of the trial, More was accused of only one thing, of remaining silent, which was judged to be malicious, and he was condemned for it.[34]

In the Guildhall Report of the trial – that is, the eyewitness report best preserved in the Guildhall manuscript[35] – More considers the indictment to consist of three "parts":

---

[32] The Latin of the quoted passage reads, "Sicque juratores praedicti dicunt quod praefatus Thomas More false, proditorie, et maliciose, arte imaginavit, inventavit, practicavit, et attemptavit ... deprivare" (p. 276).

[33] *The Reports of Sir John Spelman*, ed. Baker, 1:58: "Sir Thomas More ... fuit arraine ... de treson, de ceo que il fuit aidant, counceloor, et abettour al dit evesque, et auxi que il fauxment, maliciousment, et traitorousment desirant, voilant, et imaginant, inventa, practisa, et attempta a deprive le Roy de son dignite, nome, et title de Supreme Chiefe en Terre de l'Esglise d'Engleter." See the whole in **Doc. 18**.

[34] Reginald Pole, *Pro ecclesiasticae unitatis defensione* (Rome [1539]; repr. Farnborough, 1965), fols 89v–90, edited and translated in **Doc. 19**. See Schulte Herbrüggen, "The Process," p. 115. Pole's book was a treatise meant for Henry VIII, and it was sent to him on May 27, 1536; it had no title, and the title of the printed version was not his; it is usually referred to as *De unitate*. See Thomas F. Mayer, *Reginald Pole, Prince and Prophet* (Cambridge, 2000), p. 13, and see Mayer's entry on Pole in **ODNB**. For an English translation of the whole work, see Joseph G. Dwyer, *Pole's Defense of the Unity of the Church* (Westminster, MD, 1965).

[35] See my edition and translation in **Doc. 17**, based on Derrett, "Neglected Versions." Derrett takes the version of London, Guildhall MS 1231, as his primary text, but emends it according to other texts to produce what he calls the "reconstructed text," which he cites as "R." In contrast, I give

1 remaining silent concerning the act (cf. §§4, 8);
2 arming Bishop Fisher against the act (cf. §5);
3 conspiring with Bishop Fisher (cf. §§5–7, 9–10).

We note that the conversation with Rich (§11) is neglected entirely, whereas in William Roper's recollection, long after the event, of what he had been told, seemingly immediately after the trial, by persons who had actually witnessed it, this was the only charge that More was indicted on: "Upon whose only report was Sir Thomas More indicted of treason upon the statute whereby it was made treason to deny the king to be Supreme Head of the Church."[36]

Was part of the indictment quashed?
Derrett concludes from the discrepancy between Guildhall and Roper that More's arguments against the three first parts of the indictment were in fact "motions" made to the judges, that is to say, the members of the commission, against the validity of the indictment; that More's contentions were accepted by the judges, who dismissed those parts of the indictment, which were dropped from the indictment; and that only then did More plead not guilty.[37] This sort of analysis might strike us as very authentic, especially with reference to More's alleged "motion in arrest of judgment," but it appears to be another instance of using legal jargon anachronistically. "Motions" were not made in court until the eighteenth century, it would seem, and then only by counsel on behalf of their clients[38] – referring to civil suits. In criminal trials, we must remind ourselves, counsel was not allowed to defendants.

---

the Guildhall version throughout, unless otherwise noted. I also follow my own sense in matters of punctuation, capitalization, spacing, and spelling (as is true of all the texts I cite).
36 William Roper, *The Lyfe of Sir Thomas Moore, Knight, Written by William Roper, Esquire, Which Married Margreat, Daughter of the Sayed Thomas Moore*, ed. Elsie Vaughan Hitchcock with historical notes by R. W. Chambers, Early English Text Society original series 197 (London:, 1935), p. 86. For Roper's whole report of the trial, see Doc. 20.
37 Derrett, "Trial," p. 60: After the rejection of More's motion that the indictment was bad because the ingredients of malice had not been urged, "More moved that the first three counts disclosed no offence, giving reasons. As to the fourth count he pleaded not guilty. The court evidently upheld him on the first three counts, otherwise the attorney-general would not have dared to abandon, as he plainly did, three-quarters of the Crown's carefully prepared case. The plea of not guilty was entered. Evidence was led for the Crown on the fourth count, More made a speech to the effect that on the evidence led there was no case to answer. The submission was rejected, and the issue, whether More was guilty of high treason under the act, was delivered to the jury, which returned in a quarter of an hour with the verdict of guilty." On p. 65, Derrett sums up More's objection to the first three charges thus: "The first three counts evidenced, he submitted, no malicious acts on his part, but they were evidence of malicious misrepresentation of his conduct to the king, a possibility of which we know he had expressed apprehension to the king himself. He craved, therefore, the sympathy of the court. The first three counts were not proceeded with, and the attorney-general presented the case for the Crown on the fourth count only."
38 The *OED* gives the first citation of "motion" used in this sense as dating from 1726; the second citation, of 1729, is from a law dictionary: "In the Courts of Chancery, King's Bench, etc., motions are made by barristers and counsellors at law for what concerns their clients' causes." To argue on the other side, however, it can be shown that there were legal meanings of "motion" and "move" in pleadings already in the fifteenth century; see *MED* s.v. "mocioun" 2(c) and "meven" 6b(c). The same is true even earlier of Law Latin: see the *Dictionary of Medieval Latin from British Sources*, ed.

Sir John Baker seems to concur with Derrett's judgment that most of the indictment was dropped, though he specifically mentions only the "remaining silent" charge. He says, referring to Derrett's arguments, that the judges "apparently agreed that a refusal to answer questions was not an overt act of treason," but then he adds in a note: "It is not quite clear whether this was a ruling, or a concession by prosecuting counsel."[39]

I submit, however, that it is highly unlikely that any part of the indictment was left unprosecuted. Derrett's conclusion does not in fact make sense of Roper's statement that it was only the Rich conversation upon which More was *indicted*, which is manifestly untrue;[40] and Derrett does not take into consideration Spelman's summary of the charges.[41] It hardly seems likely that the commissioners, some of whom had undoubtedly helped to construct the case against More, would so easily have dropped most of it.

The Guildhall Report might seem to support Derrett's interpretation, in that it suggests that the jury was summoned only after More presented his arguments against the charges: "This said, immediately twelve men were called by the public minister, after the custom of the British nation, to whom were given the chapters of accusation, to deliberate and judge whether More had maliciously sinned against the statute."[42] Note that they are given charges, in the plural: *capita accusationis*.

But the Guildhall Report does not mention More's plea of not guilty, and says nothing about the confrontation of Rich and More. Moreover, Pole's account indicates that the jury heard the discussion over the charge of remaining silent.[43]

E. E. Reynolds gives a possible reason for Roper's omissions: he was simply filling in what was missing from the earlier account.[44] But this argument is not really plausible, because Roper does not talk as if he is merely supplementing what others have reported.

In sum, our best bet is to consider the two accounts – or four, counting Spelman's and Pole's – to be complementary.

Let me add a further consideration, drawing on Baker's general remarks about treason trials: "We know now that the judges were commonly consulted before indictments for treason were preferred, and that as a result of their advice

---

R. E. Latham *et al*, 12 fascs, 1975–, s.v. "motio" 7a-b and "movere" 7c; but there is no comparable usage in Law French; see J. H. Baker, *Manual of Law French*, 2nd edn (Aldershot, 1990).

[39] Baker, *Oxford History*, p. 417 and n. 38. His treatment in *Spelman's Reports*, 2:139, is similar.

[40] It is peculiar that Roper would be so imprecise in his terminology, since he was not only a lawyer himself but also the chief clerk (protonotary) of the King's Bench. See Hugh Trevor-Roper's entry on Roper in *ODNB*. As Trevor-Roper notes, Roper did not write his account of More's life for publication, but rather to supply information to Nicholas Harpsfield, whom Roper had commissioned to write More's official biography.

[41] In his revised article, "Trial," p. 56, Derrett refers only briefly to Spelman's report, without giving his summary of the indictment. Derrett does not discuss the question of when the jury appeared on the scene.

[42] Guildhall Report (**Doc. 17**), §7: "His dictis, continuo duodecim viri, de more gentis Britannicae, per ministrum publicum sunt vocati, quibus data sunt capita accusationis, ut dispicerent ac judicarent, an Morus maliciose contra decretum peccasset."

[43] Pole, *Pro defensione*, fol. 90 (**Doc. 19**), no. 6.

[44] Reynolds, *Trial of St Thomas More*, p. 106.

many accused persons were released without trial," adding: "Prosecution decisions were commonly taken in Council, with the judges present." He continues: "This being so, one would not expect the judges as a rule to countenance purely legal objections by those who had been brought to trial on their advice, at least when they were the very objections which they had already considered privately."[45] So, we should conclude that it was unlikely in More's case that the judges would have admitted legal flaws in the indictment that they had been consulted on. This is doubtless the reason why Baker gives an alternative to Derrett's conclusion, namely, that it may have been the prosecutor (that is, Sir Christopher Hales, as we will see), and any advisors that he might have had, who, in response to More's legal objections on the point of silence, decided not to press forward. We note that Baker makes no comment about the other main charge, of conspiracy with Bishop Fisher, which Spelman singled out in his summary.

More's pleading, and the significance of "maliciously"
Let us therefore start with Roper, who tells us that, when More was brought from the Tower and arraigned before the bar of the King's Bench, after the indictment was read to him, he asserted that it was not true that he denied the king's supremacy, and therefore he pleaded not guilty.

He reserved the right to "a-void" the indictment "after verdict"; that is, if the jury returned a guilty verdict, he would offer reasons why the indictment's substance ("the body of the matter") should be considered void.

But he did make an observation at the present time, just after pleading not guilty: if the words, "maliciously, traitorously, and diabolically" were not in the indictment, there would be no basis for any just charge against him.[46] He presumably meant that the actions, or lack of actions, alleged in the indictment, even if admitted or found to be true, would not constitute offenses in themselves. They could only be construed as offenses because of the assertion that his motivation in doing them was said to have been malicious.

Parliament's intention concerning malice
Cromwell originally wanted to make the Act of Succession, passed earlier in the same calendar year, 1534 (but in the previous regnal year, 25 Henry VIII), say that mere spoken words against it would be treason, but his advisers were against it, and the act as passed made words alone, when "maliciously and

---

[45] Baker, *Oxford History*, p. 415 and n. 31.
[46] Roper, *Lyfe*, ed. Hitchcock, pp. 86–7 (Doc. 20, §3): "When Sir Thomas More was brought from the Tower to Westminster Hall to answer the indictment, and at the King's Bench bar before the judges thereupon arraigned, he openly told them that he would upon that indictment have abidden in law, but that he thereby should have been driven to confess of himself the matter indeed, [which] was, the denial of the king's supremacy, which, he protested, was untrue. Wherefore he thereto pleaded not guilty; and so reserved unto himself advantage to be taken of the body of the matter, after verdict, to a-void that indictment. And moreover added that if those only odious terms, 'maliciously, traitorously, and diabolically' were put out of the indictment, he saw therein nothing justly to charge him."

obstinately" uttered, to be only "misprision" of treason (that is, similar to, but less serious than, treason).[47] But in the Act of Treasons passed six months later, any maliciously spoken words against the king's supremacy or other titles were declared to be high treason.[48]

We find out in a roundabout way, from Bishop Fisher's brother Robert, as overheard by Fisher's servant Richard Wilson, that the Commons objected to the proposed form of the new act, whereby

> speaking is made high treason, which was never heard of before, that words should be high treason. But there was never such a sticking at the passing of any act in the lower house as was at the passing of the same [the November 1534 Act of Treason Concerning Supremacy], and that was the [word] "maliciously," which, when it was put, it was not worth [*lacuna*], for they would expound the same statute themselves at their pleasure.
>
> (Wilson's testimony of June 7, 1535)[49]

John Bellamy interprets this to mean: "The government was going to expound the treason act of 1534 according to its pleasure, regardless of the inclusion of the word 'maliciously.'"[50] Whether or not this was in fact Robert Fisher's meaning, it turned out to be the case.

Robert Fisher's understanding of Parliament's intention, according to Wilson's further testimony (on June 8), was that "maliciously" was put into the statute so that "a man might answer to the questions not maliciously, and be in no danger."[51] Wilson stated that Bishop Fisher himself said that "a man may answer a question without any malice."[52]

G. R. Elton maintains that the Commons did not put the term "maliciously" into the act, but that it was already in the proposed bill as presented to them (just as it was in the Act of Succession, as we have seen). He suggests rather "that the Commons' debates turned upon the safeguard provided by the requirements of malice to make words treason."[53] Which of course amounts to the same thing: the Commons clearly intended to stipulate that only malicious words or actions violated the statute.

It will be instructive to see the accounts given by William Rastell in his *Life*

---

[47] Act of Succession, 25 H8 (1533–34) c. 22 §6 (*Statutes of the Realm* 3:474); Elton, *Policy and Police*, pp. 276–7. The word "maliciously" is also in §5 (p. 473), which declares anything done maliciously in writing or printing against the king's second marriage or its issue to be high treason.
[48] Act of Treasons, 26 H8 (1534) c. 13 §1 (*Statutes of the Realm* 3:508–9) (**Doc. 2**).
[49] LP 8, no. 856 (**Doc. 8**), i, par. 2. More himself would no doubt have disagreed that mere words had never constituted treason (if not high treason) before this, since in 1533 he said he would "advise every man for fear of treason, beware of all such lewd language, and not, under color to teach the judges their part, to tell the people without necessity that though they talk traitorous words, yet it is no treason": More, *The Debellation of Salem and Bizance*, ed. John Guy, Ralph Keen, Clarence H. Miller, and Ruth McGugan, CW 10, ch. 14, p. 69. More is opposing Christopher St German's implication that "to talk heresies is none heresy."
[50] Bellamy, *Tudor Law of Treason*, p. 14.
[51] Gairdner, loc. cit., par. 14 (**Doc. 8**)
[52] Ibid., par. 7.
[53] Elton, *Policy and Police*, pp. 283–4.

of More, even though Elton has judged them to be "artifice rather than report."[54] Rastell, born in 1508, set up as a printer of legal matters in 1529, and he was More's principal publisher. He also trained as a lawyer himself, being admitted to Lincoln's Inn in 1532, and he was undoubtedly an interested eyewitness to all of the subsequent events that we are concerned with here. He wrote his biography of More during his self-imposed exile in Louvain, between 1562 and his death in 1565, but it survives only in a few fragments, mainly dealing with Bishop Fisher.[55] Rastell not only acted as a lawyer, but he served as a justice of the Queen's Bench under Mary (beginning three weeks before her death in 1358) and Elizabeth, until 1562.[56]

Rastell speaks of six acts of the Parliament of 26 Henry VIII (1534) made in opposition to the Lords and Commons, which were "compassed by sinister and corrupt means." The second was the Act (c. 2) requiring every subject to swear an oath concerning the Succession. He notes that the Act of Succession itself (passed earlier in 1534, 25 H8 c. 22) did not require such an oath, and the holy men who refused it (before this additional act was passed) were wrongfully imprisoned for their refusal. The third act he singles out is c. 22, the act condemning Thomas More of misprision; the fourth is c. 1, the Act of Supremacy, and the fifth is c. 13, the Act of Treasons enforcing it. He says the following about this act:

> Fifthly, an act whereby it was made high treason to do or speak against the king's supremacy and other things. Note diligently here that the bill was earnestly withstood, and could not be suffered to pass, unless the rigor of it were qualified with this word, "maliciously": and so not every speaking against the supremacy to be treason, but only maliciously speaking. And so, for more plain declaration thereof, the word "maliciously" was twice put into the act. And yet afterwards, in putting the act in execution against Bishop Fisher, Sir Thomas More, the Carthusians, and others, the word "maliciously," plainly expressed in the act, was adjudged by the king's commissioners, before whom they were arraigned, to be void.[57]

The justices' previous pronouncements on malice

As was stated at the beginning, all of the professional judges (that is, the justices) who were on the commission trying More also served on the other trials of treason against the supremacy statutes. Let us listen to what they are reported to have said on the subject of malice, as well as other aspects of the trials pertinent to More's trial.

---

[54] Ibid., p. 408 n. 2.
[55] William Rastell, *The Rastell Fragments, Being "Certen Breef Notes Apperteyning to Bushope Fisher, Collected out of Sir Thomas Moores Life, Writt by Master Justice Restall*," (hereafter cited as *Life of More*) Appendix 1 of Harpsfield's *Life of More*, ed. Elsie Vaughan Hitchcock, pp. 219–52, 359–70; and see her introduction, "Rastell's Life of More", pp. ccxv–ccxix (I take it that this is by Hitchcock, but it could be by R. W. Chambers, the author of the life of Harpfield just preceding, pp. clxxv–ccxiv).
[56] See *ODNB* entry on Rastell by J. H. Baker.
[57] Rastell, *Life of More*, extract B, pp. 228–9.

Rastell describes the trial of three Carthusian priors and the Bridgettine monk Richard Reynolds on April 28–29, 1535, thus:

> The four religious persons were arraigned, and the Carthusians, by the mouth of John Houghton, their prior, confessed that they denied the king's supremacy, but not maliciously. The jury could not agree to condemn these four religious persons, because their consciences persuaded them they did it not maliciously. The judges hereupon resolved them that whosoever denied the supremacy, denied it maliciously; and the expressing of the word "maliciously" in the act was a void limitation and restraint of the construction of the words and intention of the offender. The jury for all this could not agree to condemn them; whereupon Cromwell, in a rage, went unto the jury and threatened them, if they condemned them not. And so, being overcome by his threats, they found them guilty, and had great thanks. But they were afterwards ashamed to show their faces, and some of them took great thought for it.[58]

According to the sparse records contained in the Bag of Secrets,[59] the four men were indicted, on April 28, for having made this statement on April 26: "The king our sovereign lord is not Supreme Head in earth of the Church of England." They were arraigned on April 28, and tried before a petty jury on April 29. According to Gairdner they then pleaded guilty, but a correction in the 1965 reprint of the calendar says that they were found guilty by the jury. The Rastell account is doubtless accurate: they admitting making the statement in the indictment, but argued that they made it without malice, and so did not fall under the statute.

The extract from Rastell dealing with efforts to get a damaging statement out of Bishop Fisher is taken from Chapter 55 of Book 3 of his *Life of More*. Immediately after the execution of the Carthusians and Reynolds on May 4, Rastell says, certain members of the Council came and assured Fisher that his giving an opinion "could be no manner danger to him, because it should fully appear that he did it not of any malice or evil will towards the Prince, but only for the certifying of the king of his opinion." But Fisher realized that they were trying to ensnare him, and also, "credibly hearing how this word 'maliciously' in the Statute of Treason was of none effect in the Carthusians' condemnations, he therefore would make no answer to this question." But then a messenger arrived from the king asking to know his true opinion, which he could give with impunity.[60]

---

[58] Ibid., pp. 229–30. Note that Rastell mistakenly says that Houghton was the prior of the other two (Bevall and Axholme), but they were also priors, of their own houses.

[59] *LP* 8, no. 609 (pp. 229–31) (Doc. 3).

[60] Rastell, *Life of More*, extract C, pp. 231–5. The Bollandist historian François Van Ortroy, "Vie du bienheureux martyr Jean Fisher, cardinal, evêque de Rochester († 1535)," *Analecta Bollandiana* 10 (1891), 121–365, 12 (1893), 97–247, at 10:176–8, rejects the story of the messenger as fiction, but R. W. Chambers, in his historical notes to Hitchcock's edition, pp. 363–8, argues learnedly for its authenticity. However, Elton, *Policy and Police*, p. 408 n. 2, points out that it is not in the indictment, a point made by Van Ortroy as well. Van Ortroy gives the pertinent words of the indictment on pp. 12:171–2 n. 2, and E. E. Reynolds, *Saint John Fisher*, rev. edn (Wheathamstead, 1972), pp. 285–6, gives a translation; he was charged with having explicitly denied the king's

The extract continues with Chapter 58, which recounts the bishop's trial in detail, giving the names of the commissioners who sat in judgment against him on June 17 (including Audley, Cromwell, FitzJames, and Spelman), and the names of the jury. The only witness against him was the king's messenger spoken of before, who admitted that it was by the king's command that he had assured him, on his oath, that his response would not bring him any harm. "'But all this,' quoth this wicked witness, 'do not discharge you any whit.'" Fisher replies to his judges:

> Oh, my lords, how can this only testimony burden me, that ought, as the case standeth, by all equity, all justice, all worldly honesty, and all civil humanity, to be no whit charged here withal, though in my so doing I had committed treason? And besides this, the very statute that maketh this speaking against the king's supremacy treason is only and precisely limited where such speech is spoken maliciously. And now all ye, my lords, perceive plainly that in my uttering and signifying unto the king of mine opinion and conscience, as touching this his claim of supremacy in the Church of England, in such sort as I did, as ye have heard, there was no manner of malice in me at all, and so I committed no treason.

Rastell then narrates the response of the commissioners:

> To this was it answered to the bishop by some of his judges, utterly devoid of worldly shame, and affirmed by some of the residue, both that the word "maliciously" in the statute was of none effect, for that none could speak against the king's supremacy by any manner of means but that the speaking against it was treason; and also that that message or promise to him from the king himself neither could nor did, by rigor of our law, in any wise discharge him; but that in so declaring his mind and conscience against the king's supremacy, though it were even at the king's own commandment and request, he by the statute committed treason; and nothing might discharge him now of the cruel penalty of death appointed by the statute for speaking against the king's supremacy, howsoever the words were spoken, but only the king's pardon, if it would please his Grace to grant it him.[61]

Rastell's account was obviously the source of the corresponding passages in the *Life of Fisher*, written most likely in the 1570s, and probably by John Young,[62]

---

supremacy under interrogation on May 7. The indictment is in Latin, but the statement he is charged with making is in English: "The King our Sovereign Lord is not Supreme Head in earth of the Church of England." See *LP* 8, no. 886.iii (p. 350) (Doc. 11). Elton says, "Though this seems unlikely it is probable that he said enough, for he was always inclined to say too much" (p. 408).
[61] Rastell, *Life of More*, extract C, pp. 337–40.
[62] *A Treatise Containing the Life and Manner of Death of That Most Holy Prelate and Constant Martyr of Christ John Fisher, Bishop of Rochester and Cardinal of the Holy Church of Rome* (hereafter cited as *Life of Fisher*), ed. Van Ortroy, in "Vie du bienheurex martyr," 10:202–365; 12:97–247. In his "Dissertation préliminaire," 10:200–1, Van Ortroy suggests John Young (1514–1581/2) as the likely author. In 1535, the year of Fisher's death, Young received his bachelor's degree from Cambridge, and he subsequently became an apologist for the Catholic cause. The translator of the Latin version, which Van Ortroy edits along with the original English, was Richard Hall (c. 1537–1604),

in which the king's deceitful messenger is identified as none other than Richard Rich. Fisher is represented as addressing the judges thus:

> I pray you, my lords, consider that by all equity, justice, wor[l]dly honesty and courteous dealing, I cannot, as the case standeth, be directly charged therewith as with treason, though I had spoken the words in deed, the same being not spoken *maliciously*, but in the way of advice and counsel, when it was requested of me by the king himself. And that favor the very words of the statute do give me, being made only against such as shall *maliciously* gainsay the king's supremacy, and none other.

To this, we are told, "it was answered by some of the judges that the word 'maliciously' in the Statute is but a superfluous and void word; for, if a man speak against the king's supremacy by any manner of means, that speaking is to be understand and taken in law as *maliciously*." Fisher replies: "My lords, if the law be so understood, then is it a very hard exposition, and, as I take it, contrary to the meaning of them that made the law."[63]

Perhaps we can take as truth, or as verisimilar (close to truth), the back-and-forth about *maliciously* in this account, even though the story of entrapment and the single testimony of the entrapper do not seem to be true. Fisher was indicted specifically on having denied the king's supremacy on May 7,[64] a day on which he was interrogated not by a single emissary from the royal court but by members of the king's Council, and, though the report of that interrogation does not survive, Fisher's servant Richard Wilson said that he had heard him give such an answer on that day.[65] But when Wilson told Fisher the next day (May 8) that he had said so, Fisher denied making such an answer.[66]

The Conduct of the Trial

As soon as More pleaded not guilty, the petty jury was impaneled, and, according to normal procedure, the indictment would have been explained to them, in More's presence. The explanation was presumably made by the royal procurator (proctor), as he is called in the Guildhall Report,[67] which in Harpsfield comes out as the king's attorney.[68] Pole calls him the king's advocate.[69] He was Sir

---

a protegé of Young, who published Young's treatise, *De schismate, sive de ecclesiasticae unitatis divisione*, in eight volumes in Louvain in 1573. Until Van Ortroy's demonstration to the contrary in the preface to his edition, Hall was accepted as the author of the original English version. See also the entries on Young (by Judith Ford) and Hall (by John J. LaRocca) in *ODNB*.

[63] *Life of Fisher*, section 174 (Van Ortroy, 12:178–9).
[64] Doc. 11; see n. 60 above.
[65] *LP* 8, no. 856 (Doc. 8), i, par. 3.
[66] Ibid., iii par. 19. See also Maria Dowling, *Fisher of Men: A Life of John Fisher, 1469–1535* (Basingstoke, 1999), pp. 156–7; she does not mention Fisher's denial of having so answered.
[67] Guildhall Report (Doc. 17), §3.
[68] *Harpsfield's Life*, p. 185.
[69] Pole, *Pro defensione*, fol. 89v (Doc. 19), no. 4.

Christopher Hales,⁷⁰ who, in the terminology of the time, was called the king's general attorney.⁷¹ According to Derrett, Hales "led for the Crown."⁷² By using this twentieth-century expression, however, he begs a very important question: he presumes the existence of a prosecuting "team," with one "leader" and one or more "followers." Accordingly, he adds: "Sir Richard Rich, the king's 'general solicitor' with him." This would indeed be shocking, at least to our modern sensibilities, if Rich, who figured prominently in the indictment, and who was the prosecution's sole recorded witness against More, and whom, according to the same record (Roper's account), More accused of giving perjured testimony, was also acting as a prosecutor at the trial. But Rich's participation in conducting the case seems to be a mere inference on Derrett's part, as being the sort of thing that the general solicitor would be expected to do.

It is likely, I submit (making an inference of my own), that More made his responses to the first charges in the indictment, which the Guildhall Report records, only at this time: that is, in the presence of the petty jury.

As noted, in such a trial, the prosecutor explained the indictment to the jury, perhaps even giving an opening speech (Bellamy gives examples from treason trials later in the century),⁷³ while at the same time, or subsequently, confronting the prisoner with the substance of the charges, with the prisoner/defendant responding. As Parmiter says, "The whole trial was virtually a long debate between the prisoner and the prosecuting counsel, in which they questioned each other and grappled with each other's arguments."⁷⁴

The prosecution could also bring witnesses and documentary evidence as proofs of the charges. In More's case, it was not possible to introduce letters between More and Fisher, for they had all been burned. But it was possible to introduce written testimony concerning them. The only witnesses that we hear of are Rich and the two men who were with him when he conversed with More in the Tower, but it is likely that there were other witnesses as well, whose testimony was so routine that there was no need to mention it. As Bellamy points out, "Amongst the weapons which the prosecution used in order to prove its case, pride of place went to the introduction of examinations and confessions." And he adds: "It also assisted the Crown's case if the person who had devised the examinations or confessions and also the examiner who had interrogated, made an appearance in court to vouch for their veracity in front of the accused."⁷⁵ As we will see below, servants in the Tower had been examined on the subject of letters between More and Fisher, among other things, and the chief examiner was a doctor of civil law named Thomas Legh.⁷⁶ It may well be that Doctor Legh appeared to certify his recording of the examinations, and that the servants

---

70 See *ODNB* entry on Christopher Hales by J. H. Baker.
71 25 Henry VIII (1533–34) c. 16 §2 (*Statutes of the Realm* 3:457): "the King's General Attorney and General Solicitor which for the time is …"
72 Derrett, "Trial," p. 60.
73 Bellamy, *Tudor Law of Treason*, p. 147.
74 Parmiter, "Indictment of St Thomas More," p. 165.
75 Bellamy, *Tudor Law of Treason*, p. 148.
76 *LP* 8, no. 856 (pp. 325–31), examinations of June 7–11, 1535 (Doc. 8).

themselves were not required to testify *viva voce*. And since Rich's conversation with More was the only part of the indictment that was not vouched for by formal examinations – because it was based only on a private conversation, of which Rich had submitted a report in writing after it occurred – this was doubtless why he was required to appear in person to affirm and expand upon the contents of his report.

The First Part of the Accusation: Silence

The charge of remaining silent, and More's defense
According to the Guildhall Report, More characterized "the first part of the accusation" as charging him with showing malevolence towards the king because of his second marriage. This is not in the indictment as we have it, but perhaps something of this nature came out in the explanation of the indictment given to More, or to the petty jury, or to both. More replied that he had always spoken on that matter as his conscience urged him, and that he was never willing to conceal the truth from the king. For this sin, if it should be called a sin, he had been adjudged to perpetual prison, where he had remained for the last 15 months, and to have his goods confiscated.[77] He then said that he would limit himself only to the principal head or chapter of the accusation ("solum ad praecipuum caput accusationis"), namely, that he merited the penalty specified in the statute because he had maliciously, falsely, and with unfaithful mind injured the king's majesty and name and titles, especially because, when asked by Secretary Cromwell what he thought of the statute, he replied that he did not wish to occupy himself in such matters.

> To which I clearly respond to you that it is not lawful for me to be judged to death for such silence on my part, because neither your statute nor anything in the laws of the whole world can rightly [*jure*] afflict anyone with punishment, unless one has committed a crime in word or deed, since laws have constituted no penalty for silence.[78]

To this the royal proctor responded that, on the contrary, such silence in this case was a clear sign of malign intention against the statute, since truly faithful subjects of the king, when asked their opinion of it, were bound to say it was good.[79]

---

[77] Guildhall Report (**Doc. 17**), §2 (a).
[78] Ibid., par. 2 (c): "Ad quod clare respondeo vobis, hujusmodi silentio me morti adjudicari non licere, quum quidem neque vestrum decretum neque quicquid legum in toto orbe quemquam jure supplicio afficere potest, nisi quis vel dicto vel facto crimen admiserit, cum silentio nulla poena legibus sit constituta."
[79] Ibid., §3: "Tum regius procurator, suscipiens sermonem, 'Hujusmodi,' inquit, 'silentium certum aliquod indicium erat, nec obscura significatio, malignae alicujus cogitationis contra ipsum decretum, propterea quod singuli subjecti, ut fideles suo principi, interrogati [in] sententiam super illo decreto, obligantur aperte et sine dissimulatione respondere ipsum esse bonum ac sanctum"

More replied,

> But if it is true what universal law [*jus commune*] says, "One who keeps silent seems to consent," then that silence of mine gave approval to that statute of yours more than it weakened it. But as for all the faithful being bound and obliged to make response, etc., I answer that there is a much greater obligation on the part of a good man and faithful subject to consult his own conscience and eternal salvation and to follow the prescriptions of reason than to take account of any other thing, especially since the kind of conscience that I have offers no offense to its prince and stirs up no sedition.[80]

Another version of this report, published in 1536 in a pamphlet of excerpts of letters on the English martyrs, titled *Novitates quaedam*,[81] has an ungrammatical addendum here: "asserting this to you, that my conscience had not been opened to any mortal."[82]

To sum up, More says, according to the Guildhall Report, that he could be punished only for doing or saying something offensive, not for doing nothing and saying nothing, since there is no law anywhere that punishes silence. The king's proctor objects that his silence was an offense in itself and a sign of malice, in that all subjects have an obligation to give his opinion on the statute when asked. More's rejoinder is that there is a principle of general law that silence signifies consent, and that furthermore the obligation to one's conscience is more important than any obligation to respond to interrogation (and he has never revealed his conscience on this point to anyone).

Reginald Pole and the charge of silence

Henry VIII had been expecting support for his dynastic moves from his clerical cousin, Reginald Pole,[83] who was living abroad, and he seemed not to have

---

("Then the royal proctor started to speak, saying, 'Such silence was a sure indication and a not obscure sign of some malign thinking about the statute, because all subjects, being faithful to their Prince, when interrogated on their view concerning the statute, are obliged to respond openly, and without dissimulation, that it is good and holy'").

80 Guildhall Report, §4: "Tum Morus, 'At si,' inquit, 'verum est quod jus commune ait, "Qui tacet consentire videtur," meum istud silentium plus approbavit vestrum statutum quam infirmavit. Quousque vero fidelis quisque tenetur et obligatur respondere, et cetera: respondeo, multo magis ad officium boni viri et fidelis subditi pertinere, ut suae conscientiae ac perpetuae saluti consulat, et rectae rationis praescriptum sequatur, quam [u]llius alterius rei habeat rationem, propterea quod hujusmodi conscientia qualis est mea suo principi nullam praebet offensionem neque seditionem excitat.'"

81 Derrett, "Neglected Versions," p. 206.

82 Addition to Guildhall Report, §4: "illud vobis asseverans, nulli mortalium meam conscientiam fuisse apertam."

83 Pole was Henry VIII's second cousin, being the grandson of George duke of Clarence, brother of Edward IV, Henry's grandfather. He had always been of a clerical and scholarly bent, but was as yet only in minor orders (and therefore still able to marry), even after being named cardinal in late 1536. There is no record cited of Pole's ordinations to the minor orders, which probably occurred during his early studies. Being in minor orders was the normal prerequisite for receiving benefices, and he received his first, as dean of Wimborne in Dorset, in February 1518, a month before his eighteenth birthday. See A. B. Emden, *A Biographical Register of the University of Oxford,*

thought that the elimination of Thomas More would have had any effect on his allegiance. Perhaps it was to ensure his complicit attitude that Pole's elder brother, Henry Lord Montague, was put on the commission that tried More, but, let us remember, he did not appear on the day of the trial. But Pole was appalled when he heard of the conviction and execution of Fisher and More. He was so shocked, he tells the king, that he remained stupefied for a month, until he finally brought himself to break his silence and speak his mind.[84]

Pole was living in Padua when the executions of Fisher and More took place, which must have been reported to him immediately. Doubtless his informant was not his brother, who, if he was at all troubled by the outcome of More's trial, would hardly have passed on his adverse opinion to Reginald. He was clearly very disturbed to hear of Reginald's harsh stance against the king in his treatise, not least, of course, because of the backlash that could be expected against his family, specifically himself and their mother, the Countess of Salisbury.[85]

But since Pole did not start writing his treatise until September or so, and did not finish it until the next year, he would have had time to read another account. His most likely supplementary source would be the *Expositio fidelis*, a letter purportedly written by a disciple of Erasmus, dated July 23, 1535.[86] This account incorporated the substance of the *Paris News Letter*, the French translation of the original Latin account represented by the Guildhall Report.[87]

AD 1501 to 1540 (Oxford, 1974), p. 453. He is identified as a cleric in the record: *LP* 2, ed. J. S. Brewer (1864) no. 3943, p. 1227.

[84] Pole, *Pro defensione*, fol. 107v: "Previously I remained silent, since I carried my fear with me always, but now you will see that I will not flee from speaking out what I think. Let me say, with God as my witness, what happened to me. From the time that I heard of the slaughter of those men, I do not deny that I lay senseless and unable to speak for almost a month, so stunned was I by the novelty and wonder of such unheard-of cruelty, but finally, as I collected myself, having always found myself in agreement with those men, I decided that my views should not be further hidden from sight. And not only that, but whereas I had been accustomed to whisper them now and then into a friend's ear, I now persuaded myself that they were to be preached from the housetops, as if Christ Himself were commanding it" ("Qui antea semper silerem, qui timorem semper prae me ferrem, jam vides quam non refugiam quae sentio proloqui. Equidem, ut teste jam Deo, dicam quid mihi acciderit, quo primum tempore de illorum nece accepi, quanquam certe non inficior me unum circiter mensem, quasi stupidum et sine voce jacuisse, rei novitate et miraculo tam inauditae crudelitatis perculsum, tamen, ut me collegi, qui semper cum illis viris sensissem, non modo non occultandam amplius sententiam meam esse duxi, sed si illam antea in amici aurem insusurrare interdum solitus eram, tum supra tecta depraedicandam quasi jubente Christo, mihi persuadebam").

[85] See Montague's letter to Reginald, September 13, 1536, calendared in *LP* 11 (1888), no. 451, pp. 181–2; and by Thomas F. Mayer, *The Correspondence of Reginald Pole, A Calendar*, 3 vols (Aldershot, 2002–4), 1:118 (no. 120). Montague's attitude about the matters under dispute is paraphrased by Gairdner thus: "I, who lack learning, could never conceive that laws made by man were of such strength but that they might be undone again by man, for what seems politic at one time, by abusion proves at another time the contrary."

[86] The letter was printed in 1535 by the Dutch printer Froben, in whose house Erasmus was living. Its full title is: *Expositio fidelis de morte D. Thomae Mori et quorundam aliorum insignium virorum in Anglia*; it is edited in *Opus epistolarum Des. Erasmi Roterdami*, vol. 11, ed. H. M. Allen and H. W. Garrod (Oxford, 1948), Appendix 27, pp. 368–78.

[87] As noted above, Derrett prints the French text in parallel to his reconstruction of the Latin account ("Neglected Versions"). Of Pole he says, "Cardinal Pole had some scraps of information

Pole claims to be drawing on the records (*acta*) of More's trial, while admitting in effect that he knows nothing about Fisher's trial. He says that "they" might have been able to come up with a plausible charge against Fisher, since, as befitted his position as a bishop, he had openly opposed their law. But they could find no such pretext for any likely charge against More.[88] Instead they recited a long and intricate accusation against him filled with ambiguous allegations of lese-majesty, which was designed to obscure the fact that they had nothing of substance to charge him with. It was so prolix and complex that More, even with his extraordinary memory, openly admitted that he could not remember even a third of what was said. He would, however, reply to a few of the charges, or rather to the one point that was the basis of everything else, namely, the allegation that he did not approve of their new law.[89]

More made two arguments against this charge. First, he said that, since the law had been passed after he had been committed to life imprisonment, it did not apply to him because he was legally dead, and he was not obliged to comment on any legislation that did not pertain to him. Second, he had done nothing in word or deed against the law.[90]

The judges were astounded by this response and reduced to silence, which turned into rage and fear that More would escape their net. They turned to the royal advocate to come to the rescue, and he told More that his very silence was being charged against him as a crime. Specifically, when he was interrogated in prison on what he thought about the law, More replied that all of his thoughts were now on God alone, and that he no longer had any concern about human laws, which did not apply to him. This silence, the advocate concluded, was a sign of his malicious intentions. The judges seized upon this ploy with great relief, seeing it as a way to keep the case from collapsing, and they all began to cry out, "Malice, malice!"[91]

More tried to answer this argument by saying that no one could be legitimately condemned for impugning a law merely by remaining silent about it, and in fact, according to the legal maxim, silence would signify assent, not dissent. But no attention was paid to him, and the jury was called forth to give a verdict.[92]

Pole's picture of the judges' consternation at More's initial response could hardly be true of all of them, certainly not of those who had connived in formulating the indictment or who, particularly the justices among them, were experienced enough to take in the terms of the indictment. But there may be some truth to it as far as some of the "lay" members of the panel were concerned.

---

from an eyewitness, but he used them indifferently and relied upon the *Paris News Letter*, or another version of the original account" ("Trial," p. 56 [450]).
[88] Pole, *Pro defensione*, fol. 89 (**Doc. 19**, nos. 1–2).
[89] Ibid., fols 89–89v (no. 3).
[90] Ibid., fol. 89v (no. 4).
[91] Ibid., fols 89v–90 (nos. 5–6).
[92] Ibid., fol. 90 (no. 6).

The rules of law concerning silence

For purposes of our present investigation, we can leave aside the question of the relative priority of conscience over other obligations. Let us proceed to take up More's defense in reverse order. What is the general law, *jus commune*,[93] on the significance of silence? And what does it have to say about obligations to speak or to act, and are penalties ever in order for failure to speak and act when called for?

The principle that More cites, "Qui tacet consentire videtur," is the 43rd of 88 "rules of law" (*regulae juris*) given at the end of the *Sext*, that is, the *Liber Sextus*, issued by Pope Boniface VIII in 1298.[94] This principle has proved very puzzling to students of Thomas More, and we need to examine it, and to discuss various kinds of silence, and various implications of silence in different circumstances.

Let me point out first of all that the very next rule of law, the 44th, also deals with silence: "One who remains silent neither confesses nor denies."[95]

Both of these rules seem to be outlandish: partially contradictory and of no modern relevance. But, properly understood, they are both commonsensical and fully in use today. The first rule pertains to one's reaction to an action; the second, to one's reaction to a yes-and-no question. Let me illustrate. Let's say that a beachfront property in Malibu has a path leading from the public street to the public beach. If persons ask the owner if they are allowed to use the path and he makes no answer, they don't know where they stand, whether he approves or disapproves. But if they go ahead and use the path and the owner voices no objection, their doubt is resolved: the owner assents to their actions. Another version of the first rule adds the rider, "ubi tractatur de ejus [i.e., suo] commodo,"[96] that is, "when it deals with his own interest."

---

[93] In my view, the historical meaning of the phrase *jus commune* in the Middle Ages and Renaissance was always "the general law on a specific point," and never "the body of general law." This latter meaning has been given to the phrase by modern historians, who take it to refer (both now and in the past) to a combination of canon and Roman civil law and sometimes feudal law; this new meaning (used in chap 2 below) corresponds to the Italian term, *diritto comune*. See Kelly, "Medieval *Jus commune* versus/uersus Modern *Ius commune*; or, Old 'Juice' and New 'Use,'" *Proceedings of the Twelfth International Congress of Medieval Canon Law (Washington, DC, August 1–7, 2004)*, ed. Kenneth Pennington and Uta-Renate Blumenthal (Vatican City, 2008), pp. 377–416.
[94] *Sext*, book 5, [title 13]: De regulis juris, no. 43: "Qui tacet consentire videtur"; ed. Emil Friedberg, *Corpus Iuris Canonici*, 2 vols (Leipzig, 1879–81), 2:1123. It was stated and discussed earlier, between 1234 and 1263, in Bernard of Parma's ordinary gloss to the *Decretales Gregorii IX* 2.23.5 v. *tacendo*, *CJC*, 2:787. See Christoph Krampe, "'Qui tacet consentire videtur': über die Herkunft einer Rechtsregel," in *Staat, Kirche, Wissenschaft in einer pluralistischen Gesellschaft: Festschrift zum 65. Geburtstag von Paul Mikat*, ed. Dieter Schwab et al. (Berlin, 1989), pp. 367–80. In the ordinary gloss of John Teutonicus (c. 1215) to Gratian's *Decretum* D. 65 c. 9 v. *tacuerit*, five different presumptions concerning silence are noted, depending on the circumstances: contempt, evasion, contradiction, consent, and "noncommittalness": *CJC*, 1:451–2.
[95] *Sext* 5.[13].44: "Is qui tacet non fatetur, sed nec utique negare videtur"; more literally translated: "He who is silent does not confess, nor is he seen to deny." This rule derives from Justinian's *Digest* 50.17: *De diversis regulis juris antiqui*, 142 (or 184 in medieval-Renaissance editions): "Qui tacet non utique fatetur, sed tamen verum est eum non negare."
[96] *Black's Law Dictionary*, 9th edn (St Paul, MN, 2009), Appendix B ("Legal Maxims"), p. 1866.

Qui tacet consentire videtur in convocation, 1531
More was not the first to invoke the principle of assent by silence in connection with the question of the royal supremacy; it had been done over four years earlier, when Henry first proposed this title to the southern convocation at the beginning of 1531.

After secret negotiations between councillors and justices of the king with the speaker of convocation and other members of the clergy, the title proposed for approval on February 7 was this: "Sole Protector and Supreme Head of the English Church and Clergy." We are told that "this concept of the supremacy did not well please the prelates and the clergy, and they desired it to be modified." For three sessions they negotiated with the royal councillors to change the king's mind and to express the article in milder terms. Finally, George Boleyn viscount Rochford brought back Henry's final formulation, with refusal of further discussion: "Sole Protector and Supreme Head after God." But somehow further modifications were made, and the article presented by Archbishop Warham for approval on February 11 read as follows: "As his Majesty is the singular and unique protector and supreme lord of the English Church and clergy, we recognize that he is also Supreme Head, insofar as the law of Christ allows." Bishop Fisher is thought to have been behind this saving phrase,[97] but he and the other bishops were hardly satisfied with it. The proposal seems to have been met by complete silence, whereupon Warham said, "Qui tacet consentire videtur." Then someone broke the silence, saying, "Well, then, we are all remaining silent." The record concludes: "Therefore, by unanimous consent both houses subscribed to this article."[98]

This sort of consent, whereby abstentions were turned into aye votes, was hardly a ringing endorsement, and the procedure was not quite as simple as is stated. Warham later in the day succeeded in getting the signatures of the bishops present, including Fisher's, but the lower clergy were by no means unanimous in their consent, and in fact some members, notably those who represented Fisher's diocese of Rochester, entered protests that their approval of the title in no way lessened their obedience to the pope.[99]

More had undoubtedly heard of these proceedings and therefore had precedent in using the maxim on silence in his own behalf.

Obligation to speak (silence as sin or crime)
Are there situations in which one is obliged in conscience to declare one's conscience or one's thoughts? In the criminal procedure of both English

---

[97] Dowling, *Fisher of Men*, p. 140. See Van Ortroy, "Vie du bienheureux martyr," 10:357.
[98] *Concilia Magnae Britanniae et Hiberniae*, ed. David Wilkins. 4 vols (London, 1737, repr. Brussels, 1964), 3:735. The last part of the record reads: "Tandem, 11 die Februarii, archiepiscopus articulum de suprematu regis in Synodo proposuit his verbis: 'Ecclesiae et cleri Anglicani, cujus singularem protectorem unicum et supremum dominum e[s]t, quantum per Christi legem licet, etiam Supremum Caput ipsius Majestatem recognoscimus.' Cui reverendissimus consensum fratrum suorum requisivit, dicens, 'Qui tacet consentire videtur.' Ad quod dictum quidam respondebat, 'Itaque tacemus omnes.' Unanimi igitur consensu utraque domus articulo huic subscribit."
[99] Dowling, *Fisher of Men*, p. 140; Stanford E. Lehmberg, *The Reformation Parliament, 1529–1536* (Cambridge, 1970), p. 115.

common law and international canon law (that is, the inquisitorial system), the defendant is obliged to speak to the charges, that is, about a specific past crime, not about his thoughts. In an inquisition, one would be put under oath at this point, forced to swear to tell the truth about guilt or innocence. This was an addition to the original rules, but justified from the practice of compurgation, according to which one must swear to one's innocence after suspicion is proved. This oath was an obligation in conscience, and any denial of guilt by a guilty person would constitute perjury, in the eyes of both God and man. In contrast, in the common-law tradition, no oath was taken, and a plea of not guilty meant no more than *volo contendere*.[100] In other words, the right against self-incrimination extended further in English practice, at least as eventually conceived. But remaining silent when charged, which is nowadays taken to be the equivalent of a not guilty plea, was in the past considered a serious offense, which eventually led to the barbarous custom of pressing to death.[101] In More's day, a failure to plead would result in conviction. In 1534, the year before More's trial, when Lord Dacre of the North was tried for treason, according to Spelman's report, he readily pleaded not guilty, but refused to say that he wished to be tried by his peers. The high steward then "told him that he would have judgment as a traitor, as one who refused to be tried according to law, if he would not say that he would be tried by his peers."[102] A decade later, failure to plead was declared by statute to be equivalent to a plea of guilty (or, more accurately, to being found guilty by a jury).[103] In a statute passed just after Henry VIII's death, one who refused to plead was said to "stand willfully, or of malice, mute."[104]

But outside of this special situation, was anyone ever legally or morally obliged to speak out, when remaining silent would be a crime? Yes, of course, and another legal maxim can be cited to confirm it: "Qui potest et debet vetare, tacens jubet."[105] That is, "Who can and should forbid, by being silent commands"; or, more idiomatically, "If you can and should speak against something but remain silent, you encourage it." This refers, of course, to an occurring or impending crime.[106]

Can we point to any other circumstances in which one is obliged to bring one's private thoughts to light? There was indeed such an obligation placed upon everyone in the sacrament of confession, but the confessor was himself

---

[100] Kelly, "The Right to Remain Silent," p. 996.
[101] See Baker, *Introduction to English Legal History*, pp. 508–9.
[102] Baker, *Spelman's Reports*, Crown no. 26 (1:54).
[103] 35 Henry VIII (1543–44), c. 5 ("A Bill Concerning the Six Articles") §7: "If any person ... stand mute or will not directly answer to the same offenses whereof he ... be indicted as is aforesaid, then that every such person ... for his ... contumacy shall have judgment to suffer like pains of death, losses, forfeitures, and imprisonment as if the same person ... so indicted had been thereof found guilty by verdict of twelve men" (*Statutes of the Realm* 3:962).
[104] 1 Edward VI (1547) c. 12 §9 (*Statutes of the Realm* 4:20).
[105] *Black's Law Dictionary*, p. 1866.
[106] This is the sort of situation envisaged in Justinian, *Code* 9.8.5, which says that those who were aware of treason (and did not reveal it) are to be punished. Derrett, "More's Silence and His Trial," suggests that Henry VIII's ministers may have had this law in mind when indicting More for his silence.

bound to silence by the severely strict seal of confession.[107] But what about in a court of law? Were there any circumstances in which one was obliged to answer questions posed by a judge that would reveal secret desires or thoughts?

Here is St Thomas Aquinas's opinion on a similar question, speaking from the viewpoint of the accusatorial and inquisitorial systems of criminal procedure, which of course were operative in the ecclesiastical courts in England. A judge has no right to prosecute a crime unless (1) there is an accuser, or (2) there is confirmed public suspicion, or (3) the judge witnesses the crime himself.[108] When one or other of the first two conditions is met, the defendant is morally bound to respond truthfully, even though his response will convict him, because his obligation to obey his superior supersedes his obligation or right against self-incrimination. However, if the judge were to ask a question in violation of the law (for instance, let us say, concerning deeds not connected with the charged crime, or concerning unspoken beliefs), then the defendant is not required to answer at all. What then should he do, if remaining silent will not suffice? Well, he can enter an appeal to a higher court, or extricate himself in some other licit way.[109] One may not lie, but one may conceal the truth. One is not obliged to tell a judge the whole truth, but only what the law allows him to demand.[110]

Duncan Derrett, when discussing More's defense that "silence itself is no crime," first cites, without comment, St Thomas's treatment of sins of omission, which would seem to affirm just the opposite. Thomas says that a sin of omission is the refusal to obey an affirmative precept, and he gives the example of the obligation to go to church.[111] This is a good example for us, because failure to go to church would rank as a crime as well as a sin, a crime being something punishable in the external forum, not simply a sin in the internal forum of conscience and confession.

Would there not be a similar precept in a statute that commanded Henry VIII's subjects to acknowledge his ecclesiastical supremacy? Perhaps, but this situation did not come up, precisely, since neither of the relevant statutes of November 1534 imposed such an obligation. The first, "An Act Concerning the King's Highness to be Supreme Head of the Church of England," simply recognizes him to be such.[112] The second, "An Act Whereby Divers Offenses Be Made

---

107 The seal of confession did not apply to everything said to one's confessor, but only to sins sincerely confessed. See the explanation of William Lyndwood, *Provinciale* (1432; Oxford, 1679, repr. Farnborough, 1968), 5.6.8, *Prohibemus*, p. 334, notes n–q, summarized by H. A. Kelly, "Penitential Theology and Law at the Turn of the Fifteenth Century," in *A New History of Penance*, ed. Abigail Firey (Leiden, 2008), pp. 239–317, at 256–7.
108 Thomas Aquinas, *Summa* 2–2.67.3 ad 2.
109 Ibid. 2–2.69.1 corpus; ad 1. John Andrew cites this discussion of St Thomas in his *Additiones* to the *Speculum judiciale* of William Durand, Lib. 2, pt. 2, *De positionibus*, §7: *Positiones quibus modis reprobentur, et de cautelis circa eas*, no. 40, note *a* (1: 594 of the Basel 1574 edition of the *Speculum*, repr. Aalen, 1975).
110 Thomas, *Summa*, 2–2.69.2 corpus. For the text and further explanation, see Kelly, "Right to Remain Silent," p. 1002 n. 46.
111 Thomas Aquinas, *Summa* 1–2.71.5 corpus, ad 3. See Derrett, "Trial," pp. 63, 593 n. 40.
112 26 Henry VIII (1534) c. 1 (*Statutes of the Realm*, 3:492) (Doc. 1).

High Treason," specifies as treason only the malicious use of words, writing, or craft that would deprive the king or queen of any title or dignity belonging to them.[113] Nevertheless, the king's ministers made the case (as the indictment shows) that the king's subjects had the obligation to give a supportive answer when officially required to do so.

Commanded affirmation by oath?
What if the Statute of Treasons actually had required subjects to support the king's title, or to reveal their opinions about it, under oath? Would they have had a moral and legal obligation to comply? More recorded in the letter that he sent to his daughter on June 3, 1535, that the king's Council, headed by Cromwell, claimed to be transmitting a command from Henry that More should make a plain answer as to whether he thought the statute "lawful or not," but then Cromwell further defined More's choices: not a plain "yes or no," but "that I should either [ac]knowledge and confess it lawful that his Highness should be Supreme Head of the Church of England, or else to utter plainly my malignity." More was able to avoid this command by responding that he had no malignity.[114] In other words, he was not "mute of malice."

However, when Chancellor Audley and Cromwell said that "the King might by his laws compel me to make a plain answer thereto, either the one way or the other," More replied that he would not dispute the king's authority to do so, but he responded tentatively ("under correction") that it would be "somewhat hard," or, in case his conscience were against the statutes (he was not saying that it was), it would be "a *very* hard thing," because affirmation would mean the loss of his soul (that is, a mortal sin), and denial would entail the destruction of his body.

In point of fact, More had in the previous year almost been subjected to this sort of hard case, when he had been required to take the oath supposedly called for in the Act of Succession. But he was able to evade the decision by pointing out that the text of the oath presented to him differed from the oath described in the statute, which was simply to "observe ... the whole effect and contents of this present act."[115] But it is doubtful that he would have sworn an oath that was in conformity with the statute, since the statute declared the marriage of Henry and Catherine void. As he wrote to his daughter Margaret, "Though I would not deny to swear to the succession, yet unto the oath that there was offered me I could not swear without the jeoparding of my soul to perpetual damnation."[116] The oath that More refused was presumably the same as the oath spelled out in the new Act of the Oath of Succession, passed

---

[113] 26 Henry VIII (1534) c. 13 (*Statutes of the Realm* 3:508–9) (Doc. 2).

[114] Thomas More, Letter to Margaret Roper, June 3, 1535, no 214 in *Correspondence*, pp. 555–9 (**Doc. 6**, par. 3–4). This letter is numbered as 64 in *St Thomas More: Selected Letters*, ed. Elizabeth Frances Rogers (New Haven, CT, 1961), pp. 249–53. For an edition in modern spelling, see *Last Letters*, no. 22, pp. 118–22.

[115] 25 Henry VIII (1533–34) c. 22: "An Act for the Establishment of the King's Succession," §9 (*Statutes of the Realm* 3:474).

[116] More to Margaret Roper, *c.* April 17, 1534, in *Correspondence*, no. 200, pp. 501–7, at 502 (in *Last Letters*, no. 6, p. 58).

along with the Act of Supremacy.[117] This oath is said in the act to be the one intended in the original act; it calls for faith and obedience to the king and the heirs that will be born to him and Queen Anne, and seems if anything to be less demanding than the language of the first act. There is certainly no explicit call for affirmation that the king's first marriage was null and his second one valid. But More must have decided that such an affirmation would be entailed or implied in taking the oath, and if he were ordered to take it he would have had to refuse – that is, remain silent.

The question of an oath being required to affirm the king's position as Supreme Head of the English Church had come up in 1534 even before the supremacy and treasons statutes were passed in November. By April at least, such an oath had to be taken by every new bishop in the realm.[118] Furthermore, all friars were required to take an elaborate oath combining succession and supremacy, and the earliest response was on April 17, 1534 by heads of the five orders of friars of London.[119] Similar declarations from houses of friars (and

---

[117] 26 Henry VIII c. 2: "An Act Ratifying the Oath that Every of the King's Subjects Hath Taken and Shall Hereafter Be Bound to Take for Due Observation of the Act Made for the Surety of the Succession of the King's Highness in the Crown of the Realm" (*Statutes of the Realm* 3:492–3).
[118] *LP* 8, no. 427 (p. 179).
[119] Thomas Rymer, *Foedera*, 2nd edn, 17 vols (London, 1726–35), 14:487–8, calendared in *LP* 7, no. 665 (p. 255). The formula reads, in essence:

[1] Profitemus, testamur, ac fideliter promittimus et spondemus nos … integram …fidem, observationem, et obedientiam semper praestaturos erga dominum regem nostrum Henricum Octavus et erga serenissimam Reginam Annam uxorem ejusdem, et erga castum sanctumque matrimonium nuper … contractum … sed etiam in duabus convocationibus cleri quam in Parliamento … determinatum et per Thomam Cantuariensem archiepiscopum solemniter confirmatum, et erga quamcumque aliam ejusdem Henrici regis nostri uxorem post mortem praedictae Annae…legitime ducendam, et erga sobolem dicti domini regis Henrici ex praedicta Anna [etc.], et quod haec eadem populo notificabimus, praedicabimus, et suadebimus ubicumque dabitur locus et occasio.	[1] We profess, testify, and faithfully promise and pledge that we will always give complete fidelity, observance, and obedience towards our lord king Henry VIII and towards the most serene Queen, his wife Anne, and towards the chaste and holy marriage recently contracted, and also in the two convocations of the clergy as well as in Parliament affirmed, and solemnly confirmed by Thomas, archbishop of Canterbury, and towards any other wife of the said Henry our king to be legitimately married after the death of the said Anne, and towards offspring of the said lord king Henry from the said Anne [and so on], and that we will make all this known to the people and preach to them and persuade them wherever place and occasion may be.
[2] Item, quod confirmatum ratumque habemus semperque et perpetuo habiturui simus quod praedictus rex noster Henricus est Caput Ecclesiae Anglicanae.	[2] Likewise, that we consider it confirmed and ratified and will always and perpetually do so that the said Henry our king is Head of the English Church.
[3] Item, quod episcopus Romanus… nihilo majoris…jurisdictionis habendus sit quam ceteri quivis episcopi in Anglia vel alibi gentium in sua quisque dioecese.	[3] Likewise, that the bishop of Rome is to have no greater jurisdiction than other bishops in England or elsewhere of other nations, each in his own diocese.

also nuns) soon followed.[120] But other clergy were required only to declare that the Roman bishop had no more power in England than any other bishop.[121]

Bishop Fisher was concerned to know whether the Statute of Treasons obliged one to answer by oath, like the Act of Succession, but his brother assured him that it did not.[122]

Late in the Council's interrogation of More on June 3, More was offered an oath to tell the truth about what would be asked him on the king's behalf concerning the king's person. When More replied that he never intended to take another "book oath," they thought that he was being unreasonable, since it was the sort of oath taken by persons brought before the Star Chamber and everywhere else. More replied that he could guess what the questions would be, and that it was better to refuse before rather than after. They then showed him the questions, which were two in number: whether he had seen the statute, and whether he thought it lawful. He responded that he had already answered the first, and would not answer the second.[123]

[4] Item, quod soli dicto Domino regi ... adhaerebimus atque ejus decreta ... manutenebimus, episcopi Romani legibus, decretis, et canonibus, si qui contra legem divinam et Sacram Scripturam esse invenientur, imperpetuum renunciantes.	[4] Likewise we will adhere to the said Lord king alone and maintain his decrees, forever renouncing the laws, decrees, and canons of the Roman bishop if found to be contrary to divine law and Sacred Scripture.
[5] Item, quod...quisque [nostrum] praedicabit catholice et orthodoxe.	[5] Likewise, that each of us will preach in Catholic and Orthodox manner.
[6] Item, quod unusquisque in suis orationibus ... primum omnium Regem tanquam Supremum Caput Ecclesiae Anglicanae Deo et populi precibus commendabit ...	[6] Likewise, that each of us in his prayers will first of all commend to God and the prayers of the people the King as Supreme Head of the Church of England.
[7] Item, quod omnes et singuli praedicti priores et conventus et successores nostri conscientiae ac jusjurandi sacramento nosmet firmiter obligamus quod omnia et singula praedicta fideliter imperpetuum observabimus.	[7] Likewise that each and every of us aforesaid priors and religious communities and our successors obligate ourselves in conscience and by our sworn oath that we will observe each and every one of the above provisions in perpetuity.
[8] In cujus rei testimonium huic instrumento vel scripto nostro communia sigilla nostra appendimus, et nostra nomina propria quisque manu subscripsimus.	[8] In testimony of which we append our common seals to this instrument or writing of ours, and each of us subscribe our proper names by hand.

A document describing such provisions for the friars, at least as summarized by Gairdner, *LP* 7, no. 590 (p. 236), orders that "they must acknowledge the king as Supreme Head of the Church, as convocation and Parliament have decreed." But the formula itself rightly connects such authorization only to the king's marriage and succession.

[120] Ibid., no. 665.2 (p. 255), no. 921 (p. 336). See Gairdner, *LP* 7, Introduction, pp. xxvii–xxix, for the resistance of some friars to these orders.

[121] Ibid., no. 1025 (pp. 394–8). The declaration reads: "Romanus episcopus non habet majorem aliquam jurisdictionem a Deo sibi collatam in hoc regno Angliae quam quivis alius externus episcopus" ("The Roman bishop does not have any greater jurisdiction given to him by God in this realm of England than does any other foreign bishop"). See Gairdner, *LP* 7, Introduction, p. xxvii.

[122] **Doc. 10**, q. 1; cf. *LP* 8, no. 858.

[123] More to Margaret, 3 June (**Doc. 6**), par. 11–13.

Silence and declaring conscience in inquisitorial proceedings
Just before this last exchange, Cromwell had brought up the point that More, or at least the bishops, had made a practice of examining heretics on the question of "whether they believed the pope to be the Head of the Church," and compelling them to make a precise answer. Why, then, could not the king compel an answer concerning his title? More replied in effect that an obligation imposed by the Universal Church was different from a local law.[124] So while he did not deny Cromwell's assertion that bishops were in the habit of compelling statements of belief from heresy suspects, he seemed to *assume* that what he said was true. It looks like a case of silence signifying affirmation!

I have discussed the principle of silence-as-assent in my essay, "The Right to Remain Silent: Before and After Joan of Arc," in connection with the rules of due process for defendants in inquisitorial procedure.[125] I liken our modern right to remain silent before arraignment to the implicit right accorded to defendants under the rules of inquisition, established by Innocent III at the Fourth Lateran Council in 1215. According to these rules, the first order of business is to state the charges against the summoned suspect; the charges must concern only a public crime, for which probable cause has been established: that is, it must be proved by reputable persons that there is general belief that the suspect is guilty. Only then is the suspect required to say whether he or she is guilty or innocent; if the latter, the judge must present proof of guilt (not simply proof of suspicion). But Boniface VIII in his *Sext* of 1298 authorized judges to skip the preliminaries of stating the charges and proving suspicion if the defendant does not object – that is, remains silent on the matter. The great lay canonist John Andrew in his ordinary gloss to the *Sext* defended this procedure on the grounds that lack of objection on the part of the defendant signified consent.[126] But that would be true only if the defendant knew what he was being silent about. The greatest of all English authorities on canon law and canonical procedure, William Lyndwood, says in his *Provinciale* (finished in 1432), that "through taciturnity alone no consent can be assumed."[127] By the way, we know that More possessed his own copy of the *Provinciale*, and he describes himself as consulting it in his *Dialogue Concerning Heresies*.[128]

In other words, to be strictly legal, the inquisitor would have to inform the defendant of his or her right to have charges explained before being interrogated on any subject. Inquisitors did have this obligation, of course, because they were bound to follow canon law, but it was rarely or never stressed. Similarly, in the United States, defendants always had the right to remain silent before arraignment, but it was only after the 1966 *Miranda* ruling that defendants were guaranteed *the right to know this right*.

---

[124] Ibid., par. 7–8.
[125] Kelly, "Right to Remain Silent," p. 998.
[126] John Andrew, ordinary gloss to *Sext* 5.1.2 ad v. *reclamante*; CJC (1582), 3:1:610–11.
[127] See Lyndwood, *Provinciale* 2.1.3 ad v. *aut permissionem* (p. 86 note b). See Kelly, "Right to Remain Silent," p. 998 n. 23 for the text.
[128] Thomas More, *A Dialogue Concerning Heresies* 3.14, ed. Thomas M. C. Lawler, Germain Marc'hadour, and Richard C. Marius, in *CW* 6, in two parts, 1:316.

So, what was the situation in England in More's time? Did More's silence in response to Cromwell on this question mean that bishops did regularly interrogate suspects upon their beliefs? When More defended bishops' procedures against suspected heretics in reponse to Christopher St German's charges, he repeatedly insisted that he knew of no case in which heresy suspects were ever condemned without positive proof of previous misdeeds, not simply for hitherto unexpressed beliefs.

However, the English bishops, beginning in 1382, started a policy of compelling suspected Wycliffites to state their views concerning Wyciffite doctrines,[129] and a similar policy was mandated by Pope Martin V at the end of the Council of Constance.[130] We do in fact find questions of this sort being put to heresy suspects in More's time, and in the case of the 45 questions administered to John Lambert a bit later, in 1538, two of the questions do indeed deal with the supremacy of the pope. However, I have found no instance in which anyone was actually prosecuted for their responses to such questions. All convictions that I have seen were on the basis of past deeds, such as the preaching or teaching of condemned propositions.[131]

Strictly speaking, however, admissions of belief in or support for heretical opinions would have been grounds for conviction, under the inquisitorial rules, because anything admitted in court became "notorious," an instant crime, a confession with no need of further proof, even though obtained by "unconstitutional" means.

More's conscience and speaking out

But even though More believed that the king's assumption of such a title was wrong, and believed further that to confirm it would be mortally sinful, he obviously did not believe that he had an obligation to say so in public or to convince others of his position. To do so would have been to court death needlessly, a form of suicide, and it would also have put others in danger of death. Presumably, More would have come to a different conclusion if it had been a matter of affirming his Christian faith in general, but we do not know.

Proof of the first part

As noted, no witnesses are said to have been called to prove the first part of the accusation against More, but would they have been needed, even to affirm the authenticity of the examinations taken? After all, some of the judges (that is, the commissioners), notably Chancellor Audley, witnessed the cited events. This would fall under the canonical category of notoriety, as just explained: no further proof is needed when the judge has seen the alleged crime. Moreover, More himself confessed the truth of the indicted events: he did indeed remain

---

[129] H. A. Kelly, "Trial Procedures against Wyclif and Wycliffites in England and at the Council of Constance." *Huntington Library Quarterly* 61 (1999), 1–28.

[130] H. A. Kelly, "Lollard Inquisitions: Due and Undue Process," in *The Devil, Heresy and Witchcraft in the Middle Ages: Essays in Honor of Jeffrey B. Russell*, ed. Alberto Ferreiro (Leiden, 1998), pp. 279–303 at pp. 296–303.

[131] Kelly, "Thomas More on Inquisitorial Due Process," 862–70.

silent on the subject of the act on the two named occasions when he was asked to give his opinion.

Of course, whether such silence constituted malice (as the judges decreed by acclamation in Pole's account), or whether it was necessary to prove it, is something else again. I will take up the question of malice again in the conclusion, below.

The Second and Third Parts: Collusion with Fisher

More's responses
More distinguishes as the "Second Part of the Accusation" against him, according to the Guildhall Report, the charge that he contravened the statute and worked for its abolition by a series of eight letters he wrote to Bishop Fisher, by which he armed him against the statute. He says that he would dearly like those letters to be read publicly, which is impossible since, as they tell him, the bishop burned them. Therefore he will recall their contents for them: "Some of them dealt with familiar matters, such as our old custom and friendship called for. One of them responded to his request to know how I answered when first examined on the statute. I replied that I had exonerated my conscience and followed reason, and I urged him to do the same." That was all that was in them, with nothing worthy of death.[132]

More says that the third part of the accusation charges him with telling the commissioners that the statute was like a two-edged sword, and that Fisher had made the same comparison, indicating connivance between them. More responds that he was speaking only hypothetically: "I respond that I was not speaking straightforwardly but only conditionally; that is, if there should be some statute that was like a two-edged sword, how could any person take care against coming up against one edge or the other?" ("Respondeo me non simpliciter sed sub conditione esse locutum, videlicet, si esset aliquod decretum simile gladio ancipiti, quonammodo quisquam hominum sibi possit cavere ne in alterutram aciem incurrat?") He does not know what Fisher said, but if he spoke in the same way, it was not done through any conspiracy, but rather the similarity can be accounted for by their similar training. (Just as, we might say, no collusion would be needed nowadays to account for the use of proverbial expressions like "Damned if you do, damned if you don't," or "Catch 22.") More repeats that he never said anything maliciously against the statute.[133]

Joint use of the two-edged-sword image
We can speculate that the origin of this combined set of charges against More began with the fact that both he and Fisher on the same day made use of the same simile of a two-edged sword. This would have been seen as rock-solid evidence of possible collusion between them. It could be testified to by Audley

---

[132] Guildhall Report (**Doc. 17**), §5.
[133] Ibid., §6.

and the other commissioners who had been among the group of interrogators on June 3. A fragmentary report of the interrogation of More on June 3 survives, which has him using the sword metaphor.[134] He did not include a reference to the metaphor in the detailed report of the interrogation that he sent to his daughter Margaret, discussed above.[135]

Evidence of letters having been exchanged (no evidence on contents)
Cromwell and the others who were establishing the case against More must then have set out to try to show that More and Fisher had connived together. One way of doing this would be to demonstrate that they had had a written correspondence when they were both in the Tower, which was easy to do, since it was admitted by both More and Fisher. But nothing could be proved about the malicious content of such letters, unless the letters themselves could be found, or unless Fisher or More confessed the same, or testimony to this effect could be had from someone who had read them.

They therefore set about interrogating servants in the Tower, from June 7 to June 11.[136] A series of eight interrogatories was administered to them, starting with Fisher's servant, Richard Wilson, on June 7. We can surmise the content of the questions from the answers given, and conclude that the last one or two dealt with letters or other communications between More and Fisher. Wilson said that he saw two letters from More, but did not know their content.[137] He said that when the Council interviewed Fisher about the statute, Fisher "stuck to the word 'maliciously'"; when the Council voiced their suspicion that he had had counsel from More on this point, he said, no, that his brother Robert had told him, and advised him to say so.[138] Wilson said further that he heard Fisher tell the Tower servant George Gold that "there was no peril in the statutes except it were maliciously done and spoken." He suspected that Fisher told Gold to tell More so, seven or eight days before the Council came to interrogate Fisher.[139]

Wilson never sent anything to More or More's servant concerning the king's matter, in word or in writing. He often suspected that Gold carried letters between Fisher and More. He saw Fisher burn papers, and he himself burned papers at Fisher's bidding, but did not know what they were; but among them were papers written before he came to the Tower.[140] After the Council's first examination of Fisher, Fisher gave Gold a letter to More, but he did not read it. Wilson and Gold agreed among themselves to deny that any letters were sent between More and Fisher. Wilson heard Fisher tell Gold that "he might say he

---

[134] See *LP* 8, no. 814.i (p. 309), interrogation of More, 3 June 1535 (Doc. 5).
[135] More to Margaret, June 3, 1535 (Doc. 6).
[136] *LP* 8, no. 856 (pp. 325–31) (Doc. 8). Reynolds, *Trial of St Thomas More*, pp. 94–7, mixes up the dates, thinking that Richard Wilson was interrogated only on June 11; he was in fact interrogated extensively on June 7 and 8 as well.
[137] *LP* 8, no. 856 (Doc. 8), i, par. 6.
[138] Ibid., iii, par. 7. I cited above Wilson's testimony about what Robert Fisher had reported concerning the Parliamentary debate over the term "maliciously."
[139] Ibid., par. 8.
[140] Ibid., par. 9–11.

never carried any letters on the King's business, but he would not counsel him to be forsworn for other things."[141] (As we will see below, Fisher wished them to keep as quiet as they could about the letters, without forswearing themselves.)

Wilson was again interrogated on June 8, when he said, among other things, that after the Council's second examination of Fisher, Fisher told him that they expressed displeasure with the lieutenant of the Tower for negligent keeping of Fisher and More, because they suspected that they had been counseling each other, "because both stuck much upon one point." Wilson inquired whether it was about the word "maliciously," but Fisher made no answer.[142] Wilson thought that after the last examination letters passed between Fisher and More, for he saw Gold bring Fisher a letter, and afterwards he (Gold, it seems) cast it into the fire; that was on Sunday (June 6).[143]

Also on June 8, George Gold was examined. He said that on June 6, Fisher wrote a letter to More, and the next day More sent an answer, along with Fisher's letter, and that he burned both at Fisher's command.[144] About ten days before, Fisher sent a letter to More, which More had him burn, and the next day he carried an answer to Fisher, which Fisher had him burn. Altogether he conveyed about a dozen letters between Fisher and More. Fisher, Wilson, and Gold were agreed to deny carrying any such letters, but if Gold were to swear to the matter on a book, he was to tell the truth.[145]

On June 10, More's servant John Wood, was examined, and said that about a fortnight after the Council had come to the Tower, Fisher sent Gold to More to find out what answer he had given; More replied in a letter that he would not dispute the king's title but only say his prayers. Soon after, More sent another letter, saying that he would not counsel Fisher to make the same answer, lest the Council should think that they had agreed to do so. After the Council returned to the Tower for another confrontation, Fisher told More what answer he had made, but Wood did not know if More sent a reply.[146]

Fisher's testimony on contents of letters
The interrogations continued on June 11, with no further results on any More–Fisher exchanges,[147] and on June 12, Fisher himself was interrogated.[148] Fisher recounted what his brother had told him, that the Commons were worried that the penalty specified by the act concerning treasonous words could be too easily incurred, unless the specification of malice were added. He said that about four letters had passed between him and More on the matter of the question that was being put to him. This question included pre-supremacy controversy, since he said that More asked him what answer he gave on the matter for which he

---

[141] Ibid., par. 12–13.
[142] Ibid., iv, par. 20.
[143] Ibid., par. 24.
[144] Ibid., par. 25.
[145] Ibid., v, par. 28, 33, 34.
[146] Ibid., vi, par. 41.
[147] Ibid., vi, par. 44; vii, 45–50; viii, par. 52–3; ix, p. 54.
[148] Tower Interrogation of Fisher, June 12, 1535, **Doc. 10**; cf. *LP* 8, no. 858 (pp. 331–2).

had been sent to the Tower, and Fisher sent a reply. As for More's answer to the demand to comment on the Act of Supremacy, Fisher said that he became aware of More's response from Gold's showing him the letter that More wrote to his daughter Margaret. Fisher then sent a letter to More to know his reply more precisely, but Fisher did not recall what More answered. He also wrote to More to tell him about what his brother had told him of the dispute in Parliament over the word "maliciously," but did not ask More's advice. More wrote to advise him not to give the impression that they had agreed upon their answers. He wrote to More that he told the Council that the act condemned only those who spoke with malice against the king's title, and that the act did not compel a man to answer. He burned all of More's letters as soon as he received them, because he had promised the lieutenant not to do anything to cause him to be blamed. As to whether there was any compact between him and Wilson and Gold concerning letters, he replied that "they were agreed to keep it as secret as they might."[149]

More's previous testimony
Finally, on June 14, More himself was interrogated. He said that Fisher had sent him a letter asking him what he had said to the Council, and More replied that he told the Council that he did not wish to meddle in the matter. Fisher sent him another letter, telling him that since the word "maliciously" was used in the statute, one who did not speak out of malice did not violate the statute. He replied that he agreed, but feared that it would not be interpreted in that way. More did not tell Fisher the answer he gave to the Council [that is, in full detail?] and advised him to make his own answer different, lest confederacy be suspected between them.[150]

More then added that he had written to Fisher after his last examination, which has to refer to the discussion that he had with Richard Rich, which, according to the indictment, occurred just two days earlier than the present interrogation of June 14, namely, on June 12. He told Fisher that Master Solicitor told him at that examination that remaining silent was the equivalent of speaking against the statute, "as all the learned men of Europe would justify." Therefore, More told Fisher, "he could only reckon on the uttermost" – that is, he feared the direst consequences – and he asked Fisher to pray for him, as he would for Fisher.[151]

That same day, June 14, both Fisher and More were asked to affirm Henry as Supreme Head, and to acknowledge his marriage to Queen Anne. More replied that he could make no answer to the first, and, as to the second, he had never spoken against it.[152]

---

[149] Ibid., qq. 5–30.
[150] *LP* 8, no. 867 (pp. 340–2) (**Doc. 11**), iii, q. 2.
[151] Ibid.
[152] Ibid., iv, qq. 1–3. For Fisher's replies, see i, qq. 1–3: to the first question, he stood by his previous answer; to the second, he agreed to the Act of Succession (something that More would not do). Fisher was unwilling to answer further, lest he fall under the penalties specified in the statutes.

When asked if any of the letters to or from Fisher survived, More said that Gold insisted on burning them. More tried to persuade Gold to let some friend read them so that he could testify to their contents,[153] that is, he could bear witness that they were innocuous. Gold himself, we conclude, was illiterate, and Roper tells us the same about John Wood.[154]

Upshot
The upshot of these responses is that Fisher destroyed the letters for fear of compromising the Lieutenant of the Tower, and that More wanted them preserved so that that they would exonerate him of any charge of collusion with Fisher. The servants had no knowledge of the contents of the letters, certainly of nothing incriminating. And, finally, there is no evidence yet recovered that Fisher used the metaphor of a two-edged sword in his responses to the Council on June 3, but we should probably leave open the possibility that he did actually do so. As we saw, the written report of More's usage that day survives in a very fragile condition, and it may be that a similar report on Fisher was made but failed to survive. But it is hard to see how they could have had any evidence that More used the metaphor in one of his letters to Fisher, as the indictment alleges. This part of the indictment may have been a ploy to try to get More to confess the fact, if it was a fact. However, More in effect denied it, and said that if Fisher did actually speak similarly, it was not through any communication from him.

The Last Part of the Indictment: More's Alleged Statement to Richard Rich

Absence from Guildhall and Pole reports
The Guildhall Manuscript gives nothing further of the charges against More or of More's defense; specifically, it is silent about the last part of the indictment, the purported conversation with Richard Rich, for which we will have to go to Roper's account. Instead, Guildhall speaks of the jury, as cited above, and says that after about a quarter of an hour the jurors returned with a verdict of guilty.

As stated above, Derrett's conclusion is that More's arguments against the "three counts" (as set out in Guildhall) convinced the judges, and that they found in More's favor and dismissed those charges, leaving only the charge about More's statements to Rich standing, which was prosecuted by having Rich testify, and More responding.[155] If this were true, then, as we noted above, More would have made his objections against the first three parts of the indictment before the jury was summoned. But surely he would have spoken against the rest of the indictment at that time as well, though to no avail. Then, following Derrett's scenario, he would have repeated and enlarged upon his objections to the final part of the indictment, in the presence of the jury, after which the jury

---

[153] Ibid., iii, q. 3.
[154] Roper, *Lyfe*, ed. Hitchcock, p. 75.
[155] Derrett, "Trial," pp. 65–8.

would have been sent out and returned with the verdict of guilty. That would mean that the Guildhall reporter completely ignored the whole core of the trial upon which More was convicted. It does not seem likely. Perhaps more plausible is the conclusion that Guildhall portrayed More as subsuming the whole of the Rich charge, even though it made up a full third of the indictment in length, in the first article, where he was accused of impugning the act by refusing to given an answer about it. This would fit with Reginald Pole's informant's account as well (except that he also ignored the charge of colluding with Fisher). As we will see, More maintained that he did not say anything against the act when speaking to Rich.

Weighing against Derrett's hypothesis that the judges dismissed the bulk of the indictment against More is that, as I have noted before, Spelman, one of the judges, does not mention such a dismissal, and he also says that he was convicted of aiding and abetting Fisher's treason as well as maliciously practicing against the statute.

What More really said: Parliament could not make Rich pope
That a conversation occurred between More and Rich on the date specified is beyond dispute, being admitted by More himself. A report of it, presumably filed by Rich, still exists in fragmentary form in the Public Record Office (PRO), and the indictment's account was based on it, as is particularly clear from Brian Byron's analysis.[156]

There are crucial differences between the PRO/indictment account of the conversation and the account that Roper gives. Previously, Roper has been read as saying that he is giving Rich's distorted account, as he presented it at the trial. But in Byron's plausible explanation, Roper gives the account that More himself gave at the trial, except for the crucial last words whose meaning Rich perjuriously distorted.

According to the Roper account, More told Rich that Parliament could make Rich king but could not make Rich pope, any more than it could make God not-God.

What Rich said More said: Parliament could not make Henry Supreme Head
According to the PRO/indictment account, however, More told Rich that Parliament could make him king, but could not make God not-God, and could not make the king Supreme Head of the Church of England.

In other words, Rich "changed cases": instead of the actual example he used in his discussion with More, of himself as king being made pope by Parliament, he substituted in his report the example of the present king, Henry VIII, being

---

[156] The report is noticed in *LP* 8, no. 814.ii (p. 309); it is in the PRO, S.P. 2/R, fols 24–5; a first attempt to decipher it was made by Reynolds, "An Unnoticed Document," *Moreana* 1 (Sept. 1963), 12–17, and more fully in his *Trial*, pp. 166–7, with other readings on the last part offered by Derrett, "The 'New' Document," pp. 7–8. The last part is most convincingly explained by Brian Byron, "The Fourth Count of More's Indictment," *Moreana* 10 (May 1966), 33–46. See **Doc. 9** for a transcription and conjectural expansion of the More–Rich exchange.

made Supreme Head of the English Church, and falsely claimed that More denied that Parliament had the power to make such a declaration.

The charge in the indictment is as follows: "Thomas More falsely, treasonously, and maliciously, in his words persevering in his treason and malice, and desiring to put forth and defend his aforesaid treasonous and malicious proposal, responded to the aforesaid Richard Rich," in answer to Rich's question as to why he should not affirm the king to be Supreme Head on earth of the Church of England, just as he would if Parliament were to declare Rich to be king:

> that those cases are not like, because a king can be made by Parliament, and can be deprived by Parliament, to which act any subject being at the Parliament may give his consent; but to the case of a primacy, the subject cannot be bound, because he cannot give his consent from him in Parliament. And although the king were generally accepted as such in England, yet most outer parts do not affirm it.[157]

In following the report in the PRO, the indictment would seem to preserve what must have been the actual gist of More's response, but speaking of the primacy of the whole Church, not just the Church in England. In other words, More was really saying that the English Parliament could declare Richard Rich to be pope, and even though the English might accept it, other regions of the world would not. The same gist can be found even in Roper's account of Rich's report of More's words: "'No more,' said Sir Thomas More, as Master Rich reported of him, 'could the Parliament make the king the Supreme Head of the Church.'"[158] That is (More originally meant), Parliament could not make *King Richard Rich* Supreme Head of the *Universal Church.*

The conclusion of the PRO report, giving Rich's last words to More, which was not incorporated into the indictment, is deciphered by Byron (modernizing the spelling) thus:

> Well, Sir, God comfort you, for I see your mind will not change, which I fear will be very dangerous to you, for I suppose your concealment to the question that hath been asked of you is as high offense as other that hath denied it. And this Jesu send you better grace.[159]

Byron notes that Rich here acknowledged to More that More had not revealed his mind on the act, but that Rich considered More's concealment as much of an offense as that of another who has expressly spoken against it – referring, Byron suggests, to Bishop Fisher, who had recently been tricked into an absolute denial of the statute.[160] As we have seen above, More told his interrogators

---

[157] More's indictment (**Doc. 16**), §11 (e). My translation of this section closely follows Byron, p. 35. In the passage, "cannot give his consent from him in Parliament" ("consensum suum ab eo ad Parliamentum praebere not potest"), it is not clear who "him" refers to.
[158] Roper, *Lyfe,* ed. Hitchcock, p. 86 (**Doc. 20**, §1).
[159] Byron, p. 39.
[160] Ibid., p. 40.

that, two days after his talk with Rich, he reported to Fisher that this was the substance of what Master Solicitor told him, that is, that it was just as wrong to refuse to answer as to speak out against the statute).[161]

More's defense against Rich's testimony
At the trial itself, Roper does not recount Rich's testimony, but only refers to it: "For proof to the jury that Sir Thomas More was guilty of this treason, Master Rich was called forth to give evidence unto them upon his oath, as he did."[162]

More told Rich and the jury that he was sorry to see that Rich had perjured himself; and he went on to say that he had long known Rich to be an untrustworthy character, and to urge the unlikelihood of More's making such a damning statement to him, of the sort that he had never made to any other person. Moreover, even if he had made such a statement, since the conversation was private, it could not be alleged that it was spoken maliciously, as was required by the statute to be constituted an offense: just as the Statute of Forcible Entries would not be violated by a peaceable rather than a forcible entry. There was nothing in More's history to suggest that he had any malicious intentions against the king.[163]

Then, Roper says, "Master Rich, seeing himself so disproved and his credit so foully defaced, caused Sir Richard Southwell and Master Palmer, that at the time of their communication were in the chamber, to be sworn what words had passed between them." They both testified that they had not paid any attention to what was being said.[164]

What does Roper mean by saying that Rich "caused" the two men to testify? Are we to take it that Rich did indeed have a role in prosecuting the case against More? Possibly, but it seems just as likely that what Roper intends is that Rich requested, perhaps with some insistence, that Prosecutor Hales swear the others as witnesses, in order to bolster his account.

Roper adds that More alleged in his defense "many other reasons not now in my remembrance ... to the discredit of Master Rich's aforesaid evidence, and proof of the clearness of his own conscience. All which notwithstanding, the jury found him guilty."[165] Which means, of course, that the jury heard More's statements in his own defense.

The Jury's Verdict

A rapid result
John Bellamy tells us that "the place where the jurors debated their verdict was usually apart from the courtroom."[166] The average length of time for jury

---

[161] LP 8, no. 867 (Doc. 11), iii, q. 2.
[162] Roper, *Lyfe*, ed. Hitchcock, p. 87 (Doc. 20, §4).
[163] Ibid., pp. 87–90 (Doc. 20, §§8–11).
[164] Ibid., p. 91 (Doc. 20, §12).
[165] Ibid., pp. 91–2 (Doc. 20, §13).
[166] Bellamy, *Tudor Law of Treason*, p. 168.

deliberation in Tudor treason trials (taking the rest of the sixteenth century into consideration) was about an hour.[167] The Guildhall Report says that in More's trial the jury deliberated about a quarter of an hour, whereupon they returned with a verdict of guilty.[168] In Pole's account the verdict came much sooner, as soon as the jury could assemble, which happened with almost unbelievable speed. Pole portrays them as swayed by the judges' shouts of "Malice, malice!" which were ringing through the courtroom.[169] In other words, the jury not only witnessed the debate over More's silence, but found it to be the decisive aspect of the trial.

The question of a single witness, and the jurors as witnesses
In Roper's view, as we have just seen, the evidence against More, which as he presents it consisted only of Rich's testimony, was successfully discredited, but the jury found him guilty notwithstanding. Such an outcome, conviction by a jury on the basis of a single witness, is still possible in our own day. Of course, the judge is free to nullify a guilty verdict if he thinks that the evidence was insufficient; this is an option that Tudor judges did not seem to have. An inquiry needs to be made into sixteenth-century thinking on the sufficiency or insufficiency of a single witness. For the present, we can note that this question was put into eloquent form in the *Life of Fisher*, expanded from Rastell's account in his *Life of More*. Here, Fisher says,

> "Let me demand this question: whether a single testimony of one man may be admitted as sufficient to prove me guilty of treason for speaking these words, or no; and whether my answer negatively may not be accepted against his affirmative to my avail and benefit, or no?" To that, the judges and lawyers answered that, "Being the king's case, it rested much in the conscience and discretion of the jury, and as they upon the evidence given before them shall find it, you are either to be acquitted or else by judgment to be condemned."[170]

The answer attributed to the judges and lawyers here is a good one. As Bellamy points out, although the king's case in any treason trial (or any other trial, let us add) might have been helped "to have several witnesses attesting to the guilt of the accused, he had by no means lost if he had only one, or none at all for that matter."[171] Baker puts it thus: "A jury in theory needed no formal evidence to support their verdict, since they might use their own knowledge

---

167 Ibid., p. 169.
168 Guildhall Report (**Doc. 17**), par. 7: "Qui sedentes prope quarta horae parte, deliberatione inter se habita, ut redierunt in conspectum principum ac judicum delegatorum, rogati ecquid sentirent de reo, responderunt, 'Gylthi,' quod lingua Britannica sonat, 'Condemnandus,' aut 'Dignus est morte'" ("And they, sitting about a quarter of an hour, after deliberation was had among them, when they returned to the sight of the princes and judges delegate, on being asked what they thought about the accused party, responded, 'Guilty,' which in British speech means, 'He is to be condemned,' or, 'He is deserving of death'").
169 Pole's account (**Doc. 19**), no. 6.
170 *Life of Fisher*, section 174 (pp. 179–80).
171 Bellamy, *Tudor Law of Treason*, p. 153.

acquired before the trial. It was on this footing that the common law did not require any particular number of witnesses to prove a fact."[172] Bellamy recalls John Fortescue's supreme confidence in the jury system for eliciting the truth, in contrast to witnesses, for it operates "by the oath of honest men worthy of credit, neighbours, whom the parties have no cause to challenge, and no cause to distrust their verdict."[173] Fortescue was writing in 1471, and even two generations later, in More's time, the idea was still strong that the members of juries had local knowledge and themselves served as impartial witnesses. In Fisher's trial, we recall, the jurors were to be chosen from among the inhabitants of the Tower, who would be likely to have local knowledge. Sir John Baker, in his introduction to Spelman's reports, says that "it could still be argued that the jury was supposed to proceed upon its own knowledge if there was no evidence or if the evidence was incomplete." But he also points out that Thomas More "stated quite explicitly in 1533 that jurors were not to be regarded as witnesses, but as judges of fact."[174]

Baker is citing the *Debellation*, at the point where More rebukes Christopher St German for supposing that More might have been referring to juries when he spoke of witnesses. He says:

> I never took the twelve men for witnesses in my life. For why should I call them witnesses, whose verdict the judge taketh for a sure sentence concerning the fact without any examination of the circumstances whereby they know or be led to believe their verdict to be true?[175]

More here goes to the heart of the matter, which, I repeat, holds just as true for juries now as it did then. Juries make up their mind any way they wish, and do not have to give an accounting of how they came to their decision. It still does not matter whether the evidence presented in a case would pass muster before some other kind of tribunal. They are free to decide according to emotion or prejudice or intimidation.

More found guilty on the whole indictment

In More's case, the accepted wisdom nowadays is, as I have stated, Derrett's view that the jury deliberated only on the last part of the indictment, regarding More's conversation with Richard Rich. For my part, as I have noted above, I think it probable that the whole indictment was presented to them, and that they heard the prosecutor's arguments in support of it and More's arguments against it.

Even though Baker professes to agree with Derrett's analysis, when he sums up More's case later he contradicts this view, and assumes that it was not the Rich accusation but rather the first charge, of remaining silent, that took

---

[172] Baker, *Oxford History*, p. 361
[173] John Fortescue, *De laudibus legum Angliae*, ed. and tr. S. B. Chrimes (Cambridge, 1942), ch. 32, pp. 76–7.
[174] Baker, *Spelman's Reports*, 2:109; also cited in *Oxford History*, pp. 361–2.
[175] More, *Debellation*, ch. 16, p. 149.

the greatest importance. He asserts that when More was convicted under the statute for denying the king's title of Supreme Head of the Church, "the chief complaint was of evasive answers under interrogation rather than spontaneous open denial."[176]

If the jury heard the whole indictment, it was entirely up to them to decide whether and how he had violated the statute and committed high treason: whether for refusing to give his opinion; for colluding with Bishop Fisher; and/or for speaking positively to Richard Rich against the power of Parliament to grant or affirm the king's title. They decided that he was guilty of one or all of these charges, and no accounting for their decision was forthcoming.

Post-Verdict Events: Alternative Versions

First alternative: exonerating conscience (Guildhall)
The activity described by the eyewitness account represented in the Guildhall Report, recorded just after the trial, is as follows. After the jury announced its verdict, the chancellor immediately pronounced sentence against More, as required by the statute. Thereupon, More, taking the verdict and sentence as final, seized the opportunity to finally reveal his opinion concerning the statutes upon which he had been convicted. He said, "Since I have been adjudged to death, whether rightly or not, God knows, let me speak freely to you concerning your statute, for the exoneration of my conscience." During years of study on the subject, he had never found any authority to assert that a non-ordained person could be the head of an ecclesiastical order. To Audley's taunt that he was making himself better than all of the bishops and nobles and commons of England, he replied that for every bishop on their side he could easily find a hundred, including saints, to agree with him, as well as the testimony of all of the general councils of the Church. Norfolk accused him of showing his malice, but More said, no, he was speaking to exonerate his conscience and not burden his soul, and he took God as witness to his sincerity. Their statute, he added, was wrongfully made, since it went against the Universal Church. He added that he was well aware that their underlying motive for condemning him to death was his opposition to the king's second marriage. He concluded by praying that they would all be together in heaven, like St Paul and his one-time adversary St Stephen, and he ended by praying for the king, asking God to send him salutary counsel.[177]

Second alternative: warning others against the statute (Pole)
According to Reginald Pole, More had refrained from giving his opinion about the law declaring the king Supreme Head of the English Church in order not to harm his defense. But once he was found guilty, he spoke out in order to prevent

---

[176] Baker, *Oxford History*, p. 586; cf. p. 417.
[177] Guildhall Report (**Doc. 17**), nos. 8–13.

Englishmen from accepting, out of ignorance or imprudence, what he now termed was a pestiferous statute that was inimical to them. It was against all human and divine laws, and to assent to it would produce a worse effect upon them than the death that he would suffer for allegedly dissenting from it.[178]

More then turned to his adversaries, and instead of denouncing them, prayed for them, imitating Christ on the Cross. He was now going to a place of peace, and he prayed that they too, after a change of heart (including, of course, repenting for their sin of condemning him), would come to the same place. Thus he equalled St Stephen, in praying for those who were stoning him to death.[179]

Third alternative: taking exceptions to void the indictment (Roper)
According to the Roper account, More acted on his earlier promise to speak against the indictment after an adverse verdict came in,[180] but he had to interrupt the sentencing process to do so. For as soon as the verdict was announced, Audley started to "proceed in judgment against him," until More reminded him of standard procedure: "My lord, when I was toward the law, the manner in such case was to ask the prisoner why judgment should not be given against him." Thereupon, the chancellor, "staying his judgment in which he had partly proceeded, demanded of him what he was able to say to the contrary." More thereupon "in this sort most humbly made answer."[181] At the end of his statement, Roper tells us the purpose of his speaking: "Sir Thomas More, for the a-voiding of the indictment, had taken as many exceptions as he thought meet, and many more reasons than I can now remember alleged."[182]

The main objection that More raised against the indictment was that the Act of Parliament upon which it was based was repugnant to the laws of God and the Church. One small part of the Church could not legitimately make a law contrary to the laws of the Church as a whole. It was also contrary to the laws of England still in effect, specifically, the Magna Carta provision that said that the English Church was to remain free. The Church in England could no more refuse obedience to the see of Rome than a child to its natural father. Chancellor Audley reminded him that this view of his opposed that of all the learned men of England, including bishops and members of the universities. More replied that the clergy of the past and the clergy outside England were on his side. He concluded, "And therefore am I not bound, my Lord, to conform my conscience to the counsel of one realm against the general counsel of Christendom?"[183]

A month earlier, on April 28, Richard Reynolds, after being arraigned on similar charges and pleading not guilty, gave a similar speech,[184] after being asked

---

[178] Pole's account (**Doc. 19**), no. 8.
[179] Ibid., no. 9.
[180] Roper, *Lyfe*, ed. Hitchcock, p. 86 (**Doc. 20**, no. 3).
[181] Ibid., p. 92 (**Doc. 20**, nos. 14–15).
[182] Ibid., p. 95 (**Doc. 20**, no. 18).
[183] Ibid., pp. 94–5 (**Doc. 20**, nos. 15–18).
[184] For this account here I am quoting James Gairdner's summary in his entry on Richard Reynolds in the original *DNB*. Gairdner gives the literal report of his speech, from a document in the Vatican Archives, in *LP* 8, no. 661 (pp. 247–8).

by Audley "why he persisted in an opinion condemned by the judgment of so many lords and bishops and of the whole realm in Parliament." He answered

> that he had intended to keep silence, like Our Lord; but, in discharge of his own conscience and those of others, he would say that he had all the rest of Christendom in favor of his view, besides the testimony of general councils and Fathers of the Church; and he was sure that the greater part of England at heart agreed with him.

This was said, however, *before* his trial. He was ordered to say no more, and he replied, "Well, then, judge me according to your law." A jury was summoned for the next day, with the results described by Rastell above.

On June 17, John Fisher too made a similar speech at his trial, but this time it was in the presence of the jury, after the commissioners had in effect declared him guilty of treason under the statute in spite of any plea of lack of malice on his part. Here is Rastell's account:

> Upon this point, and only by this witness of the king's own messenger sent to the bishop, were the twelve men charged to find the holy learned Bishop guilty of treason. But before the inquest of twelve men went from the bar to agree upon their verdict, there was laid to the bishop's charge, by some of his judges, high pride and great presumption, that he and a few others did dissent and vary, in this matter of the king's supremacy, from the whole number of the bishops, lords, learned men, and Commons, gathered together in the Parliament; with divers other things. Unto all which he answered in effect as the holy fathers Carthusians and Doctor Reynolds had done; wherein he showed himself excellently and profoundly learned, of great constancy, and of a marvelous godly courage; and declared the whole matter so learnedly, and therewith so godly, that it made many of them there present, and some of his judges also, so inwardly to lament, that their eyes burst out with tears to see such a great, famous cleric and virtuous bishop to be condemned to so cruel death by such impious laws and by such an unlawful and detestable witness, contrary to all human honesty and fidelity and the word and promise of the king himself.[185]

After More's speech, and after the other exceptions and reasons that Roper cannot remember (presumably from the reports of his informants all those years ago), he says that Audley, "loath to have the burden of that judgment wholly to depend upon himself, there openly asked the advice of the lord FitzJames, then chief justice of the King's Bench, and joined in commission with him, whether this indictment were sufficient or not." FitzJames, "like a wise man," answered: "My lords all, by St Julian, I must needs confess that, if the act of Parliament be not unlawful, then is not the indictment in my conscience insufficient." The rest of the commissioners took this as an affirmation of the validity of the indictment, and Audley proceeded to pass sentence.[186]

---

[185] Rastell, *Life of More*, Fragment C: book 3, ch. 58, p. 240.
[186] Roper, *Lyfe*, ed. Hitchcock, pp. 95–6 (**Doc. 20**, nos. 18–19).

Roper says that even after More was sentenced (to the horrible death stipulated for high treason), "the commissioners yet further courteously offered him, if he had any thing else to allege for his defense, to grant him favorable audience." More had nothing more to say to reverse his condemnation, but said instead that he would pray for them, hoping that one day they would meet merrily in heaven, like St Stephen and St Paul, even though Paul had consented to Stephen's death.[187]

We see, then, that whereas the Guildhall Report puts all of More's remarks after sentencing, Roper places only the reference to Saints Stephen and Paul after the sentence, and only after More is given yet another opportunity, this time by all of the commissioners as a body, to offer further arguments in his defense.

Adjudicating the alternative endings
Which of these three accounts should be given the greater credence? As noted, it can be argued that the Guildhall Report represents direct and immediate eyewitness testimony, while Pole's narrative is arguably based on the report of an independent eyewitness and Roper's account is admittedly indirect and non-immediate. As Roper says at the end,

> Thus much touching Sir Thomas More's arraignment, being not thereat present myself, have I by the credible report, partly of the right worshipful Sir Anthony Seint-Leger, knight, and partly of Richard Heywood and John Webbe, gentlemen, with others of good credit, at the hearing thereof present themselves, as far as my poor wit and memory would serve me, here truly rehearsed unto you.[188]

We can be sure that More did speak at some point about one or both of the statutes concerning the supremacy, since one of the commissioners, Sir John Spelman, says so in his report of the trial: "The said More stood firmly upon the statute of 26 Henry VIII, for he said that the Parliament could not make the king Supreme Head."[189] But this does not tell us the purpose for which More spoke, to reveal and exonerate his conscience, to warn others against acceding to it, or to argue against the validity of the indictment.

Duncan Derrett, who does not take Pole's narrative into consideration at this point, confidently asserts that Roper's version is the authentic account, and his opinion has held sway ever since. He says, "It was normal practice to await a verdict, and, if it was unfavorable, to attack the indictment on law, alleging that it was 'insufficient' to found a sentence. The heart of More's defense lies in the

---

[187] Ibid., p. 96 (**Doc. 20**, no. 20).

[188] Ibid., pp. 96–7 (**Doc. 20**, no. 21). Note that Roper uses "arraignment" in the unusual sense of "trial." There may be that meaning in John Shirley's *Death of the King of Scots* (1456), cited in the *MED*, s.v. "arreinen": "This same Earl of Athetelles was indicted, arraigned, and damned." Cf. s.v. "arreinement": "Sir Robert Grame standing there at the where he was tofore indicted of treason, ... upon his arraignment said plainly that they had no law to do him to death."

[189] Spelman's report (**Doc. 18**): "Le dit More tient fortment sur le statut de 26 Henri VIII, quar il dit que le Parlement ne point faier le roy Supreme Chiefe."

very complex motion in arrest of judgment."[190] ("Arrest" means "stopping," a sense used nowadays only in the phrase "cardiac arrest.")

However, apart from what Roper has More say in his account of the trial, there is no documentation that such an appeal *was* normal practice, or even existed at all as a possibility, in a criminal trial, not to mention a treason trial, in More's time or later in the sixteenth century. Granted, such an action, to be termed an "allegation" rather than a "motion," was starting to be used in civil trials at least a decade and a half before More's trial. We can see this in Spelman's reports. The body of cases which he deals with dates from about 1502 to about 1540, and, of course, everything is in Law French rather than in English. The phrase appears in English only much later: the *OED* gives one seventeenth-century citation (from 1660), and others from the eighteenth century onwards. Here is the entry from Blackstone's *Commentary* (1768): "Whatever is alleged in arrest of judgment must be such matter as would upon demurrer have been sufficient to overturn the action or plea."[191]

Spelman's earliest reference is in a case from 1521, in which we read: "Le consell le Senior allege ceo en arrest de jugement, pur ceo que le manas ne fuit trie" ("The Lord's counsel alleged in arrest of judgment that the menacing had not been tried.") In reply, the court "adjudged" (*ajuge*) the menace to be immaterial. Then, Spelman says, "Auter excepcion fuit pris" ("Another exception was taken.")[192]

In other words, the allegation in arrest of judgment was simply an "exception," the standard Law French term for "objection," which was also the standard term both in Latin and English,[193] and, as we have seen, it is the term that Roper uses.

Spelman mentions allegations *en arrest de jugement* in only five other cases.[194] Baker knows from another source (a yearbook) that there was an attempt to arrest judgment in one further case, but Spelman says nothing about it in his report, which leads Baker to conclude that "it is quite possible that there are more such motions in his reports than are so identified."[195] Derrett duly notes that Spelman does not mention any such "motion" in his report of More's trial.

---

190 Derrett, "Trial," p. 70.
191 The next citation, from 1772, uses "move" rather than "allege": "If the paper be not criminal ... he may move the Court in arrest of judgment." But this is not yet the modern-day idiom of "moving *that*" the court do something.
192 Baker, *Spelman's Reports*, 1: 2, Action on the Case no. 1: Reymond v. Lord FitzWauter, 1521.
193 On exceptions and demurrers in criminal cases, see Baker, *Oxford History*, pp. 523–5, and see also Baker's "Criminal Courts and Procedure," p. 284. The exception in arrest of judgment was safer than a demurrer (upon which the law was still unsettled in Blackstone's time).
194 They are: Action on the Case no. 3, 1523 (1:3–4); no. 5, 1532 (1:4–6); no. 8, 1535 (1:7–8); Information on the Statute no. 1, 1522 (1: 154); and Pledges no. 1, 1530 (1:173). A plea in arrest of judgment by reason of a jeofail (error in pleading) is to be found in a 1532 Common Bench case in *Reports of Cases from the Time of King Henry VIII*, ed. J. H. Baker, 2 vols, Selden Society 120–1 (London, 2003–4), 2:265. Earlier uses of this terminology appears in *Reports of Cases by John Caryll*, ed. J. H. Baker, 2 vols, Selden Society 115–16 (London, 1999–2000), 1:264 (1494), a demurrer on the plea in arrest of judgment; and 2:504 (1506), matter alleged in arrest of judgment.
195 Baker, *Spelman's Reports*, 2:158; the case in which Spelman neglects to mention the allegation to arrest judgment is Potkyn's Case, Feoffements no. 3, 1522, 1:136–7.

The upshot is that we do not know which of the versions of the trial to believe, whether More spoke against the statute to quash the indictment (Roper), or simply to relieve his conscience (Guildhall), perhaps with the motivation of not misleading others into thinking that it was morally acceptable to approve of the king's title of Supreme Head of the English Church (Pole).

Jury System vs. Inquisitorial System

Let us assume, however, for the sake of discussion, that the Roper presentation, which does seem very plausible, is the accurate one, and that More did attempt to void the indictment and thereby arrest the judgment against him, and that the judges acted as Roper says they did. Did the judges act properly, in keeping with their obligations of presiding over a jury?

More once told Roper that judges favored the jury system because "they see that they may by the verdict of the jury cast off all quarrels from themselves upon them [the members of the jury], which they account their chief defense."[196] That is, as Sir John Baker says, relying on juries protected judges when they knowingly gave wrong judgments. He quotes Christopher St German, More's recent opponent, as saying that judges would "sometimes give judgment against their own knowledge, and also against the truth, and yet no default to be in them, as it is in all trials."[197] If, then, it was not the place of the judges to reverse the jury's decision on the facts, it was in their realm of duty to listen to legal objections.

More made his statement about judges shirking their obligations by leaving everything to the jury after he had called a meeting of judges to dine with him in the Council Chamber at Westminster, to explain why he had modified various cases in their courts by issuing injunctions. He told them that,

> if the justices of every court, unto whom the reformation of the rigor of the law by reason of their office most especially pertained, would upon reasonable considerations by their own discretions mitigate and reform the rigor of the law themselves, there should from thenceforth by him no more injunctions be granted.[198]

---

[196] Roper, *Lyfe*, ed. Hitchcock, p. 45

[197] Baker, *Spelman's Reports*, 2:43, citing St German's *Little Treatise Concerning Writs of Subpoena*, c. 1531, in *A Collection of Tracts Relative to the Law of England*, ed. Francis Hargrave (London, 1787), pp. 332–55, at 353. A newer edition is by John Guy, *Christopher St German on Chancery and Statute*, Selden Society supplementary series 6 (London, 1985), pp. 106–26, this excerpt being from chap. 10, p. 124. St German, however, is not speaking of jury trials specifically. The last part of his comment reads in full: "as it is in all trials except death of man, where they may not give judgment against their own knowledge." This would indicate that in all felony and treason trials, which of course are held before a jury, judges are not free to rest content with a jury verdict they know to be against their own certain knowledge.

[198] Roper, *Lyfe*, ed. Hitchcock, pp. 44–5.

This is a forceful statement of the doctrine of judicial discretion, the power of judges to guide the course of justice in their courts.

We must remember that, apart from seeking relief from the chancellor, there was no provision for appeals in this court system, as Parmiter notes.[199] In a comparable situation, if a papal commission of judges-delegate had been set up to try an issue, an aggrieved or convicted party could appeal to the papal curia for a review and possibly another trial. In England, before a commission of oyer and terminer, especially one headed by the chancellor himself, a convicted person could, at most, make objections only to the commissioners themselves.

Baker seems uncertain as to whether the commissioners in the More trial could have acted in another way. In 1535, he says, there may have been a choice about accepting More's argument (to arrest judgment), but, he says, "one can state confidently that no court today" would do so.[200] This may be true, baldly speaking, but there are mechanisms today for dealing with objections about unjust laws, as there are in the United States, when allegations of unconstitutionality are raised. Baker ends by saying that "judicial review was not an established feature of the legal system" in More's time, and that the judges, though they were clearly embarrassed by More's question, were simply "recognizing the legal sovereignty of Parliament."[201] Baker's assessment is that, whether or not More received proper treatment at his trial, he was definitely treated unfairly because of actions of Parliament and king. He says, "The uneasiness which everyone feels about More's conviction stems from the obnoxious character of a statute which virtually forced a man to incriminate himself on a matter of conscience."[202]

Baker repeats this assessment in his most recent consideration of the trial, in his *Oxford History*, and he goes on to say:

> The only contemporary standard by which the fairness of a prosecution could be measured was that of the ecclesiastical courts, which was admittedly not a high standard; but it is evident that the procedures of the secular law in this intolerant age were decidedly more favourable to the accused than those which More (when in power) had thought appropriate for the eradication of those whose consciences were at odds with his own.[203]

Baker's jaundiced view of the nature and operation of ecclesiastical trials for heresy in England is not well founded; it stems, it would seem, from his acceptance of the government propaganda of the time, notably as embodied in *A Treatise Concerning the Division Between the Spiritualty and Temporalty* by Christopher St German (but published anonymously) to which More responded

---

[199] Parmiter, "Indictment of St Thomas More," p. 166.
[200] Baker, *Spelman's Reports*, 2:*139–40*.
[201] Ibid., p. *140*.
[202] Ibid., p. *139*.
[203] Baker, *Oxford History*, pp. 417–18.

in his *Apology* (1533).[204] More challenged the author, whom he refers to as "Sir John Somesay," to come up with even one instance of unfair treatment of suspected heretics, and it is a challenge that could be renewed today. St German failed to offer any example of such unfairness in his rejoinder, *A Dialogue Betwixt Salem and Byzance*, as More showed in his response, *The Debellation of Salem and Byzance*.[205] I have analyzed this debate elsewhere.[206]

In my view, More would clearly have avoided conviction in a court that abided by inquisitorial due process, which required actual proof by at least two witnesses or adequate documentary instruments. More readily admitted that the ecclesiastical procedures could be abused by unfair judges, but he said that the same was true of any other judicial process, and, I submit, it was particularly true of the jury system, especially as it existed in More's time.

As for More's denial that any such abuse had ever to taken place in England, to his knowledge, and his challenge to St German to cite cases of abuse, I have done a search myself, and I can find little to support the anti-clerical claims. Although there are cases in which suspects were required to state their views on orthodox and heterodox propositions (a procedure, which even though contrary to due process as set forth in canon law, had a papal mandate behind it), there appears to be no instance in which anyone was prosecuted by having such responses alleged as confessed crimes (which would indeed have been in accord with the inquisitorial rules). Rather, all convictions were the result of testimony by two or more witnesses, or by confessions to properly charged offenses (of actual crimes committed in the past, not presently held opinions).[207] Thus, Baker should qualify his assumption that More favored punishing persons for their consciences.

Conclusion

The trial that Thomas More received was a typical trial by jury. Specifically, there was, as always, no accountability for the decision of the jury.

By objective standards, the jury was wrong to find him guilty of violating the Statute of Treasons upon which he was convicted,[208] but they could not have been expected, given the realities of the pressures upon them, to do anything else. If any verdict could be said to have been implicitly "directed," this was it. Far greater responsibility for this miscarriage of justice rested upon the commissioners, primarily upon those who helped to formulate the indictment, but ultimately upon all of them, for not speaking out against it at the trial. The justices

---

[204] *The Apology of Sir Thomas More*, ed. J. B. Trapp, in *CW* 9, with St German's *Treatise Concerning the Division* in Appendix A, pp. 173–212.
[205] Thomas More, *The Debellation of Salem and Bizance*, ed. John Guy, Ralph Keen, Clarence H. Miller, and Ruth McGugan, *Complete Works* 10 (New Haven, CT, 1987), with St German's *Dialogue* in Appendix B, pp. 323–92. (My own modernization of these titles uses "Byzance.")
[206] Kelly, "Thomas More on Inquisitorial Due Process."
[207] Ibid., pp. 862–71.
[208] Act of Treasons (**Doc. 2**).

of the King's Bench and of Common Pleas, even before they were assigned to the commission of oyer and terminer, were at fault insofar as they participated in preparing the indictment or not protesting against it, and all of the commissioners were guilty of injustice in letting the conviction stand. More was not in fact guilty of violating the statute. He did not maliciously strive by words or deeds to deprive Henry VIII of his title of Supreme Head of the Church in England.

Sir John Baker blames Parliament for passing the statute in the first place, but the blame needs to be placed mainly upon Henry VIII and his chief factor, Thomas Cromwell, and upon everyone else who for fear or favor fell into line behind them. Baker refers, as we have seen, to "the obnoxious character of a statute which virtually forced a man to condemn himself on a matter of conscience." This is indeed what king and secretary wished for, and this is how the modified and ratified statute was implemented, but the Commons, to their credit, resisted as far as they could. The statute, as passed, did *not* require one to voice one's conscience on the king's new title. It did *not* make private talk a matter of high treason, unless actual statements could be proved, and even then only when malicious intent could also be proved. It would have been clearly obvious to everyone, jurors and judges alike, that More did everything he could to avoid giving his opinion on the king's new title. His arguments against putting a malicious interpretation upon any of his actions, or upon his silences, should have been accepted. It was also obvious, of course, that he did not approve of the title; but he did nothing to oppose it.

The king and his secretary interpreted More's refusal to approve the title, when requested, to be the equivalent of a malicious attempt to deprive him of it, and this is the way the indictment read. The same interpretation was placed on More's and Fisher's other attempts to avoid falling under the statute. According to Derrett, the judges accepted More's explanations concerning these parts of the indictment – which the judges had presumably helped to draw up – and dismissed them from contention, leaving only the conversation with Rich. Even if this were true, it is clear from the recounting of this conversation in the indictment itself (based on Rich's original twisted report of his conversation with More) that More was continuing his efforts to avoid falling under the statute. These efforts should have led automatically to the conclusion that he was not attempting, out of malice or otherwise, to deprive the king of his title.

However, I do not believe that the judges dismissed any part of the indictment. Spelman's testimony that More was convicted on the conspiracy charge as well as the direct-depriving charge is proof of that. But the judges *should* have dismissed all of the charges, since the alleged actions, as stated, did not come close to violating the statute, because there was no justification offered for the constantly reiterated "surcharge" of malice.

Derrett and Baker basically accept the Roper scenario. According to Rich, More told him that Parliament did not have the power to declare Henry Supreme Head. More denied having said this; but then he argued that, even if he had said so, no malice could be proved, and therefore the statute would not have been violated. Nevertheless, the jury convicted him on this point. Then (the Derrett–Baker script goes) More tried to get the charge dismissed by the judges because, in actual fact, Parliament did not have the power to declare Henry Supreme Head. Even though he had not said so to Rich, he was now telling the judges that this had been his belief all along, and he offered reasons for it, and he requested them to strike down the law and vacate the verdict. Baker considers this "the only legal difficulty in the case,"[209] and believes that the judges did not disgrace themselves by refusing to answer it.

I, on the contrary, am inclined to follow the basic outline of the Guildhall Report and Sir John Spelman's summary. More was accused of violating the statutes concerning Henry as Supreme Head by maliciously seeking to deprive him of his title (which would include the part of the charge connected with Richard Rich), and conspiring with Bishop Fisher in the same treason. More denied that his refusal to give his opinion about the statutes violated them, especially since nothing he did could be construed as malice towards the king. He was found guilty by the jury, whereupon he decided to finally declare his conscience on the statutes.

Baker agrees with Derrett that More's discourse on Parliament's exceeding its powers was a vain attempt to "arrest judgment," a new procedure that can be found only in a few civil cases before the time of More's trial. There is no evidence, apart from Roper's hearsay account, that the procedure was available in criminal cases, specifically treason, and no example has been cited from the sixteenth century as a whole.

The legal question that the judges should have addressed was not whether the statutes declaring and enforcing Henry's headship were "constitutional" or not, but rather whether the actions cited in the indictment fell under the statutes. The judges avoided their responsibility by leaving the full burden upon the unlearned jury, who were forced to decide that there was malice even though no malice had been demonstrated. Rather, innocuous acts were construed as malicious without further ado. Or, according to Pole's account, the judges declared vociferously in the hearing of the jury that More's very refusal to declare his mind on the statute constituted an act of malice in itself.

I noted above that John Baker agrees with Derrett in concluding that the judges dismissed the charge that More remained silent when asked about the king's supremacy. But elsewhere he contradicts this analysis of the trial, when he speaks of the distorted enforcement of the supremacy acts perpetrated by the government and acceded to by the courts:

> Now the mere private expression of opinion could be treason. The Commons are said to have insisted on the qualifying adverb "maliciously," but it proved a worthless safeguard in practice. Within seven months Prior Houghton of the Charterhouse, Bishop Fisher, and Sir Thomas More were convicted under this statute for denying the king's title of supreme head of the Church in England. Moreover, the expression of opinion did not have to be public: in the case of

---

[209] Baker, *Spelman's Reports*, 2:139.

More, the chief complaint was of evasive answers under interrogation rather than spontaneous open denial."[210]

In saying that the provision of malice proved worthless, Baker should acknowledge that it was because of the judges who oversaw the prosecution. To bring it home to our case, More was convicted against the letter of the law, a miscarriage of justice that the judges should have prevented (not to mention not encouraged).

The question of More's purpose in speaking against the statutes after the guilty verdict came in, whether it was to exonerate his conscience, or to give guidance to others, or to void the indictment, turns out to be not very important. One could answer that all three purposes were intended, but that the first two were more important than the third (voiding the indictment), since it had no hope of success. Therefore, any effort to "arrest judgment" was not seriously intended. This is, in fact, Derrett's own understanding of the maneuver, as he makes clear in his 1964 *Moreana* article, written after his 1964 *English Historical Review* article on the trial. He believes that More was guilty of saying what Rich claimed he said, in spite of his vehement denial at his trial; it was, after all, what he really believed, and, if he was tricked into revealing his views, he should have been clever enough to avoid the trap; More denied that he had spoken against Parliament's power, and that he had compared the statute to a two-edged sword, and the jury disbelieved him.[211]

But then Derrett conjectures that More deliberately courted disaster; he kept his discourse hypothetical, but he must have known, as Cromwell certainly did, that such a hypothetical discussion would be good enough to convict him. More had certainly committed a crime within the Act of Treasons, and the jury was right to disbelieve his denials. More must have known the risk he was taking: his motive was far higher than any disburdening of his conscience; rather he spoke as a patriot, and "placed his country's constitutional health above his own convenience." "At the risk of his own life More was prepared to have yet another attempt to show where the government's view of the constitution was faulty; if they could profit from this discovery and amend the statutes accordingly it would be to the profit of the nation."[212] It should be quite obvious that, in Derrett's view, More's judges were not expected to step forward and amend the constitution in accepting his "motion." Rather he was speaking for the future.

E. E. Reynolds's reaction to Derrett's *Moreana* account is simple: "After many years studying the life and works of Thomas More, I believe that when, at his trial, he denied having said the words reported by Rich, he was speaking the truth. Dr Derrett doubts this."[213] Two years later, in 1966, Brian Byron published an article in *Moreana* with a plausible explanation of what More had really

---

210 Baker, *Oxford History*, p. 586. In a note he adds that even an error in a coat of arms could be treason.
211 Derrett, "The 'New' Document," pp. 10–11.
212 Ibid., pp. 16–18.
213 E. E. Reynolds, Comments on "The 'New' Document on Thomas More's Trial." by J. Duncan M. Derrett. *Moreana* 3 (1964), 20–2, at p. 22.

told Rich: that the English Parliament had power to make Rich king, but not pope. Rich then falsely reported that More had denied Parliament's power to declare Henry Head of the English Church. Derrett did not cite Byron's article or respond to his argument in his 1977 revision.

My own judgment on the trial is that the judges could not have been reasonably expected to declare the act of Parliament illegal, but they did have the obligation to enforce it as Parliament intended it to be enforced, not as Henry VIII and Thomas Cromwell wanted it enforced. More succeeded, I believe, in his attempt to remain silent about the king's supremacy, and therefore he did not come close to uttering words that, if spoken maliciously, could be declared to fall under the act.

But the judges should have admitted More's further argument: that even though his efforts to avoid giving his opinion on the act were a deliberate evasion (which he admitted), and even if he had discussed the matter with Fisher, and even if he had said the words ascribed to him by Rich (which he denied), he did not do so maliciously; and that no attempt was made to prove malice on his part. The judges were at fault for not ruling in his favor on this point. Instead they ruled that the qualification of malice as a necessary constitution of treason under the act, which Parliament had insisted on, was of no force. Or, to follow Pole's scenario, they ruled that any manifestation of refusal of the title was automatically malicious, and required no further proof. This seems to be a strikingly modern view of malice and "malice aforethought," as is discussed in the judicial comments later in this book. I pose, however, that the contexts of More's case and the cases of the Carthusians and Bishop Fisher before him, in which the importance of malice is stressed, show that there was real meaning to the qualification intended by Parliament, and for the judges to dismiss it was, I hold, a clear violation of their duty to enforce the law, and a manifestation of malice on their part. The chief blame for More's conviction, therefore, lies with king and secretary, and secondarily with the commissioned judges, and only residually with the members of the jury.

We can be sure that an extremely detailed account of More's trial was contained in the vast *Life of More* by Master Justice Rastell, which has long gone missing, except for a few chapters dealing with Bishop Fisher. Many of the questions raised by the fragmentary reports of More's trial that do survive and are available to us will be answered as soon as anyone can discover the whereabouts of Rastell's complete book and bring it to light. Meanwhile, we can only be guided by our own lights.

2

Natural Law and the Trial of Thomas More

R. H. Helmholz

Introduction

Political motives stood behind the decision to put Thomas More on trial for treason. Who can doubt it? In the circumstances of the times, they often did. Even today, politically motivated prosecutions have not been wholly banished from the criminal law. Accepting this as an unfortunate fact of life, deciding whether the person being prosecuted has been given a fair trial is always a separate question. A judgment about the fairness of the proceedings is not determined by the government's motives. The trials themselves – the procedures they use and the ways they are conducted – are what matter most in deciding whether a defendant has been treated lawfully.[1] It is this second question as it relates to More's trial that this chapter addresses.

It does so by taking one of the several perspectives from which More's trial can be viewed: its relation to natural law. The treatment appropriate to that perspective begins with the law of nature as it was then understood to relate to criminal procedure. It then seeks to apply its tenets to the legal issues that arose in the course of More's trial. Although a certain amount of overlap does exist, this chapter's approach is different from that taken elsewhere in this volume. Professor Kelly raises questions about the currently accepted account of the trial itself. He seeks to uncover what actually happened (and what should have happened) under English law as it then stood. This is a fruitful approach. We need to know as much as we can about the mechanics of the trial itself. The legal issues raised during its course help us to understand and assess its consistency with contemporary legal practice. However, it is not the approach taken in this chapter. This chapter contains nothing about the novelty of motions in arrest of judgment in English procedural law or about their place in the evolution of trial by jury. It also has little to contribute to understanding the requirement of malice under the English treason statutes. This chapter's subject is the trial and natural law.

---

[1] For discussion, see the treatment, including discussion of Thomas More's trial, in Baker, *Oxford History*, pp. 415–19; see also James Fitzjames Stephen, *History of the Criminal Law of England*, vol. 3 (London, 1883), pp. 321–4.

Is this a subject worth investigation? Is it a helpful way to evaluate More's trial? By my lights at least, it is. The subject is both important and useful, because the law of nature was accepted as a valid source of law by all the participants in this trial. Like virtually all lawyers and theologians prior to the nineteenth century, they regarded it as a proper standard against which a trial's fairness (and even validity) could be measured. Although it has fallen out of favor in mainstream jurisprudence today, natural law was common coin in the sixteenth century, accepted as a matter of course by English common lawyers and Continental jurists.[2] It was regarded as a legitimate source of law, indeed the most fundamental source of law. In other words, the approach taken here attempts to assess the trial under a standard that was pertinent and widely accepted at the time – by More himself[3] as well as by those who controlled the trial that would sentence him to death.[4] This approach may be limited in scope, but it is not anachronistic.

One of the functions the law of nature then served was to guide and to assess positive laws. It did two things: it helped legislators to draft good statutes and it allowed jurists to determine whether an enacted statute or a custom was a legitimate law. Under the second of these – obviously the one most relevant in More's trial – the positive law was itself evaluated by asking whether a specific rule or practice it contained stood in accord with the precepts of the natural law. For example, could condemnation of a person for having committed a crime be legitimate if he had not been given a legal summons and allowed to state his side of the case? The late medieval and sixteenth-century jurists said: No. Or rather: Usually no. Proof by notoriety had a long history in European law, but it had come to be widely accepted that, unless there were exceptional circumstances, even if it were undoubted that a person had in fact committed a crime, the law had to accord him a chance to be heard in his own defense.[5] He must be cited and he must be listened to. The law of nature so required. The positive law should (and did) guarantee it. Thomas More, of course, could not complain on this score; he had been lawfully summoned and he was allowed to speak. However, he might find other inconsistencies with the law of nature in the procedures by which he was convicted of treason.

The argument for examining the trial from the perspective of the law of nature is even stronger than its general relevance in earlier centuries suggests. More himself must have had natural law in his own mind as he presented his case. He had never been content to assess the quality of justice by the common

---

[2] Norman Doe, *Fundamental Authority in Late Medieval English Law* (Cambridge, 1990), pp. 132–54.

[3] See, e.g., *A Dialogue Concerning Heresies* 4.14, pp. 414–15 ("Nature, reason, and God's behest bindeth").

[4] D. J. Ibbetson, "Natural Law and Common Law," *Edinburgh Law Review* 5 (2001), 4–20; S. B. Chrimes, *English Constitutional Ideas in the Fifteenth Century* (Cambridge, 1936), pp. 200–6. I have compiled a partial list; see R. H. Helmholz, "Natural Law and Human Rights in English Law: From Bracton to Blackstone," *Ave Maria Law Review* 3 (2005), 1–22, at pp. 5–11.

[5] C. 3 q. 9 c. 2; Dig. 48.17.1. The abbreviations to the texts of the *Corpus Juris Canonici* and the *Corpus Juris Civilis* as used here are explained in the Appendix to this chapter, p. 70.

law's procedures alone,[6] and some, although not all, of the arguments he made during his trial tracked contemporary understanding of what natural law required. Four questions arising from More's trial raised questions to which the law of nature was relevant:

1. the claim that More could lawfully refuse to answer questions about his views of the statute that recognized the king's title as Head of the English Church. More had remained silent when asked, and he argued that he had the right to remain silent;
2. the contention that because there were not two witnesses against him, More's conviction was invalid. No person could be convicted of a crime, much less the crime of treason, without proof, including the testimony of at least two creditable witnesses;
3. the assertion that requiring More to accept the statute as valid violated the fundamental rights of conscience. Under the natural law, in the absence of urgent necessity no person should be compelled to act in a way that was contrary to deeply held convictions of conscience;
4. the argument that a statute making it a crime to intend by words or writing to deprive the king of the title or name of his estate, which estate included the headship of the English Church, was contrary both to the law of nature and to the law of God.

These were weighty contentions. More has earned a reputation for standing on technicalities in his trial,[7] and it is true that he approached his trial as a lawyer would. He gave little away. He raised procedural points. He insisted on them. However, these four arguments were not technicalities. They raised four fundamental objections to the legitimacy of the prosecution, all of which were available under the law of nature as it was understood at the time. There was also support for all four to be found within the Roman and canon laws that made up the contemporary *ius commune*; the latter were held to have been based upon the natural law in the sense that they put into positive form the more general principles of the law of nature. When jurists of the time spoke of the natural law, they often cited texts of the *ius commune* to show what the law of nature should mean in practice.

Of course, invoking general principles drawn from the natural law did not necessarily mean that More's prosecution was unlawful. There was also something to be said on the other side. The law of nature often left room for disagreement when applied to specific cases, and More's critics might answer him in kind. I shall take the questions up in order, attempting to summarize both sides of the four arguments.

---

[6] See the evidence collected in Martin Fleisher, *Radical Reform and Political Power in the Life and Writings of Thomas More* (Geneva, 1973), pp. 20–32; J. H. Hexter, *More's Utopia: The Biography of an Idea* (Princeton, NJ, 1952), pp. 145–53.

[7] Brian Cormack, *A Power To Do Justice: Jurisdiction, English Literature and the Rise of Common Law, 1509–1625* (Chicago, 2007), pp. 85–129. On More's work as a lawyer, see Richard J. Schoeck, "Sir Thomas More, Humanist and Lawyer," *University of Toronto Quarterly* 34 (1964), 1–14; John A. Guy, *The Public Career of Sir Thomas More* (New Haven, CT, 1980).

The Right to Silence

That no person should be punished solely for his thoughts was a fundamental axiom of Western law, accepted both in the English common law and in the European *ius commune*. *De occultis non judicat Ecclesia. Nemo tenetur prodere seipsum.* These were not just counsels of prudence. They stated a rule of the natural law, one that had been made part of the *ius commune*.[8] Its purpose, broadly speaking, was to protect men and women from overzealous prosecution and punishment. Without such protection, anyone would be subject to investigation and punishment, because every man or woman falls short of compliance with the law in one way or another.[9] If we could be forced to make public our innermost thoughts and own up to our secret actions, and then be prosecuted for what we had admitted, the result would not only be devastating for us. It would upset the right order of society. Of course we are required to acknowledge our faults, including our thoughts, before Almighty God, who knows our hearts in any case. But that acknowledgment was to be made to God alone,[10] not to other men, not in a public forum. This rule – a privilege to keep silent and not suffer for it – was regarded as a salutary principle of the natural law.

Even today, when we have cast away most of the assumptions that accompanied the law of nature in prior centuries, we have not cast away this principle. It remains the basis for the privilege against self-incrimination recognized in the Fifth Amendment to the United States Constitution.[11] Much has been written about the history of this privilege,[12] and more about its modern relevance. It embodies an old assumption of the common and civil laws, and an important one.

More sought shelter under it.[13] During his trial and beforehand, he maintained that he had not done or said anything to deny the validity of the statute recognizing King Henry's title. He insisted he would continue to say nothing. Nothing at all. The Tudor treason statute required that a defendant have denied

---

[8] See Hans Peter Glöckner, *Cogitationis poenam nemo patitur (D. 48. 19. 18): Zu den Anfängen einer Versuchslehre in der Jurisprudenz der Glossatoren* (Frankfurt, 1989). See below, p. 79.
[9] See, e.g., Innocent IV (d. 1254), *Apparatus in quinque libros decretalium* (Frankfurt, 1570), ad X 1.6.54, no. 11; "[S]uper criminibus non debet iurare de veritate dicenda cum si a quolibet inquireretur de suis criminibus occultis vix quisquam sine crimine reperiretur." ("In criminal matters, no one should be required to take an oath to tell the truth, because if such inquiries were made into secret crimes, scarcely any person would be found free from guilt.")
[10] De pen. Dist. 1 d. p. c. 87 §6. Exceptions existed; see, e.g., James A. Brundage, "The Ethics of Advocacy: Confidentiality and Conflict of Interest in Medieval Canon Law," in *Grundlagen des Rechts. Festschrift für Peter Landau*, ed. Jörg Müller et al. (Paderborn, 2000), pp. 454–66.
[11] See the essays in R. H. Helmholz, ed., *The Privilege against Self-Incrimination: Its Origins and Development* (Chicago, 1997).
[12] See, e.g., H. A. Kelly, "Inquisitorial Due Process and the Status of Secret Crimes," in *Proceedings of the Eighth International Congress of Medieval Canon Law*, ed. Stanley Chodorow (Vatican City, 1992), pp. 407–27.
[13] See Kelly, chapter 1 above, pp. 8–30.

the royal title "by word or writing."[14] More had done neither. And he would do neither. He had refused to answer the question when asked whether he accepted the statute, saying, "I will not meddle with any such matters, for I am fully determined to serve God."[15]

His accusers took note of More's silence in the face of demands that he state his opinions. It told against him. It showed his mind. But this would not do, he replied. If anything his silence supported his innocence. "Qui tacet consentire videtur" (*Sext* 5.12.43).[16] If he was thought to have consented through silence, he could scarcely be accused of denying the statute's validity by having remained silent about it. More's argument here may have been more clever than convincing, but in the context of a formal trial, it made some sense to argue that silence should not be punishable under principles of positive or natural law.

The difficulty with More's argument, one that is still present today, is that the right to silence has never been without exceptions. Some civil libertarians take an absolutist view of the Fifth Amendment, but in fact it cannot be, and never has been, a blanket permission to refuse to answer relevant questions. There are situations where a person has a duty to answer yea or nay, even about his personal conduct and opinions. If the person refuses, a judge or jury is entitled to draw appropriate – indeed inevitable – conclusions about the person's guilt or innocence.

That limitation was as forceful then as it is now. It was widely recognized. Here is an example taken from the medieval canon law. A papal letter, one included in the *Decretals of Gregory IX*, stated that a man elected to an ecclesiastical office should be subject to an inquest to determine his fitness for the post before he could be confirmed in it. Among other things, the inquest was expected to determine whether he was guilty of any crime that might disqualify him from holding the office. The questioners were entitled, indeed required, to ask the man whether he had committed a crime.[17] Thus, for example, one might ask him "Have you paid any money to anyone for his vote?" Particularly was this true if there were reasons for suspicion, such as "public fame" that money had changed hands as part of the election.[18] By the same token, the nominee should be asked about his past conduct. Had he committed some other crime?

---

14 26 Henry VIII (1534), c. 13 (**Doc. 2 §1**) on the history of treason by words, see G. R. Elton, *The Tudor Constitution: Documents and Commentary* (Cambridge, 1962), pp. 59–60; and see generally Rebecca Lemon, *Treason by Words: Literature, Law, and Rebellion in Shakespeare's England* (Ithaca, NY, 2006).
15 Derrett, "Trial," esp. at p. 63. See the indictment, **Doc. 16 §4**.
16 Guildhall Report, **Doc. 17 §4**: Pole, **Doc. 19 §6**.
17 See *gl. ord.* ad X 5.1.21, s.v. *conversatus*: "Alias non posset de ipsius vita constare." The Rome, 1582 edition of the *CJC*, complete with the *glossa ordinaria*, can be seen online on the UCLA Library site: http://digital.library.ucla.edu/canonlaw/. For modern comment, see generally, William J. Dohar, "*Sufficienter litteratus*: Clerical Examination and Instruction for the Cure of Souls," in *A Distinct Voice: Medieval Studies in Honor of Leonard E. Boyle, OP*, ed. Jacqueline Brown and William Stoneman (Notre Dame, IN, 1997), pp. 305–21.
18 See Julius Clarus (d. 1575), *Sententiarum receptarum liber [seu] Practica criminalis* (Venice, 1595), Quaest. 6, no. 1.

Was he suspected of any? If the man refused to answer, standing as it were on a right to silence, the inquest was entitled to quash his election.

That may seem obvious. Indeed it is obvious. One might raise an objection, however. Disqualifying a man from an office is a far cry from convicting a man of treason, with the terrible penalties the latter could entail. And differences, even differences in degree, often matter in law. However, this distinction was not one drawn in late medieval thought, at least not in a way that would have helped More. Indeed something like the opposite conclusion was reached. The jurists assumed that the more serious the crime, the more urgent was the compulsion for the accused to tell the truth. The law of nature left room for what we would call a "balancing test". Greater danger meant greater necessity. Treason was regarded as a *crimen enormissimum et gravissimum*.[19] It posed the gravest danger to society, and where a person was publicly suspected of having committed this special crime, where suspicion to that effect was widespread among good and reliable men, and where there were other indicia of his guilt, the rule that permitted silence under ordinary circumstances did not apply. The defendant must answer. He must say whether he had committed the crime of which he stood defamed.[20] If he refused, the law would take its course.[21] This was regarded as quite consistent with the law of nature. It did not eliminate the right to silence altogether; but it did stand as a qualification to its assertion in many situations.

In some ways, this was a dangerous limitation. It invited abuse on the part of government officials and prosecutors. More was caught by it, as indeed had been hundreds of lesser men and women who had stood before the tribunals of church and state and been compelled to forego their right to be silent. One may not like the results. I do not much like them myself. Few of us do when we stand in jeopardy. But that does not change the fact. At the time, the exceptions to the privilege against self-incrimination were regarded as perfectly consistent with a procedural law founded upon the law of nature. Natural law was not meant to be a tool for unravelling the ties of civil obedience that guaranteed public order. Aggressive use of a right to silence could serve as a means of

---

[19] See Hieronymus Gigas (*fl.* sixteenth century), *Tractatus de crimine laesae maiestatis* (Lyon, 1557), tit. *Quomodo et per quos*, Quaest. 29, no. 3.
[20] E.g., Johannes Petrus de Ferrariis (*fl.* 1400), *Aurea practica* (Venice, 1690), tit. *Forma excipiendi contra positiones*, §*Detegentes*, Additiones v. *Positioni*.
[21] What was that course? It is not so easy to know. The law of nature did not descend to this level of particularity. It would have been limited to showing that the right to silence did not apply where a legitimate reason existed for requiring an answer. Nevertheless, this was (and is) a relevant question. The ordinary practice in England in the Church courts was to excommunicate the person for contumacy. See, e.g., Ex officio c. Agnes Harvey (Diocese of Lincoln 1526), Lincolnshire Archives Office, Act book Cj/3, f. 14: "Tamen adhuc recusavit iurare quam dominus excommunicavit in scriptis." ("She nonetheless refused to take the oath, for which his lordship excommunicated her in writing.") In the parallel case of heresy under the canon law, the defendant who obstinately refused to answer the questions put to him was thus not to be convicted of heresy, but if he persisted in this refusal for a year, thereby remaining excommunicate, he would be condemned as a heretic: *Sext* 5.2.7. Thomas More knew and apparently approved of this provision; see *Debellation*, ch. 15, in *CW* 10:118. The English criminal law dealt with the same underlying problem through the notorious *peine forte et dure*.

subverting the right order of society, even the demands of justice itself. The resulting limitation of the right to silence was designed to ensure that this did not happen. It was a limitation that could well apply in More's case.

The Necessity of Proof

What actual proof was there of More's guilt? Was the evidence enough to convict him? It was a rule, based upon the law of nature and well demonstrated by many texts from the *ius commune* and even in the Bible itself, that there must be positive evidence before a person could be convicted of a crime. Some jurists insisted, following the Roman law,[22] that the evidence must be "clearer than the noonday sun."[23] The English common law, under which the trial was conducted, did not go quite that far, but it did require satisfactory proof before any person could be convicted. The presentment of a grand jury might be based upon suspicion – it could establish a prima facie case. But presentment was not a conviction. Only the petty jury could convict, and the jurors were required to acquit unless there was convincing evidence against the defendant. English law had a somewhat looser definition of evidence than the *ius commune*. The institution of the jury, whose members were assumed to know the truth, provided a direct means of satisfying the evidentiary requirement. But the requirement was there nonetheless. The jurors were not to convict unless what they themselves knew or had heard during the trial satisfied their consciences that the defendant was guilty. As Sir Edward Coke wrote, evidence against a man on trial for his life could only be convicted "upon direct and manifest proof," and "not upon conjectural presumptions, or inferences, or strains of wit."[24]

Again, today we recognize the centrality of this principle, though we rarely connect it with the law of nature. It is recognized in several concrete ways in our own law. The well-established presumption of innocence is the most obvious.[25] The directed verdict in criminal cases is another. Where the evidence put on by the prosecution does not rise to a sufficient level, the judge will take the case from the hands of the jury and direct an acquittal.[26] A judge may even enter a judgment *non obstante veredicto* after a guilty verdict has been given by the

---

[22] Cod. 4.19.25.
[23] E.g., Julius Clarus, *Practica criminalis* (above n. 18), Quaest. 66, no. 4: "Debent autem esse in criminalibus probationes luce meridiana clariores ... [e]t hoc omnes sciunt et dicunt." ("In criminal matters, the proof must be clearer than the midday sun ... This is known to all and stated by all.")
[24] Edward Coke, *Institutes*, Part 3 (London, 1644), ch. 12. The heavy responsibility thereby placed on the jurors is one theme of James Q. Whitman, *The Origins of Reasonable Doubt: Theological Roots of the Criminal Trial* (New Haven, CT, 2008), pp. 125–57.
[25] The history of the presumption in European law is usefully discussed by Kenneth Pennington, "'Innocent until Proven Guilty': The Origins of a Legal Maxim," in *A Ennio Cortese*, ed. Domenico Maffei and Italo Barocchi, 3 vols (Rome, 2001), 3:59–73, and by Richard Fraher, "*Ut nullus describatur reus prius quam convincatur*: Presumption of Innocence in Medieval Canon law," in *Proceedings of the Sixth International Congress of Medieval Canon Law*, ed. Stephan Kuttner and Kenneth Pennington (Vatican City, 1985), pp. 493–506.
[26] See Wayne R. LaFave, *Principles of Criminal Law* §1.8(a) (St Paul, MN, 2003), pp. 43–4.

jury. Its availability is regarded as a protection against speculation or prejudice on the part of the jury, but it is more than that. It is part of a fundamental guarantee in our law that no person should be convicted of a crime in the absence of satisfactory proof.

In the medieval *ius commune*, as one part of this guarantee of justice, stood a well established rule founded upon the law of nature: two witnesses were necessary to prove a fact (*testis unus, testis nullus*).[27] The Bible itself so stated, nowhere more dramatically than in the story of Susanna and the Elders in the Apocrypha. Jurists recalled how the two elders conspired to accuse the virtuous Susanna of adultery after she refused their sexual advances, only to be tripped up by Daniel, who interrogated the elders separately and thereby uncovered a basic contradiction in their stories. That story was taken by the learned jurists to point to a lesson of the natural law: only evidence that agrees in substance and that comes from two witnesses will constitute satisfactory proof (*testes singulares nihil probant*). Under the common understanding of the day, in treason or heresy trials, the *ius commune* allowed that the testimony of a single witness might be sufficient to put a suspect to torture but it was not enough to condemn him.[28]

More sought shelter under this rule of law.[29] At the trial only one witness had appeared to give evidence against him, and an unsatisfactory witness at that: Richard Rich. The other two men who had been placed in the Tower, presumably with the purpose of listening to the conversation between Rich and More, both said they had not been able to overhear the conversation between the two men. They did not count. That left Rich. More sought to discredit him, as is well known, although Rich's credibility was properly a question for the jury which decided it against More. However, even with Rich's testimony, that still made only one witness. Everything else amounted to suspicion or presumption, not evidence. Thus, it seems, the case against More was insufficient under a standard founded upon natural law as it had been elaborated in many texts from the *ius commune*.

This assertion raised an old point, one on which the English common lawyers had long been sensitive, even sometimes defensive. They had an answer, however. Indeed they had several answers. Sir John Fortescue, writing in the 1460s, defended the English law against the charge that it ignored the two-witness requirement. Far from condemning men on the testimony of a single

---

[27] Dig. 22.5.12; see generally Giovanni Minnucci, "Diritto e processo penale nella prima trattatistica del XII secolo," in *"Ins Wasser geworfen und Ozeane durchquert": Festshcrift für Knut Wolfgang Nörr*, ed. Mario Ascheri *et al*. (Cologne, 2003), pp. 581–608.

[28] Josephus Mascardus (d. 1588), *Conclusiones probationum omnium quae in utroque foro quotidie versantur* (Frankfurt, 1587), vol. 1, concl. 462, no. 18: "[T]estis unicus sufficiat ad faciendum indicium ad torturam, ... ex unico enim indicio videtur procedi posse ad torturam in crimine laesae maiestatis." ("A single witness is sufficient to authorize torture ... And from a single piece of evidence it seems that one may proceed to torture in cases of treason."). See also Gigas, *Tractatus*, tit. *De pluribus et variis quaestionibus*, Quaest. 3, nos. 4–5: "[Q]uia crimen laesae maiestatis est crimen exceptum, ... ideo in isto crimine recedimus a communibus regulis." ("Because the crime of treason is a *crimen exceptum*, in it we depart from the ordinary rules.")

[29] See Derrett, "Trial," p. 68; Kelly, chapter 1 above, pp. 31–39.

man, he wrote, English law required the decision of twelve, the twelve honest men that made up the jury, before any defendant could be punished.[30] He went on to ridicule the Romano-canonical procedure by throwing up the textbook case in which a person who had first entered into a clandestine marriage and then a public marriage would be condemned to commit perpetual adultery with the second, where only the public marriage could be proved by two witnesses. He suggested that this was "the case, of which Job spoke, in which Leviathan's testicles were perplexed." So he ended his discussion. The case was, he thought, a clear instance where the civil law's requirement of two witnesses led to injustice.

The spirit of contest lived on – the question of comparative merit was widely discussed in later civilian literature in England.[31] It even appears in the great modern treatise on the law of evidence by John Henry Wigmore (d. 1943); he dealt at length with its merits, deriding the Continental law on this point as "the numerical system."[32] But which was actually better? It is difficult to be sure. The jury system had its critics at the time. Parsons the Jesuit described this aspect of the English criminal trial as "against very reason and justice itself."[33] He was, of course, answered in kind. Twelve was more than two. Was it not therefore better than two? Moreover, the requirement that the jury be unanimous spoke strongly in favor of the compatibility of the English system with the law of nature's requirement of proof before conviction.[34] So did the absence of torture from judicial proceedings in England. Unreliable confessions induced by torture, the English common lawyers argued, were the inevitable result of following the Continental path.[35] The law of proof in the *ius commune* had tempted the jurists to take this shortcut. Fully considered, therefore, the English law was in greater harmony with the law of nature.

Even if one ignores the English side of the argument, as a modern critic might do even though More could not, a further difficulty is that the jurists of the *ius commune* themselves held that the two-witness requirement was subject to limitations. It could not be abolished consistently with natural law, but it could be interpreted so as to admit of exceptions. For example, a father testifying that his son had been made a monk against the son's wishes could count as sufficient proof of the coercion.[36] The situation was one in which circum-

---

[30] See *De laudibus legum Angliae*, cc. 31–2, pp. 72–9.
[31] See the treatment by the Regius Professor of Civil Law at Cambridge, Francis Dickins (d. 1755), in "Summary of judicial proceedings," Suffolk Record Office, Ipswich, MS. E 14/11/10, f. 12 (giving both sides of the argument).
[32] John Henry Wigmore, *Evidence in Trials at Common Law*, vol. 7, rev. James H. Chadbourn, 1978 (St Paul, MN, 2003), §§2030–5.
[33] Robert Parsons, *The Jesuit's Memorial for the Intended Reformation of England under Their First Popish Prince*, ed. Edward Gee (London, 1690), p. 248. See generally, J. S. Cockburn, "Twelve Silly Men? The Trial Jury at Assizes, 1560–1670," in *Twelve Good Men and True: The Criminal Trial Jury in England, 1200–1800*, ed. J. S. Cockburn and Thomas A. Green (Princeton, NJ, 1988), pp. 158–81; James Oldham, *Trial by Jury: The Seventh Amendment and Anglo-American Special Juries* (New York, 2006), pp. 128–30; Bellamy, *Tudor Law of Treason*, p. 140.
[34] See, e.g., Thomas Smith (d. 1577), *De Republica Anglorum*, ed. Mary Dewar (Cambridge, 1982), Lib. 2, c. 23, pp. 110–16.
[35] See J. H. Langbein, *Torture and the Law of Proof: Europe in the Ancien Régime* (Chicago, 2006).
[36] C. 20 q. 3 c. 4.

stances made it unlikely that more than one witness would ordinarily exist. So, it was concluded, one witness must be enough. The exceptions seemed to multiply. William Durantis (d. 1296), the procedural encyclopedist, managed to elucidate some 30 separate exceptions to the rule requiring two witnesses.[37] His followers did more, and this was to be a question of the greatest complexity in the *ius commune*.

In addition, under the common understanding of the time, presumptions and reasonable conjectures might reasonably be added to the testimony of a single witness to convict a man of treason.[38] More himself had endorsed the essential correctness of criminal convictions based in part on the existence of legal presumptions.[39] This was not necessarily unreasonable. Treason is a crime men try to hide from the world, especially after the fact. Exceptions to the two-witness requirement, based on a clear-eyed recognition of the special nature of the crime of treason, were not regarded as inconsistent with the requirements of justice established by divine and natural law. Other factors and other kinds of evidence could give to the testimony of one witness a guarantee of veracity. Moreover, canonists and civilians held that more effective measures of efficient criminal prosecution were justified by the contemporary need to suppress crime.[40] The enormity of the crime might excuse a certain flexibility in the law of proof. That is the way the law of nature was applied and understood at the time.[41]

In the face of this attitude, could More have hoped to gain anything by invoking the two-witness rule? Perhaps not in terms of immediate result, but there is a possibility that it might have helped him in the court of public opinion. The two-witness rule for treason trials was very much in the air at the time of More's trial.[42] Indeed it became a statutory rule in England just a few years later.[43] More sought to raise the principle that underlay those statutes. And even without those statutes, More may have hoped to show the injustice of his trial under the law of nature as that law was understood in his day.

---

[37] William Durantis, *Speculum judiciale*, Basel, 1574, Lib. I, Pt. 4 §*De teste*, tit. De numero testium, nos. 8–11.

[38] See Mascardus, *De probationibus*, Lib. I, concl. 462, no. 20: "[E]tiam crimen istud probari possit per coniecturas et praesumptiones" (Also this crime can be proved by conjectures and presumptions"). The reason he gives is that "crimen laesae maiestatis sit difficile probatum" ("the crime of treason is only to be proved with difficulty"). In the next paragraph, no. 21, he goes on to say, however, that the conjectures and presumptions must be "evidentes et apertae" ("undoubted and manifest").

[39] See *Debellation*, ch. 15, CW 10:117: "A man may sometime be so suspect of felony by reason of sore presumptions, that though no man saw him do it, ... yet may he be founden guilty of it."

[40] For discussion and references, see Winfried Trusen, "Rechtliche Grundlagen der Hexenprozesse und ihrer Beendigung," in *Gelehrtes Recht im Mittelalter und in der frühen Neuzeit* (Goldbach, 1997), pp. 297–320; Richard Fraher, "The Theoretical Justification for the New Criminal Law of the High Middle Ages: *Rei Publicae interest, Ne crimina remaneant impunita*," University of Illinois Law Review (1984), 577–95.

[41] See generally Paul Foriers, "La conception de la preuve dans l'école de droit naturel," in *La Preuve*, Recueils de la Société Jean Bodin, 17:2 (Brussels, 1965), pp. 169–92.

[42] The evidence is set out by Wigmore, *Evidence*, §2036.

[43] 1 Edw. VI, c. 12 §22 (1547), and 5 & 6 Edw. VI, c. 11 §12 (1552).

Even if the English judges were not free to accept his argument under current common law, he may have supposed it would avail him something in the minds of thoughtful men steeped in the law of nature. Indeed it could have. However, it could not have been decisive in anyone's evaluation of the trial itself, given the contemporary understanding of the law of nature's scope and the porous character of the two-witness rule.

The Rights of Conscience

The most seemingly compelling argument More raised in his own defense was his invocation of the rights of conscience.[44] He had been emphatic, even stubborn, on this score.[45] And here too, his position found support in the natural law. It was, for instance, by human conscience that men understood the dictates of the law of nature. As one writer has put it, "the individual conscience serves as our guide in fulfilling the duty to obey [the] natural law."[46] It is "an inner judge."[47] It sets limits on the obedience ordinary men and women owe to the positive law. So it might have been said at the time. Since the law of nature stood higher than positive law (which was itself regarded as a creature of the natural law), a person's conscience might in effect dictate that he obey the former rather than the latter. This was pretty much the situation in which More found himself.

One can speak about this subject in a little more detail. The positive law of the Tudor era itself recognized the relevance of the individual conscience. It played a central role in the English courts of equity, where regular reference was made to the "law of conscience" as a source of legitimate obligation.[48] It figured also in the common law courts, although to a lesser extent. A feoffee to uses, for example, was said to be under a duty to perform the wishes (or last wishes) of the feoffor "in conscience."[49] Conscience was a standard held up for regular application in the English criminal law; even the notorious common law judge, Sir William Scroggs, told a jury "Follow your own consciences; do wisely; do honestly."[50]

The place of conscience was even more emphatically stated in the contemporary canon law; it furnished one measure by which human actions could and should be judged. "Those whom conscience justifies need not fear the curses

---

[44] See, e.g., More's letter to Margaret Roper, c. April 17, 1534, in *Conscience Decides: Letters and Prayers from Prison Written by Sir Thomas More*, ed. Dame Bede Foord (London, 1971), pp. 25–32; cf. *Correspondence*, no. 200, pp. 501–7.

[45] Gerard Wegemer, *Thomas More: A Portrait of Courage* (Princeton, NJ, 1995), pp. 171–81.

[46] J. Rufus Fears, "Natural Law: The Legacy of Greece and Rome," in *Common Truths: New Perspectives on Natural Law*, ed. Edward B. McLean (Wilmington, DE, 2000), pp. 19–56 at 22.

[47] John T. Noonan, Jr., *The Lustre of Our Country: The American Experience of Religious Freedom* (Cambridge, MA, 1998), p. 44.

[48] Anon. (1508), in *Carylls' Reports*, 116, no. 421. See also A. W. B. Simpson, *History of the Common Law of Contract* (Oxford, 1975), pp. 396–402; Mike Macnair, "Equity and Conscience," *Oxford Journal of Legal Studies* 27 (2007), 659–81.

[49] See *Gervys v. Cooke* (1522), in *Yearbooks of Henry VIII: 1520–1523*, ed. J. H. Baker, Selden Society 119 (London, 2002), no. 5.

[50] *Rex v. Langhorn*, in *State Trials*, ed. T. B. Howell and T. J. Howell, 33 vols (London, 1816–26), 7:484. See Barbara J. Shapiro, *Beyond Reasonable Doubt and Probable Cause* (Berkeley, CA, 1991), pp. 63, 263, n. 52.

of the crowd." "An action taken against the dictates of conscience builds to Gehenna." "One should suffer any ill before committing a mortal sin against conscience." So proclaimed the texts of the canon law and its *glossa ordinaria*.[51] They purported to be derived ultimately from the law of nature.

No exact modern equivalent to such enthusiastic recognitions of the force of conscience exists, at least in the United States Constitution or in the law built upon it. Conscience has nonetheless retained a toe-hold in our law. Most notable, of course, is the case of the conscientious objector to military service. Excepted from the reach of our armed forces are persons who are "conscientiously opposed to participation in war in any form."[52] Doctors, too, commonly have no duty to perform abortions if doing so would require them to act contrary to the dictates of their conscience.[53] True, the rise of legal positivism has restricted the attention explicitly accorded to the inherent rights of conscience in our law. The exceptions allowed today are normally based on legislation, and the jury instruction given by Judge Scroggs might actually be impermissible today, at least if he included the word "God" in any part of it. Nevertheless, the force of conscience in our public life is something we still recognize and respect. The Civil Rights Movement found its anchor in conscience.

It is not surprising to find that More invoked the rights of conscience during his trial, although so far as the record indicates he did so only after the jury had brought in a verdict against him.[54] He had not done so directly, and probably could not have done so while he maintained his silence, but at this point he advanced to "speak my mind plainly" and this "in discharge of my conscience."[55] More's conscience compelled him to refuse the commands of his sovereign. He must put God first. This amounted to an invocation of a higher law than an act of Parliament.

There was, it seems, a good reason that More made this argument only after his fate had been determined. Despite the seemingly unambiguous statements taken from the Church's law, conscience by itself played only a limited role in contemporary thinking about the relations between positive and natural law.[56] It was a fallible guide. Any person's conscience might be mistaken. King Henry VIII had been moved by his conscience in divorcing Catherine of Aragon.[57] More

---

[51] See C. 11 q. 3 c. 55; *gl. ord.* at Dist. 13, v. *item adversus*; X 5.39.44, v. *humiliter sustinere* (*CJC* 2:1916).
[52] See generally Charles Moskos and J. W. Chambers, II, eds, *The New Conscientious Objection: From Sacred to Secular Resistance* (Oxford, 1993).
[53] E.g., *Wolfe v. Schroering*, 541 F.2d 523, 527 (6th Cir. 1976); *Doe v. Hale Hospital*, 500 F.2d 144, 147 (1st Cir. 1974).
[54] See Derrett, "Trial," 71; Kelly, chapter 1 above, pp. 41–43.
[55] See Reynolds, *Trial of St Thomas More*, pp. 120–4 (**Doc. 17, no. 8**).
[56] See Brian Tierney, "Religious Rights: An Historical Perspective," in *Religious Human Rights in Global Perspective*, ed. John Witte, Jr. and Johan D. van der Vyver (The Hague, 1996) pp. 17–45, esp. pp. 24–6; Doe, *Fundamental Authority*, pp. 137–54.
[57] See Kelly, *Matrimonial Trials of Henry VIII*, pp. 14–18; Geoffrey de C. Parmiter, *The King's Great Matter: A Study of Anglo-Papal Relations 1527–1534* (London, 1967), p. 18, no. 1; J. J. Scarisbrick, *Henry VIII* (Berkeley, CA, 1968), pp. 153–4; J. Christopher Warner, *Henry VIII's Divorce: Literature and the Politics of the Printing Press* (Woodbridge, 1998), pp. 47–62.

had found himself asserting as much before Parliament in 1531.[58] He came to lament his parliamentary position soon enough, but if King Henry had invoked his conscience with effect, surely More could do the same?

The problem was that if fully respected, individual conscience could easily become a recipe for anarchy. For this reason, in the sixteenth century the invocation of conscience would no more free a man from the law's commands than it will free a modern science teacher from the duty to teach the theory of evolution. If he refuses, the authorities say to him, "You are mistaken." They do not say, "We respect your rights of conscience." So it was under the law of nature as understood in the sixteenth century. An "erroneous conscience" counted for little in the public forum. A man's conscience had to be aligned with right reason to serve as a legitimate justification for action.[59] Indeed, as one reads the early evidence, the conviction grows that conscience normally imposed additional obligations on those it touched; it did not free them from the commands of the positive law. It said to the man in possession of stolen property after the statute of limitations had run, "You have a duty in conscience to return it to the true owner." It did not say "The statute of limitations is invalid." It did not permit the statute to be ignored in a court of law.

A matter worthy of note, it must appear, is that here More himself moved quickly to the fourth point in speaking on his own behalf – the invalidity of the statute under which Henry VIII laid claim to the title of Head of the English Church. Reynolds stated the point carefully when he wrote, "the individual Christian has a duty to obey conscience in consonance with the teaching of the Church."[60] An objective view of what conscience dictated was, in the end, what counted most heavily in the balance, not the dictates of a particular individual's mind. It was because he believed his own conscience was consistent with the Church's law and the opinion of the learned men More respected that he could reasonably invoke it in his own defense. Otherwise, he would himself have been open to reproach for having hurried Protestants to their deaths. They had consciences too. But for More, the rights of conscience did not extend to Protestants. And under the most commonly accepted position taken in that era, More had been right about this – this time, he found, to his own disadvantage. The law of nature was not read to protect him.

---

[58] *Hall's Chronicle: Containing the History of England during the Reign of Henry the Fourth ... to the End of the Reign of Henry the Eighth*, ed. Henry Ellis (London, 1809), p. 780.

[59] See, e.g., Angelus de Clavasio (d. 1523), *Summa Angelica* (Venice, 1569), v. *conscientia*, nos. 1–2, distinguishing conscience that was in accordance with God's commands and to be followed and conscience that was contrary to God's law and not to be followed. A considerable casuistic literature grew up around the normal situation, in which one's conscience pushed towards disobedience to the law, but in which the person involved could not be wholly certain of his position. As I read the literature, the *communis opinio* held that in these circumstances the positive law should be obeyed and conscience safely disregarded, because thereby the person would be excused "propter bonum obedientiae."

[60] Reynolds, *Trial of St Thomas More*, p. 122.

The Invalidity of the Henrician Statute

More maintained that his indictment was "grounded upon an Act of Parliament directly repugnant to the laws of God and his Holy Church."[61] The overlap between fundamental law and canon law was not complete, but that some overlap existed few men doubted, and in any case both stood as fundamental laws all Christians were bound to respect. A statute contrary to the law of nature was void.[62] It was beyond the legitimate competence of Parliament to enact such a law. This was an accepted part of the law of More's time, almost a cliché. If Parliament enacted a statute requiring men to worship Baal rather than the Trinity, the statute would be invalid. Christians must obey God, and if it came to a choice, they must disobey any ruler who directed them not to.

The principle underlying this had been stretched in More's day by a long-standing clerical tendency to equate divine law with the advantage of Church and clergy. The medieval Church had not erred on the side of modesty, and clerical assertion of a special status in law had caused stresses and strains over the centuries – in England's case most famously in the quarrel that ended in the martyrdom of Thomas Becket in the twelfth century. However, this particular bit of history only strengthened More's position in disputing the merits of the Henrician statute. A statute contrary to the liberty of the church was held to be invalid. That is what Thomas Becket's example was said to prove. Support for this position could also be found in the positive law: the canon law,[63] the Roman law,[64] and in the provision in England's Magna Carta that the Church should remain free.[65] The charter's provision was regarded as a recognition placed in the positive law itself of an important principle necessary in all just law. Ecclesiastical liberty could not be transgressed. More invoked this traditional understanding of the limits of secular power and applied it to his own case.

Today's controversies about the extent of religious freedom under the United States Constitution remind us of what a difficult area of law this is, but I think most participants in the recent controversies will admit that there is a sphere of human life – the sphere of religious belief – that secular government is bound to leave untouched. Just how large that sphere is remains a subject of disagree-

---

[61] Derrett, "Trial," pp. 70–5; Kelly, Chapter 1 above, pp. 42–44.
[62] The *locus classicus* for this principle in English law is *Dr Bonham's Case*, 8 Co. Rep. 107a, 117b–118a, *The English Reports*, 178 vols (Edinburgh, 1900–32), 77:646, 652 (1610): "[W]hen an Act of Parliament is against common right and reason ... the common law will controul it and adjudge such Act to be void." This report drew upon the law of nature; see R. H. Helmholz, "Bonham's Case, Judicial Review, and the Law of Nature," *Journal of Legal Analysis* 1 (2009), 324–53.
[63] X 5.39.49.
[64] See the novel of Justinian, *Cassa et irrita*, commonly placed after Cod. 1.2(5).12 in early editions of the *Corpus Juris Civilis*. It stated that "omnia statuta et consuetudines contra libertatem ecclesiae" ("all statutes and customs contrary to the freedom of the church ") in Italy should be null and void. The gloss, v. *per Italiam*, added that it was in Italy "ubi maxime fiebant" ("where they are particularly frequent").
[65] *Stubbs' Select Charters from the Beginning to 1307*, 9th edn, H. W. C. Davis (Oxford, 1921), pp. 292–3; the meaning of the clause is more fully discussed by W. S. McKechnie, *Magna Carta: A Commentary on the Great Charter of King John*, 2d edn (Glasgow, 1914), pp. 190–5.

ment. Disputes about matters like animal sacrifice for religious purposes are reminders that we have not "solved" the problem.[66] They do serve as a reminder that we still recognize something akin to the principle which More invoked during his trial.

He invoked it with eloquence. The statute commanded something that was contrary to the laws of God and God's holy Church; therefore an indictment founded upon it was "insufficient to charge any Christian man" with its violation. More was unmoved by the argument that many learned men, including virtually all of those on the episcopal bench, had accepted the statute's validity. He claimed he could vouch the opinions of a far greater number of men through the ages who had been of his opinion. No one realm had any right to "make a particular law disagreeable with the general law of Christ's Universal Catholic Church."[67]

This was a crucial point, and More stressed it in claiming the moral high ground. Why, then, did his position not make more of an impact than it did on the judges? Fear, perhaps. But there were other reasons too. One was that "particular laws disagreeable with the general law" of the Church were in fact very common at the time, in England as elsewhere across the Channel. More himself had defended their validity on previous occasions. The Statutes of Praemunire (1393) and Provisors (1390) were evident examples.[68] They were "disagreeable with the general law" of the Church. bishops and popes themselves had said so emphatically.[69] But no one, and certainly not More, supposed the statutes could be ignored or invalidated in an English court on that account.

A particularly clear example of the strength of such laws was the English law that subjected the clergy to the jurisdiction of secular courts in civil cases. We take that rule for granted today; the clergy are subject to suit for debt or trespass in a secular court. However, it was quite otherwise with the medieval canonists. For them, the *privilegium fori* was a fundamental part of God's law, and the English custom that ran counter to it was invalid. The Rota Romana had itself so held in what must have been a test case brought in the 1370s: the *Domini* of the Rota held that even in civil causes the English secular courts had no jurisdiction over the clergy and could have none.[70] When More had been asked about this aspect of the Church's law during his controversy with St

---

[66] E.g., *Church of the Lukumi Babalu Aye, Inc. v. City of Hialeah*, 508 US 520 (1993).
[67] See Reynolds, *Trial of St Thomas More*, p. 121 (Doc. 20, §15).
[68] See *Debellation*, chap. 18, CW 10:187; and *The Supplication of Souls*, CW, 7:132–4.
[69] See letter of Pope Martin V (1427), in *Calendar of Entries in the Papal Registers Relating to Great Britain and Ireland. Papal Letters*, vol. 7: AD 1417–1431, ed. J. A. Twemlow (London, 1905), pp. 36–7, warning that no one who observed this "execrable statute against ecclesiastical liberty" could be saved; see also R. G. Davies, "Martin V and the English Episcopate," *English Historical Review* 92 (1977), 309–44, esp. pp. 343–4; E. F. Jacob, *The Fifteenth Century 1399–1485*, Oxford History of England 6 (Oxford, 1961), pp. 266–7.
[70] *Decisiones Antiquae Rotae Romanae* (Turin, 1579), tit. *De consuetudine*, Dec. 10 (840) (Turin, 1579), fols 8v–9. The case is discussed by Walter Ullmann, "A Decision of the Rota Romana on the Benefit of Clergy in England," *Studia Gratiana* 13 (1967), 455–89.

German, he had defended the English practice.⁷¹ In other words, he had adopted a position seemingly opposed to the one he was taking at the end of his trial.

No change of mind or logical inconsistency is necessarily implicit in More's actions and statements. Without Herculean effort, the two might be reconciled. However, the seeming contradiction does point to the difficulty with More's position. In fact, it points to a problem inherent in the law of nature itself when it came to be applied to actual cases. Natural law did not reach down to the level of specificity required to distinguish between the Henrician statute and this long-established English jurisdictional rule. It did not allow the former to be disregarded as invalid whereas the latter passed muster. Divine and natural laws were guides in making and interpreting the law. They left room for difference of opinion about the specifics of procedural law. Except in the clearest cases, they did not require a specific result, though they might suggest one. For a practical-minded lawyer, they could be maddeningly abstract.

There was an additional problem inherent in More's position. The law of nature as then understood did not permit judges to "strike down" (as we would say) the considered actions of their sovereigns. It is unlikely that More was asking the judges to do this. He was a sixteenth-century lawyer. However, so ingrained among us is the assumption that judges have the power to refuse to enforce unconstitutional statutes that we are likely to read that attitude back into earlier centuries. It is too easy to suppose that natural law must have served that same function. We so readily assume that the law of nature was a fundamental law and roughly equivalent to our own federal Constitution, that it has become necessary to emphasize that the law of nature did not include the power of judicial review in the modern sense of that term.⁷² In the courts, "even the errors of the prince" were to be treated as binding upon the judges.⁷³

According to More's earlier writings, duly enacted statutes did not even permit public contention about their merits.⁷⁴ Some room for manoeuvre, it is true, was left to conscientious judges in making use of the law of nature when interpreting statutes. Where the lawmaker had not been specific or had not fully considered the potential results of the enactment, it might be assumed that he had not intended to violate the law of nature. The statute could be interpreted accordingly to avoid any conflict. That standard applied to acts of Parliament. However, interpretation, even aggressive interpretation, did not amount to judicial invalidation of statutes, and it could scarcely be maintained that this approach provided a way around the Henrician statute. Its stated purpose

---

⁷¹ See *Debellation*, chap. 19, *CW*, 10:195.
⁷² The evidence is convincingly reviewed in Helen K. Michael, "The Role of Natural Law in Early American Constitutionalism: Did the Founders Contemplate Judicial Enforcement of 'Unwritten' Individual Rights?" *North Carolina Law Review* 69 (1991), 421–90. The failure to appreciate this point lies behind much of modern criticism of natural law; it is easy to show that the maxim *lex iniusta non est lex* is mistaken if one thinks about law mainly in terms of what courts are authorized to do. But that attitude was not that of lawyers schooled in the *ius commune* of earlier centuries.
⁷³ See *gl. ord.* ad D. 4 c. 3: "[E]tiam error principis ius facit" ("Even the errors of the prince constitute law"), citing Dig. 33.10.3 (*CJC* 1:11).
⁷⁴ *The Apology*, chap. 26, in *CW*, 9:96–7.

was to extinguish the power which popes had unlawfully exercised within the English Church. There was no ambiguity about that. On that score, the judges in More's trial were doing what they were obliged to do under the law of nature as it was then understood. If fault there was in the trial, it could not have been because the Henrician statute failed a test supplied by the law of nature.

Conclusion

An unusual feature of the trial's course deserves brief mention in assessing the arguments More's raised by this trial. Once the verdict against him had been given and after he had finished his legal argument, More went on to remark to the judges before him that he looked forward to the time when he and they would meet in heaven. Invoking the biblical story of St Paul's presence at the stoning of Stephen, he looked forward to a "merry" reunion with these men, whom he certainly knew well. They would meet, he said, just as surely as Paul and Stephen had met together and shared a happy time in paradise.[75]

It seems a strange comment. Why say this to the men who, More argued, had just violated fundamental tenets of justice in condemning him to death? To pray for them to see the light might have been appropriate, but not a seemingly confident prediction that they would all meet again in heaven. One might of course suppose that More meant this as an indirect call for their repentance. If he did, it was a very subtle call, an odd choice from a man who no longer had anything to lose and who had just owned up to his opinions. His words had a more friendly tone.[76] It is true that one might also speculate that More still had a hope of being reprieved and wished to curry favor with the judges who might yet make it possible. But this too seems unlikely. It is overly cynical. More knew he was to die. But why did he say what he did?

We cannot know his motivation with certainty. However, there is a plausible explanation that fits within an assessment of the trial based upon the law of nature. It is that the judges had done their duty. Judged against natural law standards, they had done what they were supposed to do.[77] The procedure they had followed was in accord with the laws of England, and the laws of England were consistent with the law of nature. These laws did not allow all men to escape punishment by remaining silent; they did leave evaluation of the evidence to the jury; they did not allow pleas of conscience to overturn positive law in public courts; and they did not provide authority for judges to strike down duly enacted statutes. The law of nature provided arguments for More – arguments of substance. He had made them. But he must have realized that, as it was then understood, natural law proved too weak a reed to support

---

[75] See Roper's Account, **Doc. 20**, §20.
[76] It is ascribed to More's undoubted talent for friendship in the introduction to Gerard Wegemer and Stephen Smith, eds, *A Thomas More Source Book* (Washington, DC, 2004), pp. xviii–xix.
[77] See Jean-Marie Carbasse, "Le juge entre la loi et la justice: approches médiévales," in *La conscience du juge dans la tradition juridique européenne*, ed. Jean-Marie Carbasse and Laurence Depambour-Tarride (Paris, 1999), pp. 67–94, esp. pp. 84–6.

the contention that these judges should have done something other than what they did. The fault lay elsewhere. Even had they been so inclined, judges were not entitled to substitute the testimony of their own consciences for a decision reached under existing positive law.[78] Even had a motion in arrest of judgment been available in the circumstances of the trial, and even had the question of the trial's consistency with the law of nature been raised as directly as I have sought to raise it, the judgment against More could not have been overturned on the basis of invocation of the law of nature as it then stood.[79] Great things have been claimed for natural law as the foundation for justice.[80] But at least as applied to More's trial, a trial held at a time when natural law's legitimacy was accepted without question, its tenets proved inadequate to protect this victim of Tudor politics. This is the unmistakable, if disappointing, conclusion that is reached by working through the natural law arguments as they applied to this famous trial. Even when advanced by as astute a lawyer as Thomas More, invocation of the law of nature was not enough to change the trial's outcome. It played a part in the trial, but not a decisive part, at least not in the sense that it provided real protection for him. In the end, those who argue that More did not receive a fair trial must look for support to the arguments that are raised and discussed by Professor Kelly in chapter 1.

Appendix: Abbreviations to the texts of Corpus Juris Canonici and Corpus Juris Civilis

Dist. 1 c. 1	*Decretum Gratiani*, Distinctio 1, canon 1
C. 1 q. 1 c. 1	*Decretum Gratiani*, Causa 1, quaestio 1, canon 1
De pen.	*De penitencia*
X 1.1.1	*Decretales Gregorii IX*, Book 1, tit. 1, cap. 1
Sext. 1.1.1	*Liber sextus*, Book 1, tit. 1, cap. 1
Clem. 1.1.1	*Constitutiones Clementis V*, Book 1, tit. 1, cap. 1
gl. ord.	*glossa ordinaria*
Dig. 1.1.1	*Digestum Justiniani*, lib. 1, tit. 1, lex 1
Cod. 1.1.1	*Codex Justiniani*, lib. 1, tit. 1, lex 1
Inst. 1.1.1	*Institutiones Justiniani*, lib. 1, tit. 1, lex 1
Nov. 1.1.1	*Novellae Justiniani*, lib. 1, tit. 1, lex 1

---

[78] The conundrum, including citations to the literature of the *ius commune*, is discussed at length in Didacus Covarruvias (d. 1577), *Variarum resolutionum libri quatuor* (Geneva, 1723), Lib. I, cap. 1, nos. 1–4. Among modern treatments, see esp. K. W. Nörr, *Zur Stellung des Richters im gelehrten Prozeß der Frühzeit: Iudex secundum allegata non secundum conscientiam iudicat* (Munich, 1967); Richard Fraher, "Conviction According to Conscience: The Medieval Jurists' Debate Concerning Judicial Discretion and the Law of Proof," *Law and History Review* 7 (1989), 23–88; Antonio Padoa-Schioppa, "Sulla coscienza del giudice nel diritto commune," in *Iuris Vincula: Studi in onore di Mario Talamanca* (Naples, 2001), pp. 119–62.

[79] The writ of error that, if successful, might lead to a new trial also seems to have been a matter of grace only at the time of More's trial. See Stephen, *History*, 3:308–11.

[80] See, e.g., Hadley Arkes, "The Natural Law, the Laws of Reason, and the Distractions of History," *Journal of Law, Philosophy and Culture* 3 (2009), 203–20.

3

A Guide to Thomas More's Trial for Modern Lawyers

Louis W. Karlin and David R. Oakley

Introduction

The trial of Sir Thomas More is a touchstone for examining our sense of injustice, whether understood in terms of legalistic notions of due process or in the most fundamental sense of human rights. Until very recently, however, such examinations were conducted without a sound historical basis either as to the legal background of the time or the events of the trial itself. That has changed, thanks to the pioneering work of twentieth-century scholars such as J. H. Baker,[1] John G. Bellamy,[2] and J. Duncan M. Derrett.[3] Further implications of the law of sixteenth-century England for the trial are developed by H. A. Kelly and R. H. Helmholz in chapters 1 and 2 of this volume.

In this chapter, we seek to provide an account of More's trial from the modern lawyer's perspective in such a way as to minimize the distorting effects of hindsight and partisan prejudices. Any such account, however, will necessarily remain incomplete because there remain as yet unbridged gaps in our historical knowledge, due mainly to the lack of a contemporaneous record of the trial proceedings. Authorized court reporters and trial transcripts are a thing of our, not More's, time.

Important questions remain unresolved as to major aspects of the proceedings themselves. For instance, did More successfully move to dismiss a large portion of the indictment? A recent consensus, deriving from Professor Derrett, is "yes." If so, we may look to More's trial as evidencing an early example of judicial courage and independence. In his chapter, however, Professor Kelly offers strong reasons to reconsider that conclusion. Still more fundamental, what was the legal significance of the concept of malice as used in the indictment? Was it an element of the offense, requiring positive proof of an intent to harm, as More himself seems to have understood, or was it a mere term of art, meaning any conduct deemed by a jury to violate the Act of Treasons?[4] If More

---

[1] See Baker, *Oxford History*, vol. 6, and earlier works.
[2] Bellamy, *Tudor Law of Treason*.
[3] Derrett, "Trial."
[4] Act of Treasons, 26 Henry VIII c. 13 (Nov.–Dec. 1534), in *Statutes of the Realm*, 3:508–9 (**Doc. 2**).

was correct – as Professor Kelly argues – we must consider whether the judges betrayed More by failing to give deserved credence to a defense consistent with Parliament's intent in limiting the reach of that statute.

In the pages that follow, we present a chronological account of the trial process from King Henry's invocation of the special court's jurisdiction, to jury selection, and through the trial and judgment. In so doing, we draw on the scholarship of Professors Baker, Bellamy, Derrett, Kelly, and Helmholz, while including examples of contemporary American jurisprudence to provide a comparative, contemporary perspective. Our hope is to help provide a surer foundation from which scholars, jurists, and students can assess whether More's trial was unjust and, if so, to better understand the nature of the injustice – whether it was one of legal process or of substantive law or a failure of the participants' personal virtue.

Jurisdiction

The trial proceedings commenced with Henry VIII's decision to appoint a special commission of oyer and terminer for Middlesex County to adjudicate More's alleged treason. Having been specially invoked by the Crown and being comprised of the realm's highest judges and ministers, an oyer and terminer commission was, in effect, the king's Council acting in a judicial capacity. The king himself almost certainly chose the commission's members. To the modern sensibility, there would appear to be a serious conflict of interest in his doing so, and in fact the commission included some of More's known enemies: Anne Boleyn's father, brother, and uncle, Thomas and George Boleyn and Thomas Howard. At the time, however, this was likely the accepted practice, and there is no record of any challenges to the commission's composition. Additionally, there was no prescribed number of commissioners. The historical record shows commissions comprising as few members as three and as many as a score. Commissions often included judges from the King's Bench and the Court of Common Pleas, along with notable royal lawyers and prominent ministers. More's trial featured seven justices, including the chief justices of the King's Bench and Common Pleas, John FitzJames and John Baldwin, supplemented by Lord Chancellor Thomas Audley and Secretary Thomas Cromwell.

The court's jurisdiction was final; there was no right to appeal – except to the commissioners themselves who included the chief justices of the realm's most important courts.

Such a commission was the kind of court typically used to try cases of high treason. Indeed, this same procedure of commission of oyer and terminer (without all the illustrious participants) was used in the trial of the three Carthusian priors, including Prior Houghton, and the Bridgettine monk Richard Reynolds in late April 1535.[5] Rather than proceed by this special commission, King Henry could have obtained a bill of attainder for high treason. By such

---

[5] Doc. 3 below.

an end-run around the judicial system, Parliament could have convicted More of treason and imposed punishment, including execution and confiscation of property. The king had used that approach in December 1534, when he arranged for the passage of the act of attainder against More, by which Parliament found him guilty of misprision of treason for his original, pre-commitment refusals to take the oath of succession.[6] The Act of Succession made such refusal akin to a strict liability offense, which was punishable not as high treason but as the lesser offense of misprision of high treason. As explained below, under the Act of Succession, high treason was reserved for "any word without writing or any exterior deed or act" done *maliciously* against the king, queen, or succession.[7] As it turned out, however, Parliament was not in session at the time of More's trial in June 1535.

Then, as now, a bill of attainder is a legislative act that inflicts punishment without a judicial trial.[8] The United States Constitution provides: "No bill of attainder or ex post facto law shall be passed,"[9] and "no State shall ... pass any bill of attainder, ex post facto law, or law impairing the obligation of contracts."[10] In *United States v. Brown*, the Court stated that the Bill of Attainder Clause was to be read broadly "in light of the evil the Framers had sought to bar: legislative punishment, of any form or severity, of specifically designated persons or groups."[11]

Substantive Law of Treason and More's Defenses

The Act of Treasons made it high treason to

> maliciously wish, will, or desire by words or writing, or by craft imagine, invent, practice, or attempt any bodily harm to be done or committed to the king's most royal person, the queen's, or their heirs apparent, or to deprive them or any of them of their dignity, title, or name of their royal estates, or slanderously and maliciously publish or pronounce, by express writings or words, that the king our sovereign lord should be a heretic, schismatic, tyrant, infidel.[12]

Thus, to *maliciously* deprive Henry VIII of his title as Supreme Head of the Church in England, as conferred by Act of Supremacy of 1534,[13] became high treason.

The Act of Succession, previously enacted in March 1534 and effective May 1, 1534, some months before the Act of Treasons was passed, legitimized

---

6 Act of Attainder of More, 26 Henry VIII, c. 23 (*Statutes of the Realm* 3:528).
7 Act of Succession, 25 Henry VIII (1533–34) c. 22 §6 (*Statutes of the Realm* 3:474).
8 *Cummings v. Missouri*, United States Reports 71 (1867), 277, 323 (4 Wall.).
9 *Constitution of the United States*, Art. I, §9, cl. 3: *United States Code*, 2006 edn (Washington, DC, 2008), vol. 1 (Title 1).
10 Ibid., Art. I, §10.
11 *United States v. Brown*, United States Reports 381 (1965), 437, 447.
12 Doc. 2.
13 Doc. 1.

the marriage of Henry and Anne Boleyn. It required all citizens to swear a corporeal oath "that they shall truly, firmly, and constantly, without fraud or guile, observe, fulfill, maintain, defend, and keep, to their cunning, wit, and uttermost of their powers, the whole effects and contents of this present act." If any person commanded to take "the said oath afore limited, obstinately refuse that to do, in contempt of this act, that then every such person so doing, to be taken and accepted for offender in misprision of high treason; and that every such refusal shall be deemed and adjudged misprision of high treason."[14] Again, misprision of treason was a lesser offense. Whereas high treason was punishable by hanging, drawing and quartering, misprision was punishable by imprisonment for life and loss of all property.

Under the Act of Succession, the element of malice was not the criterion used to distinguish high treason from the lesser offense of misprision of treason. The act specified that anything done "by any word without writing or any exterior deed or act maliciously and obstinately" against the king's marriage was misprision of treason,[15] whereas writing or printing any such thing maliciously was high treason.[16] However, to the extent the act criminalized omissions or silence, it was only in terms of a silent (and obstinate) refusal to affirm the oath, which did not amount to high treason. The Act of Treasons increased the punishment for malicious speaking from misprision to high treason, but made no mention of the oath requirement and said nothing about refusals to speak. Thus, as the Act of Treasons neither made it high treason to refuse the oath nor imposed any further obligation to affirm the king's title, it is reasonable to infer the Commons intended to reserve the offense of high treason to those who spoke, wrote, or acted to impugn the king's title. Mere silent refusal to affirm the royal title would presumably fall outside the scope of the Act of Treasons.

The American constitutional and statutory law of treason serves as a counterpoint. Article III of the Constitution defines treason as "only in levying war against [the United States], or in adhering to their enemies, giving them aid and comfort. No person shall be convicted of treason unless on the testimony of two witnesses to the same overt act, or on confession in open court."[17] Federal law provides:

> Whoever, owing allegiance to the United States, levies war against them or adheres to their enemies, giving them aid and comfort within the United

---

[14] Act of Succession, 25 Henry VIII (1533–34), c. 22 (*Statutes of the Realm* 3:471–4). The quoted portion is taken from §9 (p. 474). When More was ordered to take a fuller version of the oath, he refused to do so, on grounds that the oath did not comport with the statute. This was remedied by giving the full text in the Act Ratifying the Oath That Every of the King's Subjects Hath Taken and Shall Hereafter Be Bound to Take for Due Observation of the Act Made for the Surety of the Succession in the next session of Parliament, 26 Henry VIII (Nov.–Dec. 1534), c. 2 (*Statutes of the Realm* 3:492–3). As we explain below, More perceived that the oath went beyond affirming the succession and likely implied an affirmation of the severing of the English Church from the Church of Rome.

[15] Act of Succession, §6 (p. 474) (*Statutes of the Realm* 3:474).

[16] Ibid., §5 (p. 473).

[17] *Constitution of the United States*, Art. III, §3, cl. 1.

States or elsewhere, is guilty of treason and shall suffer death, or shall be imprisoned not less than five years and fined under this title but not less than $10,000; and shall be incapable of holding any office under the United States.[18]

Misprision of treason under federal law applies to persons who know about treasonable acts, but conceal that information from the president or other official. The lesser offense is punishable by a fine or imprisonment of not more than seven years, or both.[19] Thus, in contemporary American jurisprudence, treason

> consists of two elements – adhering to the enemy; and giving him aid and comfort. One may think disloyal thoughts and have his heart on the side of the enemy. Yet if he commits no act giving aid and comfort to the enemy, he is not guilty of treason. He may on the other hand commit acts which do give aid and comfort to the enemy and yet not be guilty of treason, as for example where he acts impulsively with no intent to betray. Two witnesses are required not to the disloyal and treacherous intention but to the same overt act.[20]

In the first Parliament held after Henry's death in 1547, the penalty for mere speaking against the king's supremacy was reduced from high treason to imprisonment during the king's pleasure and forfeiture of goods.[21] Under the Act of Treasons, however, "traitorous words were really the centre-piece. To wish or attempt bodily harm to the king, queen or the royal heir or to try to deprive the king of his title by malicious deeds, writings, and spoken words, was now laid down as treason."[22] More would therefore have understood that the act made words alone high treason. Nor was there a requirement that the actionable words need be made public: "In the case of More, the chief complaint was evasive answers under interrogation rather than spontaneous open denial."[23]

Did the Commons insist on inserting the qualifying adverb "maliciously" as means of limiting persons subject to high treason to those who impugned the king's title with a proven intent to harm? Although Professor Baker does not take a position, other scholars dispute whether the insertion of the word "maliciously" was superfluous (Bellamy) or a limitation on the definition of treason (Kelly). Bellamy says,

> Both of these different types of treason, causing bodily harm to the king, his queen or heir or seeking to deprive him of his title by spoken words or writing, and calling him a heretic, tyrant or the rest had to be uttered mali-

---

[18] *United States Code*, vol. 18 (Title 18), §2381.
[19] Ibid., §2382.
[20] *Tomoya Kawakita v. United States*, *United States Reports* 343 (1952), 717, 736.
[21] See Treason Act of 1547, 1 Edward VI, c. 12 (*Statutes of the Realm of the Realm* 4:18–22), section 5 (pp. 19–20). This is the penalty for the first offense; a second offense brings forfeiture of lands and life imprisonment, and a third constitutes high treason, with the death penalty. Section 6 (p. 20) stipulates that any such opposition to the supremacy by writing, printing, or overt deed is high treason.
[22] Bellamy, *Tudor Law of Treason*, p. 31.
[23] Baker, *Oxford History*, p. 586.

ciously if they were to be traitorous ... More argued apparently that but for the word "maliciously" nothing in the indictment disclosed an offence. The judges, however, rejected the argument. Fisher also questioned the word and to him the judges replied that malicious was superfluous. They were probably correct.[24]

Thus, according to Professor Bellamy, "maliciously" was merely substituted for the usual term, "traitorously."

Whether viable or not, according to Roper, More's defense seized on the statutory reference to malice – "where there is no malice, there can be no offense."[25] Analogizing to the requirement that an entry be "forcible," and not merely peaceable, to constitute a crime under the Statute of Forcible Entries, More argued that his lawyerly trading of hypothetical arguments with Master Rich – the "putting of cases" – could not amount to malice. It was merely "familiar secret talk, nothing affirming."[26] According to the Guildhall Report, More argued his refusal to affirm the supremacy was mere silence, which was not punishable under the Statute of Treasons or indeed any law in the whole world.[27] Lawful punishment must be premised on the commission of a crime "in word or deed."[28] According to the same report, More told the court that he had already been punished for his refusal to support the king's second marriage, being "adjudged" (*adjudicatus*) to life in prison and his property confiscated.[29] (Actually, no conviction took place until his attainder in the Parliament of November 1534, declaring him guilty of obstinately refusing to take the oath which Parliament had contemporaneously formulated, making it an apparent violation ex post facto.) More seems to have been arguing that the Act of Succession made his "obstinate" refusal misprision of high treason, not high treason; but now, by his subsequent refusals – all instigated by the Crown *after* the Acts of Supremacy and Treasons had been passed – he was being prosecuted for a new, separate, and greater offense based on precisely the same kind of conduct. That is, if More committed high treason under the Act of Treasons – rather than repeated instances of misprision of treason under the Act of Succession – the prosecution should be required to prove additional, affirmative acts of misconduct beyond that of refusing to make an affirmation. In response, the prosecution would almost certainly have argued that More was being prosecuted not for his original refusals of the oath of succession, which resulted in the bill of attainder, but for his subsequent actions while in custody, including his refusal to affirm the king's supremacy at that later time.

Reference to More's prison letters is instructive here too. In the famous letter of August 1534 (ascribed to Margaret Roper), More refers to the fact that Parliament was still in session and could make new laws affecting his cause. At the

---

[24] Bellamy, *Tudor Law of Treason*, pp. 32–3.
[25] Roper's Account, Doc. 20 §10.
[26] Ibid.
[27] Guildhall Report, Doc. 17 §2c.
[28] Ibid.
[29] Ibid., §2a.

time, neither the Act of Treasons nor the Act of Supremacy had been enacted; More's concern was about the Act of Succession, for which his silent refusal still appeared sufficient to avoid high treason. He says to Margaret, "Albeit I know well that if they would make a law to do me any harm, that law could never be lawful."[30] Similarly, in a subsequent letter, More stated:

> Now have I heard since that some say that this obstinate manner of mine, in still refusing the oath, shall peradventure force and drive the king's Grace to make a further law for me. I cannot let [prevent] such a law to be made. But I am very sure, that if I died by such a law, I should die for that point innocent afore God.[31]

He eventually saw the "new statutes made at the last sitting of the Parliament," but he told Cromwell, as he reported to his daughter in a letter written after the death judgments for treason against the Charterhouse priors and Master Reynolds, he did not spend much time studying them.[32]

The prosecution viewed More's silence negatively. Under the circumstances, his refusal to affirm the king's supremacy was evidence of malice. The prosecution argued that More's silence when interrogated in the Tower "was a sure indication and a not obscure sign of some malign thinking about the statute" because a faithful subject was obliged to respond openly and without dissimulation "that it is good and holy."[33] It was here that More invoked the legal maxim under "universal law" that "one who keeps silent seems to consent."[34] From the Guildhall Report, we can see that More was realistic about the chances that this technical argument would succeed. Considering the circumstances surrounding his trial, and given that, since his resignation, More had been publishing anti-Reformation tracts, there was no good reason to think his refusal to affirm the supremacy bespoke consent to the king's new title as Head of the Church. Accordingly, More explained why that evidentiary presumption should nevertheless be respected. Contrary to the Crown's position, there was a good-faith basis for remaining silent, which was compatible with one's obligations as a "good man and faithful subject" – respect for the "greater obligation" to consult one's "own conscience" and to "follow the prescriptions of reason," especially where the dictates of his conscience can be followed without offending his prince or stirring up sedition.[35]

---

[30] *Last Letters*, no. 12 (*Correspondence*, no. 206), August 1534: Margaret Roper to Alice Alington, p. 87.
[31] *Last Letters*, letter no. 15 (*Correspondence*, no. 210), To Margaret Roper, from the Tower, 1534, p. 101.
[32] *Last Letters*, letter no. 20 (*Correspondence*, no. 214), at p. 115; Doc. 4 §3.
[33] Guildhall Report, Doc. 17 §3. Pole's account is to similar effect – the prosecution arguing that More's silence was positive evidence of "an evil mind," with More countering with the legal presumption that "silence was an indication of a mind that assented to a law rather than one that opposed it." Doc. 19 §6.
[34] Guildhall Report, Doc. 17, §4; cf. Pole, Doc. 19, §6.
[35] Guildhall Report, Doc. 17, §4. From this argument, we can infer what must have been More's political/ethical theory of liberty of conscience and religious toleration: While obligations to God trump those owed to one's sovereign, those obligations should work in harmony – and will in a

The problem with More's appeal to conscience, at least from the Crown's perspective, is that it implies a reasonable doubt as to the supremacy's legitimacy. In any event, if there were no recognized substantive right to remain silent when required to affirm an oath, as Professor Helmholz argues, the prosecution's argument was a reasonable one. Indeed, even if silence alone could not support a conviction, a legitimate question would remain as to whether More's silence and the circumstances surrounding his exchange of letters with Fisher could be viewed as corroborating Rich's testimony that More expressly denied the king's title. As Professor Bellamy concludes: "The important trials [including More's] which occurred between 1535 and the end of the reign, much though they have been commented on adversely, reveal, in the main, little that was unfair in the interpretation of treason."[36]

In contrast, as Professor Kelly demonstrates, that conclusion follows only if one accepts the notion that malice had little or no substantive meaning in the language of the Act of Treasons. For if malice meant an intent to harm, there was no solid evidence that More acted maliciously to deprive the king of the legislatively conferred supremacy: mere refusal to affirm the supremacy was not punishable as high treason; More made every effort to avoid giving his opinion on the supremacy; and all the words and deeds alleged as amounting to high treason were committed after More was jailed and attainted for misprision of treason for refusing the oath, consistent with the Act of Succession.

Arrest and Detention

After arrest, a treason suspect was placed in jail, there to remain until he was either arraigned or released on bail. More, like most notorious treason suspects, was jailed in the Tower of London. The time during which a prisoner suspected of treason had to remain in jail before his arraignment varied enormously, from a few days to a decade. More was committed in mid-April 1534 and only put on trial on July 1, 1535.[37] But in More's case, he never was arraigned for the original charge, misprision of treason, instead being convicted by attainder, and handily already present in the Tower when charged under the new statute.

> Conditions under which treason suspects lived in prison varied considerably but in general they were harsh even by the standards of the times. The intention was quite clear to both officials and captives: to weaken the prisoner's body and thus his resolution so that incriminating evidence ... should be forthcoming.[38]

---

just state. In striving to harmonize these potentially competing obligations, moreover, the citizen's respect for political authority remains such that it proscribes positive violation of duly enacted laws. Conscientious objection counsels persuasive efforts – not violent overthrow – and when those efforts fail, silence remains the only viable alternative.

36 Bellamy, *Tudor Law of Treason*, p. 39.
37 Ibid., p. 94.
38 Ibid., pp. 93–4.

At that time, common law did not concern itself with conduct occurring between arrest and trial. Hence, the Council's discretion was practically untrammeled; and torture – although not employed against More – became, in Tudor times, increasingly common.[39]

As discussed above, More was convicted of treason based on conduct and statements made in the Tower. At that time there was no right to remain silent as that right is understood in light of contemporary American jurisprudence generally and more particularly in terms of the Fifth Amendment. Indeed, "once the suspected traitor had been arrested and placed in custody, there followed the examination or questioning."[40] "Articles, or interrogatories as they were sometimes called, which were leading questions the suspect must answer, were composed by king, minister or council or all three."[41] "The choice of examiners depended largely on the degree of importance of the treason, the rank of the suspect, and where he was being held." Sir Thomas More was examined "by the attorney-general, the solicitor-general, two civilians and Cromwell himself."[42]

As Professor Helmholz explains, the accepted law of More's time usually compelled suspects to affirm or deny wrongdoing.[43] In light of that understanding, More's silence should not be understood as the invocation of some recognized legal privilege, but as his good-faith effort to avoid giving offense under the Act of Treasons – not showing malice, which he understood as an element of the offense requiring affirmative evidence of ill will. Of course, even if not recognized in treason prosecutions, such a strategy accorded with, and likely had its roots in, a fundamental axiom of Western canon law "accepted both in the English common law and in the European *ius commune. De occultis non judicat Ecclesia. Nemo tenetur prodere seipsum.*"[44]

Grand Jury/Indictment

Again, the Crown alleged violations of the Act of Treasons, which criminalized as high treason a vague array of offenses, understood as mainly directed towards any act or attempt to deprive Henry VIII of his title as Supreme Head of the Church in England, as conferred by the Act of Supremacy. To the eyes of a modern lawyer, More's indictment[45] appears to consist of a number of separate charges. However, there is good reason to believe that the "counts" were not separate charges, but a series of material facts alleged in support of the single charge of treason.[46] At the same time, while there is no indication that the

---

[39] See ibid., pp. 130–1.
[40] Ibid., p. 104,
[41] Ibid.
[42] Ibid., p. 105. Bellamy here follows the date of the indictment, May 7 (Doc. 16, §4), but More, writing on May 2 or 3, dates it to April 30 (Doc. 4, §2).
[43] R. H. Helmholz, chapter 2 above, p. 58.
[44] Ibid., p. 56. That is, "The Church does not judge concerning secret things" and "No one is obligated to betray himself."
[45] Doc. 16.
[46] Parmiter, "Indictment of St Thomas More," pp. 162–3.

indictment was organized by separate counts, the document is so prolix that for purposes of discussion it is helpful to view it as setting forth eight charges: That More's act or attempt to deprive Henry VIII of his title as Supreme Head of the Church in England was shown by:

1. maliciously remaining silent on May 7, 1535, while being interrogated;
2. maliciously writing to Fisher on May 12, 1535 to consent in Fisher's denial of the supremacy, informing Fisher of his own silence, and calling the Act of Treasons a "two-edged sword";
3. maliciously writing to Fisher on May 26, 1535, telling him not to use the same words to interrogators in order to avoid imputation of conspiracy;
4. Fisher's remaining silent and using the "two-edged sword" metaphor (thus, evidencing a conspiracy between More and Fisher);
5. More's maliciously persevering in his silence when interrogated on June 3, 1535;
6. using the "two-edged sword" statement when questioned concerning the act on June 3, 1535;
7. More and Fisher's burning their letters (thus, evidencing conspiracy); and
8. More's maliciously telling Rich on June 12, 1535 that subjects could not be obligated by an act of Parliament making the king the Supreme Head of the Church.

Although there was no public prosecutor, typically in important cases,

> the king's "learned counsel," that is to say the royal legal advisers, sent to the grand juries bills they had compiled themselves which described the offences, the culprits and the particular laws broken. This was done in a way which was so comprehensive and already so close to the form of actual indictment that the jurors needed only to approve and send them on to the justices.[47]

Ministers of the Crown had a greater or lesser involvement and influence in proposing an indictment, depending on the importance of the target. Thus, in More's case, Cromwell probably drafted the indictment based on answers to interrogatories submitted to More, Rich, and other witnesses.

> Indicting juries usually contained twelve jurors, although there could on occasion be twice as many. They were all supposed to be men of substance and, in practice, a fair proportion had held offices in local government. There was no bar on their being related to the accused and some definitely were.[48]

As in contemporary American jurisprudence, grand jury proceedings were conducted in secret.

If Professor Kelly is correct that the Crown's ministers should have understood that Parliament intended the term "maliciously" in the Act of Treasons as an element of the offense and an affirmative limitation on the statute's reach,

---

[47] Bellamy, *Tudor Law of Treason*, p. 126.
[48] Ibid., pp. 127–8.

then we must question whether the ministers followed through to insure that malice was proved at trial. While the indictment was technically correct in that it pleaded "maliciously" throughout, it is questionable whether the allegations could support a good-faith inference of malice. In any event, as we have seen, from More's perspective, the defense strategy depended greatly on the interpretation of "maliciously."

Arraignment/Plea

More entered his not guilty plea after listening to the indictment in Latin.

According to Professor Derrett's 1964 analysis of the trial, More not only successfully challenged most of the allegations and had them dismissed, but he also attempted to challenge the final charge (his statement to Rich) in a post-verdict motion in arrest of judgment.[49] Because Roper does not set out the first-named charges (as outlined in the Guildhall Report and detailed in the indictment itself), we cannot be sure of the timing, nature, or scope of any such demand for dismissal on More's part. However, the fact that Roper states that More's conviction was entirely based on the testimony of Richard Rich would support the inference that More successfully interposed such a motion to dismiss all allegations save those pertaining to Rich's interrogation in the Tower. This motion, like a modern day demurrer in civil practice, or a motion to dismiss in criminal matters, would argue that the charges should be dismissed because, even if the alleged facts were true, they did not amount to a crime.[50]

According to Geoffrey de C. Parmiter's study, published in 1957, after the indictment was read to the prisoner, he had the right to make pleas in abatement. These were technical challenges to the form of the indictment, based on the rigorous pleading requirements, and there was a limited right to assistance of counsel for the making of such motions. Demurrers were permitted, says Parmiter; however, they were risky because the prisoner was required to admit the facts he contended were insufficient to constitute a crime. Accordingly, if he lost, he had effectively entered a guilty plea.[51] In modern Anglo-American practice, the motion is made conditionally with no such precipitous downside risk.

In Roper's rendition (as construed above), More argued that the alleged facts – remaining silent, writing to Fisher – were not in themselves malicious, but were made so only by attaching the conclusory allegation of malice. Professor

---

[49] The question of arrest of judgment is discussed below, p. 89.
[50] For instance, Rule 34 of the Federal Rules of Criminal Procedure provides that "upon the defendant's motion or on its own, the court must arrest judgment if: 1) the indictment or information does not charge an offense; or 2) the court does not have jurisdiction of the charged offense." In the civil context, for example, the California Code of Civil Procedure, section 430.10 provides that a civil defendant may object by demurrer to a pleading on the ground that it "does not state facts sufficient to constitute a cause of action." (Cal. Code Civ. Proc., §430.10, subd. (e).) Rule 12 of the Federal Rules of Civil Procedure provides that a party may move to dismiss on the ground of a "failure to state a claim upon which relief can be granted." (Fed. R. Civ. Proc. 12(b)(6).)
[51] Parmiter, "Indictment of St Thomas More," p. 164.

Baker sides with Professor Derrett in concluding that the judges ruled that failure to answer a question was not treasonous and removed those parts of the indictment. From that conclusion, Professor Baker cites More's case as an instance of "judicial independence."[52] Acceptance of the Baker/Derrett view, drawn from the Roper account, leads to the conclusion that More's trial and conviction hinged entirely on the allegations concerning the conversation with Rich. In chapter 1 of this book, however, Professor Kelly assesses the persuasiveness of the Baker/Derrett view in light of the historical record and concludes it "highly unlikely that any part of the indictment was left unprosecuted."[53]

Role of Petty Jury

The twelve men presumably "of the Tower" who sat as jurors in More's trial were the finders of the facts, including guilt or innocence. They were freeholders from the London neighborhood near the Tower. With the aim of enlisting jurors who were less susceptible to bribes, "petty jurors were supposed to men of substance who lived in the hundred where the crime was committed."[54] Selection of the members of the "petty" – as opposed to the "grand" – jury was very much in the hands of the Crown since, although in theory they were appointed by local electors, in practice the task was given to the sheriff.[55] Even today, in most American jurisdictions, when necessary, local sheriffs will round up prospective jurors from restaurants, bars and coffeehouses near the courthouse.

Parties were generally permitted to exercise as many as 35 peremptory challenges – motions to dismiss prospective jurors without a showing of good cause. "The accused person was not, however, supplied with the panel of the jurors, so that the value of his right of challenge was considerably diminished."[56] Moreover, Professor Baker questions whether such challenges were available in treason trials. His inference is corroborated by the absence of indication in the historical records that More sought to strike any of the jurors, despite the strong likelihood that the venire included persons predisposed to find against him. Among the twelve jurors seated was John Parnell, who seems to have been "the fast-talking Lutheran and vintner to the Boleyns who had tried to have [More] impeached."[57]

Although deliberations occurred in secret, "juries were easily corrupted."[58] Additionally, after the case was submitted, if the jury was inclined to delay, the jurors were not allowed to separate but would be locked up with no light or fuel. Unanimity was the only clear rule guiding the jury's decision-making.

[52] Baker, *Oxford History*, p. 417.
[53] Kelly, chapter 1, p. 10.
[54] Bellamy, *Tudor Law of Treason*, p. 166.
[55] Ibid.
[56] Parmiter, "Indictment of St Thomas More," p. 164 n. 68.
[57] Guy, *A Daughter's Love*, p. 259; but see R. W. Chambers' notes to *Harpsfield's Life of More*, 343–4, 349–50, indicating that the identity of this Parnell as the one who had accused More of bribery is not definite.
[58] Parmiter, "Indictment of St Thomas More," p. 163

The accused did not enjoy a presumption of innocence. Jurors would have been likely to be swayed by the fact that the accused had been charged. Jurors, however, had the power to render a verdict on a lesser crime.[59]

On June 25, 1535, the day before More's court was appointed, King Henry had issued a "circular letter" or proclamation, decrying the abuses of the "Bishop of Rome," asserting the king's title as "Supreme Head in earth immediately under God of the Church of England," and enjoining the bishops, clergy, and justices of the peace to take all steps necessary to promote and ensure the supremacy. Within that proclamation, the king ordered that public declarations be made of "the treasons traitorously committed against us and our laws by the late bishop of Rochester and Sir Thomas More, knight, who thereby and by divers secret practices of their malicious minds against us intended to" spread sedition. Lest there be any question as to the king's seriousness of purpose, the members of the public were to understand that, upon pain of their allegiance and at their uttermost peril, they must follow the dictates of the proclamation "most effectually, earnestly, and entirely," or they would incur the king's "high indignation and displeasure."[60] Today, it is common to conduct voir dire (the questioning of prospective jurors by the court and/or counsel) to ferret out whether jurors have heard media reports that might prejudice them, and even to order sequestration during trial, especially in notorious matters. Henry, however, used his office to publicly declare More a traitor and order his subjects – on pain of incurring his wrath – to consider him as one just before the trial began.

Obviously, no amount of procedural protections can insure a fair trial if the jury is corrupt or otherwise unfairly influenced by fear or hope of reward. In More's case, not only is there scant historical evidence that he could move to strike jurors with potential biases, but the Crown made overt efforts to convince the jury pool of More's guilt before the trial began.

In More's time, as now, exercising the impartiality expected of a juror required some degree of courage – and this was and is particularly so in notorious trials and where the stakes are especially high. It is well accepted among practitioners that jurors will tend to approach their tasks differently in, for instance, a garden-variety drug possession trial and a capital murder trial. Cases involving celebrities and politicians often come with inherent extra-judicial influences, as jurors cannot help but think of how the parties or public might potentially reward or punish them for their verdict. Moreover, as Professor Kelly indicates, given the way the judges chose to interpret the statute (by effectively reading malice out of it), More's legal strategy may have been doomed from the outset. Furthermore, given the Crown's overt influence and the undeniable fact that the jurors would have known they had much to lose or gain depending on their verdict, it is hard to see it as other than a foregone conclusion.

---

[59] Ibid., p. 166.
[60] Doc. 14. See Schulte Herbrüggen, "The Process Against Sir Thomas More," p. 127.

Role of Judges

As was typically the case with noblemen or high officials such as More, the chancellor or some other senior peer was appointed to act as lord high steward and preside over the trial. In More's trial it was the chancellor himself, Thomas Audley, who pronounced judgment.[61] Then, as now, the judges' role was to rule on the law.

> Sometimes four or five were named in the commission as being members of the quorum, that is to say of an inner group whose presence was essential when sessions were held. The reason for this device was to ensure there should be available in court proper legal expertise and sufficient knowledge about the background of the case, the members of the quorum often being judges of the two benches, notable royal lawyers, even prominent ministers. Thus for the trial of Sir Thomas More there were named in addition to six judges the Lord Chancellor (Sir Thomas Audley) and Thomas Cromwell.[62]

According to Professor Bellamy, it would have been expected that Cromwell, who presumably had drafted the indictment, would have also taken it upon himself to demonstrate how guilt might most easily be demonstrated in court. Indeed, he frequently advised the attorney-general in similar matters.[63] But though he is named in the commission, there is no sign that he actually sat among the judges.

By one school of thought, the Act of Treasons left the judges precious little room for legal interpretation. Commenting on the Act of Treasons, Professor Bellamy concludes there can be "little doubt" as to its fairness,

> as long as by fairness we mean its observing of legislative and legal precedents and we do not set out to judge the severity of the sixteenth century by the relative tolerance of the twentieth. Basically, the statute was intended to outflank the judges' power of declaration in cases of suspected treason where the overt act was spoken words only, and this it did successfully.[64]

Consistent with trying to avoid anachronistic judgments, we must remember that the separation-of-powers doctrine had not yet been conceived, much less the doctrine of judicial review or anything like modern conflict-of-interests doctrines.

Nevertheless, even accepting a sixteenth-century perspective, it can be argued that all the players must have seen that the king was arrogating to himself powers traditionally vested in the Parliament, the courts and the clergy. Indeed, through an overtly anti-Catholic legislative project, Henry had effectively severed the Church in England from Rome's jurisdiction: the submission of the

---

[61] Baker, *Oxford History*, pp. 265–6.
[62] Bellamy, *Tudor Law of Treason*, p. 122.
[63] Ibid., p. 145.
[64] Ibid., p. 35.

clergy of 1532; the Act of Submission of the Clergy and Restraint of Appeals, 1534; the Act of Ecclesiastical Appointments, 1534; and the Act Concerning Papal Dispensations and Peter's Pence, 1534. Thus, the question of whether the judges acted justly should be evaluated in the overarching context of the king's incremental path toward despotic rule. Opposing this tide would require extraordinary courage. More himself had provided a recent historic example of such courageous action when, as speaker of the House of Commons, he faced down Cardinal Wolsey when the cleric broke the traditional liberty of the House in an effort to "browbeat the Commons into accepting his tax bill" in 1523.[65]

In the contemporary political context, the historical question of whether the judges in fact dismissed most of the indictment on the ground that More's silence and refusal to affirm the king's supremacy could not support a finding of treason takes on added significance. If they did, it would have been an especially honorable, courageous exercise of judicial independence. Of course, doing so would not have dictated a defense verdict, for it left the jury to make the factual findings as to what More said to Rich and whether it supported an inference of malice. On the other hand, the judges' conduct would look far different under Professor Kelly's interpretation, in which they left the indictment intact and refused to give effect to the meaning of malice intended by Parliament.

Trial Rights and Practice

Detailed knowledge of sixteenth-century trial practice is limited by the absence of contemporaneous transcripts of proceedings. In a trial of the magnitude of More's, the clerk of the King's Bench was given the task of preserving the official records in the *Baga de Secretis*.[66] Unfortunately, his record was sparse indeed and provides no insights into the conduct of the trial.[67] (The unofficial report of Sir John Spelman,[68] one of the commissioners, was contained in a private notebook of memoirs.) The "law required a public hearing, with a clear accusation, evidence given on oath, an opportunity to challenge the evidence and present a defence, and a sworn jury of twelve each satisfied in his conscience that the charge was true."[69] "With possible exception of the process of indictment, and the withdrawal from the courtroom of the petty jury in order to consider its verdict, all parts of a criminal trial under the English common law were held in public."[70] As Professor Bellamy explains, the government seems to have approved of large crowds of spectators for propaganda purposes.[71]

In treason trials, the Crown was afforded the right to make an opening statement. "The main part of a treason trial, the offering of evidence, frequently

---

[65] Gerard B. Wegemer, *Thomas More on Statesmanship* (Washington, DC, 1996), p. 188.
[66] Baker, *Oxford History*, p. 417.
[67] Doc. 15.
[68] Doc. 18.
[69] Baker, *Oxford History*, p. 68.
[70] Bellamy, *Tudor Law of Treason*, p. 133.
[71] Ibid., p. 134.

began with a speech by the king's counsel, often in the person of the king's serjeant." The accused did not necessarily enjoy a similar opportunity, although it was sometimes afforded him.[72] The accused enjoyed no right to counsel in criminal trials – in contrast to the practice on the Continent and in ecclesiastical courts. The accused had no right to confront adverse witnesses. Nor did the accused have the right to offer witnesses or present evidence.[73]

In chapter 2 above, Professor Helmholz examines whether there was a requirement of at least two witnesses to support a conviction. He concludes that the general rule was recognized under natural law, but it may not have been applied in treason trials – and even if it was, it was subject to a myriad of exceptions such that it would have been of little practical use to More.[74] According to Professor Bellamy, there was no such requirement:

> Although it may have helped the king's case to have several witnesses attesting to the guilt of the accused, he had by no means lost if he had only one, or none at all for that matter. There was nothing at that time in any treason law which demanded two witnesses.[75]

On Derrett's reading of More's trial, and in the opinion of others who consider only the Roper account, More was convicted on the testimony of one witness, Richard Rich, the solicitor-general. English law was changed during Edward VI's reign to adopt the two-witness rule, likely in reaction against Henry's treason laws.[76] As pointed out above, the United States Constitution specifies that a treason conviction requires two witnesses as to the same overt act.

At the time of More's trial, there were practically no rules of evidence. Hearsay was freely admitted and originals of documents not required.[77] Evidence usually consisted of examinations and confessions. "Amongst the weapons which the

---

[72] Bellamy, *Tudor Law of Treason*, pp. 147–8; cf. Parmiter, "Indictment of St Thomas More," pp. 164–5.
[73] "Throughout the seventeenth century the defendant had no right to subpoena unwilling witnesses. Indeed, in the sixteenth century there were prominent occasions on which trial courts refused to hear defense witnesses who were present in court and willing to testify. When defense witnesses were received, they were forbidden to testify upon oath, although accusing witnesses were routinely sworn. The defendant always spoke unsworn – he was forbidden the right to testify upon oath until 1898." John H. Langbein, "The Historical Origins of the Privilege Against Self-Incrimination at Common Law," *Michigan Law Review* 92 (1994), 1047–85 at p. 1955, footnotes omitted. As Professor Langbein points out, "The Treason Act of 1696 granted compulsory process and allowed defense witnesses to be sworn, but only for treason cases" (p. 1956). Through the Treason Act of 1696, Parliament granted the right to counsel to those charged with treason. However, as is explained by Professor Randolf H. Jonakait, "The Origins of the Confrontation Clause: An Alternative History." *Rutgers Law Journal* 27 (1995), 77–168, it was only in 1730 that defense counsel were "increasingly allowed to question witnesses," a force that served to transform the trial system toward the adversarial model (pp. 87–8).
[74] Helmholz, chapter 2, pp. 60–63. Baker, *Oxford History*, p. 518, holds that conviction on treason charges on the basis of a single witness was allowed, but as evidence he cites the dubious cases of Fisher and More.
[75] Bellamy, *Tudor Law of Treason*, p. 153.
[76] Ibid., p. 154.
[77] Parmiter, "Indictment of St Thomas More," pp. 164–5.

prosecution used in order to prove its case, pride of place went to the introduction of examinations and confessions."[78] "In the same category ... were incriminating documents like letters and memoranda which had been discovered in the possessions of the accused or his confederates."[79] Far from there being a right against self-incrimination, "each statement by counsel alleging confession, examination, documents, witnesses' evidence, or point of law, tended to take an interrogative form and the accused was expected at natural junctures to deny or explain away the allegations."[80]

Geoffrey Parmiter explains a key structural difference from modern trial practice: In More's time,

> the central and vital feature of every trial was the examination of the accused person in a manner which is, to-day, scrupulously avoided; indeed, the whole trial was virtually a long debate between the prisoner and prosecuting counsel, in which they questioned each other and grappled with each other's arguments.[81]

Not surprisingly, the debate tended to be one-sided.

> Even when the trial had got under way the accused was not allowed time or opportunity to view the indictment so as to marshal his arguments or make sure he had tried to answer every point laid against him. He must think on his feet and woe betide him if his memory was not good. Realization of this accounts in part for the numerous lamentations made by prisoners at the start of their trial about the way their wits were dulled and their memory impaired through the arduous imprisonment they had suffered. They often tried to make the best of circumstances by asking for *aides memoires*, the chance to take notes, or simply to have reasonable comfort in the courtroom. Thus, Sir Thomas More obtained permission to sit down in a chair.[82]

Nevertheless, we can assume that More's own training and natural gifts would have evened the odds. While modern procedural and evidentiary requirements would have strengthened More's defense immeasurably, the debate-like quality of trials would have tended to play to More's rhetorical strengths. He was likely the most able lawyer of his day and he had about a year and the greatest possible incentive to prepare, albeit without a law library.

It is possible that Solicitor-General Rich functioned as a prosecutor at the trial, even though he was a witness. This dual role would not have been surprising. Needless to say, the contemporary ethical proscription against being witness while acting as an attorney had not been formed. Today, for instance, the American Bar Association's Model Rules of Professional Conduct counsel that a lawyer "shall not act as advocate at a trial in which the lawyer is likely to

---

[78] Bellamy, *Tudor Law of Treason*, p. 148.
[79] Ibid., p. 149.
[80] Ibid.
[81] Parmiter, "Indictment of St Thomas More," p. 165.
[82] Bellamy, *Tudor Law of Treason*, p. 144. See Doc. 17, §2a.

be a necessary witness unless: (1) the testimony relates to an uncontested issue; (2) the testimony relates to the nature and value of legal services rendered in the case; or (3) disqualification of the lawyer would work substantial hardship on the client."

In More's day, the justices decided when the evidentiary phase of the trial was complete and the prisoner had been given sufficient time to respond. At that point, one of the justices would sum up the case for the jury's benefit.[83] Today, most American jurisdictions eliminate or strictly limit the court's role in that regard, leaving summing up to counsel. While trial judges are typically afforded the discretion to ask questions of witness, such examinations must not tend to favor either side. For instance, the California Supreme Court explains:

> A trial court has both the discretion and the duty to ask questions of witnesses, provided this is done in an effort to elicit material facts or to clarify confusing or unclear testimony. The court may not, however, assume the role of either the prosecution or of the defense. The court's questioning must be "temperate, nonargumentative, and scrupulously fair"

and it must not convey to the jury the court's opinion of the witness's credibility.[84]

Upon the completion of the trial's evidentiary phase, modern trial courts will instruct the jury impartially on the applicable laws. As part of those instructions, a jury will typically be told not to take any cue from the judge:

> Do not take anything I said or did during the trial as an indication of what I think about the evidence, the witnesses, or what your verdict should be. Now, I will comment on the evidence only to help you decide the issues in this case. However, it is not my role to tell you what your verdict should be. You are the sole judges of the evidence and believability of witnesses. It is up to you and you alone to decide the issues in this case. You may disregard any or all of my comments about the evidence or give them whatever weight you believe is appropriate.[85]

There is no indication that any such formal instructions were supposed to be given to More's jury. Indeed, if the 1536 account of the trial by Reginald Pole is credited, the justices voiced their agreement with the attorney-general's rebuttal of More's argument that silence could not constitute a criminal violation by crying out "Malice, malice!"[86]

---

[83] Bellamy, *Tudor Law of Treason*, p. 164.
[84] *People v. Cook*, California Reports, 4th series, 39 (2006), 566, 597; *West's Pacific Reporter*, 3rd series, 139 (Cal. 2006), 492, 515–16, internal citations omitted.
[85] *Judicial Council of California Criminal Jury Instructions* (CALCRIM; Eagan MN 2006–7), no. 3530.
[86] Doc. 19, §6.

Post-Trial Rights and Practice

The sufficiency of the evidence to convict was left to the judgment of the petty jury.

> The delivery of judgment on a convicted prisoner, and any speech by the latter in the arrest of this delivery, might follow immediately on the return of a verdict by the jury. On the other hand, when the jury had pronounced the accused guilty, the court might then be adjourned for several days or even weeks if the crown wanted it so.[87]

It does not appear that a prisoner could make a pre-sentence argument that there was insufficient to support the verdict, in the manner of a modern-day motion for judgment notwithstanding the verdict (known by the initialism JNOV, for *judicium non obstante veredicto*). Today, a defendant can typically move the trial court to throw out the jury's verdict upon a finding of insufficient evidence to support the conviction.

Nevertheless, Bellamy and Parmiter agree that the prisoner could make a post-verdict motion in arrest of judgment or to quash the indictment.[88] "Of the few prisoners who sought to arrest judgment by showing the indictment was insufficient the most famous by far was Sir Thomas More."[89] More argued (1) the indictment was invalid because the statute on which it was founded was invalid as contrary to God's laws and those of the Universal Church – and England, as a small part of the Church, could not properly make a law which was odds with the "general law ecclesiastical"; and (2) the Act of Supremacy was contrary to traditional liberties of the Church as recognized by the Magna Carta and the coronation oath. According to Roper, Lord Chancellor Audley

> there openly asked advice of the lord FitzJames, then lord chief justice of the King's Bench, and joined in commission with him, whether this indictment were sufficient or not. Who, like a wise man, answered, "My lords all, by St Julian" – that was ever his oath – "I must needs confess that if the act of Parliament be not unlawful, then is not the indictment, in my conscience, insufficient."[90]

Because there was no right to appeal, and the judges almost certainly lacked the power to rule the jury's finding invalid because the evidence presented could not support a conviction, the jury's verdict was effectively unreviewable. So, for instance, in the absence of the judges' granting a special defense motion requiring a second witness or finding insufficient evidence of malice to over-

---

[87] Bellamy, *Tudor Law of Treason*, p. 173.
[88] Bellamy, *Tudor Law of Treason*, p. 175; Parmiter, "Indictment of St Thomas More," p. 166. For Kelly's argument that such motions in arrest of judgment are not documented in criminal trials at this time, see chapter 1 above, pp. 44–46.
[89] Bellamy, *Tudor Law of Treason*, p. 175.
[90] Doc. 20, §18.

come the presumption of acquiescence arising out of More's silence, the question of whether More had acted with malice would have been an unreviewable question of fact.

More's Initial Refusal of the Oath of Succession and His Final Argument at Trial

More was jailed for his refusal to take the oath concerning succession; he was convicted of misprision of treason for this offense by an act of attainder. He was then convicted of treason for refusing to affirm the king's supremacy as Head of the Church, even though affirmation was not specifically required in the Act of Treasons passed in the same Parliament that passed the act of attainder against him (November–December 1534). In this final section, we seek to place More's trial strategy and final argument in the larger context of the beliefs that More refused to compromise. The essence of his attempt to avoid falling under the Treasons act, and the primary focus of his trial defense, was to rely on his silence or, more accurately, his refusal to explain why he would not affirm the supremacy. Simply put, he knew that his reasons would offend the Crown, and so he remained silent. The same was true when he refused the oath of succession. As More wrote to his daughter Margaret while in the Tower before the Acts of Supremacy and Treasons had been enacted, he was at pains to show the Council that he was not being stubborn in refusing to explain why he would not swear the oath, and even though he would rather fall under the statute than offend the king by telling his reasons, he would agree to tell them if he could do so with impunity, and he would be willing to change his mind if his objections could be satisfactorily answered.[91]

Once found guilty, however, for the purpose of "exonerating of his conscience,"[92] More finally publicized his reason. In making Henry the Supreme Head of the English Church, Parliament had divorced itself from the Universal Church:

> Your statute was wrongly made, because you deliberately swore your oaths against the Church, which alone is whole and undivided through the whole Christian world. And you alone have no power to enact anything, without the consent of all other Christians, which is contrary to the unity and concord of the Christian religion.[93]

In the same manner, More disputed the lord chancellor's assertion that he should follow the example of the many high-ranking English bishops and scholars who had endorsed the supremacy: "therefore am I not bound, my

---

[91] *Last Letters*, no. 15 (*Correspondence*, no. 210), 1534, p. 100; it reads in part, "I rather would endure all the pain and peril of the statute than by the declaring of the causes give any occasion of exasperation unto my most dread sovereign."
[92] Guildhall Report, Doc. 17, §8.
[93] Ibid., §12.

lord, to conform my conscience to the counsel of one realm against the general counsel of Christendom."[94] It followed that, for More, swearing allegiance to Henry entailed the denial of the greater allegiance owed to the true Church – a denial that would exclude him from its jurisdiction and protection.

More had developed the theme of the true Church's essential unicity, informed by consensus throughout Christendom – as contrasted with the sectarianism and divisiveness he found inherent in the Reformation project – as early as 1528 when he composed his *Dialogue Concerning Heresies*.[95] There, he had argued that Christ and the apostles intended the Church to be identifiable in the world and active in guiding and correcting God's people. Through apostolic succession, the primitive Church developed over years under the Holy Spirit's direction so that it was visible in his time as consisting of "all the Christian people whom we call the Church, under obedience of the pope."[96] Indeed, in the *Dialogue* More cited St Paul's First Letter to the Corinthians for the proposition that, for the Universal Church, the essential mark was agreement itself, rather than the object of agreement:

> [Paul] maketh no mention of agreement upon the best and upon the truth, but only [biddeth them] to avoid all discord and division, and by common consent exhorteth them to agree all in one, meaning thereby, as me thinketh, that if the Church of Christ, intending well, do all agree upon any one thing concerning God's honor or man's soul, it cannot be but that thing must needs be true. For God's Holy Spirit, that animateth His Church and giveth it life, will never suffer it all [to] give consent and agree together upon any damnable error.[97]

Returning to More's refusal of the oath of succession, we see remarkable consistency. As explained above, the Act of Succession imposed an oath requirement without specifying its terms – that was done later in the Act Regarding the Oath of Succession, enacted in the same session as the Act of Supremacy. Since we do not know the exact terms of the oath that was ministered to him, we do not know with precision the reason why More was prepared to go to jail, lose his property, and even risk his life. We can be sure, however, that the oath commanded allegiance to more than the king's succession through Anne Boleyn. We can also be fairly sure that More must have understood the oath as advocating a break with Rome, implicitly or explicitly. It seems probable that the Act Regarding the Oath of Succession confirmed and set forth the oath that had been used generally and presented originally to More.[98] That oath required each person to swear that Anne and her progeny would be rightful rulers: "You shall observe, keep, maintain, and defend the said Act of Succession, and all the whole effects and contents thereof, *and all other acts and statutes made in confirmation or for execution of the same or of anything therein contained*" (emphasis

---

[94] Roper, **Doc. 20**, §17.
[95] More, *A Dialogue Concerning Heresies*, CW, vol. 6
[96] More, *Dialogue* 2.4, 1:204
[97] Ibid., 2.9, 1:224.
[98] See n. 14 above.

added). When More first refused the oath, a number of anti-Catholic statutes had already been passed, which effectively severed the Church in England from Rome's jurisdiction. Thus, the oath administered to More likely embraced the disestablishment of the English Church.

From More's last letters and Roper's biography, there is little doubt that More was willing to sign off on the king's pronouncement of succession. In his letter to Margaret of April 17, 1534, More explained that after comparing the Act of Succession with the text of the oath, he told the king's commissioners that "though I would not deny to swear to the succession, yet unto the oath that there was offered me I could not swear without the jeoparding of my soul to perpetual damnation."[99] Roper reports that his father-in-law, after reading the oath for the first time, objected that oath presented went beyond the terms of the Act of Succession.[100] Thus, given that the oath must have enlarged upon the Act to the extent More believed affirmance would jeopardize his soul, we can safely assume the oath approved of the English Crown's arrogation of unprecedented ecclesial authority.[101] Interestingly, the timing of More's resignation supports this understanding: it came on the heels of the submission of the clergy.[102]

When we compare More's exoneration of conscience at trial with his statements to Thomas Cromwell before his arrest and those to Margaret in the Tower, it becomes clear that More's legal strategy of silence/refusal was a means of preserving his integrity before God.[103] Writing to Cromwell shortly before his arrest, More used the phrase "corps of Chistendom" to refer to the essential unity of the Church under the pope.[104] Later, as he recounted to Margaret, when interrogated by Cromwell after his arrest, More sought to explain why acceptance of the pope and acceptance of King Henry as Head of the Church were

---

[99] *Last Letters*, no. 6 (*Correspondence*, no. 200), c. April 17, 1534.

[100] Roper, *Lyfe*, ed. Hitchcock, pp. 77–8. Note that Roper consistently calls the Act of Succession the Act of Supremacy or the Act of Supremacy and Matrimony.

[101] This position is substantially the same as that offered by Peter Ackroyd, in his biography, *The Life of Thomas More* (London, 1998), pp. 364, 378–9. Professor Richard Rex argues persuasively that in terms of the Henrician revolution, royal supremacy was not just a short step away from elimination of papal jurisdiction, but contained in it. Richard Rex, *Henry VIII and the English Reformation*, 2nd edn (London, 2006), pp. 149–59.

[102] One could certainly argue that even if the oath hewed very closely to the Act of Succession, More would have still objected. The act refers to Anne Boleyn as Henry's "lawful" wife. One thing is succession – for More, an arrangement entirely within the competence of the Crown and Parliament – and another thing is the divorce/remarriage, which was a matter belonging to ecclesiastical authority. To swear that Anne was the lawful wife of the king could certainly be seen as importing all the legislation that had declared the Church in England beyond Rome's jurisdiction. Thus, at a minimum, in any oath of succession, More could well have seen himself as being asked to sign off on the separation of the English Church from what More understood as the Universal Church.

[103] The editors of More's translation of Pico de Mirandola's *Life of Pico* identify over eighty words that are either the first recorded usage of them, or antedate the first recorded usage, according to the *OED*, including "integrity." See More, *English Poems, Life of Pico, Last Things*, ed. Anthony S. G. Edwards, Katherine Rodgers, and Clarence H. Miller, in *CW*, vol. 1.

[104] *Last Letters*, no. 5 (*Correspondence*, no. 199), March 5, 1534, p. 54. More explains: "Therefore sith all Christendom is one corps, I cannot perceive how any member thereof may without the common assent of the body depart from the common head."

fundamentally different matters, even if the law were to require allegiance to the latter instead of the former: it was one thing where the person is bound by the "law of one realm," but quite another "where there is a law of the whole corps of Christendom to the contrary in matter touching belief."[105] While a violation of a mere "local" law commanding allegiance could mean death by beheading, violation of a universal law to the contrary was punishable eternally in hell.[106] More made the same point in his famous paradox: "I thanked God that my case was such in this matter through the clearness of mine own conscience that though I might have pain I could not have harm, for a man may in such case lose his head and have no harm."[107]

Of course, More failed in convincing the judges and jury with his defense, just as he failed in convincing King Henry and Cromwell of his good faith. To the Crown, opposition to the supremacy was malicious *per se*, whatever the Act of Treasons said – likely making his defense doomed from the start. Nevertheless, because the danger posed to liberty of conscience by the state's creeping despotism is not a relic of More's time, crucial questions remain for contemporary historians and lawyers. What would have happened if More's judges had recognized Parliament's inclusion of malice as a substantive limitation on the crime of treason – and the judges and jury had had the courage to enforce the legislative will?

---

[105] *Last Letters*, no. 22 (*Correspondence*, no. 216), June 3, 1535, p. 120, **Doc. 6**, §10.
[106] *Last Letters*, no. 22.
[107] Ibid., §4.

4

Thomas More's Three Prison Letters Reporting on His Interrogations

Elizabeth McCutcheon

Overview

Among the thirteen extant letters that More wrote between mid-April 1534 and July 5, 1535 are three important letters about an interrogation at Lambeth in 1534 and two later interrogations at the Tower of London in the spring of 1535 that he sent to his daughter, Margaret Roper:[1]

1. Letter of *c.* April 17, 1534 (no. 200 [6]).
2. Letter of May 2 or 3, 1535 (no. 214 [20]) (**Doc. 4**).
3. Letter of June 3, 1535 (no. 216 [22]) (**Doc. 6**).

They are, in some sense, personal letters, and it was important for both More's sake and his daughter's that they be perceived so. On June 14, 1535, 11 days after he wrote the third letter, More was asked about letters he had written "touching" "the Acts of Succession, of Supreme Head, or the act wherein speaking certain words of the king is made treason."[2] After discussing his letters to and from John Fisher, More added that he had sent letters to Margaret Roper by way of George Gold, "both after his first examination and after his last" (presumably April 30 and June 3, 1535) out of worry that his daughter, "being (as he thought) with child … might take harm" when she heard that the Council had interrogated him.[3] He had told "her the answers he had given" and stressed his obedience. He also pointed out that "she had written to him before divers

---

[1] There is no simple way to refer to More's letters, which are numbered differently in different editions. The most complete edition is *The Correspondence of Sir Thomas More*, ed. Rogers, (*Correspondence*). The letters associated with More's arrest and imprisonment have been edited as *The Last Letters of Thomas More* by Alvaro de Silva (*Last Letters*). I will note the number assigned by Rogers followed by de Silva's. In addition, the second and third of these three letters, that of May 2 or 3, 1535, no. 214 [20], and that of June 3, 1535, no. 216 [22], are in the Documents section below, and will be referred to as **Doc. 4** and **Doc. 6**, respectively. See my Appendix, pp. 109–10, for more on these and other interrogations.
[2] *LP* 8, no. 867 iii, item 2 as cited in "Tower Interrogations of Fisher and More, June 14, 1535," Doc. 11.
[3] Ibid.

letters, to exhort him and advertise him to accommodate himself to the King's pleasure."[4] This did not allay the Council's suspicions, then or later. Stapleton writes that, following More's death, Margaret

> was brought before the King's Council, and charged with keeping her father's head as a sacred relic, and retaining possession of his books and writings. She answered that she had saved her father's head from being devoured by the fishes, with the intention of burying it: that she had hardly any books and papers but what had been already published, except a very few *personal letters*, which she humbly begged to be allowed to keep for her own consolation.[5]

But More could hardly have intended these letters for Margaret alone, regardless of the explanation he gave to his servant, John Wood, who testified on June 11, 1535 that "on the morning after the Council came to the Tower his master (More) told him that his daughter, Roper's wife, wished to know what had taken place, and he wrote her three letters."[6] This becomes quite evident when we compare the first letter (200 [6]) with number 210 [16], another extraordinary and deeply felt letter that More sent to Margaret in the latter part of 1534. Number 210 [16] echoes some of the material about his first interrogation and adds details missing from his earlier letter. But it is more clearly personal, albeit even here the personal is, in some sense, political, especially since Margaret was his closest confidante, he had already made her his personal representative (no. 204 [10]),[7] and she was doing her best to help both her father and John Fisher. Answering a poignant letter (no. 209 [15]) from Margaret, who is alarmed because More has been shut up again "in close prison,"[8] he reminds her of their earlier conversation in a garden at the Tower, anticipates further searches, and warns her that a law might be (and soon after was) made against him. He also pointedly repeats Cromwell's oath at Lambeth, "that he had liefer [rather] than I should have refused the oath, that his own only son (which is a goodly young gentleman of whom our Lord send him much joy) had had his head stricken off."[9] But now this reminiscence and other matter from the Lambeth interrogation are embedded in words designed to strengthen his daughter, and More writes feelingly about his love for her even as he acknowledges that his stance could well result in his death.

Despite the overlap in content, the focus and tone are different in our three letters, where More obviously has multiple addressees and several purposes

---

[4] *State Papers*, as cited by E. E. Reynolds, *Margaret Roper: Eldest Daughter of Sir Thomas More* (New York, 1960), p. 103, which is slightly more detailed than the paraphrase in *LP* 8, no. 867 iii, item 2, **Doc. 11**.
[5] Thomas Stapleton, *The Life and Illustrious Martyrdom of Sir Thomas More*, tr. Philip E. Hallett, ed. E. E. Reynolds (New York, 1962), p. 193: emphasis mine. See too Elizabeth McCutcheon, "Margaret More Roper: The Learned Woman in Tudor England," in *Women Writers of the Renaissance and Reformation*, ed. Katharina M. Wilson (Athens, GA, 1987), pp. 449–80 at pp. 457–8, and Guy, *A Daughter's Love*, notes on p. 325.
[6] *LP* 8, no. 856 viii, item 52, "Interrogations of Tower Servants," **Doc. 8**.
[7] *Last Letters*, p. 68.
[8] Ibid., p. 97.
[9] Ibid., p. 101. Cf. ibid., p. 61.

in mind.¹⁰ I count at least five possible sorts of readers and one auditor in addition to his eldest daughter: (1) interceptors, spies, or representatives of the king, including Audley and Cromwell, an unwelcome possibility, but one that More had to be aware of and guard against; (2) other members of his immediate and extended family; (3) friends and interested allies of the Mores, including Catholic families in England and on the Continent, to whom a copy of the letters might have been shown (in what Richard Marius calls a "sort of sixteenth-century *samizdat*");¹¹ (4) a wider audience still, should Margaret preserve these letters (as she did) and have them published; (5) More himself; and, finally, (6) God.¹²

Writing these letters let More set down an important record of his interrogations, indirectly broadcasting his point of view and counteracting any misrepresentation or manipulation of it by the king or his representatives. Indeed when Fisher was interrogated on June 12, 1535, he recalled that "George, Master Lieutenant's servant, showed him a letter from More to Mrs Roper, stating that when the Council had proposed to him the matter about which they came, he said he would not dispute the king's title, and Master Secretary gave him good words."¹³

Writing these and other letters from the Tower also let More gain some psychological distance and sense of control over a process in which he was a prisoner, his execution a matter of time if he refused to capitulate.¹⁴ It let him reach out to others in the community, always important to him. The action involved in writing out his letters would have sharpened his already prodigious memory with respect to these interrogations, too, and would have been helpful on July 1, 1535, when he challenged his indictment. The letters are also a moving testament to his love of his family, his fears, and his faith at a time when an understanding of God, His Church, and the English nation was being radically redefined in England. In sum, these are extremely complex and rhetorically sophisticated letters that served any number of purposes, personal, legal, political, psychological, and spiritual. In the discussion that follows, I will be emphasizing More's rhetoric and that of his interrogators, seen in a variety of contexts.¹⁵

---

¹⁰ See Richard Marius, *Thomas More: A Biography* (New York, 1984), p. 503, and Guy, *Thomas More*, pp. 176–7.
¹¹ Marius, *Thomas More*, p. 503.
¹² Guy, *A Daughter's Love*, discusses plans for publication, pp. 266–7 and unnumbered note on p. 325.
¹³ *LP* 8, no. 858, item 5, "Tower Interrogation of Fisher, June 12, 1535," **Doc. 10**, item 5. Fisher could have been referring to our second letter (May 2 or 3, 1535, **Doc. 6**).
¹⁴ Furthermore, writing was an essential part of More's life and sense of identity. The following anecdote is telling. After his books, ink, and paper were taken away from him on June 12, 1535, he had all the windows of his cell shut. Asked why, he answered: "Is it not meet ... to shut up my shop windows when all my ware is gone?" Ro. Ba., *The Lyfe of Syr Thomas More, Sometymes Lord Chancellor of England*, ed. Elsie Vaughan Hitchcock and P. E. Hallett, with additional notes and appendices by A. W. Reed (London, 1950), p. 115, spelling modernized.
¹⁵ The rhetorical analysis that follows supports the conclusion of Henry Ansgar Kelly, in the conclusion of chapter 1 above, that the justices and other commissioners were far more responsible than the jury for the guilty verdict rendered at his trial, while the ultimate blame is Henry VIII's

The last two of the three letters that we are focusing on cover the interrogation of April 30, 1535 and that of June 3, 1535, but not that of May 7 (which may be spurious) or that of June 14.[16] Together with the first letter about his interrogation at Lambeth in the spring of 1534, they document significant moments in the course of his imprisonment. When read in sequence, moreover, they constitute key scenes in the more complete drama that Roper reports in his biography of More. These letters are indispensable in understanding that drama, although Roper quickly passes over them, simply referring to copies in manuscript or in More's *English Works*, first published in 1557 by William Rastell.[17] In the first, of April 1534 (200 [6]), More refuses to swear to the oath that the government had drawn up to enforce the Act of Succession. The second, of May 2 or 3, 1535 (214 [20]), is concerned with an interrogation several months after Henry was declared Supreme Head of the Church in England. And in the third, of June 3, 1535 (216 [22]), which takes place hardly more than a month before his execution on Tower Hill, More refuses to swear an *ad hoc* oath then offered him "on the king's behalf, concerning the king's own person,"[18] declaring that he will not swear "any book oath more" while he lives, and definitively spells out the limits to the king's authority and power, as he understands them, acknowledging that the king can kill his body, but not his soul.[19] This was hardly designed to placate the king, as More surely knew, and threats of the king's indignation (a code word for his death-dealing power) become increasingly overt in the course of these letters, even as More's position becomes increasingly adamantine. This third letter is invaluable for other reasons. Here More makes a hypothetical answer to the question Cromwell put to him about his opinion of the statutes. The question is a loaded one, which presumes More's guilt, while his answer, which the indictment cites, albeit with small but crucial alterations that misrepresent him, anticipates his strategy in a conversation on June 12, with Richard Rich.

Letter of c. April 17, 1534 (no. 200 [6])

Like his subsequent letters, the letter written in April of 1534 presents a detailed account of events from More's point of view, letting him lay out his position and that of the king and his advisors in something like a legal record. In fact our first letter (200 [6]), an account of what turned into an interrogation at

---

and Thomas Cromwell's. Discrepancies between More's descriptions of his interrogations and the official records and subsequent indictment show how More's testimony, which many of these men had heard, was distorted and manipulated so as to establish his guilt.

[16] See my Appendix below, p. 109.

[17] William Roper, *The Life of Sir Thomas More*, ed. Richard S. Sylvester, in *Two Early Tudor Lives: The Life and Death of Cardinal Wolsey*, by George Cavendish, and *The Life of Sir Thomas More*, by William Roper, ed. Richard S. Sylvester and Davis P. Harding (New Haven, CT, 1962), pp. 238 and 244.

[18] The oath would commit him to answer truthfully any question that might be put to him; see Kelly, Chapter 1 above, pp. 26–28.

[19] *Last Letters*, p. 121 (**Doc. 6**).

Lambeth on April 13, 1534, is so detailed and comprehensive, and so masterfully written, that Richard Marius and Peter Ackroyd repeat much of it, sometimes verbatim, in their biographies.[20] In contrast to his usual letters, there is no salutation or mention of an addressee, no closing, and no signature in the copy as we have it, which make it much more like a report or memorandum.[21] There is no date, either. Its first printer (and editor), William Rastell, followed by later editors and biographers, dated it *c.* April 17, when More was taken to the Tower of London.[22] But More could well have written it a few days earlier, while he was temporarily under the custody of the abbot of Westminster, and had it smuggled out after he was taken to the Tower.[23] It is focused throughout on the scene at Lambeth, while certain details also suggest that he was writing very shortly after April 13.[24] In either case, he wrote soon after his interrogation, while his memory was fresh, which is important from a legal perspective.

More begins letter 200 [6] abruptly, like the lawyer he is, by positioning himself and his "interrogators," that is, the king's commissioners who had gathered at the archbishop's palace to administer the oath of succession to various select persons. He notes that he was the first to be called in, though not the first one there, and that, more remarkable still, he was the only layman called. Then he takes us step by step as he reacts to a cat-and-mouse game that has been carefully staged on the king's behalf. First the cause of his summoning is declared and the oath enforcing the Act of Succession is shown to him. Then More asks to see the act itself, which he reads silently from a printed roll, and states his position – he would swear to the succession but not to the oath, lest he jeopardize his soul. In turn he is warned that his refusal to swear (unlike that of everyone else listed on the roll) would cause the king's Highness "to conceive great suspicion of me and great indignation toward me."[25] The stakes laid out, the interrogation is suspended, and More is commanded to go down to the garden at Lambeth Palace, although he keeps to himself "in the old burned chamber" instead.[26]

The longer part of the letter shows how More parleys with Audley, the lord chancellor; Cranmer, the archbishop of Canterbury; William Benson, the abbot of Westminster; and Thomas Cromwell (Master Secretary). Cromwell, who will prove to be the master manipulator, relays the words of the king, who remains

---

[20] Marius, *Thomas More*, pp. 461–63; Ackroyd, The Life of Thomas More, *The Life of Thomas More*, pp. 351–5.
[21] Contrast the next extant letter to his daughter, no. 201 [7], with its loving greeting and closing, a formal signature, and a postscript sending greetings to his family and friends, *Last Letters*, pp. 62–3.
[22] See *The Workes of Sir Thomas More 1557*, facsimile edition, introduction by K. J. Wilson (London, 1978), 2:1428; this notation is included in *Last Letters*, p. 57, and *Correspondence*, p. 501. Cf. Marius, *Thomas More*, p. 461, and Guy, *A Daughter's Love*, p. 233.
[23] According to Guy, *A Daughter's Love*, p. 233, it was one of at least two letters carried out of the Tower by More's servant, John Wood.
[24] See the discussion of Dr Wilson, below. In an email of December 8, 2008, Germain Marc'hadour mentioned that he believes this letter was written before More entered the Tower. This led me to look even more closely at the language in the letter and the stance that More took.
[25] *Last Letters*, p. 58.
[26] Ibid.

behind the scenes. Soon what More began as a report also becomes a dramatic dialogue. Reminiscent of scenes in his *History of King Richard III*, it could easily be staged, as first one and then another of More's adversaries urges him to swear to the oath, to which so many others have already sworn. More even refers to the king's advisors as players in a pageant. Here, as in his subsequent interrogations, he is both an observer and a performer or participant, and simultaneously subject and object, a position that requires tremendous control, which is complicated by the high stakes involved and his sense that he is already on trial. More's attitude or attitudes are a correspondingly complex mix of irony, bravado, sarcasm, innuendo, caution, anxiety, and humility. Consider his brief sketches of Hugh Latimer and Nicholas Wilson, formerly the king's chaplain and confessor. We see Latimer walking in the garden, "very merry ... for he laughed, and took one or twain about the neck so handsomely, that if they had been women, I would have went [supposed] he had been waxen wanton."[27] On the other hand, we see Nicholas Wilson, who "was with two gentlemen brought by me, and gentlemanly sent straight unto the Tower."[28] More's language here obviously contains a covert message; he must suspect that he will soon find himself, like Dr Wilson, "gentlemanly" sent to the Tower of London.[29] In fact, More's apparently artless or improvisational prose is both artful and devious in the extreme.[30] It can also be as important for what it doesn't say, or only hints at, as for what it does – a point to which I will return.

At a tense moment in this first interrogation More offers a compromise: were he to receive a special license from the king, he would be content to declare to him in writing the reasons why he wouldn't swear to the oath, adding that if he found those causes answered to the satisfaction of his conscience, he would swear the principal oath.[31] His offer is immediately rejected by Cromwell, who points out that it would not "serve against the statute."[32] More repeats this exchange in a letter written later in 1534 to his daughter (no. 210 [16]), as evidence of his good faith and of Cromwell's kindness towards him.[33] He was very anxious to demonstrate that he was not obstinate.[34] And he certainly wanted to reassure Margaret. But his offer and Cromwell's response also let More take the measure of the opposition to him and show just how isolated and yet how important he was to the government. Cromwell's quick response also signals a total collapse of the verbal agreement that More thought he had with King Henry VIII regarding his conscience; now the regime is going to employ the full force of the law, as it interpreted it. As Marius notes, "Cromwell's

---

[27] Ibid.
[28] Ibid.
[29] This oblique message suggests that More is writing before he was actually imprisoned in the Tower.
[30] See Louis L. Martz, *Thomas More: The Search for the Inner Man* (New Haven, CT, 1977), pp. 55–64, and Louis L. Martz, "Thomas More: The Tower Works," in *St Thomas More: Action and Contemplation*, ed. Richard S. Sylvester (New Haven, CT, 1972), pp. 57–83.
[31] *Last Letters*, p. 59.
[32] Ibid.
[33] Ibid., p. 101; cf. ibid., p. 59.
[34] Guy, *Thomas More*, p. 179.

government had an almost compulsive desire in these years to preserve the form of the legalities, as if meticulous attention to the processes of the law would cast a spell over the actuality that might ensure the survival of the new order."[35]

Letter of May 2 or 3, 1535 (no. 14 [20]) (Doc. 4)

Shortly after More refused to take the oath of succession on April 13, 1534, he was sent to the Tower in anticipation of being convicted on misprision of treason for violating the Act of Succession. This conviction eventually came in the form of an act of attainder passed by Parliament in its sitting in November–December of 1534.[36] At the same time Parliament passed the Act of Supremacy and the Act of Treasons enforcing it, which was to come into force on February 1, 1535.[37] While any malicious opposition by word or deed to any of the king's titles would be high treason, the main title at issue was the new one of Supreme Head of the Church of England. Three months later, on April 30, 1535, Cromwell, now clearly in the ascendant, and a number of lawyers and judges, including Sir Christopher Hales (the attorney-general), Mr Bedill (clerk of the Privy Council), Richard Rich (the solicitor-general), and Sir John Tregonwell, came to the Tower either to seek More's approval of the new title or to collect evidence of his disapproval.

By May 2 or 3, 1535, soon after this interrogation, More wrote our second letter to Margaret, no. 214 [20]) (Doc. 4), explaining his position. He notes that he had refused, again and again, to answer the direct question that Cromwell put to him: What is his opinion of the new statute? More's major points are essentially four. First, that he had already "discharged my mind of all such matters, and neither will dispute king's titles nor pope's."[38] Secondly, that he was the "king's true faithful subject ... and daily I pray for him and for all his, and for you all that are of his honorable Council, and for all the realm."[39] His third point counters implicit and explicit threats of execution – he is dying already and would welcome death. As he says, "I do nobody harm, I say none harm, I think none harm, but wish everybody good. And if this be not enough to keep a man alive, in good faith, I long not to live."[40] Related to this is his fourth point: "That that shall follow lieth in the hand of God." He beseeches God to "put in the king's Grace's mind that thing that may be to His high pleasure, and [to put] in mine, to mind only the weal of my soul, with little regard of my body."[41]

Unlike his letter of mid-April 1534, which almost bristled with energy as More and the Council probed and counter-probed, this second letter, written

---

[35] Marius, *Thomas More*, p. 482; see too p. 479, on a "fearful and insecure government."
[36] See Karlin and Oakley in chapter 3 above, p. 73.
[37] Docs. 1–2.
[38] *Last Letters*, p. 113 (Doc. 4 §5).
[39] Ibid.
[40] Ibid., p. 114 (Doc. 4, §9).
[41] Ibid., p. 115 (Doc. 4, §11).

over a year later, is more sober, reflective, and inward-looking, though not devoid of wordplay, as when More, who thought that Margaret might be pregnant, alludes to her "heaviness."[42] Rhetorically and psychologically, two elements are exceptionally telling. Most obvious are the many antitheses. In the sentences I just quoted, More oscillates between harm and good, life and death, soul and body. These antitheses, and others, such as conformable versus obstinate, and the king's mercy and pity versus his rigor, spell out the painful situation in which he finds himself. It is equally clear, from what More says and from what he does not say, that he has already made up his mind and is hardly going to be swayed by promises of mercy or talk of his being "abroad in the world again among other men as I have been before."[43] Indeed, as Cromwell makes clear, More's very existence is seen as a threat: "And his Mastership said further that my demeanor in that matter was of a thing that of likelihood made now other men so stiff therein as they be."[44]

Even more striking are the rhetorical elements that so often accompany More's antitheses and make this letter so very muscular and analytical. Here, as elsewhere, More is fond of litotic expressions, which engage and energize the mind, are inherently antithetical, and often ambiguous.[45] He also establishes careful balances between words, phrases, and whole sentences, so that one is increasingly conscious of alternatives either being weighed or having been weighed and judged. His very first words, for example, are "I doubt not," followed shortly by "it is not unlikely."[46] A more complicated sentence follows: "I have thought it necessary to advertise you of the very truth, to the end that you neither conceive more hope than the matter giveth, lest upon other turn it might aggrieve your heaviness, nor more grief and fear than the matter giveth, on the other side."[47] You can almost feel the contrasting parts of the sentence on a balance or scale, as More ponders the delicate movement between hopes raised and then dashed, on the one hand, and grief and fear, on the other hand. Subsequently he manages to imply agreement, albeit ambiguously, with Cromwell's point that "the king's Grace might exact of me such things as are contained in the statutes and upon like pains as he might of other men," by remarking that "I would not say the contrary."[48] Thus he circumvents a direct challenge to the king's authority even as he refuses to answer any question about

---

[42] Ibid., p. 112 (**Doc. 4**, §1).
[43] Ibid., p. 113 (**Doc. 4**, §6).
[44] Ibid., p. 114 (**Doc. 4**, §8).
[45] See Elizabeth McCutcheon, "Denying the Contrary: More's Use of Litotes in the *Utopia*," in *Essential Articles for the Study of Thomas More*, ed. R. S. Sylvester and G. P. Marc'hadour (Hamden CT 1977), pp. 263–74 and 623–5, reprinted from *Moreana* 31-2 (1971), 107–21. For another famous (or infamous) instance that combines a conditional statement with litotes, see Roper on Chief Justice FitzJames's answer to Lord Chancellor Audley during More's trial as to whether or not his indictment was "sufficient": "I must needs confess that, if the act of Parliament be not unlawful, then is not the indictment, in my conscience, insufficient" (**Doc. 19**, §18). See too Roper, *Life*, ed. Sylvester, p. 250. Audley chooses to interpret this very nuanced and ambiguous, even ironic, declaration as a ringing affirmation.
[46] *Last Letters*, p. 112 (**Doc. 4**, §1).
[47] Ibid.
[48] Ibid., p. 114 (**Doc. 4**, §8).

the statutes. Finally, towards the end of the letter, he sums up his situation in another carefully weighed and weighted sentence: "Here am I yet in such case as I was, neither better nor worse."⁴⁹ This last statement is More at his most economical and declarative best.

Letter of June 3, 1535 (no. 216 [22]) (Doc. 6)

The third letter that we are dealing with, written on June 3, 1535 (no. 216 [22]), reports his interrogation of that day to Margaret in a cunning and complex mix of plain and deliberately evasive English. Compared with that of April 30 (and that of May 7, if not a misdating of the April 30 event),⁵⁰ this interrogation was attended by even better-placed men with ties to the king or Anne Boleyn, most of whom were also present at his trial. More names the archbishop of Canterbury, the lord chancellor (Audley), the lord of Suffolk (Charles Brandon), the lord of Wiltshire (Thomas Boleyn, Anne's father), and Cromwell. This letter of June 3 is also the tipping point, as it were, indirectly handing the government material that it subsequently manipulates to formulate a quasi-legal case against him. More correctly sensed his danger; he writes that "Master Secretary said that he liked me this day much worse than he did the last time, for then he said he pitied me much, and now he thought that I meant not well."⁵¹

During this interrogation More talks and talks and talks, all the while skillfully avoiding what he identifies as its "whole purpose": "Either to drive me to say precisely the one way, or else precisely the other" about the Act of Supremacy.⁵² This is exactly what he refuses to do. What ensues is a no-holds-barred exchange between Cromwell and Audley, on the one hand, and More on the other, which includes a nasty *ad hominem* attack on More's conscience.

The interrogation starts calmly enough, as Master Secretary "made rehearsal in what wise he had reported unto the king's Highness, what had been said by his Grace's Council to me, and what had been answered by me to them at mine other being before them last."⁵³ More's response sounds cordial: Cromwell had "rehearsed [them] in good faith very well."⁵⁴ But Cromwell swiftly moves to the main charge: the king was not satisfied with More's answer. He thought that he had "been occasion of much grudge and harm in the realm," and "had an obstinate mind and an evil toward him." Now he wants a "plain and terminate answer whether I thought the statute lawful or not and that I should either acknowledge and confess it lawful that his Highness should be Supreme Head of the Church of England or else to utter plainly my malignity."⁵⁵

More immediately rejects the charge of "malignity," a crucial word that echoes

---

⁴⁹ Ibid., p. 115 (**Doc. 4**, §11).
⁵⁰ See Appendix, p. 109.
⁵¹ *Last Letters*, p. 121 (**Doc. 6**, §16).
⁵² Ibid., p. 118 (**Doc. 6**, §1).
⁵³ Ibid. (§2).
⁵⁴ Ibid.
⁵⁵ Ibid., p. 119 (**Doc. 6**, §3).

the notion of malicious intent and prejudges his motives, insinuating his guilt. He insists that he has no malignity, so nothing to answer for. Nor could he add anything to his earlier answers to the king's first question, either. Instead, he repeats, at some length, his innocence and his trust that the truth would ultimately be known, insisting on the clearness of his conscience: "though I might have pain I could not have harm, for a man may in such case lose his head and have no harm."[56] Undeterred, Audley and Cromwell press on, reminding More that the king might by his laws compel him to "make a plain answer thereto."[57] And now More becomes even more evasive, employing a hypothetical "if" and a denial:

> I answered I would not dispute the king's authority, ... but I said that verily under correction it seemed to me somewhat hard. For if it so were that my conscience gave me against the statutes (wherein how my mind giveth me I make no declaration), then I nothing doing nor nothing saying against the statute, it were a very hard thing to compel me to say either precisely with it against my conscience to the loss of my soul, or precisely against it to the destruction of my body.[58]

Part of More's very subtle statement reappears in the indictment against him. But it reads differently there. It includes a comparison of the statute to a two-edged sword, a simile which does not appear in his letter but which the government will cite as evidence of collusion between More and Fisher.[59] Moreover, what More treated as a hypothetical case is now represented as a virtually open denial of the king's supremacy and interpreted as malicious and thus treasonable.

Here is the relevant passage from the indictment:

> Rather, falsely, treasonously, and maliciously then and there imagining, inventing, practicing, and attempting, and willing and desiring, to deprive the aforesaid lord our king of a dignity, title, and name of his royal condition, and to raise up and generate sedition and malignity in the hearts of true subjects of the lord king against the same lord king, he openly spoke to the aforesaid subjects and councilors of the said lord king then and there the following English words, namely, "The law and statute whereby the king is made Supreme Head, as is aforesaid, be like a sword with two edges; for, if a man say that the same laws be good, then it is dangerous to the soul; and if he say contrary to the said statute, then it is death to the body. Wherefore I will make thereunto none other answer, because I will not be occasion of the shorting of my life."[60]

---

[56] Ibid. (§4).
[57] Ibid., p. 120 (**Doc. 6**, §5).
[58] Ibid. (§6).
[59] See Kelly, chapter 1 above, pp. 31–2. See too Cecilia A. Hatt, "The Two-Edged Sword as Image of Civil Power for Fisher and More," *Moreana* 45, 175 (2008), 67–86.
[60] **Doc. 16**, §9.

Pace John Guy, I do not think that "More's reply was taken down verbatim."[61] Even if More did use the simile of the two-edged sword in his interrogation,[62] the indictment truncates and thus distorts More's nuanced and very precise statement, and has shifted the location of his all-important "if." More's refutation of this charge at his trial is to the point: "to this part of the accusation I respond that I was not speaking straightforwardly but only conditionally; that is, if there should be some statute that was like a two-edged sword, how could any person take care against coming up against one edge or the other?"[63] Only by a misleading paraphrase of More's hypothetical words, which More spells out so precisely (and characteristically) in his letter, could the government claim that he spoke both openly and maliciously, another point that he repeatedly denies. Furthermore, as the rest of his letter of June 3 to Margaret makes clear, More was anything but "open," to Cromwell and the Council's obvious fury.

In fact, More's refusal plainly to incriminate himself during this interrogation precipitated an even sharper question. More had himself examined heretics, and, Cromwell thought, like the bishops, "used to compel them to make a precise answer" as to whether they believed the pope to be head of the Church. Well then, "why should not then the king sith it is a law made here that his Grace is Head of the Church here compel men to answer precisely to the law here as they did then concerning the pope."[64] More's initial response is a legal one; he points out that the two cases are not alike, because "at that time, as well here as elsewhere," the pope's power was recognized "through the corps of Christendom."[65] But Cromwell simply sweeps this aside, exclaiming that "they were as well burned for the denying of that, as they be beheaded for denying of this."[66] At this grim moment, More relates the differences between the law of Christendom and local law to the fundamental issue of his conscience. The difference, he says, is "not in the respect or difference between heading or burning," but "between heading and hell."[67]

At last Audley and Cromwell show him the blanket interrogation oath, which he declines.[68] This is not the end of the letter, however, and More backtracks to speak once more about his conscience, or rather, his adversaries' attempt to impugn it, by suggesting that he "was not sure therein."[69] More's response is a telling and unusually personal one that he universalizes by way of St Paul. He says that he has well enough informed his conscience with respect to his own salvation, and adds that "I meddle not with the conscience of them that think otherwise, every man *suo domino stat et cedit*. I am no man's judge."[70] This is just the middle part of a long verse from Romans 14:4: "Who are you to pass

---

[61] Guy, *A Daughter's Love*, p. 255.
[62] See the partial summary in *LP* 8, no. 814 i (Doc. 5).
[63] See Guildhall Report (Doc. 17, §6).
[64] *Last Letters*, p. 120 (Doc. 6, §7).
[65] Ibid. (§8).
[66] Ibid. (§9).
[67] Ibid. (§10).
[68] On the particular dangers of this oath, see Guy, *Thomas More*, pp. 181–3.
[69] *Last Letters*, p. 121 (Doc. 6, §14).
[70] Ibid.

judgment on servants of another? It is before their own lord that they stand or fall. And they will be upheld, for the Lord is able to make them stand." By what he quotes, by what he omits, and by what he adds, More appropriates St Paul's reproach to his present situation. With those few Latin words he creates a miniature drama that indicts his adversaries, who sit in judgment upon him, while gaining comfort from St Paul's promise that each of us stands or falls in his lord. These words resonate ironically throughout the rest of the letter, moreover, since Paul began by talking about serving a secular master, but ended by referring to God as Lord.

More's adversaries, frustrated by his refusal to speak plainly, and anxious to have legal grounds for charging him with treason, have one further taunt. "If I had as lief [rather] be out of the world as in it, as I had there said, why did I not speak even out plain against the statute. It appeared well I was not content to die though I had said so."[71] More answers them by acknowledging his fear of presumption and his fallibility as a human being. But "if God draw me to it Himself, then trust I in His great mercy, that He shall not fail to give me grace and strength," he adds.[72] His language is plain and simple enough, but hardly the sort of plainness that the king and Council demanded. And the Council's arguments contradict the charge made in the indictment: had More spoken plainly, their subsequent questions would have been irrelevant. Furthermore, the indictment insinuates that More was a coward and afraid to die, misrepresenting his explanation for his stance. Those who were present at this interrogation and his trial had to know that the indictment misrepresented him. The indictment, in other words, used the law rhetorically, to make a case against More.

By June 11, Cromwell and the Council knew about some of More's letters to Fisher and his daughter. This was followed by the interview between More and Richard Rich on June 12 and the removal of his books and writing materials; More's final interrogation on June 14; the king's circular of June 25, declaring the treasons of the late John Fisher and of Thomas More; the grand jury's acceptance of More's indictment on June 28; his trial on July 1; and his execution on July 6, 1535. Cromwell and the king were closely implicated in these events: see Cromwell's "remembraunces," which include notes to be remembered when next he went to the court, jotted down sometime before June 22, when Fisher was executed. "Item," one note reads, "to knowe his [Henry's] pleasure touchyng Maister More," adding, "and to declare the oppynion of the Judges theron and what shalbe the kynges plesure"; another, "Item, when Maister Fissher shall go to execucion with also the other"; and yet another, "Item, what shalbe done farther touching Maister More."[73] It has been surmised that "the other" refers to

---

[71] Ibid.
[72] Ibid. (§15).
[73] See Doc. 13. I cite the text of the memos from the exhibition catalogue guest-curated by David Starkey, *Henry VIII: Man and Monarch*, item 157 (p. 1 pictured), p. 159, with a description by John Guy, "What To Do about Sir Thomas More?" The memos are also discussed in an earlier exhibition catalogue edited by Trapp and Schulte Herbrüggen, *"The King's Good Servant": Sir Thomas More, 1477/8–1535*, item 245, p. 126, and the relevant page of the Remembrances is reproduced on the back of the front cover. All of the contents of the Remembrances are summarized by Gairdner, *LP* 8, no. 892 (p. 353).

More or, alternatively, to the three Carthusians who were executed on June 19.[74] In either case, it seems that these trials were what we today would call "show trials." This would not have surprised More, who once wrote that "kings' games" were like stage plays "for the more part played upon scaffolds."[75]

Only one later letter to Margaret is extant – the tender personal letter of July 5 (no. 218 [24]), in which More says farewell to her, his family, and his friends, blessing them and hoping that "we may merrily meet in heaven."[76] For More's plain answer to the question put to him so many times in the course of his interrogations we need to turn to his trial. After the verdict, guilty of treason, was rendered, More stated his position vis-à-vis the statute: the act of Parliament was "directly repugnant to the laws of God and His holy Church."[77]

Recapitulation

Although they would have had no *legal* knowledge of More's views,[78] no one who heard him speak during his interrogations, or read these letters, could have had much doubt as to why More was opposed to the statutes and would not sign any oath. More hinted at his opinion again and again, while denying that he was doing so.[79] And this was the sticking point: he would not say *plainly* what he was willing to give up his life for. It is a typically Morean strategy, at once rhetorical, political, psychological, and spiritual. It was also risky, as he must have known: on the one hand, he was able to communicate his point of view without seeming to do so; on the other, nothing could have been better designed to infuriate and frustrate the king and Council. From one point of view it is amazing that More remained in prison as long as he did before he was tried and beheaded. His status as a layman rather than a religious and as a lawyer who was once the lord chancellor meant that his hidden or not-so-hidden statements and his very existence would have been seen as a serious threat by the king, Cromwell, and the Council, while his usefulness, had he capitulated, would have been incalculable. And this precipitated a massive exercise of rhetoric, cloaked in law, against him. Given his understanding of the law and his religious convictions, More (like Fisher, with whom he was implicated by the Council) did not speak

---

[74] Trapp and Schulte Herbrüggen conjecture that the reference is to More, reading: "with also the other [?More]"; and they say that the memo shows that More's conviction and execution were a foregone conclusion. Guy, "What To Do about Sir Thomas More?" simply assumes that the reference is to More, and comes to the same conclusion. On the Carthusians rather than More as "the other," see Kelly, chapter 1 above, p. 5.
[75] Thomas More, *The History of King Richard the Third: A Reading Edition*, ed. George M. Logan (Bloomington, IN, 2005), p. 95.
[76] *Last Letters*, p. 128.
[77] Roper, **Doc. 20**, §15; cf. Roper, *Life*, ed. Sylvester, p. 248.
[78] As an anonymous reviewer of this chapter pointed out.
[79] See G. R. Elton, "Sir Thomas More and the Opposition to Henry VIII," in *Essential Articles for the Study of Thomas More*, ed. Richard S. Sylvester and Germain Marc'hadour (Hamden CT 1977), pp. 79–91 and 596–9, repr. from *Bulletin of the Institute of Historical Research* 41 (1968), 19–34, and the analysis in Guy, *Thomas More*, pp. 214–15.

maliciously. But More also "feared," as he wrote to Fisher, that "it would not be so interpreted."[80] Sometime after his interrogation on June 3, 1535, More wrote Fisher again, telling him that "Master Solicitor (Richard Rich) had informed him it was all one, [on the one hand] not to answer, and, [on the other hand] to say against the statute what a man would: as all the learned men of England would justify."[81] Juan Luis Vives had anticipated such a situation in a prescient letter that he sent to Erasmus on May 10, 1534: "The times are difficult, and one can neither speak nor be silent without danger. Vergara, his brother Tovar, and other learned men have been arrested in Spain, and in England the bishops of Rochester and London and Thos. More."[82]

I want to give the last words to More, although they are not wholly recoverable. More would have spoken in English. But "none of Henry's subjects was allowed to publish anything approaching an eyewitness account during his lifetime,"[83] and the earliest extant accounts of his brief remarks on the scaffold are in French or Latin.[84] R. W. Chambers came up with what has become the best-known English version, that More "died the King's good servant *but* God's first," in his influential biography of More, first published in 1935.[85] This is close to the French account in the *Paris News Letter*, Chambers's source, which ends "qu'il mouroit son bon serviteur *et* de Dieu premierement."[86] But Chambers substituted "but" for the French *et* (and), only later changing "but" to "and."[87] Gairdner's report of the *Paris News Letter* in 1885, which reads "faithful" instead of "good," also ends with "but God's first."[88] Any translation from one language to another is an interpretive act; a translation of a translation is even more so.

---

[80] *LP* 8, no. 867 iii, item 2 (**Doc. 11**).
[81] Ibid. Notice, in particular, Rich's stress on "the learned men *of England*" (emphasis mine). This reflects the new regime's ideology.
[82] *LP* 7, no. 635.
[83] Guy, *A Daughter's Love*, p. 265.
[84] For the French manuscript, traditionally considered earliest, see *The Paris News Letter* included in *Harpsfield's Life of More*, Appendix 2, pp. 258–66. For the early Latin version that Chambers would have known see *Expositio fidelis*, printed as Appendix 27 in *Opus epistolarum Des. Erasmi Roterodami*, ed. P. S. Allen, vol. 11 (Oxford, 1947). Derrett, "Neglected Versions," discusses these and other early accounts. Derrett argues that a Latin text preceded the French and reconstructs a different Latin account, which he juxtaposes with a copy of *The Paris News Letter*; cf. the Guildhall Report, **Doc. 17**. But the problems that are inherent in any translation remain.
[85] See R. W. Chambers, *Thomas More* (London, 1935, repr. Ann Arbor, MI, 1958), p. 349, emphasis mine. For evidence of its popularity, see Marius, *Thomas More*, p. 514; Ackroyd, *The Life of Thomas More*, p. 394; Guy, *Thomas More*, p. 210; Guy, *A Daughter's Love*, p. 266. In his biography of More, Guy questions whether or not More would have said any part of the last phrase in that way: see discussion below.
[86] Chambers, *Thomas More*, p. 334; he used *The Paris News Letter* in *Harpsfield's Life of More*, p. 266. Cf. Derrett, "Neglected Versions," p. 223.
[87] Germain Marc'hadour evaluates this and other changes and argues for the French "et" in "Raymond Wilson Chambers," *Moreana* 105 (April 1991), 61–80 at p. 71. Oddly, Chambers's "but" is closer to the *Expositio*'s *ac* ("and yet") in *Expositio fidelis*, p. 373, and the *tamen* in Derrett's reconstructed account in "Neglected Versions," p. 223, than to his French source. Other scholars, including Gerard Wegemer, prefer "yet" or "and yet" to "and" or "but" in translating *ac*. Cf. the Guildhall Report, **Doc. 16**, §16.
[88] *LP* 8, no. 996, p. 395.

It is hard to know, then, whether "but" represents a general anglophone predilection, a different interpretation of More's nuanced relationship between the king and God, or both.

Like Chambers, though, the *Paris News Letter*, the *Expositio*, other Latin manuscripts (including Derrett's reconstructed account and the Guildhall Report), and the English version from 1885 agree that More ended his speech by speaking first of the king and then of God. This reverses Henry VIII's charge when More first entered the king's service, to look "first upon God and next upon the king."[89] Roper records More's recollection of this "virtuous lesson" in his biography of his father-in-law.[90] And More himself cited it three times between 1534 and 1535 in letters to Thomas Cromwell, Nicholas Wilson, and his daughter Margaret.[91] Obviously it was much on his mind and seems almost formulaic. This makes his pointed reversal of the king's own words singularly ironic.[92]

It is this irony that the final sentence in Chambers's version highlights: "He then begged them earnestly to pray for the *King*, that it might please *God* to give him good counsel, protesting that he died the *King's* good servant but *God's* first."[93] The cadence, the parallelism between "King" and "God" and "King's" and "God's," and the weight of the last two words all serve to emphasize God. By contrast, the *Paris News Letter*, which has a pronoun instead of "King's," depends upon a final long adverb, *premièrement*, so unlike the short English "first," for emphasis. Early Latin versions also understate the parallelism and are wordier and too long for what More had been told must be kept very short.[94]

It is not surprising that Chambers's 1935 English version remains popular. Chambers was sensitive to Tudor English, steeped in More's style, and familiar with his letters.[95] We will never know just what More said before he was executed. In any case, thanks to that ironic reversal of the king's words – a reversal that early Latin and French manuscripts agree upon and Chambers's version underscores – More surely reaffirmed that his primary loyalty was to God, whose servant he was and with whose help he trusted to stand.

---

[89] Letter of June 3, 1535 to Margaret Roper, no. 216 [22], *Last Letters*, p. 119 (**Doc. 6**, §4).
[90] Roper, *Life*, ed. Sylvester, p. 224.
[91] Letter of March 5, 1534 to Thomas Cromwell, no. 199 [5], *Last Letters*, p. 51; letter of 1534 to Dr Nicholas Wilson, no. 208 [14], *Last Letters*, p. 92; letter of June 3, 1535 to Margaret Roper, no. 216 [22], *Last Letters*, p. 119 (**Doc. 6**, §4).
[92] Guy, *Thomas More*, argues that this reversal would have been too dangerous and that More "threw back in Henry's face the words which he had spoken to More at his 'first coming' into royal service," p. 211. But the early accounts I have referred to agree that More both echoed and reversed them – hence the extraordinary irony.
[93] Chambers, *Thomas More*, p. 349 (emphasis mine).
[94] See Guy, *Thomas More*, p. 210.
[95] In this connection see Chambers' long study, "The Continuity of English Prose from Alfred to More and His School," in *Harpsfield's Life of More*, pp. xlv–clxxiv.

Appendix: Interrogations of Thomas More between April 13, 1534 and June 14, 1535

1 April 13, 1534. Lambeth Palace
See *Last Letters*, no. 6, pp. 57–61. (Cf. *Correspondence*, no. 200, pp. 501–7.) A headnote by William Rastell states that it was written from the Tower of London and sent to Margaret Roper. Rastell and later editors date it *c.* April 17, 1534, but More could have written it before he was sent to the Tower, while under the custody of the abbot of Westminster.

More mentions the following persons in attendance: the lord chancellor, Sir Thomas Audley; the lord of Canterbury, Archbishop Cranmer; the abbot of Westminster, William Benson; Master Secretary, Thomas Cromwell.

For references to this same interrogation see *Last Letters*, no. 16, pp. 99–103 (cf. *Correspondence*, no. 210, pp. 540–4.) This letter was written from the Tower of London to Margaret Roper, undated, but sometime in the late fall of 1534.

2 April 30, 1535. Tower of London
See *Last Letters*, no. 20, pp. 112–15, **Doc. 4**. Cf. *Correspondence*, no. 214, pp. 550–4. Written from the Tower of London to Margaret Roper on May 2 or 3, 1535.

More names the following in attendance: Master Secretary, Thomas Cromwell; Mr Attorney, Sir Christopher Hales; Mr Solicitor, Richard Rich; Mr Bedill, clerk of the Privy Council; Sir John Tregonwell, principal judge of the Court of Admiralty.

[3 May 7, 1535. Tower of London?]
No known letter from More.

But his indictment lists Thomas Cromwell, Thomas Bedill, John Tregonwell, and "divers other persons," **Doc. 17**, section 4.

The indictment also reports the following by More, cited in English: "I will not meddle with any such matters, for I am fully determined to serve God and to think upon His Passion and my passage out of this world," **Doc. 17**, section 4.

Compare More's letter about his interrogation of April 30, 1535 (item 2, above), which names three of the same persons and includes the following: "I had fully determined with myself, neither to study nor meddle with any matter of this world, but that my whole study should be upon the Passion of Christ and mine own passage out of this world" (*Last Letters*, no. 20, p. 114, **Doc. 4**).

It is not surprising that these two interrogations are sometimes confused. I wonder, however, if there were two such similar interrogations. Kelly, in chapter 1 above, p. 7, also has his doubts, and suggests that this is the same interrogation as the above, rightly dated by More as on Friday, April 30, and mistakenly post-dated in the indictment to the following Friday, May 7.

4 June 3, 1535. Tower of London
See *Last Letters*, no. 22, pp. 118–22 (*Correspondence*, no. 216, pp. 555–9), **Doc. 6**. Written from the Tower of London to Margaret Roper, June 3, 1535.

More identifies the following in attendance: The lord of Canterbury, Thomas Cranmer; the lord chancellor, Thomas Audley; the lord of Suffolk, Charles Brandon; the lord of Wiltshire, Thomas Boleyn; Master Secretary, Thomas Cromwell.

See too *LP* 8, no. 814, **Doc. 5**, and More's indictment, which reports More as saying:

> The law and statute whereby the king is made Supreme Head, as is aforesaid, be like a sword with two edges; for if a man say that the same laws be good, then it is dangerous to the soul; and if he say contrary to the said statute, then it is death to the body. Wherefore I will make thereunto none other answer, because I will not be occasion of the shorting of my life. (**Doc. 15**, section 9)

Compare More, *Last Letters*, no. 22, p. 120 (*Correspondence*, no. 216), **Doc. 6**:

> But I said that verily under correction it seemed to me somewhat hard. For if it so were that my conscience gave me against the statutes (wherein how my mind giveth me I make no declaration) then I nothing doing nor nothing saying against the statute it were a very hard thing to compel me to say either precisely with it against my conscience to the loss of my soul, or precisely against it to the destruction of my body.

5 *June 14, 1535. Tower of London*
No letter from More. His writing materials had been removed on June 12, and this interrogation focused on his correspondence while he was in the Tower, making any attempt at communication very dangerous.

See *LP* 8, no. 867 iii–iv, **Doc. 11**. Cf. Trapp and Schulte Herbrüggen, "*The King's Good Servant,*" item 244, p. 126.

The following were in attendance; Thomas Bedill, Dr Aldridge, Dr Layton, Dr Curwen, in the presence of Harry Polstede, John Whalley, and John apRice, notary public.

As Trapp and Schulte Herbrüggen summarize it, "More was interrogated twice that day, on his communications and correspondence with others regarding the Succession, the Supremacy, and the Act of Treason, and his silence." Specifically, in the second part of the interrogation, three questions were put to More: "Whether he would obey the King as Supreme Head"; "Whether he will acknowledge the King's marriage with Queen Anne to be lawful, and that with Lady Katharine invalid"; and why he wouldn't answer the first question "and re[cogni]se the King as Supreme Head, like all other subjects." More is recorded as saying he could make no answer to any of the questions, while pointing out that he had never spoken against the king's marriage to Anne (*LP* 8, no. 867 iv, items 1–3, **Doc. 11**).

5

Judicial Commentary on Thomas More's Trial

Preliminary Comment
MICHAEL TUGENDHAT

The term "maliciously"
What did the word "maliciously" mean in a criminal statute in the sixteenth century?

The noun "malice," and its adverb, "maliciously," have long been used as terms of art in legal English (as in "malice aforethought"). According to the OED,[1] these words are derived from Latin and French. The example given for Latin is the word *malitia* (as in *malitia praecogitata*"), and for French is the word *malice* (as in "malice prepensé"). Examples given in the dictionary from English sources show that, in English by the fourteenth century, the word malice had acquired the meaning "ill will," which it bears to this day. That is a secondary meaning that the word bore in Latin.

In legal English the adverb "maliciously," and Law Latin *maliciose*, are used to mean the same as "with malice." Examples are in the indictment of Thomas More.[2]

In legal English the words "malice" and "malicious" each have two distinct meanings. They are commonly referred to as "malice in law" (or "legal malice") and "malice in fact" (or "actual malice").[3]

J. H. Baker discusses murder in the period 1483–1558. He states that what premeditation was required for murder was not precisely defined. None of the cases Baker cites suggests that ill will (or any other motive) was ever required as a constituent of the offense of murder, in addition to intent to do the act in question (*actus reus*). Another crime he discusses is arson, or malicious burning. Again there is no suggestion that any mental element (or *mens rea*) was required other than intent to do the act in question.[4] This is not surprising. A crime for which the mental state (*mens rea*) required was not only intent, but ill will in addition, would give much less protection to the public, and be a recipe for anarchy (see below).

---

[1] OED s.v "malice," online edition, draft revision 2009.
[2] See **Doc. 17**.
[3] *Black's Law Dictionary* refers to John Salmond, *Jurisprudence*, 10th edn, ed. Glanville L. Williams (London, 1947), p. 384.
[4] Baker, *Oxford History*, pp. 555–6.

Malice in law is defined by Coke in his *Institutes*.⁵ Coke was writing less than 100 years after More's trial. A statute of Henry IV (1399–1413) provided that "If any man do cut out the tongue, or put out the eyes of any of the king's lieges, of malice prepensed, it is a felony." Coke commented: "Malice prepensed: that is, voluntary and of set purpose, though it be done upon a sudden occasion; for if it be voluntary the law implieth malice."

This is the meaning of the word malice which has been consistently applied in the criminal law ever since that time.⁶

"Malice in fact" carries its ordinary meaning of ill will, although it may include other forms of wrongdoing.

An example of "actual malice" which means more than either intent to do the act in question, or ill will, is to be found in defamation law. In defamation a common form of malice is stating what you know to be false.

Defamation was another field of the law in which malice was required to be proved in the sixteenth century. At that time defamation was part of the ecclesiastical law, and not the common law (still less the criminal law). That was so at least until 1533, as Baker notes.⁷ But the meaning of "malice" was the same.

R. H. Helmholz states that in the ecclesiastical law of defamation, "Malice simply meant *animus iniurandi*, the intent to cause harm ... It could be presumed from the nature of the words spoken and the surrounding circumstances."⁸ But in certain circumstances a person could speak in situations where malice would not be presumed in that way, for example, a master giving a reference for a servant. In those cases there developed the use of the word malice in the sense of ill will or some improper motive, that is to say "actual malice." Plaintiffs then alleged that the speaker had spoken "out of hatred."⁹ The use of the word malice in the law of defamation remained unchanged until the 1960s, when developments of the law, first in the USA, and then in other common law countries, introduced the requirement for the plaintiff in a certain case to allege actual malice in order to prove his claim. Actual malice is required in many contexts in the civil law.

The two different meanings of malice in the law reflect the origins of the word in classical Latin. According to Lewis and Short, *malitia* meant first "badness" in general, and second, "ill will, spite."¹⁰ As to the adjective and adverb, *malitiosus* and *malitiose*, they give meanings such as "wicked" and "wickedly." They do

---

⁵ Coke, *Institutes*, Part 3, p. 62, cap. 13, commenting on 5 Henry IV (1403–4) cap 5. Coke died in 1632, and the third part of the *Institutes* was published posthumously: Catherine Drinker Bowen *The Lion and the Throne* (London, 1957), pp. 446, 460.
⁶ Glanville Williams, *Criminal Law: The General Part*, ed. 2 (London, 1961), pp. 72–3, identifies two cases where the word "maliciously" in criminal statutes has been understood to connote more than intent to do the act in question. They are not before the nineteenth century, and in each case the word is in conjunction with another adverb: *White v. Feast* (1872) LR & QB 353, 359 ("wilfully and maliciously"); *Roper v. Knott* [1998] 1 QB 868, 871, 873 ("unlawfully and maliciously").
⁷ Baker, *Oxford History*, 6:796.
⁸ R. H. Helmholz, *The Oxford History of the Laws of England*, vol. 1: *The Canon Law and Ecclesiastical Jurisdiction from 597 to the 1640s* (Oxford, 2004), p. 579.
⁹ Ibid., p. 581.
¹⁰ *A Latin Dictionary*, ed. Charlton T. Lewis and Charles Short (Oxford, 1879, repr. 1969).

not give for the adverb *malitiose* an English word indicative of a motive. There is a separate word in Latin for spite or ill will: *malevolentia*. Roper pointed this out in his account.[11] Roper then goes on to refer to a third meaning of *malitia*, namely "sin," omitting any reference to its legal meaning of "intent." Justice William Rastell describes the trial of three Carthusian priors and the Bridgettine monk Richard Reynolds on April 28–29, 1535, thus:

> The four religious persons were arraigned, and the Carthusians, by the mouth of John Houghton, their prior, confessed that they denied the king's supremacy, but not maliciously. The jury could not agree to condemn these four religious persons, because their consciences persuaded them they did it not maliciously. The judges hereupon resolved them that whosoever denied the supremacy, denied it maliciously; and the expressing of the word "maliciously" in the act was a void limitation and restraint of the construction of the words and intention of the offender. The jury for all this could not agree to condemn them; whereupon Cromwell, in a rage, went unto the jury and threatened them, if they condemned them not. And so, being overcome by his threats, they found them guilty, and had great thanks. But they were afterwards ashamed to show their faces, and some of them took great thought for it.[12]

This passage suggests that the jury thought that "malice" meant "ill will," and that they disregarded the direction of the judges to the contrary. An English jury might well behave in the same way today, if asked to try a case such as that of the Carthusians. Juries acquit, whatever the judge directs them as to the law, if they think the prosecution is political or oppressive. A relatively recent example is *R. v. Ponting*, where a British civil servant who had disclosed official secrets about the Falklands War was acquitted against the direction of the judge.[13] The classic example is *Bushell's Case* (1670), where the jury acquitted William Penn, who had unlawfully held a meeting for worship outside the Church of England.[14]

Until *Bushell's Case*, juries could be punished for their decisions. Baker records that on occasions in the sixteenth century juries were punished for supposed perversity when they acquitted, citing *R. v. Throckmorton* (1554).[15]

Rastell represents Bishop Fisher at his trial as speaking thus:

> The very statute that maketh this speaking against the king's supremacy treason is only and precisely limited where such speech is spoken maliciously. And now all ye, my lords, perceive plainly that in my uttering and signifying unto the king of mine opinion and conscience, as touching this his claim of supremacy in the Church of England, in such sort as I did, as ye have heard, there was no manner of malice in me at all, and so I committed no

---

[11] Doc. 20, par. 10.
[12] Cited from chapter 1 above, p. 14.
[13] *Criminal Law Review* 1986, August, 491–510.
[14] Reports of Chief Justice Vaughan, ed. 1677, pp. 135ff., in Howell and Howell, *State Trials*, 6:999; also in *The English Reports*, 124:1006.
[15] Baker, *Oxford History*, 6:373.

treason ... I cannot, as the case standeth, be directly charged therewith as with treason, though I had spoken the words in deed, the same being not spoken *maliciously*, but in the way of advice and counsel, when it was requested of me by the king himself. And that favor the very words of the statute do give me, being made only against such as shall *maliciously* gainsay the king's supremacy, and none other.

To this, Rastell says, some of the judges answered "that the word 'maliciously' in the statute is but a superfluous and void word; for, if a man speak against the king's supremacy by any manner of means, that speaking is to be understand and taken in law as *maliciously*"; to which Fisher replied: "My lords, if the law be so understood, then is it a very hard exposition, and, as I take it, contrary to the meaning of them that made the law."[16]

If the judges' ruling was that "maliciously" is "superfluous and void," then that gives the word no meaning at all. That would be a poor example of legal reasoning. But if the judges' ruling were that "maliciously" meant "malice in law," or "intent to do the act in question," then it would be orthodox law. On this interpretation, maliciously is not superfluous: in a criminal statute it serves to exclude any unintentional act (most commonly careless or accidental acts). But the result would have been the same for the Carthusian defendants, whichever of these two rulings the judges made. If the word "maliciously" referred to malice in law, the word "maliciously" would not have helped Fisher either. Words said in good conscience would still be said intentionally, and so with malice in law.

Fisher's argument that what is said in good conscience cannot be said "maliciously" is addressed by Professor Helmholz above:

> The problem was that if fully respected, individual conscience could easily become a recipe for anarchy. For this reason, in the sixteenth century the invocation of conscience would no more free a man from the law's commands than it will free a modern science teacher from the duty to teach the theory of evolution.[17]

In the criminal law the legal meaning of the word malice was not only relevant to the state of mind (*mens rea*) required for an offense to be committed. As Kelly has pointed out,[18] a person arraigned had an obligation to plead guilty or not guilty. If he did not plead, but stood mute, there had to be a decision on the question whether he was "mute of malice" or "mute by the visitation of God" (i.e., deaf and dumb). If he was found to be mute by the visitation of God, there then had to be a decision as to whether he was fit to be tried. Today if a defendant is mute of malice, a plea of not guilty will be entered, but in the sixteenth century the consequences were serious, as Kelly describes.

In this context the word "malice" again means no more than intent to remain

---

[16] Above, chapter 1, p. 16.
[17] Above, chapter 2, p. 65.
[18] Above, chapter 1, p. 24.

mute. If he was not mute by the visitation of God, but voluntarily, then it did not matter whether his silence was motivated by conscience or by ill will.

In Pole's account the judges are said to have cried out, "Malice, malice!"[19] From a modern perspective, and whatever may have been the meaning of the words, it is very hard to understand how judges could have said that at all, and especially in what appears to be the middle of a trial, at a stage before they came to give a ruling on the law, or a charge to the jury. And there is nothing in the reports that indicates that they ever did give a ruling on the law or a charge to the jury. From a modern perspective, for the judges to have cried out in the way described would have been a usurpation of the function of the jury. The function of the judge today is to rule on questions of law, and to direct the jury as to what the law is that they are to apply. It is the function of the jury alone to decide the facts. If the judges did cry out as Pole describes, then, by today's standards at least, it would be the plainest possible unfairness. But the facts that such an intervention by the judges would be so gross an unfairness, and that it is not mentioned in the other reports of the trial, give rise to the question whether it really happened, at least in the way described in the report. In the Guildhall Report the attribution of malice to More at this stage of the proceedings is said to have been made, not by the judges, but by the royal proctor ("silentium certum aliquod indicium erat ... malignae alicujus cogitationis contra ipsum decretum").[20] But whoever said the words, they are consistent with the speaker meaning that More was showing that he had acted intentionally. It is not necessary to interpret them as meaning that he had acted out of ill will.

The Carthusians and Fisher were not lawyers. More was a lawyer. He is recorded as addressing the issue of malice (in terms which do not refer to conscience or ill will), in the following passage:

> And yet, if I had so done in deed, my lords, as Master Rich hath sworn, seeing it was spoken but in familiar secret talk, nothing affirming, and only in putting of cases, without other displeasant circumstances, it cannot justly be taken to be spoken maliciously. And where there is no malice, there can be no offense.[21]

What More appears to be saying in this passage is that he did not affirm anything, but merely discussed hypothetical cases. If that evidence were accepted by the jury, then I would agree with Duncan Derrett that that would raise a defense to the charge, even on the footing that "maliciously" means no more than "intent to do the act in question."[22] A statement made by way of hypothetical example is not an intentional affirmation of the truth of that statement. On the other hand a jury might not have accepted More's evidence. The jury could have

---

[19] See **Doc. 19**.
[20] **Doc. 17**, par. 3.
[21] Roper's Account (**Doc. 20**), par. 10.
[22] Derrett, "The 'New' Document," p. 15.

considered that what More said was not in fact just hypothetical, but was what he really meant. That would have been an issue of fact for the jury, and not for the judges, to decide.

Assuming silence could ever constitute an offense in this context, then "maliciously" (in the sense of "intent to do the act in question") would not provide a defense for More, if the silence was deliberate.

It is on the issue of silence, rather than on the issue of malice, that I agree with Kelly's conclusion. I take him to be saying that it was because More was silent that More did not "maliciously strive by words or deeds to deprive Henry VIII of his title of Supreme Head of the Church in England." On that basis I would agree with Kelly.

Nullifying a guilty verdict on insufficiency of evidence
Kelly in his review says that a judge nowadays "is free to nullify a guilty verdict if he thinks that the evidence was insufficient; this is an option that Tudor judges did not seem to have."[23] It is correct that judges do nowadays have that power, in very limited circumstances. It is not enough that the judge should disagree with the jury. It has to be a case where the jury would be perverse to convict on the evidence that they have heard. There is a harsh fact about the right to trial by jury: a judge can be obliged by law to condemn a defendant when the judge doubts that he is guilty. Fortunately I do not know of any judge who has had that experience (the converse does occur: many judges have experience of juries acquitting a defendant when the judge has no doubt of that defendant's guilt).

Whether Tudor judges had the power to withdraw a case from the jury is crucial as to whether More's judges could have done other than as they did. If they did not have the power, they cannot be criticized for not exercising it.

Nullifying a guilty verdict on a point of law, and the question of unjust laws
Duncan Derrett put forward the theory that More made a motion in arrest of judgment after the guilty verdict was returned. Kelly casts doubt upon whether such an action was yet available in More's time in criminal or treason cases. He also notes Baker's doubt as to whether the commissioners could have accepted such a motion to arrest judgment and his confidence that no court today would do so. Baker ends by saying that "judicial review was not an established feature of the legal system" in More's time, and that the judges, though they were clearly embarrassed by More's question, were simply "recognizing the legal sovereignty of Parliament."[24]

The words of Baker quoted were written by him in 1977. It is strictly correct that an English court cannot even today, by judicial review, strike down as unlawful a statute that has been passed by Parliament. What Helmholz says applies in England to this day: "The law of nature as then understood did not permit judges to 'strike down' (as we would say) the considered actions of their sovereigns." He cites *Dr Bonham's Case*.[25] That case has never been accepted

---

[23] Above, chapter 1, p. 39.
[24] See chapter 1, p. 47.
[25] Above, chapter 2, p. 68.

as the law in England, although that principle is still a matter for debate in England.[26]

To an English lawyer it does not appear that that power exists in the USA either. The power of the US Supreme Court to strike down a law is a power to do so because the law is not compatible with the Constitution, not because it is contrary to the law of nature as derived from some source other than the Constitution. The US Supreme Court accepts the legal sovereignty of the Constitution.

But the fact that a court cannot strike down a law as contrary to the law of nature did not, and does not, mean that modern English judges are powerless when faced with unjust laws. Since the passing of the Human Rights Act 1998, an English court can declare a statute to be contrary to fundamental rights as set out in the European Convention on Human Rights. On the occasions when it has done so, Parliament has changed the law. Even when Baker wrote in 1977, a declaration to a similar effect could be obtained from the Court of Human Rights in Strasbourg under the European Convention on Human Rights 1950 (as it still can today). Such judgments were and are rare, but the UK Parliament has invariably altered the law when such declarations were made by the European Court of Human Rights.

In earlier times, the English courts responded to apparently unjust laws by adopting rules of interpretation of statutes that strained to give a meaning which was consistent with fundamental rights. English judges still do adopt that rule of interpretation: Parliament is presumed not to intend to infringe fundamental rights.

Fundamental rights were already set out in More's day in Magna Carta. More did refer to Magna Carta. It is not clear on what basis he referred to it. If he meant that it made Henry VIII's legislation illegal and void, that would not be an argument that a modern English judge could accept. But if More referred to it as giving rise to a presumption that Parliament did not intend that the provisions of Magna Carta be infringed, then that would today be an acceptable argument in law, in principle. But it would be difficult to persuade a judge to accept that argument, given the plain words of the statute. Henry VIII's Parliament did not repeal Magna Carta, and the provision of it which More cites remains in force in England to this day.

Kelly in his conclusion says:

> The judges were at fault for not ruling in his favor on this point. Instead they ruled that the qualification of malice as a necessary constitution of treason under the act, which Parliament had insisted on, was of no force. Or, to follow Pole's scenario, they ruled that any manifestation of refusal of the title was automatically malicious, and required no further proof. This seems to be a strikingly modern view of malice and "malice aforethought," as is discussed in the judicial comments later in this book. I pose, however, that the contexts

---

[26] See the lecture of Sir Anthony Clarke on June 16, 2008, "Constitutional Justice: Lessons from Magna Carta," delivered at Royal Holloway, University of London, Surrey: Available online at http://www.runnymede.gov.uk/portal/site/magnacarta/menuitem.d12521181aaae4bdc534227c9f8ca028

of More's case and the cases of the Carthusians and Bishop Fisher before him, in which the importance of malice is stressed, show that there was real meaning to the qualification intended by the Parliament, and for the judges to dismiss it was, I hold, a clear violation of their duty to enforce the law, and a manifestation of malice on their part.

For reasons set out above, I cannot agree that it is clear that there was a violation of their duty and a manifestation of malice on the part of the judges. What is recorded in the contemporary documents is consistent with all the judges (that is the judges of the Carthusians, of Fisher and of More), and with More himself, all understanding the words "malice" and "maliciously" in the sense spelt out by Coke.

If a modern English judge were to be faced with such an unjust law which required the *actus reus* to have been done "maliciously", and if he had no other means at his disposal, he might strive to interpret "maliciously" as requiring something more than intention or recklessness. It is not obvious what interpretation of "maliciously" might have been given in More's case (an allowance for conscience would be too vague, for the reasons given by Helmholz). And if the modern judge did find such an interpretation, he would (if he could) withdraw the case from the jury, and direct them to enter a not guilty verdict, on the grounds that there was no evidence to support the charge. But if he did follow this course, it would be because his duty is to read statutes as being consistent with fundamental rights. And he would be giving "maliciously" a meaning which it does not normally bear in criminal statutes.

The role of the judges
Except as discussed above, none of our position papers help us as to what a sixteenth-century judge would have been expected to say at different stages of a trial. The absence of any reference to a charge to the jury (or summing up) is a striking feature of the reports.

Baker states in relation to the period 1483–1558, that "when the jurors had heard the evidence, they received their charge from the court. Very little is known about the nature of the directions they were given."[27] A modern judge directing a jury on a charge for which the *mens rea* is expressed as malice (e.g., murder) will tell the jury that malice means no more than that the killing must have been intentional or reckless. This is a direction which benefits the prosecution. The reason why it benefits the prosecution is that if the direction is not given, it is likely that the jurors would assume that the *mens rea* required was what is meant ordinarily by the word malice, that is ill will or some other similar motive. If malice meant what Coke says it meant in statutes such as the fifteenth-century statute that he was commenting upon, then judges must in practice have given that direction to the jury from the earliest times. If judges, including More's judges, did not give that direction to the jury, then by their omission to do so, they would have left the jury to understand that

---

[27] Baker, *Oxford History*, 6:369.

malice bore its ordinary meaning of ill will. That is the meaning most favorable to the defense, and so to More, because it requires the prosecution to prove an additional fact, namely the defendant's ill will. The prosecution is always entitled to adduce evidence of ill will, but is not obliged to do so. In practice prosecutors do adduce such evidence if it is available, because ill will may be evidence of intent. There was no evidence of ill will on More's part referred to in any account of his trial. But there was evidence from Rich as to what he alleged More had said. Whether More said what Rich alleged, and if so what More's intentions were (that is, whether he was merely expressing hypothetical propositions, or asserting the proposition as true), were each issues of fact for the jury alone to decide.

Round Table[28]

Moderator: Louis Karlin

Panelists:
  Judge Edith Jones – Chief Judge, US Court of Appeals, Fifth Circuit
  Judge Sidney Fitzwater – Chief Federal Judge, N. District of Texas
  Judge Jennie Latta – Bankruptcy Judge, W. District of Tennessee at Memphis
  Sir Michael Tugendhat, Judge of the High Court (Queen's Bench), London
  With comments by H. A. Kelly, David Oakley, and Seymour Baker House.

Karlin: Do you consider More's trial to be unjust, and if so, what do you understand to be the primary injustice?

Jones: This question, and questions about the broader issues, seem to me to embody what we are really all about here – the responsibility that the legal system bore in More's conviction. Before reading the conference papers, especially those of Professors Helmholz and Kelly, I was mainly familiar with More through Robert Bolt's play, *A Man for All Seasons*. There it's portrayed as a fundamentally unjust trial with Richard Rich as a clear perjurer. More was railroaded to an unjust verdict. Now, after reading these papers and the accounts of the trial, I am still convinced that he was unjustly convicted. However, one can make the argument that he was convicted pursuant to standards that were at the time not much different from what was understood as the ordinary rule of law. And that is what is extremely disturbing and provocative in the long run here. Now you can take it on several levels – and now I will be brief so that the others can comment:

First of all, you have a king who is determined to work his will, and anyone who challenges him has to be put aside, so there is

---

[28] Editors' note. The audiotape of this discussion, which took place on November 7, 2008, was transcribed by Matthew Mehan of the University of Dallas and subsequently edited by the participants.

certainly excessive hubris there. Second, you pass a statute and the statute has rather specific language – in essence, "by words or deeds or maliciously done" – against challenging the king's headship of the Church of England. Why would anyone pass such a statute? To the modern mind – and even after Locke, who of course was more than a hundred years in the future – you do not normally have statutes that challenge mere words in opposition to the government's status. But even in More's time, it is clear that the statute was passed to get at More and the king's opponents. There is room to speculate as to legislative intent: did the Commons stress "malice" because there was a known body of law or common understanding of malice, because they wanted to assuage their own consciences: "Well, we will stick this in and make it look as if it offers stronger protections." But even then you have Cromwell preparing an indictment where he knows he is relying on all sorts of things that are – again to the modern eye but, I think, even for the time – highly questionable in terms of whether More is being condemned for what he did or for what danger he posed – or whether it was simply an attempt to find a way to get him killed.

And then finally, you have the problems concerning valuation of the evidence before the jury. This afternoon, Judge Latta and I were talking about whether Rich committed perjury or not. I think it is clear he committed perjury. But I am an appellate judge; I don't have to read the nuances of behavior. I just look at cold records, and this cold record looks like "liar" to me.

So you can say, in short, that there is arguably substantive injustice, and there is arguably procedural injustice as well. And then you have the fundamental crux of it: the man is condemned because his conscience opposed that of the king. But what this shows to me is the inherent weakness of any human system of justice. Even if you assume everything had gone according to or consistent with due process as it existed, More's conviction shows the ultimate infirmity of the law to insure justice in every instance. The most we can hope for in this world is that judgments will not come out seriously wrong and that those of us involved in the justice system, whether as jurors or judges or witnesses, have not seriously compromised the processes or our legacy to the future.

Tugendhat: I agree with everything Judge Jones has said. It is easy coming at this time in November 2008 to look at it and say, "Well, this would never have happened with us." And of course it would not, in the sense that we would not have had to face this statute. The procedures are different; everything is different. There is a saying which is quoted quite often in England, "The past is a foreign country: they do things differently there."[29] And that is how it seems to us. But More's trial

---

[29] The first sentence of L. P. Hartley's novel, *The Go-Between* (London, 1953).

had a recognizable procedure, and, although it was 500 years ago, we can understand, or at least we think we can understand, some of the things that were going on, especially with the assistance of those who have studied it, like Professor Kelly and Professor Helmholz, and who can explain the legal landscape at the time.

There are two things I would like to say. One is, of course, that if we were looking at this as modern judges, we would have a full record of the trial proceedings. And the most important thing would be, if we were sitting in an appellate jurisdiction, what the judges actually said at the time in terms of making rulings and directing the jury. But I do not think we have got anything like an accurate record of what the judges actually said at the time. So, I would not feel it to be at all possible to say that they made any ruling at all or that whatever they said to the jury, if they said anything, was wrong.

Nevertheless, if I had been a judge, and the evidence of Richard Rich was given as part of the prosecution case – and if I had not made any ruling of law which had the effect that the case could not proceed as a matter of law – I would have to say that I would have left to the jury the decision whether Richard Rich's testimony was to be accepted or not and what it meant. And if the jury had – following a proper direction – returned a verdict of guilty, that might have made me feel unhappy and uneasy. But judges must respect the role of the jury, and, if you cannot withdraw the case from the jury – except on the basis that no reasonable jury properly directed could possibly convict – if you cannot satisfy that really high standard, then you have to live with the verdict. So I, perhaps at the risk of professional sympathy with the judges at the time, prefer to suspend judgment as to whether they had done anything wrong or not.

Latta: A few comments in line with Judge Jones and Justice Tugendhat. First of all, it is very difficult for me to understand the exigencies of the time. In none of the papers that I heard over the weekend did we really think about and get inside of the head of citizens, bishops, legislators, administrators – whether they felt that the Act of Supremacy or Act of Treasons was of such a weight that they would go to these extreme lengths to enforce it. And as a judge I do try to suspend judgment until I am overwhelmed with evidence. It is easy enough to paint Henry as simply a villain and a victim of his own sensuality – I think that is maybe too easy. So that will be an area of further study for me. I think too that, from the four accounts that we have, I keep coming back to the fact that I cannot point to anything demonstrating that the judges actually ruled on a legal question. And I think that was Sir Michael's point as well. The closest that we seem to get is this outcry of "Malice!" in the Pole account,[30] which I am cynical enough to say sounds as if – especially after hearing the dramatic

---

[30] Account of Reginald Pole (**Doc. 19**), §6

account today[31] – More's trial was being shaped to fit a certain other trial that we are all familiar with. That does not sound like a very judicial thing for a panel of judges to shout. So maybe I am guilty of professional bias as well.

I think that if More was trying to ask the judges to set aside the indictment, the judges' answer was absolutely the right answer: If the statute be valid, the indictment is good.[32] There was nothing wrong with the indictment. Therefore I agree that the question of fact as to whether Rich's testimony was to be credited was certainly to be given to the jury. And so I am left uneasily asking, "Do we think this is an unjust trial simply because our hero died?"

Perhaps another way to look at it is by recognizing that many of the constitutional protections that we enjoy today came to be as a direct result of this trial. In the United States we take it for granted that the Supreme Court has the ability to rule upon the constitutionality of statutes. And while everybody loves to hate judges right now in the United States, the unsettling aspects of More's trial show us why the separation-of-powers doctrine and the independence of the judicial branch are so important to us – that is, why the United States Constitution's guarantee of an independent judiciary is crucial. Judges are fair game for almost anybody these days, and we seldom get to say what we think, but the truth is, our judicial system is the envy of the world.

Fitzwater: I would make two final points on this subject. First, a trial can be carried out properly and be consistent with what we, in our modern way, describe as due process and still be an unjust trial if the result is incorrect. That is, if Sir Thomas More were convicted based on the perjured testimony of Richard Rich, then it was an unjust result. Second, if he was convicted because of so-called malicious silence, it could be unjust in the sense that one really could not violate that statute simply by remaining silent.

Karlin: Judge Jones, I want to pursue the question of freedom of conscience, and I propose to the panel a hypothetical: Counsel for the Crown argues that in light of many benefits the king bestowed on More, the refusal to affirm the king's supremacy as approved by Parliament would have had the easily anticipated results of causing embarrassment to the Crown and giving comfort to its enemies abroad, since More was England's highest statesman and most renowned scholar. So, in spurning the king's request to affirm the supremacy, can we not infer a most pernicious ingratitude on More's part, one that can only bespeak malice? That is, what good reason could he have for refusing to affirm what Parliament enacted and so many other loyal subjects and leading citizens have affirmed? So my question is, was there any

---

[31] See below, Appendix 2.
[32] See Roper's Account (Doc. 20), §18, statement by Chief Justice FitzJames.

real way that conscience could have legally helped More, and, if it could not, are there other ways of protecting this very important right that perhaps he did not have under the law? Or are these really extra-judicial concerns?

Specifically, did More have a right to remain silent, and did it provide him with a legal defense, or was it really more of an appeal to fundamental human dignity?

Jones: Let me begin by referring to the best-evidence rule: "Judge, it is the best evidence that I have." I certainly understand your argument, and one can make a very good prosecutor's argument, that if you put all the allegations in the indictment together, you see a reasonable inference that in fact More had exhibited malice under the statute. I'm referring to a modern-day scenario in which the prosecutor in a drug case argues that the defendant was found at the place where the drugs were stored; his car had drug residue found inside; and "indeed, we found his fingerprints on a one-kilo bundle of cocaine." Therefore, even though he was not caught in the act, he is guilty of transporting for sale a thousand kilos of cocaine. Goodness knows we rely on inferences every day in reaching criminal convictions. But I suppose the difference here is that the statute required words or deeds maliciously undertaken against the king's status. And the facts in that part of the indictment are certainly neither words nor deeds. And whether silence could be taken somehow as an act, I would defer to Sir Michael, but it seems to me that that would require a very difficult logical leap, since silence is the exact opposite of an act. So, I think that his reliance on silence was his strongest defense to show why the facts alleged did not amount to a violation. I do not think that he was making that argument just as a matter of conscience, but also as a significant matter of legal importance.

Karlin: So really, if we leave aside the charges of More's colluding with Fisher and their use of the two-edged sword comment (which could have been proved by witnesses), the testimony of Rich is critical because that is the only statement we get?

Jones: That is what I think, yes. But now I would like to follow up on Judge Fitzwater's comment that, if More was convicted on the basis of perjury, then it would be an unjust result. I had thought about it in these terms earlier: suppose on appeal that there was evidence which proved that Rich had perjured himself, and therefore you had to decide whether to sustain the verdict notwithstanding the perjured testimony – whether it was harmless error, in other words. I do not think that you can find a reasonable evidentiary basis to support the verdict absent Rich's testimony. And I think that this is what led Professor Derrett to his conclusion that the judges must have dismissed those other charges – they do not support a guilty verdict.

Tugendhat: Let me take up Judge Jones's invitation to speak on the question of silence. When I started reading these papers – I think probably like everybody else, following the Derrett analysis – it looked as if there were, say, four counts. And if there really were four separate counts, and as a judge I had been asked to rule on whether the first three should go forward, I would not have had any hesitation in saying that they should not go forward because silence is not words for the purpose of the statute – on my personal, modern interpretation. But if there was, in effect, only one count that went forward, as in the Roper account, then, unless the jury were given directions of law which prevented them from doing so, I think a jury probably would have used the silence in the first part of the indictment (if they heard it) to assist them in interpreting what More actually meant, if he said the words that Rich attributed to him. In English law, we do have limited circumstances where an accused is given an opportunity to set forth his answer to the evidence against him, and, if he chooses not to and then comes to court and gives an account which he could have given earlier, then our juries are allowed to draw inferences from that earlier silence. For instance, if the prosecution puts forward a case which would be easy to answer if it were untrue and if the accused chooses to be silent and not to answer, then he cannot be criticized for exercising his right not to give evidence – but that does not stop the jury from drawing the inference that if he did not give an answer, then maybe there was not one.

Fitzwater: To pick up on the original question, "Could his silence have meant anything other than intention to act with malice?" I think the answer is that it could, but it might not. For example, if one's conscience forbids one from even speaking on the topic, then one's refusal would not be speaking with malice or with intent to deprive the king's titles. It would simply indicate that this is not something on which I can speak without violating my conscience. On the other hand, as More's prosecutors had characterized the facts, one could draw that conclusion of malice from the evidence.

Tugendhat: If I could add something: we have two ways of dealing with conscience in English criminal procedure. Normally, conscience and motive have got nothing to do with whether you have committed the offense or not. If you put a knife into somebody and they die, it is no good saying that you were obeying the commands of whoever your deity happens to be. None of those things will help you. But one way that we address issues of conscience – and I expect it is the same here – is through prosecutorial discretion. We don't live in a country where every time there is evidence of an offense having been committed, the state has to prosecute. In our system the prosecuting authorities have a choice whether to prosecute or not, and they will exercise that choice according to whether it is in the public interest that the prosecution be brought. In certain cases they will not bring a prosecution, in order to reflect deference to a person who acted according to conscience. The other way in which we deal with it is in sentencing. In our system the sentence is solely for the judge to determine; the jury is never involved in sentencing. And there are cases – even cases of homicide – where there is no doubt about the guilt of the accused, but, equally, because of the personal circumstances, we can reflect the question of conscience in the sentence.

Karlin: Judge Fitzwater, I wonder if you would focus on the question of political coercion brought to bear on the judges and jurors during the trial, and the likelihood that many of the judges and jurors had strong biases in favor of Anne Boleyn. In light of those circumstances, would it have mattered whether the law provided greater procedural and substantive protections for criminal defendants in More's day?

Fitzwater: My sense from reading the literature is that it would not have. King Henry was going after More – and others, but More in particular – and had been doing so no later than 1534. When you look at the trial of the Carthusian priors at the end of April, in the account of Rastell,[33] and see the approach that was taken when the jury initially refused to convict, what occurred? You had Cromwell going into the jury room, haranguing and threatening the jury. My sense is that this was a legal killing. My sense – and this is a lay perspective – is that King Henry, whether out of personal animus, insanity, or reasons of state – felt he had to get rid of More. More was respected as a voice of conscience. More's silence spoke volumes. For state reasons or political reasons, the king could not just have More murdered and then hide his bones under the Tower. He had to have this done in a way that appeared to be consistent with the law, and that's what he did.

Latta: I will try to play devil's advocate. I cannot understand the political exigencies of the time. I cannot personally understand – perhaps because I have not studied it as thoroughly as I would like – what it was that King Henry feared from other powers, what he feared from the fact that, as Judge Fitzwater said, More's silence did speak volumes. We can dispute all we want to about whether he had the right to remain silent, but the fact is that his silence resounded throughout the Christian world. I am certainly not defending Henry, but I am trying to better understand – from the perspective of a statesman under a monarchical system with a Parliament that did his bidding – what he was trying to accomplish. None of us lives in that kind of system, and it is hard to see things from such a different point of reference.

Karlin: As a follow-up to that, even if we assume that Parliament was coerced into passing the supremacy and treasons statutes and that Cromwell overstepped his bounds in bringing the prosecution, there are various times during the trial when the overreaching could have been stopped – for instance, if the jurors had performed their role differently. Juries sometimes choose to acquit when the evidence is clearly against someone if they feel there is some underlying unfairness with the prosecution. Now, of course, you have the spectacle of Cromwell barging in and telling the jurors to convict. That kind of thing is an

---

[33] See above, chapter 1, p. 14.

obvious problem. But is there anything in your own experience that gives you a sense of the courage needed to be a true and honorable juror? I am sure that you have had cases where juries have sat out for a long time and the voting proceeded through numerous pollings. Is there a judicial role for insuring that they deliberate conscientiously?

Fitzwater: Well, yes, there is, answering in terms of modern times. What we do now is try to make it clear to jurors that they do not have to explain their verdict; they do not have to answer for their verdict; but that the public expects them to return a verdict based on the evidence. And we encourage jurors to do their duty and, if they are not satisfied that there is proof beyond a reasonable doubt, to return a verdict of not guilty – we make that very clear. I do not know from the historical record whether that was typically made plain in More's time. But from what I have read in his case, the jurors returned the verdict in 15 minutes, which would indicate that they either were under tremendous pressure regardless of how bad Rich's testimony was, or they believed it. And I have problems with a jury either way under those circumstances. But I think in that era – perhaps Sir Michael would like to comment on how this has developed over the last several hundred years – I am not under the impression that the judges made these points clear to the jury in this case. Of course, one other point, we are also talking about an era when originally the jurors were themselves considered to be witnesses. In some ways, that was preferable to our modern notion that jurors should not have any information about the case or, if they do, they must set it aside for purposes of deliberation.

Tugendhat: It is interesting to compare the trial of More to the trial of William Penn. He made an issue of not going to the Anglican Church on Sundays for Communion when the law obliged him to do so. And that was seen as a sufficient challenge to the authorities that he was prosecuted, which was obviously what he intended. And in his case, as was attempted in the Carthusians' case, the jury did not come back with a guilty verdict, although it was perfectly obvious that he had no legal defense at all. And in those days, as we know, the juries were not allowed to separate overnight and they did not get food or heat, which were encouragements to prompt decision-making. But as they did not come back in the Penn case, the judge for some reason got impatient. And I cannot remember what sanction it was that he imposed on them; I think he may actually have put them all in prison with the result that some friend of a juror obtained a writ for habeas corpus. And it is that decision which decided in England that juries must not be threatened, nor be put under any pressure. But the implication to me is that, however disreputable one might think Cromwell's behavior was, until the decision a hundred years later that it was unlawful, it was part of what was permitted to happen.

Latta: Well, there was no indication that this jury was sworn to any particular duty or what their understanding of their role might have been.

	As noted, originally jurors were supposed to represent the community out of which the defendant came and would have their own knowledge of what had happened, and could rely on their own understanding of events – and practically anything else.
Karlin:	The problem of jurors' fear of retribution is certainly one that is alive today. So many violent crimes are gang-related, and I think that often jurors fear retribution. So in many jurisdictions, one way of protecting against this is juror anonymity, where judges will instruct the jurors that their personal information will be kept confidential.
Fitzwater:	Well, another protection against improper influence is the source of the jury pool. At More's trial, the jurors come from the vicinity of the Tower. And so you have jurors returning to the very environment that involved the allegations, which would certainly make objective decision-making difficult.
Karlin:	Let's move to a very general and difficult question: How should jurists and citizens act when they find themselves caught up in a corrupt process? I take it that there is no simple answer to this.
Jones:	I think that first you have to reconsider the question and take a step back – because how does one make the decision that the process is corrupt? We can all think of one or two cases that have been in the news in the last few years where it would appear that a prosecution was undertaken for less than honorable motives, and that somebody was convicted who probably was a law-abiding citizen – and again, all with due process. So does that mean that one part of the system is corrupt or that the whole system is corrupt? It is very hard sitting in a jury box to make that assessment. I am afraid that quite often the judgment of the corruption is best made in hindsight because it is a very difficult thing to pin down at the particular time when it's happening.
Latta:	These are all good points. I think, though, that where the question was headed was, how do we explain the phenomenon of Thomas More, as one who was able to stand up in the face of overwhelming pressure and say, "No, no. That is not what my conscience tells me"? That *is* the lesson of Thomas More. On recalling my reading of More's *Dialogue Concerning Heresies*, which he wrote in 1529, what strikes me is that he had spent a good bit of his life effectively preparing for the moment of his trial. When he instructed the tutors for his children, he wanted his children trained in the formation of their conscience and in truth; and when he had considered other vexing questions facing him and his country, he spent much time considering how conscience informs one's response to those questions. He goes to great lengths in the *Dialogue* to talk about what it is that binds a Christian's conscience, which I think, perhaps, is the answer to the heresy trials of More's time. While I do not claim to be an expert, I am convinced that for More, clearly, conscience was not "me and God." For More, conscience had to be in relation to the Church precisely because he claimed to be a Christian. He says that the Church is the fellowship

of those who claim Christ as Lord. If you do not claim that, then you are not bound by the teachings of the Church. I think he would say that. There is, of course, a natural law and a common law that bind persons simply as persons. Beyond that, however, there are the claims of the Church that bind Christians precisely because they are Christians. And I think that is what is implicated in this trial.

I do not know that he would say that there is something inherently wrong about a king claiming to be the head of a religious body within his sovereign territory. But to More there was something inherently wrong about a Christian agreeing that this king was the head of the Christian Church. This leads me to perhaps a narrow understanding of conscience, but certainly a better understanding: that it is not simply some freewheeling hope to find a rule of life out there somewhere; but that once one has pledged allegiance to Christ, the Church itself has a right to make demands upon our conscience. And that is clearly not the way we understand conscience in the United States today. Conscience is something else. Usually, I think, even in the Church, it is often heard as the right to dissent. I think conscience nowadays gets invoked more often than not as the right to dissent from the teachings of the Church. I think that would have been foreign to Thomas More.

Karlin: I want to make sure that all of our panelists get to address this question of concern to us all: That is, in light of what you have seen in this conference, what do you come away with as the primary lesson from More's trial? We will start with Judge Jones.

Jones: I have been working on some thoughts on another subject recently and reading various things that Justice Robert Jackson wrote. He and a number of other famous jurists from the 1930s, 1940s, and 1950s were, in various ways, objecting to the growing role of Supreme Court review in trying to resolve moral and social disputes, and especially that the manner of review went beyond the text of the Constitution. And these advocates of judicial restraint kept emphasizing that the rule of law will not ultimately save a people from ruin. The rule of law, much as we – those of us who work in the system – are inclined to extol it, and recognizing as I do that the rule of law is an indispensable precondition to liberty, is still a human, and therefore imperfect, institution. Now I am still strongly inclined to think that a fundamental miscarriage of justice occurred in respect to Thomas More's conviction. However, on another level, we can say that God had purposes that were ultimately served, despite or beyond the trial's injustice. And that may be the case in every legal miscarriage of justice, but it is to me just another example of the fact that one has to take the enterprise in which we are engaged very seriously as a moral enterprise and not simply a way to make a living every day.

Fitzwater: I think there are several lessons. One is that, if a sovereign has sufficient power and sufficient structure, he can carry out an injustice that cannot be stopped. And that should tell us a great deal about the importance of an independent judiciary, the rule of law, the rights that we take for granted in the United States especially by virtue of the Bill of Rights.

Another lesson would be what the trial says about Sir Thomas More as a person – that this is a man of tremendous courage who could very easily have done what his daughter had said to him: "Father, say the words but believe something different." Yet he refused this easier option, as when he refused to swear to the succession, saying, in effect: "What is an oath but when you speak to God?" And so I think the lesson we have from him is a living example of what courage meant to someone who truly had courage.

Tugendhat: I hope we are not the only country in the world that, as we look back on this trial in the England of Thomas More, sees it as a miscarriage of justice. I think I could cite a number of cases over the last 500 years, which, on hindsight, we would regard as miscarriages of justice. They are not the most troubling ones; the most troubling ones are the ones that are very near to us. We all know, as we preside over trials, that we might be presiding over a miscarriage of justice. And we all, I think, spend a great deal of time and effort to try to ensure that we do not. Usually, but not always, if there is a miscarriage of justice, there is an appellate system that can put it right, which, in the case of More, did not exist. But I agree with Judge Jones that we are just part of the world and however hard we try there will be miscarriages of justice. In considering the merits of More's case, I think there was probably more substance in the argument that More put forward, on the requirement of malice in the statute, than has been given credit for. Obviously in England we never had a superior law like the Constitution of the United States; Magna Carta was never a superior law. We only had one level of law, but we always have had a way of addressing laws which seemed unjust to the judges, which was and still is a well-established rule: that where a statute appears capable of two meanings, one of which is consistent with fundamental rights and one which is not, we can interpret – we must interpret – the statute in a way that is consistent with fundamental rights. This is not judicial review; this is statutory interpretation. And confronted by a statute as obscure as the Treasons Act in this case, a modern judge, certainly – and when I say a modern judge, I think I am talking now about a judge in the last 200 years, certainly, if not 300 – would have had open to him a juridically permissible route to interpret the statute in a way that did not lead to the conviction that occurred in this case.

I do not know whether the judges deliberated on that or not. According to the record, it rather looks as if they did not. So if they did do anything wrong, then it would seem to me that is probably the strongest argument against them – that they could have read the statute down in a number of respects. For my part, I am not sure that the word "malice" or "malicious" is the important word. That is, to me, a word that appears in the common law, as in "malice aforethought" for murder and in lots of statutes. Personally – I am not a

Latta: legal historian – I would be surprised if that was the significant word. But other devices could have been found. But it does not look as if the judges were looking for such devices or interpretations or other available procedures. It may be that it is unrealistic to expect that they could have found one. But the statutory interpretation route would be available to us, even without a superior law of the type that exists in the United States.

Latta: I too agree with Judge Fitzwater and Judge Jones. Even though I can raise real questions whether the trial was in fact just – and I think the argument could be made that it was – I think Judge Jones has raised the right question. We always have to keep in mind that our courts, as good as they are, are human institutions, and we can follow all of the rules and nevertheless reach a result that does not resonate with whatever that integral, interior part of us is – our conscience. You have already heard me say that for me, especially after studying the *Dialogue Concerning Heresies* and then again this year focusing on the trial, the lessons I will take away from these last two conferences have been about More the person. And I do not know if they are so much lessons as perhaps they are sources for questions and admiration. And indeed, of course, he is *Saint* Thomas More. He is held up to us for our learning and emulation. And what is that telling us? What is it about him that enabled him to remain silent when his silence did in fact speak volumes? Again, we can say whatever we want to say, but clearly he was sending a message to the world in the face of overwhelming pressure. And so, for me, the study of Thomas More is the study of what kind of preparation brings a person to that point in his or her life. If called upon to do that, would I be able to do it? Those to me are the central questions.

Karlin: These comments cause me to reflect on the letter that More wrote in collaboration with his daughter, which we refer to as the "Dialogue on Conscience," while he was in the Tower for refusing the oath of succession.[34] In it, he is trying to explain why he is not going along and taking the oath and why this is not obstinacy and why – despite the fact that everyone else is doing it, all these learned people – he is not. And it is fascinating to me that he chooses to tell a story – his own fable – concerning a jury. There is a trial at a fair, and the person on trial as well as the members of the jury, who are his buddies, are all from the same town. So, they pick up this man named Company, a stand-in for More, and he is the twelfth juror. And they say to him, "Well, we do not really have to talk very long; we know which way we are all going to go." And Company says, "Well, wait. I do not agree." And there is pressure brought on him: "Why do you not just come along with us?" And Company explains that he cannot pin his

---

[34] *Correspondence*, no. 206 (pp. 514–32): Margaret Roper to Alice Allington (August 1534); also *Last Letters*, ed. de Silva, no. 12 (pp. 72–89).

conscience, his soul, to someone else. Well, I found it would be a beautiful lawyers' argument to the jury in a trial today. But it also points to something that I think Judge Jones focused on, which is that perhaps the question can never be purely one of legal process in a legal regime. Often it will come down to questions of personal virtue in the individual's circumstances.

Latta: What More tells us – and we are so quick to forget, I think, in this day – is that there are things worse than death. That is almost a heretical statement in the United States today as we see the kinds of debates going on, but that is what he tells us: There are things worse than death. It is a sobering prospect.

Kelly: Let me focus on the laws that were at issue in More's trial. In November of 1534 Parliament passed the Act of Supremacy and the Act of Treasons enforcing it.[35] There was no reported difficulty about passing the first act, since almost four years earlier the convocation of Canterbury had recognized Henry as Supreme Head "so far as the law of Christ allows,"[36] and the new statute claimed to be following the clergy's recognition of the title. More's trial was about the second statute, which said that it was high treason to deprive the king and queen of any title. The first statute was questioned only after the trial was over, when More said that that statute was not valid. More was charged only on the Treasons Statute, and he had two lines of defense. One was "I did not do it." He admitted remaining silent about the king's supremacy title, but the statute required some overt action by word or deed; and he denied the actions named in the other charges, of colluding with Fisher and making a statement against the supremacy in speaking with Rich. More's second defense was to insist that whatever he did was not done maliciously, and malice was required by the statute. Now this was an argument that was very important because, according to Justice Rastell's account, it was used by the Carthusian priors and the Bridgettine monk Richard Reynolds in their trial at the end of April, and by Bishop Fisher in his trial just two weeks before More's trial. I would like to return to this point because Sir Michael, in his position paper,[37] and in his remarks just now, noted that the comment of the judges in the Carthusian trial was uncannily like the idea of malice in many of our current understandings of it, as in the requirement of malice aforethought for first-degree murder. That is, that the deed itself is malicious, and if you thought about doing it, it was malicious. But there are other instances in which malice is an additional requirement. For instance, the California Civil Code has a provision like this on the non-criminal side, specifying that, for purposes of punitive damages, if the jury finds someone guilty of violation of an obligation, then they can also look and see whether

---

[35] See below, Docs 1–2.
[36] Declaration of February 11, 1531; see Chambers, *Thomas More*, p. 248, citing *LP* 5, no. 171.
[37] See above, pp. 111–19.

the defendant was guilty of oppression, fraud, or malice. And each of those terms is defined. Malice is defined as "conduct which is intended by the defendant to cause injury to the plaintiff or despicable conduct which is carried on by the defendant with a willful and conscious disregard of the rights or safety of others."[38]

Tugendhat: The first way I made a response to that has got nothing to do with the law. I think we all know now what Henry was trying to achieve by this legislation. He was trying to compel the submission of More, Fisher, and people who thought like them. But if he could not procure their submission, he was trying to procure their elimination. And I think it is unlikely that a man as sophisticated as Henry, who knew these individuals personally, was unaware that they were claiming to maintain their positions as matters of conscience. I do not think there was a constituency out there of people who were going to deny the title of the king out of ill will to the king. It seems a strange concept. So, if you were trying to get the people who were in your sights and were claiming to act according to conscience, and you were not facing a hostile opposition who claimed to be acting out of malice, then I do not see why you would have used the word "malice" in the sense of ill will. That certainly is a sense which exists in other areas of the law. There is no doubt about it that there are areas of the law where "malice" does mean what it means in the California statute. But if it meant that in the Statute of Treasons, I am not sure who would ever have been convicted because I do not think there was anyone who fit that description.

Jones: Well, I guess that is why I suggested at the beginning that it is possible the Commons demanded that the word be put in there as a way to salve their own consciences. And I do not know what the make-up of the Commons was at this time, whether they tended to be lawyers, or whether they were henchmen of the king, or from rotten boroughs or what-not. But I am not as willing – just on the face of it – just to look at it with a post-legal realist view that it was such a malleable concept. I know it has gained protean meanings over the years, but the fact that those other defendants relied on it so heavily means, to me, that they must have thought it meant something. So I would be more inclined to say that I could see that it might have been ambiguous in the statute. Of course, it being a criminal statute, in this day, you have to apply the rule of lenity, in fact, so as not to convict. But I am inclined to think that "maliciously" was probably put in there as a device to say: "And we really mean it; you really have to be bad in denying the king whatever titles he and the queen might hold." And in fact there were plots, over the next hundred years or so, with a high point in Guy Fawkes. There were plots all over the place. How

---

[38] California Civil Code, §3294, subd. (c) (1).

many plotters did Elizabeth end up executing? Were there not, in fact, plenty of people who would maliciously will bad things like this?

Latta: Is not the malice just that – in denying the title? Did it add anything? The malice is this: "I deny this title of the king for the purpose of depriving him of this power that he has arrogated to himself."

Fitzwater: One thing it does do is to eliminate the possibility of an effects test along the lines of strict liability: "You said the following and it had the effect of doing this." That is not what they are after. Rather, with "malice," you have to at least intend the negative consequence. So More, as I understand the literature, gives the example of the Statute of Forcible Entry and points out that in that case the entry must be forcible and not peaceful.[39] And that would indicate to me that there is something required more than the mere denial of Henry's title.

Latta: But, in other words, would not More be saying: "I did not do this with malice; I did it for the king's good. I intended him good because I am trying to save his immortal soul by preventing him from denying the supremacy of Rome." However, the statute is saying: "No, it is malicious to propose that any authority trumps the authority that is vested by this title." That was what I understood the Treasons Statute to be saying.

Fitzwater: Well, you know, we get into the idea of "state of mind" when More, as a defense says: "Look, when I am talking to Rich, this is just the putting of cases."[40] That is, we were just talking hypothetically. And if I were to say, hypothetically, that Parliament cannot do this, then that is not a malicious act because we were just debating the point as lawyers do.

Jones: Let me turn to the question of More and the general public. I think that to have tried him in this way and executed him for high treason would have been somewhat equivalent to executing Benjamin Franklin, because like him More was a man of international renown. He was renowned both for his position in churchly matters and for his significance in the government. And therefore, when he was one of the only two prominent men in England who was standing against the king's assertion of authority against the Church, this was a very bold proclamation. You have all sorts of things happening on the Continent in the wake of Martin Luther. I am a Protestant, but I understand that this was a cataclysmic political period, and for More to stand up in this way was certain to have consequences.

Latta: I agree; I think people on the street were talking about More. They certainly knew that Henry had abandoned Catherine for Anne Boleyn, and that the legitimacy of their issue depended on the likes of More being out of the way.

---

[39] Roper's Account (**Doc. 20**), §10.
[40] Ibid.

House: Let me return to the question of malice. The statute itself gives examples of what might be malicious speaking, including saying that "the king, our sovereign lord, should be a heretic, schismatic, tyrant, infidel, or usurper of the Crown."[41] That is different from, say, casually expressing an opinion that the king should not be Head of the Church. When More was a judge in the Star Chamber, up to 1532, he presided over cases of people being charged with speaking ill of Anne Boleyn, not just saying that she should not be queen, but really nasty and libelous things. Therefore, I think that "malice" had a substantive meaning when the Commons put it into the Treasons Act. Otherwise why would they have used these words: "heretic, schismatic, tyrant, infidel"?

Latta: I think that what we were responding to is the idea that in order to show malice you had to show some sort of plot to deprive him of his title. And, again, maybe it is just my sense of More, but I really believe that what More wanted to do was to convert Henry because he was afraid for his immortal soul. And I think the very fact that he did not acknowledge the title absolutely indicated malice in this sense: "Henry, if you persist in this you *are* a schismatic; you are an infidel; you have put yourself outside the Church." I think that is what was at stake, and that is why he is St Thomas More. Not only did he die for his conscience, but he died for his king. I think that is very important for us to understand.

Fitzwater: To return to the question of silence: presently, to my knowledge, we do not punish mere silence. We punish either actions or failures to act. A failure to act might be a failure to stop and render aid in the case of an auto accident. The mere failure to act is never a crime or an overt act for the purpose of such criminal statutes. We do not punish, indeed I think it would be unconstitutional to punish, merely what a person thinks. It must be combined with an action or failure to act, where there is a duty to act, that can be measured.

Oakley: Thomas More received a lot of process. Is there not some value in this fact? Are we the beneficiaries of this emphasis on process, even if it had an unjust result for More? I ask this especially of Sir Michael, as the most direct heir of this whole problem.

Tugendhat: I think there is a fundamental point here. For good or ill, I do not think that we in England are the direct heirs any more than you in the United States, the people of Canada, the people of Australia, or for that matter the people of India. I think this is a common heritage, and we all know it is a common heritage. It is something which we value enormously, and the fact that territorially Westminster Hall stands in England and not in the District of Columbia or New Delhi is neither here nor there. I think this is truly our common heritage. I also think you are right that we should say more about that process that he got.

---

[41] Act of Treasons (Doc. 2).

There were many parts of the world then where he might have gotten a very different treatment – no trial at all. And I think we should also remember places where the discussion we are having today would be impossible. There are many parts of the world with the common law tradition where there are rulers like Henry VIII and where even the forms are not respected and judges who attempt to respect them disappear. These things happen. For us, this is all rather academic, but it is not in many parts of the world. So I think you are right. I think we should say: "Look, he was not just murdered like Thomas Becket. He had a trial." And although we would not try it like that now, we would try him according to our best lights. We have got to hold very firm to the fact that the rule of law is something which is so important to us that we must never forget how far back it goes. It is not something that started in 1791 with the passage of the Bill of Rights. That year was an enormously important event in the development in law and rights, but it did not start in 1791 and it did not start in any place at any time. It is our heritage, and we should bear this very much in mind.

Appendix 1

Documents

Document 1

Act of Recognizing Henry VIII as Supreme Head of the Church in England: 26 Henry VIII (November–December 1534) c. 1[1]

An Act Concerning the King's Highness to Be Supreme Head of the Church of England and to Have Authority to Reform and Redress All Errors, Heresies, and Abuses in the Same

[The King shall be reputed Supreme Head of the Church of England, and shall correct all heresies and offenses]

ALBEIT the King's Majesty justly and rightfully is and ought to be the Supreme Head of the Church of England, and so is recognized by the Clergy of this realm in their Convocations,

YET NEVERTHELESS for corroboration and confirmation thereof, and for increase of virtue in Christ's religion within this Realm of England, and to repress and extirp all errors, heresies, and other enormities and abuses heretofore used in the same,

BE IT ENACTED by authority of this present Parliament, that the King our Sovereign Lord, his heirs and successors, Kings of this Realm, shall be taken, accepted, and reputed the only Supreme Head in Earth of the Church of England, called *Anglicana Ecclesia*; and shall have and enjoy, annexed and united to the Imperial Crown of this Realm, as well the title and style thereof, as all honors, dignities, pre-eminences, jurisdictions, privileges, authorities, immunities, profits, and commodities to the said dignity of Supreme Head of the same Church belonging and appertaining; and that our said Sovereign Lord, his heirs and successors, Kings of this Realm, shall have full power and authority from time to time to visit, repress, redress, reform, order, correct, restrain, and amend all such errors, heresies, abuses, offenses, contempts, and enormities, whatsoever they be, which by any manner spiritual authority or jurisdiction ought or may lawfully be reformed, repressed, ordered, redressed, corrected, restrained, or amended, most to the pleasure of Almighty God, the increase of virtue in Christ's religion, and for the conservation of the peace, unity, and tranquility

---

[1] *Statutes of the Realm*, 3:492.

of this realm; any usage, custom, foreign law, foreign authority, prescription, or any other thing or things to the contrary hereof notwithstanding.

Document 2

Act of Treasons: 26 Henry VIII (November–December 1534) c. 13[2]

An Act Whereby Divers Offenses Be Made High Treason, and Taking Way All Sanctuaries for All Manner of High Treasons

[I. Maliciously to wish or attempt bodily harm to the King or Queen or their heirs, or to deprive them of their title, or to slander the King as an heretic, etc., or to detain any fortresses, ships, etc., declared to be high treason]

FORASMUCH as it is most necessary, both for common policy and duty of subjects, above all things to prohibit, provide, restrain, and extinct all manner of shameful slanders, perils, or imminent danger or dangers which might grow, happen, or rise to their Sovereign Lord the King, the Queen, or their heirs, which when they be heard, seen, or understood, cannot be but odible and also abhorred of all those sorts that be true and loving subjects, if in any point they may, do, or shall touch the King, his Queen, their heirs, or successors, upon which dependeth the whole unity and universal weal of this Realm, without providing wherefor too great a scope of unreasonable liberty should be given to all cankered and traitorous hearts, willers and workers of the same; and also the King's loving subjects should not declare unto their Sovereign Lord now being, which unto them has been, and is most entirely both beloved and esteemed, their undoubted sincerity and truth,

BE IT THEREFORE ENACTED by the assent and consent of our Sovereign Lord the King and the Lords Spiritual and Temporal and Commons in this present Parliament assembled, and by the authority of the same, that if any person or persons, after the first day of February next coming, do maliciously wish, will, or desire, by words or writing, or by craft imagine, invent, practise, or attempt any bodily harm to be done or committed to the King's most royal person, the Queen's, or their heirs apparent, or to deprive them or any of them of their dignity, title, or name of their royal estates, or slanderously and maliciously publish and pronounce, by express writing or words, that the King our Sovereign Lord should be heretic, schismatic, tyrant, infidel, or usurper of the Crown, or rebelliously do detain, keep, or withhold from our said Sovereign Lord, his heirs, or successors, any of his or their castles fortresses, fortalices, or holds within this Realm, or in any other the King's dominions or marches, or

---

[2] *Statutes of the Realm*, 3:508–9.

rebelliously detain, keep, or withhold from the King's said Highness, his heirs, or successors any of his or their ships, ordnances, artillery, or other munitions or fortifications of war, and do not humbly render and give up to our said Sovereign Lord, his heirs, or successors, or to such persons as shall be deputed by them, such castles, fortresses, fortalices, holds, ships, ordnances, artillery, and other munitions and fortifications of war, rebelliously kept or detained, within six days next after they shall be commanded by our said Sovereign Lord, his heirs, or successors, by open proclamation under the Great Seal,

THAT THEN every such person and persons so offending in any the premises after the said first day of February, their aiders, counselors, consenters, and abettors, being thereof lawfully convict according to the laws and customs of this Realm, shall be adjudged traitors, and that every such offense in any the premises that shall be committed or done after the said first day of February, shall be reputed, accepted, and adjudged high treason, and the offenders therein and their aiders, consenters, counselors, and abettors, being lawfully convict of any such offense as is aforesaid, shall have and suffer such pains of death and other penalties as is limited and accustomed in cases of high treason.

[II. Traitors shall not have any benefit of sanctuary]

AND TO THE INTENT that all treasons should be the more dread, hated, and detested to be done by any person or persons, and also because it is a great boldness and an occasion to ill-disposed persons to adventure and embrace their malicious intents and enterprises, which all true subjects ought to study to eschew,

BE IT THEREFORE ENACTED by the authority aforesaid that none offender in any kinds of high treasons whatsoever they be, their aiders, consenters, counselors, nor abettors, shall be admitted to have the benefit or privilege of any manner of sanctuary, considering that matters of treasons touch so nigh both the surety of the King our Sovereign Lord's person, and his heirs and successors.

[III. Treason committed out of the Realm may be tried in any County within the Realm, etc.; process and outlawry against offenders out of the Realm]

AND OVER THAT, BE IT ENACTED by authority aforesaid that, if any of the King's subjects, denizens, or other do commit or practise out of the limits of this Realm, in any outward parts, any such offenses which by this Act are made or heretofore have been made treason, that then such treasons, whatsoever they be or wheresoever they shall happen so to be done or committed, shall be inquired and presented by the oaths of twelve good and lawful men, upon good and probable evidence and witness, in such Shire and County of this Realm and before such persons as it shall please the King's Highness to appoint by commission under his Great Seal, in like manner and form as treasons committed within this Realm have been used to be inquired of and presented; and that upon every indictment and presentment found and made of any such treasons, and certified into the King's Bench, like process and other circumstance shall be there had and made against the offenders as if the same treasons so presented had been lawfully found to be done and committed within the limits of this Realm. And that all process of outlawry hereafter to be made and had within this Realm against any offenders in treason, being resident or inhabited out of the limits of this Realm, or in any of the parts beyond the sea, at the time of the outlawry pronounced against them, shall be as good and as effectual in the law to all intents and purposes as if such offenders had been resident and dwelling within this Realm at the time of such process awarded and outlawry pronounced.

[IV. Traitors shall forfeit all their estates of inheritance]

AND BE IT FURTHER ENACTED by authority aforesaid that every offender and offenders, being hereafter lawfully convict of any manner of high treasons, by presentment, confession, verdict, or process of outlawry, according to the due course and custom of the common laws of this Realm, shall lose and forfeit to the King's Highness, his heirs, and successors all such lands, tenements, and hereditaments which any such offender or offenders shall have of any estate of inheritance in use or possession by any right, title, or means, within this Realm of England or elsewhere, within any of the King's dominions, at the time of any such treason committed, or any time after;

[General saving]

SAVING to every person and persons, their heirs, and successors (other than the offenders in any treasons, their heirs, and successors, and such person and persons as claim to any their uses) all such rights, titles, interests, possessions, leases, rents, offices, and other profits which they shall have at the day of committing such treasons, or any time afore, in as large and ample manner as if this Act had never been had nor made.

Document 3

Trial of Charterhouse Priors Houghton, Webster, and Lawrence and the Bridgettine Monk Reynolds, April 23–29, 1535 (Bag of Secrets)[3]

609

Proceedings against John Houghton, prior of the Charterhouse, Middlesex; Augustine Webster, prior of the Charterhouse, Axholme, Lincolnshire;

---

[3] Summary of pertinent sections of PRO KB 8/7, part 1, in The National Archives, Kew. Adapted from the calendared entry in *LP* 8, no. 609 (pp. 229–31).

Robert Lawrence, prior of the Charterhouse of Bevall, Nottinghamshire; and Richard Reynolds, brother of the house of Syon, Middlesex; for high treason. (NB: The commission's actions against the clerks Robert Feron and John Hale on other charges are omitted here.)

609 i

April 23 (Friday) 1535, Westminster. Special commission of oyer and terminer for Middlesex to Sir Thomas Audley, chancellor; Thomas, duke of Norfolk, treasurer; Henry, marquis of Exeter; William, earl of Arundel; John, earl of Oxford; Henry, earl of Essex; Thomas, earl of Rutland; Henry, earl of Cumberland; Thomas, earl of Wiltshire; Henry, lord Montague; George, lord Rochford; Thomas Cromwell, chief secretary; Sir John FitzJames; Sir John Baldwin; Sir Richard Lister; Sir John Porte; Sir John Spelman; Sir Walter Luke; Sir Anthony FitzHerbert; Sir Thomas Inglefield; and Sir William Shelley.

609 ii

April 24 (Saturday) 1535, Westminster. The justices' precept to the sheriff for the return of the grand jury.

609 iii

April 27 (Tuesday) 1535, Westminster. The justices' precept to the constable of the Tower to bring up John Houghton, Augustine Webster, Robert Lawrence, and Richard Reynolds at Westminster on Wednesday next after one month of Easter (April 28).

609 vi

April 28 (Wednesday) 1535, Westminster. Indictment against Houghton, Webster, Lawrence, and Reynolds for declaring, on April 26 (Monday) 1535, at the Tower of London, "The king our sovereign lord is not Supreme Head in earth of the Church of England."

609 vii

April 28 (Wednesday) 1535, Westminster. The justices' precept to the sheriff for the return of a jury of inhabitants of the Tower for the trial of Houghton, Webster, Lawrence, and Reynolds.

609 viii

April 28 (Wednesday) 1535, Westminster. Trial before the above justices. Houghton, Webster, Lawrence, and Reynolds, being brought to the bar by Sir Edmund Walsingham, pleaded not guilty. *Venire* awarded returnable at Westminster on Thursday after one month of Easter (April 29).

April 29 (Thursday) 1535, Westminster. The jury found the prisoners guilty.[4]

Judgment as usual for high treason.

(May 4, 1535: Execution at Tyburn by hanging, drawing, and quartering.)

Document 4

More's Letter of May 2/3, 1535[5]

A Letter Written and sent by Sir Thomas More to his daughter Mistress Roper, written the second or third day of May, in the year of Our Lord 1535 and in the 27th year of the reign of King Henry VIII

[Tower of London,
May 2 or 3 1535]

Our Lord bless you, my dearly beloved daughter.

[1] I doubt not but by the reason of the councilors resorting hither, in this time (in which Our Lord [be] their comfort) these fathers of the Charterhouse and Master Reynolds of Syon [that be now] judged to death for treason, whose matters and causes I know not, may hap to put you in trouble and fear of mind concerning me, being here [prisoner], specially for that it is not unlikely but that you have heard [that I] was brought also before the Council here myself, I have thought it necessary to advertise you of the very truth, to the end that you neither conceive more hope than the matter giveth, lest upon other turn it might aggrieve your heaviness, nor more [grief and] fear than the matter giveth of, on the other side.

[2] Wherefore shortly [ye] shall understand that on Friday the last day of April in the afternoon, Master Lieutenant came in here unto me, and showed me that Master Secretary would speak with me. Whereupon I shifted my gown and went out [with] Master Lieutenant into the gallery to him, where I met many, some known and some unknown, in the way, and in conclusion coming into the chamber where his Mastership sat with Master Attorney, Master Solicitor, Master Bedill, and Master Doctor Tregonwell, I was offered to sit with them, which in no wise I would.

[3] Whereupon Master Secretary [showed] unto me that he doubted not but that I had by such friends [as] hither had resorted to me seen the new statutes made at the [last] sitting of the Parliament. Whereunto I answered, "Yes, verily. [Howbe]it, forasmuch as being here I have no conversation with

---

[4] Gairdner has the prisoners pleading guilty; a correction in the 1965 reprint reads: "This is not in the R.O. Manuscript. They were found guilty by the jury."
[5] *Correspondence*, no. 214, pp. 550–4; text respelled and repunctuated.

any people, I thought it little need for me to bestow much time [upon] them, and therefore I redelivered the book shortly, and the effect of the [statutes] I never marked nor studied to put in remembrance."

[4] Then [he] asked me whether I had not read the first statute of them, of [the] king being Head of the Church. Whereunto I answered, "Yes." Then [his] Mastership declared unto me that, since it was now by act of Parliament ordained that his Highness and his heirs be, and e[ver] right have been and perpetually should be, Supreme Head in the earth of the Church of England under Christ, the king's pleasure was [that those] of his Council there assembled should demand [mine opinion] and what my mind was therein.

[5] Whereunto I [answered that in] good faith I had well trusted that the king's [Highness would never] have commanded any such question to [be demanded of me], considering that I ever from the beginning well and truly from time to time declared my mind unto his Highness. "And since that time I [had]," I said, "unto your Mastership, Master Secretary, also, both by mouth and by writing. And now I have in good faith discharged my mind of all such matters, and neither will dispute king's titles nor pope's, but the king's true faithful subject I am and will be, and daily I pray for him and for all his, and for you all that are of his honorable Council, and for all the realm. And otherwise than thus I never intend to meddle."

[6] Whereunto Master Secretary answered that he thought this manner of answer should not satisfy nor content the king's Highness, but that his Grace would exact a more full answer. And his Mastership added thereunto that the king's Highness was a prince not of rigor but of mercy and pity, and though that he had found obstinacy at some time in any of his subjects, yet when he should find them at another time confirmable and submit themselves, his Grace would show mercy. And that, concerning myself, his Highness would be glad to see me take such confirmable ways as I might be abroad in the world again among other men, as I have been before.

[7] Whereunto I shortly, after the inward affection of my mind, answered, for a very truth, that I would never meddle in the world again, to have the world given me. And to the remnant of the matter, I answered in effect as before, showing that I had fully determined with myself neither to study nor meddle with any matter of this world, but that my whole study should be upon the Passion of Christ and mine own passage out of this world.

[8] Upon this, I was commanded to go forth for a while, and after, called in again. At which time Master Secretary said unto me that though I was prisoner and condemned to perpetual prison, yet I was not thereby discharged [of] mine obedience and allegiance unto the king's Highness. And there[upon] demanded me whether I thought that the king's Grace might exact of me such things as are contained in the statutes and upon [like] pains as he might of other men. Whereto I answered that I would not say the contrary. Whereto he said that, likewise as the king's Highness would be gracious to them that he found conformable, [so his] Grace would follow the course of his laws toward such [as he shall find] obstinate. And his Mastership said further [that my demeanor in that matter] was of a thing that of [likelihood made] now other men so stiff therein as they be.

[9] Whereto I answered [that] I give no man occasion to hold any one point or the other, nor [never] gave any man advice or counsel therein one way or other. [And] for conclusion I could no further go, whatsoever pain should [come] thereof. "I am," said I, "the king's true faithful subject and daily beadsman, and pray for his Highness and all his and all the realm. I do nobody harm, I say none harm, I think none harm, but wish [everybody] good. And if this be not enough to keep a man alive, in [good faith] I long not to live. And I am dying already, and have since I came here been divers times in the case that I thought to die [within] one hour, and I thank Our Lord I was never sorry for it, [but rather] sorry when I saw the pang past. And therefore my poor body is [at the] king's pleasure; would God my death might do him good."

[10] After [this] Master Secretary said, "Well, ye find no fault in that statute, find [you] any in any of the other statutes after?" Whereto I answered, "Sir, whatsoever thing should seem to me other than good, in any of the statutes, or in that statute either, I would not declare what fault [I] found, nor speak thereof." Whereunto finally his Mastership said full gently that of anything that I had spoken, there should [none] advantage be taken. And whether he said further that there be none to be taken, I am not well remembered. But he said [that] report should be made unto the king's Highness, and his gracious [pleasure] known.

[11] Whereupon I was delivered again to Master Lieutenant, which was then called in, and so was I by Master Lieutenant brought again into my chamber, and here am I yet in such case as I [was], neither better nor worse. That which shall follow lies in the hand [of God], whom I beseech to put in king's Grace's mind that thing [that] may be to His high pleasure, and in mine, to mind only [the] weal of my soul, with little regard of my body.

[12] And you with all yours, and my wife and all my children and all our friends, both bodily and ghostly heartily well to fare. And I pray you and all them, [pray for] me, and take no thought whatsoever shall happen me. For [I verily] trust in the goodness of God; seem it never so evil to this world, it shall indeed in another world be for the best.

Your loving father,
Thomas More, knight.

Document 5

Tower Interrogation of More, June 3, 1535[6]

814 i

June 3 (Thursday) 1535. Answers of Sir Thomas More to questions put by Thomas Audley, lord chancellor, and others.

1   Whether he knew the statute making the king Supreme Head, etc. Replied that he did.

2   When asked whether the king was, as by statute decreed, Head of the Church [in England] or not, he answered that "the [statute made in the Parliament] whereby the king's Highness was made Supreme Head, as is aforesaid, [was like unto a sword] with two edges, for if he said that the same law were good,[7] then [it] was dangerous to the soul. And if he said contrary to the said statute, [then] it was death to the body. Wherefore he would make thereto none other answer, beca[use] ... o*u*ld not ... ..f... of the shorting of his life."

Document 6

More's Letter of June 3, 1535[8]

[June 3, 1535]
[Tower of London]

Another Letter Written and Sent by Sir Thomas More to his daughter Mistress Roper, written in the year of Our Lord 1535, and in the 27th year of the reign of King Henry VIII

Our Lord bless you and all yours.

[1] Forasmuch, dearly beloved daughter, as it is likely that you either have heard or shortly shall hear that the Council was here this day, and that I was before them, I have thought it necessary to send you word how the matter stands. And verily, to be short, I perceive little difference between this time and the last, for as far as I can see the whole purpose is either to drive me to say precisely the one way or else precisely the other.

---

[6]   Summary of PRO SP 2/R, fols 24–5, in The National Archives, Kew. Adapted from the calendared entry in *LP* 8, no. 814 (p. 309).

[7]   The text originally read "were not good," but the "not" was apparently crossed out, making sense of the text: More would then be reported as saying that he would be endangered whether he said that the statute was good or bad.

[8]   *Correspondence*, no. 21, pp. 555–9; text respelled and repunctuated.

[2] Here sat my lord of Canterbury, my lord chancellor, my lord of Suffolk, my lord of Wiltshire, and Master Secretary. And after my coming, Master Secretary made rehearsal in what wise he had reported unto the king's Highness what had been said by his Grace's Council to me, and what had been answered by me to them at mine other being before them last. Which thing his Mastership rehearsed in good faith very well, as I acknowledged and confessed and heartily thanked him therefore.

[3] Whereupon he added that the king's Highness was nothing content nor satisfied with mine answer, but thought that by my demeanor I had been occasion of much grudge and harm in the realm, and that I had an obstinate mind and an evil toward him, and that my duty was being his subject; and so he had sent them now in his name upon my allegiance to command me to make a plain and terminate answer whether I thought the statute lawful or not, and that I should either knowledge and confess it lawful that his Highness should be Supreme Head of the Church of England, or else to utter plainly my malignity.

[4] Whereto I answered that I had no malignity and therefore I could none utter. And as to the matter, I could none other answer make than I had before made, which answer his Mastership had there rehearsed. Very heavy I was that the king's Highness should have any such opinion of me. Howbeit if there were one that had informed his Highness many evil things of me that were untrue, to which his Highness for the time gave credence, I would be very sorry that he should have that opinion of me the space of one day. Howbeit if I were sure that other should come on the morrow by whom his Grace should know the truth of my innocence, I should in the meanwhile comfort myself with the consideration of that. And in like wise now, though it be great heaviness to me that his Highness have such opinion of me for the while, yet have I no remedy to help it, but only to comfort myself with this consideration, that I know very well that the time shall come when God shall declare my truth toward his Grace before him and all the world. And whereas it might haply seem to be but a small cause of comfort because I might take harm here first in the meanwhile, I thanked God that my case was such in this matter through the clearness of mine own conscience that though I might have pain I could have no harm, for a man may in such case lose his head and have no harm. For I was very sure that I had no corrupt affection, but that I had always from the beginning truly used myself to looking first upon God and next upon the king, according to the lesson that his Highness taught me at my first coming to his noble service, the most virtuous lesson that ever prince taught his servant. Whose Highness to have of me such opinion is my great heaviness, but I have no means, as I said, to help it, but only comfort myself in the meantime with the hope of that joyful day in which my truth towards him shall well be known. And in this matter further I could not go nor other answer thereto I could not make.

[5] To this it was said by my lord chancellor and Master Secretary both that the King might by his laws compel me to make a plain answer thereto, either the one way or the other.

[6] Whereunto I answered I would not dispute the king's authority, what his Highness might do in such case, but I said that verily under correction it seemed to me somewhat hard. For if it so were that my conscience gave me

against the Statutes (wherein how my mind giveth me I make no declaration), then I, nothing doing nor nothing saying against the Statute, it were a very hard thing to compel me to say either precisely with it against my conscience to the loss of my soul, or precisely against it to the destruction of my body.

[7] To this Master Secretary said that I had before this, when I was chancellor, examined heretics and thieves and other malefactors and gave me a great praise above my deserving in that behalf. And he said that I then, as he thought, and at the leastwise bishops, did use to examine heretics whether they believed the pope to be the Head of the Church, and used to compel them to make a precise answer thereto. And why should not then the king, since it is a law made here that his Grace is Head of the Church, here compel men to answer precisely to the law here as they did then concerning the pope?

[8] I answered and said that I protested that I intended not to defend [= deny] any part or stand in contention; but I said there was a difference between those two cases because at that time, as well here as elsewhere through the corps of Christendom, the pope's power was recognized for an undoubted thing, which seems not like a thing agreed in this realm and the contrary taken for truth in other realms.

[9] Whereunto Master Secretary answered that they were as well burned for the denying of that as they be beheaded for denying of this, and therefore as good reason to compel them to make precise answer to the one as to the other.

[10] Whereto I answered that since in this case a man is not by a law of one realm so bound in his conscience, where there is a law of the whole corps of Christendom to the contrary in matter touching belief, as he is by a law of the whole corps, though there hap to be made in some place a local law to the contrary, the reasonableness or the unreasonableness in binding a man to precise answer standeth not in the respect or difference between heading and burning, but, because of the difference in charge of conscience, the difference standeth between heading and hell.

[11] Much was there answered unto this both by Master Secretary and my lord chancellor, overlong to rehearse. And in conclusion they offered me an oath by which I should be sworn to make true answer to such things as should be asked me on the king's behalf, concerning the king's own person.

[12] Whereto I answered that verily I never purposed to swear any book oath more while I lived. Then they said that I was very obstinate if I would refuse that, for every man doth it in the Star Chamber and everywhere. I said that was true, but I had not so little foresight that I might well conjecture what should be part of my interrogatory, and as good it was to refuse it at first as afterward.

[13] Whereto my lord chancellor answered that he thought I guessed truth, for I should see them, and so they were showed me; and they were but two. The first whether I had seen the statute. The other whether I believed that it were a lawful made statute or not. Whereupon I refused the oath and said further by mouth, that the first I had before confessed, and to the second I would make none answer.

[14] Which was the end of the communication, and I was thereupon sent away. In the communication before, it was said that it was marveled that I

stuck so much in my conscience, while at the uttermost I was not sure therein. Whereto I said that I was very sure that my own conscience, so informed as it is by such diligence as I have so long taken therein, may stand with mine own salvation. I meddle not with the conscience of them that think otherwise, every man *suo domino stat et cadit* ["by his own master stands or falls" (Rom. 14.4)]. I am no man's judge. It was also said unto me that if I had rather be out of the world as in it, as I had there said, why did I not speak even out plain against the statute. It appeared well I was not content to die, though I had said so.

[15] Whereto I answered as the truth is, that I have not been a man of such holy living as I might be bold to offer myself to death, lest God for my presumption might suffer me to fall; and therefore I put not myself forward, but draw back. Howbeit, if God draw me to it Himself, then trust I in His great mercy, that He shall not fail to give me grace and strength.

[16] In conclusion, Master Secretary said that he liked me this day much worse than he did the last time, for then he said he pitied me much, and now he thought that I meant not well. But God and I know both that I mean well, and so I pray God do by me.

[17] I pray you be, you and my other friends, of good cheer whatsoever fall of me, and take no thought for me, but pray for me as I do and shall do for you and all them.

> Your tender loving father,
> Thomas More, knight.

Document 7

Trial of Charterhouse Monks Middlemore, Exmew, and Newdigate, June 1–11, 1535 (Bag of Secrets)[9]

886 i

June 1 (Tuesday) 1535, at Westminster. Special commission of oyer and terminer for Middlesex to Sir Thomas Audley, chancellor; Charles, duke of Suffolk; Henry, marquis of Exeter; Thomas, earl of Rutland; Henry, earl of Cumberland; Thomas, earl of Wiltshire; Thomas Cromwell, secretary; Sir John FitzJames; Sir John Baldwin; Sir William Paulet; Sir Richard Lister; Sir John Porte; Sir John Spelman; Sir Walter Luke; Sir Anthony FitzHerbert; Sir Thomas Inglefield; and Sir William Shelley.

---

[9] Summary of pertinent sections of PRO KB 8/7 part 2 in The National Archives, Kew. Adapted from the calendared entry in *LP* 8, no. 886 (p. 350).

886 ii

June 5 (Saturday) 1535, Westminster. The justices' precept to the sheriff of Middlesex for the return of the grand jury at Westminster, on Tuesday after the quinzaine of Holy Trinity (June 8). With panel annexed.

June 9 (Wednesday) 1535: The panel bears an endorsement stating that the jury found one bill against Fisher and others on this date, the Wednesday after the quinzaine of Trinity. They adjourned until June 11 (Friday), when they presented another bill, and day was given to them until June 16 (Wednesday) for further inquiry; on which day they appeared, and were discharged.

886 iii

June 9 (Wednesday) 1535. Grand jury indictment, setting forth the Act of Supremacy, etc. and finding that John Fisher, etc. [see **Doc. 11** below for the finding on Fisher]. Also that Humphrey Middlemore, William Exmew, and Sebastian Newdigate, late monks of the Charterhouse, London, under the obedience of John Houghton, prior, now deceased, did at Stepney, Middlesex, on May 25 (Tuesday) 1535, each of them say to several of the king's true subjects, "I cannot nor will consent to be obedient to the king's Highness as a true, lawful, and obedient subject, to take and repute him to be Supreme Head in earth of the Church of England under Christ."

886 iv

June 9 (Wednesday) 1535, Westminster. The justices' precept to the constable of the Tower, commanding him to bring up Middlemore, Exmew, and Newdigate at Westminster, on Friday next after the quinzaine of Holy Trinity (June 11).

886 v

June 11 (Friday) 1535, Westminster. The justices' precept to the sheriff of Middlesex for the return of a jury of inhabitants of the Tower for the trial of Middlemore, Exmew, and Newdigate, on Friday next after the quinzaine of Holy Trinity (June 11). With panel annexed.

886 viii

June 11 (Friday) 1535. Record of the first session held before the above justices, citing the preceding documents, and showing that the indictment was found on Friday next after the quinzaine of Trinity (June 11). That same day (June 11), Middlemore, Exmew, and Newdigate were brought to the bar by Sir Edmund Walsingham, deputy of Sir William Kingston, constable of the Tower, and severally pleaded not guilty. *Venire* awarded, returnable same day (June 11). Verdict, guilty. Prisoners have no lands, goods, or chattels. Judgment as usual in high treason.

(June 19, 1535: Execution at Tyburn by hanging, drawing, and quartering.)

Document 8

Interrogations of Tower Servants, June 7–11, 1535[10]

856 i

June 7 (Monday) 1535, Tower of London. "Answers by confession of Richard Wilson, servant to Master John Fisher, doctor of divinity, late bishop of Rochester," before Sir Edmund Walsingham, lieutenant of the Tower, and Thomas Legh, doctor of civil law, and in presence of Henry Polstede, John Whalley, and John apRice, to certain interrogatories ministered to [him].

[1] To the first interrogatory, he says that about midsummer come twelve months [c. June 24, 1534] he heard his master say to Master Wilber, Master Johnson, commissary of Rochester, and Master Robert Fisher his brother, when they would have persuaded him to take the oath of succession, that he wished himself some great misfortune if he went to any place for that purpose.

[2] To the second, touching the Act of Supreme Head, about Candlemas last [c. February 2, 1535], Robert Fisher came and told him of it in the Tower, when he "took up his hands and blessed him, saying,'Is it so?'" Robert Fisher also told him of an act "by reason whereof men should come to the Tower thick and th[in] ... For now, said he, speaking is made high treason, which was never heard of before, that words should be high treason. But there was never such a sticking at the passing of any act in the lower house as was at the passing of the same, said he; and that they stuck at the last to have one word in the same, and that was the [word] 'maliciously,' which, when it was put, it was not worth ... for they would expound the same statute themselves at their pleasure." Cannot remember if Dr Fisher made any answer to this.

[3?] On Friday after Ascension Day last [May 7, 1535], Master Secretary and others of the Council came to examine Bishop Fisher on the Act of the Supreme Head, and this respondent, standing in the chamber without the partition, heard some part of the examination. Master Secretary said they were sent for two things, first touching the Act of Supremacy; the second point the respondent did not hear. Master Secretary read the act, and Fisher replied that he could not consent to take the king as Supreme Head. The act was also read to him making it treason to deny the king to be Supreme Head. After supper, respondent told his master that he thought Master Bedill's reasons weak when he said the king was head of his people, and the people was the Church; with some further observations. The bishop asked if he thought he had been too quick with Master Bedill, and respondent said no. Had no conversation with the bishop afterwards till he was examined again, but how they looked for the

---

[10] Summary of PRO SP 1/93, fols 52–62, in The National Archives, Kew. Adapted from the calendared entry in *LP* 8, no. 856 (pp. 325–31). The superscript numbers are numbers of the paragraphs found in the original. For the most part, the text of the interrogatories is not extant.

Council every day to come to them again. Cautioned the bishop to beware what answer he made as to the supremacy. During the interval Edward White, the bishop's brother-in-law, was twice with him. Heard no words between them but salutations, and touching the Anabaptists, of whom the said Edward spoke to him.

To the third [and fourth] interrogatories, says he never had communication of those matters with his master other than is above said, but had heard his master say since he was last examined that he had heard one of the statutes read but not the other.

[4] To the fifth and every part of the same he says no, except as above rehearsed.

[5] To the sixth, seventh, and eighth he also answers no.

[6] Further examined whether he knew any letter, writing, or intelligence to be between Master More or any other man and his master since he came to the Tower; said that Dr Adyson brought his master about Michaelmas last [September 29, 1534] two letters which he found in his master's books, and after he had showed them to him he took them with him again; but what their contents were he cannot tell.

Notarial signature of John apRice

856 ii

[Canceled heading referring to the testimony of John Wood, More's servant.]

856 iii

[June 7 (Monday) 1535, Tower of London. Replies of Richard Wilson, apparently in his own hand.]

[Response to the question:] "What communication has been between my lord and me since the first co[ming of the Council]." My answer:

[7] "I remembered unto him ... this word 'maliciously' to be put in that Statute or some other like, for so heard I my lord's brother, Robert Fisher, tell my lord." Moved my lord (Bishop Fisher) to send for the statute book, and asked Edward White to send it. Read the two statutes to my lord, and he read them himself, and on Friday or Saturday last [4 or June 5] the book was burned. Said that a man may answer a question without any malice; but my lord would not tell him what he would answer. After his last answer before the Council, my lord said he had stuck to the word "maliciously," and that the Council suspected that he had counsel from Master More. But he said nay, but his brother Robert had told him of the word and bade him so say.

[Response to the question:] "Whether I suspect any note between my lord and Master More."

[8] Heard my lord tell George that there was no peril in the statutes except it were maliciously done and spoken, and suspects he bade George tell More so about seven or eight days before the last coming of the Council. Heard from George that Master More said Master Secretary gave him very good words,

but he would say nothing about his answer but that my lord was certified. Told George he thought my lord would suffer death if he gave no other answer, and asked him to get the statute book, but he would not.

[Response to the question:] "What I have sent to Master More or his servant."

[9] Never sent anything concerning the king's matter, either in word or writing. Sent to Master More's servant half a custard on Sunday last [i.e., yesterday], and, long since, greensauce. More or his servant sent him an image of St John, and apples and oranges after the snow that fell in winter. On New Year's Day More sent him a paper with writing, £2000 [sic!] in gold, and an image of the Epiphany.

[10] Has often suspected George of carrying letters between my lord and Master More.

[11] Has seen my lord burn papers, and has burned them at his bidding, but never was so bold as to look at them, "and for such causes I did suspect the matter the more." Has also burned old papers that were written before he came to the Tower.

12 Gave George a letter to More from my lord since the first examination, but read it not.

13 "We" were agreed to deny any letters being sent between them. Thinks my lord gave many letters to George, and heard him tell George he might say he never carried any letters on the king's business, but he would not counsel him to be forsworn for other things.

856 iv

June 8 (Tuesday) 1535. [Further examination of Richard Wilson, servant of Bishop Fisher] [Heading mostly illegible, except for the date.]

14 First: he says he has put in writing and sent by Master ... certain things omitted in his first examination. When the books were here. Master More sent word to "the said" Master Fisher by George G[old], the lieutenant's servant, that he heard that his own books should be condemned, but he does not remember Master Fisher's answer. After the said Master Fisher's first examination, said to him that he remembered that Master Robert Fisher said to his brother that "maliciously" was in the statute, and therefore a man might answer to the questions not maliciously, and be in no danger; and the Respondent asked George and Master White to get the book, which the latter at length did.

15 Read the book to his master, and said there was nothing to bind him to answer.

16 And afterwards heard him say to George that he saw no great peril in the statute, unless it were done or spoken maliciously. The next night Fisher wrote a letter to More, which was not sealed or closed, and told him, if George was sober, to give it to him to be delivered; which he did. Knows nothing of the contents.

17 Thinks Fisher told George to show more about the statute.

18 Does not know whether George brought any answer, but heard

him say that Master More was merry, and that my lord was satisfied. Then within a few days came the Council again to the second examination.

[19] At supper, Fisher, in answer to his questions, said he had not made answer, "but the [Co]uncil was gone even as they came. Then said my master to this respondent, '[You] remember, sir, that the last day before this that the Council was here, the Council should ask me two questions or two points.' And this respondent said, 'Yes,' for he heard Master Secretary say then and purpose that he had come then principally for two things, [on]e was touching the Act of Supreme Head, and the other this deponent could [n]to hear." Then said his master that the Council bore him in hand that they purposed to ask him two questions, of which one was whether he would accept the king as Supreme Head; "'and I remember no such thing.' 'Nor I neither,' said this deponent then." But a while after he came to his master as he was saying evensong, and said, Yes, that he had answered that he did not think the king might be Supreme Head; but his master denied having said so. The next day he remarked to his master that he had been a long time with the Council yesterday.

[20] His master said the Council had blamed Master Lieutenant sore for keeping him and Master More so negligently, thinking that they had counsel of each other, and it was not so, but they supposed it, because both stuck much upon one point. Said that if it was upon the word "maliciously," the book was worth sending for; but he answered nothing.

[21] On Saturday next "the said George" said to Fisher that he heard he was made a cardinal. "Then said Master Fisher, 'A cardinal! Then I perceive it was not for nought that my lord chancellor did ask me when I heard from my master the pope, and said that there was never man that had exalted the pop[e a]s I had.'"

[22] A further conversation between the respondent and Fisher, the former saying that if the [king] were Head of the Church, he would have power to [make] the Body of Christ, and hear confessions.

[23] Between the examinations George brought Fisher certain scrolls of paper, [written] with lead in some places, and in some other with an agg[let or] dry point, so that they could not be well read; which George said his master had bade him cut out of one of the monks' books. In one was written, "Pasce oves meas," etc.; "and I am sure that these words Christ spake Himself, and dare take that quarrel to my death." In another place he [this respondent] read, "My lord, ye should not judge me to death this day, for, if ye should, ye should first condemn yourself and all your predecessors, which were not simple sheep in this flock, but great bellwethers. And, my lord, if ye would, in detestation of this opinion, dig up the bones of all our predecessors and burn them, yet should not that turn me from this faith." Could not read any more. Showed them to his master, who said, "T[h]ey be gone. God have mercy on their souls!" And when they were alive, Fisher said, referring to the said monks under examination, "I pray God that no vanity subvert them."

[24] Thinks that letters have passed between Fisher and More since the last examination, for he saw George bring his master a letter, and afterwards cast it in the fire, last Sunday [i.e., two days ago, June 6].

856 v

June 8 (Tuesday) 1535. Depositions of George Gold, [servant u]nto Master Lieutenant. Before Master Ch ......, John apRice, and ......

[25] Says that on Sunday last [June 6] ... "Master Fisher" wrote a letter to Master More, and sent it by him. The next day More sent back an answer, with Fisher's letter. Burned both at Fisher's order.

[26] About 10 days ago, told Fisher he heard that he should be a cardinal; to which he answered that "he set as much by that as by a rush under his foot."

[27] Heard this from John, some time Fa[lconer] to the said Master Fisher, who heard it from one Noddy and one Andrew, servants of Anthony Bonvis[e].

[28] No one else told him of this. About 10 days ago Fisher sent a letter to More by him, and More caused him to burn it. The next day More wrote an answer and sent it by him. Fisher told him to burn it.

[29] About six days after the monks of the Charterhouse were executed, Master Lieutenant caused him to carry to the Charterhouse six books which the monks had left in the prison, out of which books Master Lieutenant caused him to cut six leaves of parchment, "which leaves were as though it were with lead or like thing." Laid them up in the lieutenant's parlor under a cupboard cloth. Two days after gave them to Richard Wilson, Fisher's servant, and, on their being returned, burned them.

[30] Two days after the execution, Fisher said to him that he saw not so great peril in the statute, unless it were done or spoken maliciously, and he marveled much that the monks were put to execution, [say]ing that they did nothing maliciously nor obstinately.

[31] Delivered a letter from Wilson for the buying of the book of the statutes to the Falconer, but does not know whether it was directed to the Falconer or to Edward White, Fisher's brother. Received the book from the Falconer, and gave it to Wilson.

[32] When the Lubecks were lately in London, More caused him to tell Fisher that he heard say thow ... works should be condemned; unto whom the said Master Fisher ... that so they would condemn his ...

[33] Has conveyed about a dozen letters between More and Fisher, some being written with ink, and some with coal.

[34] It was agreed between Master Fisher, his servant, and this Deponent, both times the Council came to the Tower, to deny having carried any letters between them; but, if he were sworn on a book, that he should speak the truth.

[35] More also wrote four letters to his wife and Mrs Roper [his dau]ghter.

[36] Does not know of Fisher sending letters, except to More.

June 9 (Wednesday) 1535. Further examination [of George Gold?]

[37] About a week ago, went to William Thornton's house in Thames Street for Master Fisher's diet, as he was accustomed, and asked him if he had

heard that Fisher should be made cardinal. Thornton replied that he had heard it from a servant of Lord Rochford.

[38] About five days ago, took a pot of conserve from Fisher to Anthony Bonvise, *but he would not have it, saying that Fisher had more need or it than he* [passage struck out]. There were no letters in the pot.

[39] Bonvise sent to More, two or three times every week, meat and a bottle of wine, till a quarter of a year ago, since when he has sent none. Before the said time he sent Fisher a quart of French wine every day, and three or four dishes of jelly.

[40] Heard of Fisher being made cardinal, on Friday or Saturday last [June 4 or 5], from Mrs Roper, and the same day told Fisher. Mentions Falconer and Noddy in connection with the report.

856 vi

June 10 (Thursday) 1535. Depositions of John Wood, servant to Sir Thomas [More], knight, taken by Master Thomas Legh, doctor of laws, Henry Polstede, and John apRice.

[41] Being examined as to the intercourse between his master and Fisher, said that about a fortnight after the first being of the Council in the Tower, George, the lieutenant's servant, came to More, and asked him, from Fisher, what answer he had made. More replied that he would not dispute of the king's title, but give himself to his beads and think on his passage hence; and this he wrote in a letter to be given to Fisher. Soon after he sent another letter by George to the effect that he would not counsel Fisher to make the same answer, lest the Council might think they were agreed, and that he would meddle with no man's conscience but his own. After the Coun[cil were at the] Tower, Fisher sent to tell More what answer he had made. Does not know if More sent an answer.

[June 10 (Thursday) 1535. Examination of William Thornton.]

[42] William Thornton, of London, says that he heard of Fisher's being made cardinal from George, the lieutenant's servant, and the Falconer, who serves Fisher with his meat.

[June 10 (Thursday) 1535. Examination of Andrew, servant of Anthony Bonvise.]

[43] Andrew, servant to [Anthony] Bonvise, about 12 days ago [c. May 30] heard Florence Volusene say at his master's house at dinner, that he heard at the French ambassador's house that Fisher was made Cardinal, and since heard others speak of it.

June 11 (Friday) 1535. [Further examination of John Wood?]

[44] Never carried any letters or other intell[igence], but bare stewed meat d[ivers times] ...... passed, for the which Mrs Roper did give ...... buying of the same, when she was .... Also that John the Falconer came to his master.

856 vii

[June 11 (Friday) 1535.] Examination of John Pewnoll, *alias* Falconer, [somet]ime servant to Master Dr Fisher, sometime Bishop of Rochester.

[45] Last Lent carried a letter from Fisher, about his disease, to Master Bonvise, who consulted Master Clement, and sent back word that Fisher's liver was wasted, and he should [ta]ke goat's mi[lk] and other things. Carried another letter to Dr Fre ... concerning physic, and others to Master White, to desire him to seek relief for the said Master Fisher.

[46] Fisher had money from his brother Robert, and, since he is dead, of Master ... and Master Thornton.

[47] Twice or thrice Master Anthony Bonvise sent him a dish of stewed meat, before ... six weeks passed, and a quart of French wine and ... when Fisher sent for it.

[48] Heard that Fisher was made a cardinal first from George, the lieutenant's servant, who heard it from Andrew ...

June 11 (Friday) 1535. [Deposition of George White.]

[49] George White deposes that last Saturday [June 5] William Thornton told him Fisher was made a cardinal, and afterwards John the Falconer. Asked about letters and communications between Fisher and others, "saith that he knowe[th] .... but that he hath received himself bills of [the said Master Fisher's] diet, which he hath got to show." Was also asked to send him a book of the statutes, which he did by Falconer.

[50] Examined who [conv]eyed to him any book or letters; says he sent himself a book of divinity.

[51] [Illegible]

856 viii

June 11 (Friday) 1535. Further examination of John Wood.

[52] Says that on the morning after the Council came to the Tower his master (More) told him that his daughter, Roper's wife, wished to know what had taken place, and he wrote her three letters. Gives the substance of them.

June 11 (Friday) 1535. Further examination of Richard Wilson.

[53] Says that he does not know of anyone encouraging Fisher. About two ... past he found the copy of a letter in Fisher's chamber to the effect that his opinion concerning the matrimony was true, and he should no[t] doubt therein, i[nsomu]ch as the pope ha[d] ... as stipulat ... Whether it was direct to [Fisher] or not he does not know.

856 ix

June 11 (Friday) 1535. Further examination of William Thornton.

[54] Says he first heard that Fisher was made cardinal of Master Thornam, steward to my lord of Wiltshire, in Paul's, eight or nine days ago [*c.* June 2 or 3], in presence of another priest. The same day, or the next, John

Falconer and George both told him. Does not know whether any letter was sent to Fisher from beyond sea or on this side. Does not know or suspect anyone of counseling or encouraging Fisher.

Document 9

Richard Rich's Report on Thomas More, June 12, 1535

I Transcription of the Conversation between Sir Thomas More and Sir Richard Rich, June 12, 1535[11]

Key:
* * *   missing paper:
_____   faded ink
abc   conjecture from partial or faded letters
I distinguish between allographs (different forms of the same letters) thus:
a/*a*/A b/B c/C d/D e/E/E f/F g/G h/*h* i/y/I m/M n/N/N p/P r/R/R
s/*f*/s/z t/T u/v

[f. 20 bottom (marked by Gairdner as "ii")]

```
1  *                      Theffect of the   * *_____* * between Rychard Ry * * * * * * * * *
2  *                      & the seyd Sir Thomas More in the prefence of * * * * * * * * * *
3  *                      Edmund Walfyngham Rychard southewell                              *
4  *                      Palmer  And            Berleght                                   *
5  * * * * * * * * yche charitably movyd the seyd sirThomas More to be conformable          *
6  * * * * * * * * nd lawez as were made concernyng the cafe that he knew of                *
7  * * * * *_pon condycion that yf the seyd More wold so be that he wold god                *
```

[f. 21]

```
-2  * * * * * * * * * *_____    * * * * * * * * * * * * * * * * * * * * * * * * * * * *
-1  *          _____            * * * *_____* * * * *          _____               *
 0  * * * * * *_____   * * * * * * *                              *
 1  * * * *_And on  hy f_____To whome  the  seyd  More gave thanke sayng that your conf* * *
 2  * * * *_d save  you  And  my  conscience fhall save me . wheruppon the   seyd Rych* * * * * *
 3  * * * * * * *_d to  the seyd  More  sir for  me  to gyve yow advyfe or counfell  beyng A     *
 4  * * * * * * * * * * * peryence  lernyng  &  wysedome . . yt were lyke  As yf A man wold take *
 5  * * * * * * * * * * * * * * *_of  water  And cast yt  in to Temmys by cause yt shold not be* * *
```

[11] The National Archives: PRO SP 2/R, fols 21 and 22 (new foliation). Mentioned by Gairdner, *LP* 8, no. 814, 2, ii.

In deciphering this text, I have been aided by past efforts, beginning with the transcription by Reynolds, *Trial of St Thomas More*, pp. 166–7, and other readings by Derrett, "The 'New' Document," with Reynolds, comments on "The 'New' Document"; by Byron, "The Fourth Count"; and a further transcription by Reynolds, in *The Field Is Won: The Life and Death of Saint Thomas More* (London, 1968), pp. 385–6. In addition I have been greatly assisted by the specific readings and comments of Guy Albert Trudel, OP, for which I am very grateful. H. A. K.

6   * * * * * ent sir proteſtynG wt   yow   that   I haue noo commyſſion or   commaundment to   *
7   * * * * * * * *   __wt yow oF the   mater   ye   wott oF Neuertheleſſe wt   your fauour I aſk *
8   *oF yow this   caſe IF   yt were   Inactyd   by   parlyament that I shold   be   kynG   *
9   * And *who so * * uer sayd   nay   yt   shold * * treſ * * * * what offence were   yt to yo* *
10 *IF ye seyd t * * t   I were   kynG for soth* * * my   confcyence yt werre   none   off* *
11 *h*t ye were bound so to say   And to * * accept   me   for   so   muche   as   your confent *
12 * * * * hen   b* * * * *as   whervnto * * seyd More sayd   that   he   shold offende* * * *
13 * * * * * * * * * * * * foR he * * * * boun* * * by the   act   by   cauſe   he might gyve his * *
14 * * * * * * * * * * And   he sayd   further *h*t the same   caſe   was a sma*l* * * caſe *_* * *
15 * * * * * * * * * * *putt   A nother   hyer   caſe   whiche   was   this . sir I put caſe* * * *
16 * * * * * * * * * * yd by   parlyament that   god   werre   not god . And yF Any Repug*y * * *
17 * * * * * same   act   that   yt   shold   be   treſon   yF the queſtion were aſkyd oF   yow * * *
18 * * *ld ye say   that   god were * * t god Accordyng to the statute . And yF he   dyd . dyd * *
19 *yow offende   yes   foR sothe   wher vnto   the   seyd   Ryche sayd that   that   act *was not * *
20 *poſſyble to be made to make god vngod but sir by cauſe   your   caſe   ys * * * * * * * * * * * *
21 * * *_t to yow & me* * * * * * * * * that ys s_* * * * * * * * * *   to be p__* * * * * * * * * * *
22 * * * * *   __ * * * * * * * * * * * * * * * * * * F Inglo* * *   * * * * * * * * * * * * * * * * * * *
23 * * * * * * * Aſirme & accept h * *   so as welle *s in the caſe that I were made   kynG * * * * * *
24 * * * * yche caſe ye agre that ye were bound so to affirme & accept   me to be kynG   __ * * * * *
25 * * * * *er vnto the seyd More sayd that   the caſez were not lyke by cauſe that A kynG   * * * * *
                        (canceled caret:) sygg   * *
26 * * * y be made by parlyament And A kyng depryved by parlyament to whiche act eny /   * *
27 * * * ett (canceled)   subgett beyng of the parliament may gyve his   concent   but to the caſe *
28 * * * * F A * p * * m * * *e A subgett can not be bound by cauſe he cannot gyve his confen* *
29 * *m hym * * * the parliament   sayng further that although   the kyng were acceptyd   *
30 *in Inglond yet   moſte   vtter   partE DOO   not   Affirme   the   same whervnto the seyd * * *
31 *Ryche   sayd   well   sir   god   comfort   yow   foR   I   see your mynd wyll not change *
32 *which I fere wyll be very daungerous to yow foR I suppoſe   your concelement to the   * * * * *
33 *ueſtyon   that   hath ben aſkyd oF yow ys as high offence   as   other   that hath DenyD   *
34 * * t And this Jheſu send yow better gr__e

II Modernized version

Lacunae conjecturally filled, based in part on the indictment; respelled with modern punctuation

[f. 20, last 7 lines]

1   The effect of the [conversation] between Richard Ri[ch]
2   and the said Sir Thomas More in the presence [o]f
3   Edmund Walsingham, Richard Southwell (   )
4   Palmer, and (   ) Berleght.
5   [Richard R]ich charitably moved the said Sir Thomas More to be conformable
6   [to statutes a]nd laws as were made concerning the case that he knew of
7   [well] upon condition that if the said More would so be, that he would, God

[f. 21]
-2 [willing, take it upon himself to intercede at the hands of Master Secretary]
-1 [and other of the king's Council on his behalf, because, as Master More must]
0   [know well, it did him great pain to see him so beset, with sorrow upon his]

1   [family] and on hi[m]s[elf.] To whom the said More gave thanks, saying that "Your cons[cience
2   [shoul]d save you, and my conscience shall save me." Whereupon the said Rich[ard]
3   [Rich said] to the said More, "Sir, for me to give you advice or counsel, being a
4   [man of great ex]perience, learning, and wisdom, it were like as if a man would take
5   [a small vessel] of water and cast it into Thames, because it should not be
6   [expedi]ent. Sir, protesting with you that I have no commission or commandment to
7   [commune here] with you of the matter ye wot of, nevertheless, with your favour I ask
8   [o]f you this case: if it were enacted by Parliament that I should be king,
9   and [w]hoso[e]ver said nay, it should [be] treas[on], what offence were it to yo[u],
10 if ye said t[ha]t I were king? Forsooth, [in] my conscience, it were none off[ence],
11 [that] ye were bound to say and to accept me, forsomuch as your consent
12 [was due w]hen b[id, as it w]as." Whereunto [the] said More said that he should offend
13 [if he were to refuse] for he [should be] boun[d] by the act, because he might give his
14 [consent and approval.] And he said further [t]h[a]t the same case was a smaller case [than]
15 [him liked. He] put another, higher, case, which was this: "Sir, I put case [that]
16 [it were now enact]ed by Parliament that God were not God, and if any repug[n] i[t],
17 [by this] same act, that it should be treason. If the question were asked of you [now],
18 [wou]ld ye say that God were [no]t God, according to the Statute? And if [y]e did, did
19 you offend? Yes, forsooth?" Whereunto the said Rich said that that act was not
20 possible to be made, to make God un-God. "But, Sir, because your case is [so greatly exalted]
21 [I put] to you a mi[ddle case for you], that is, Sir, [you know our king] to be p[roclaimed]
22 [as the Supreme Head of the Church o]f Engla[nd on earth, why ought not you, Master]
23 [More, him] affirm and accept h[im] so, as well [a]s in the case that I were made king, [in]
24 [the wh]ich case ye agree that ye were bound so to affirm and accept me to be king?
25 [Wher]erunto the said More said that the cases were not like, because that a king
26 [ma]y be made by Parliament and a king deprived by Parliament, to which act any
27 subject, being of the Parliament, may give his consent; but to the case
28 [o]f a p[ri]m[ac]y, a subject cannot be bound because he cannot give his con[sent]
29 [from hi]m [in] the Parliament." Saying further that although the king were accepted
30 [so] in England, yet most outer parts do not affirm the same. Whereunto the said
31 Rich said, "Well, Sir, God comfort you, for I see your mind will not change,
32 which I fear will be very dangerous to you, for I suppose your concealment to the
33 [q]uestion that hath been asked of you is as high offence as other that hath denied
34 [i]t. And this Jesu send you better gr[ac]e."

Document 10

Tower Interrogation of Fisher, June 12, 1535[12]

The Answers made by Master John Fisher, doctor of divinity, to the interrogatories ministered to him, the 12th day of June, anno R.R. Henry VIII 27, within the Tower of London, examined thereupon by Master Thomas Bedill and Master Richard Layton, clerks of the king's Council, in the presence of Sir Edmund

---

[12] Edited by John Lewis, *The Life of Dr John Fisher, Bishop of Rochester in the Reign of King Henry VIII*, 2 vols (London 1855), 2:407–13 from London, British Library MS Cotton Cleopatra E.6, fols 169 ff. Cf. the calendared entry in *LP* 8, no. 858 (pp. 331–2). The text here is a modern-spelling version of Lewis's edition.

Walsingham, knight, lieutenant of the said Tower, Henry Polstede, John Whalley, and John apRice, notary, underwritten and sworn *in verbo sacerdotii*, that he would truly answer to the said interrogatories and to every part of the same as far as he knoweth or remembreth.

[The numbers correspond to the interrogatories, which are not extant.]
1   To the first interrogatory he said that when the act by the which words are made treason was a-making, Robert Fisher his brother came to him to the Tower and said that there was an act in hand in the common house by the which speaking of certain words against the king should be made treason; and because it was thought, by divers of the said house, that no man lightly could beware of the penalty of the said statute, therefore there was much sticking at the same in the common house, and unless there were added in the same that the said words should be spoken maliciously, he thought the same should not pass. And then this respondent asked him whether men should be bound to make any answer to any point upon an oath, by the virtue of the same act, like as they were by the other Act of Succession. And he said no. And no other communication had this deponent with him, to his remembrance, at any time touching the said acts or any or them.
2   To the second interrogatory, he hath answered afore, and no other answer can he make to the same, as he saith.
3   To the 3rd, he doth not remember that ever he had such communication with his brother.
4   To the 4th, he answereth as afore, and no otherwise can he answer.
5   To the 5th interrogatory this examined answered that there hath been letters sent between him and Master More to and fro upon a four [times] or thereabouts from either of them to other since they came to the Tower, touching the matters specified in this interrogatory. And, declaring the contents and effect of the same as far as he can remember, saith that he remembreth not the effect of any of the letters that either he sent to Master More, or that he received of Master More, before the first being of the Council here with this examined; but he doth well remember that there were letters sent to and fro between him and Master More before that time.

And the first occasion of writing between them proceeded of Master More; and now, being better remembered, saith that the effect of the first letter that Master More did write unto him after they came to the Tower was to know the effect of this deponent's answer which he had made to the Council in the matter for the which he was first committed to the Tower. And then this deponent signified unto him by his letters what answer he had made them.
Examined whether he doth remember the effect of any other letters that went between him and Master More before the first being of the Council with them, saith No.

And further examined what letters went between them since that time, saith that soon after that the Council had been here first to examine this respondent, George, Master Lieutenant's servant, showed this examined a letter which Master More had directed to his daughter, Mistress Roper, the effect whereof was this, that when the Council had proposed unto him the matter for the which they came for, he said that he would not dispute the king's title, and that Master

Secretary gave him good words at his departure. And that is all that he can remember of the effect of the same letter. And by the occasion of that letter this respondent wrote to Master More a letter to know a more clearness of his answer therein, which letter he did send him by the said George. And thereupon he received a letter again from the said Master More by the hands of the said George concerning his answer, but what the same was, he saith he hath not in his remembrance.

And after a deliberate time, about a three or four days, this respondent calling to his remembrance the words that his brother Robert Fisher had spoken unto him long before, viz., how that the Commons did stick and will not suffer the said statute to pass unless the word "maliciously" were put in it, wrote a letter containing the same words in effect, adding this, that if this word "maliciously" were put in the said statute, he thought it should be no danger if a man did answer to the question that was proposed unto him by the Council after his own mind, so that he did not the same maliciously.

But, he saith, he nothing required or demanded in the said letters the advice or counsel of Master More therein, as he is sure that the same Master More himself would testify if he be examined.

And thereupon, as this deponent thinketh, Master More, supposing that this respondent's answer and his should be very nigh and like, and that the Council thereby would think that the one of them had taken light of the other, would that the same suspicion should be avoided, and thereupon wrote a letter to this respondent accordingly.

Further examined whether any other letters or intelligence were between them, saith that soon after the last being of the Council in the Tower, and after the taking away of Master More's books from him, the said George came to this deponent and told him that Master More was in a peck of troubles, and that he desired to have either by writing or by word of mouth certain knowledge what answer this respondent had made to the Council. And thereupon this respondent wrote unto him a letter that he had made his answer according to the statute, which condemneth no man but him that speaketh *maliciously* against the king's title; and that the statute did compel no man to answer to the question that was proposed him; and that he besought them that he should not be constrained to make further or other answer than the said statute did bind him, but would suffer him to enjoy the benefits of the same statute – which was all the effect of the said letter, as far as this deponent doth remember. And saith further that he doth not remember any other letters or message sent from him to Master More, or from Master More to him, since that time, nor the effect of any other letter or message going between them at any time other than are before expressed.

6–17 To the 6th, 7th, 8th, 9th, 10th, 11th, 12th, 13th, 14th, 15th, 16th, and 17th interrogatories he hath answered before, and otherwise he cannot answer to the same, as he saith.

18 To the 18th he saith, and answered, no: he knoweth where none is.

19 To the 19th he saith that they were all burned as soon as [he] had read them, and to the entent that the effects thereof should have been kept secret if it might be. For he was loath to be reproved of his promise made to Master

Lieutenant that he would not do that thing for the which he might be put in blame. Albeit if that there were more in the said letters than is before touched, he is sure it was nothing else but exhortation either of other to take patience in their adversity, and to call God for grace, and praying for their enemies, and nothing else that should hurt or offend any man earthly, as he saith.

20 To the 20th, he answereth that he received no other letters than afore touched.

21 To the 21st interrogatory he saith that he received the same book from Edward White by the hand of the said George in the time specified in this interrogatory.

22 To the 22nd interrogatory, he saith that he remembereth no communication between him and Edward White; but he saith that there was certain communication between Wilson and him about the time that they read the said statutes, and saith that he threppened upon [remonstrated with] this respondent that the Council had proposed unto this respondent two points, and this respondent said that he remembered not, that it was but one, which was this, how the Council was sent hither to know his opinion touching the Statute of Supreme Head, and no other did he remember that they should propose unto him; and said further that Wilson said that he stayed behind the door and heard partly what this Respondent did answer unto them, and how he heard Master Bedill's reasons that he made then.

And saith that, after that the said Wilson had read the said statutes to this respondent once or twice, this respondent caused them to be burned, because he thought that if Master Lieutenant had found them with this examinate, he would have made much business thereupon.

23 To the 23rd interrogatory he saith that he doth not remember that ever he declared to Wilson or to any man what answer he was disposed to make, whatsoever communication were between them thereof.

24 To the 24th he saith that he received no such letters to his knowledge or remembrance but one that Erasmus did send unto him, which this respondent's brother Robert Fisher showed first to Master Secretary ere it came to him.

25–6 To the 25th and 26th he saith that George aforenamed brought him word since the last sitting of the Council here that he heard say of Mistress Roper that this respondent was made a cardinal. And then this respondent said, in the presence of the same George and Wilson, that if the cardinal's hat were laid at his feet he would not stoop to take it up, he did set so little by it.

27 To the 27th he saith he received no other letters touching the same business.

28 To the 28th he saith that he received no such letters nor message, to his knowledge or his remembrance.

29 To the 29th he saith that he wrote oftentimes letters touching his diet to him that provided his diet, as to Robert Fisher while he lived, and to Edward White; and a letter to my lady of Oxford for her comfort; and letters of request to certain of his friends that he might pay Master Lieutenant for his diet, to whom he was in great debt, and he was in great need.

30 To the 30th, he received certain money of each of them according to his request, and no other answer, as he saith.

31 Item, examined whether there were any such confederacy or compaction

between this respondent and his servant Wilson and the said George, that [the] said conveying of letters and messages to and fro should be kept close, if they were examined thereof, saith they were agreed so together to keep the same as secret as they might.

[Each page is signed:]

Jo. Roff. [Johannes episcopus Roffensis]

Document 11

Tower Interrogations of Fisher and More, June 14, 1535[13]

867 i

June 14 (Monday) 1535, Tower of London: "Interrogatories ministered on the King's behalf [unto] John Fisher, DD, late bishop [of Rochester]," by Master Thomas Bedill, [Dr Aldridge], Richard Layton, and Richard [Curwen], of the king's Council, in presence of Harry [Polstede and John] Whalley, and of John apRice, notary public; with Fisher's answers.
1   Whether he would obey the king as Supreme Head of the Church of England?
– He stands by the answer he made at his last examination, but will write with his own hand more at length.
2   Whether he will acknowledge the king's marriage with Queen Anne to be lawful, and that with the lady Katharine to be invalid?
– He would obey and swear to the Act of Succession; but desires to be pardoned answering this interrogatory absolutely.
3   For what cause he would not answer resolutely to the said interrogatories?
– He desires not to be driven to answer, lest he fall in danger of the statutes.

Signed by John apRice as notary: J. R. (mutilated)

867 ii–iii

June 14 (Monday) 1535, Tower of London. Interrogatories ministered to Sir Thomas More before Master Bedill, Dr Aldridge, Dr Layton, Dr Curwen, in the presence of Polstede, Whalley, and apRice aforesaid; with More's responses.
1   Whether he had any communication with any person since he came to the Tower touching the Acts of Succession, of Supreme Head, or the act wherein

---

[13]   Summary of PRO SP 6/7, fols 5–9, in The National Archives, Kew. Adapted from the calendared entry in *LP*, 8 no. 867 (pp. 340–2). All of the papers calendared here (867 i–iv) are in the same hand, and form one document.

speaking certain words of the king is made treason; and, if so, when, how often, with whom, and to what effect?

— Never had any communication of such matters since he came to the Tower.

2 Whether he received letters of any man, or wrote to any, touching any of the said acts; and, if so, how many, of whom, etc.?

— Had written divers scrolls or letters since then to Dr Fisher, and received others from him, containing for the most part nothing but comforting words and thanks for meat and drink sent by one to the other. But about a quarter of a year after his coming to the Tower he wrote to Fisher, saying he had refused the oath of succession, and never intended to tell the Council why; and Fisher made him answer, showing how he had not refused to swear to the succession.

No other letters passed between them touching the king's affairs till the Council came to examine this deponent upon the Act of Supreme Head; but after his examination he received a letter of Fisher, desiring to know his answer. Replied by another letter, stating that he meant not to meddle, but fix his mind upon the Passion of Christ; or that his answer was to that effect.

He afterwards received another letter from Fisher, stating that he was informed that the word "maliciously" was used in the statute, and suggesting that therefore a man who spoke nothing of malice did not offend the statute. He replied that he agreed with Fisher, but feared it would not be so interpreted. Did not report to Fisher his answer to the Council, with the advice to make his own answer different lest the Council should suspect confederacy between them.

After his last examination, sent Fisher word by a letter that Master Solicitor had informed him it was all one, [on the one hand] not to answer, and, [on the other hand] to say against the statute what a man would; as all the learned men of England would justify. He therefore said he could only reckon on the uttermost, and desired Fisher to pray for him as he would for Fisher.

Also, considering that it would come to the ears of his daughter, Master Roper's wife, how the Council had been with him, and other things might be reported which would cause her to take sudden flight, and fearing that, being (as he thought) with child, she might take harm, he sent to her, both after his first examination and after his last, letters telling her the answers he had given, and that he could not tell what the end might be, but whatever it were he prayed her to take it patiently and pray for him. She had written him before divers letters advising him to accommodate himself to the king's pleasure, especially urging this in her last. Other letters he neither sent nor received from any person. George, the lieutenant's servant, carried the letters to and fro.

3 Whether these letters are forthcoming; and, if not, why they were done away, and by whose means?

— There is none of these letters forthcoming, where he knoweth. He would have had George to keep them, and George always said there was no better keeper than the fire. When he saw this he desired George to let some trusty friend read them, and if he saw any matter of importance in them he might report it to the Council and get thanks before any man, otherwise that he should deliver them. But George said he feared his master the lieutenant, who had ordered him not to meddle with such matters, and so burned them.

4   Whether any man of this Realm or without this Realm sent him any letters or message exhorting him to persist in his opinion; and, if so, how many, of whom, when, and to what effect?

– No.

Examined further, why he sent the said letters to Dr Fisher?

– Replies that as they were both in one prison, and for one cause, he was glad to sent to him, and hear from him again.

Signed as above: J. R.

867 iv

June 14 (Monday) 1535, Tower of London. Interrogatories ministered to Sir Thomas More by the Council aforenamed, and in the presence of the said witnesses; with his answers.

1   Whether he would obey the king as Supreme Head?

– He can make no answer.

2   Whether he will acknowledge the king's marriage with Queen Anne to be lawful, and that with lady Katharine invalid?

– Never spoke against it, "nor thereunto [can] make no answer."

3   Where it was objected to him that by the said statute he, as one of the king's subjects, is bound to answer the said question, and re[cogni]ze the king as Supreme Head, like all other subjects?

– He can make no answer.

Notarial signature (mutilated)

Document 12

Trial of Bishop Fisher, June 1–17, 1535 (Bag of Secrets)[14]

886 i

June 1 (Tuesday) 1535, at Westminster. Special commission of oyer and terminer [as above, **Doc. 6**].

886 ii

June 5 (Saturday) 1535, Westminster. The justices' precept for the return of the grand jury on June 8.

---

[14] Summary of pertinent sections of PRO KB 8/7 part 2 in The National Archives, Kew. Adapted from the calendared entry in *LP* 8, no. 886 (pp. 350–1).

June 9 (Wednesday) 1535: The grand jury found one bill against Fisher and others.

886 iii

June 9 (Wednesday) 1535. Grand jury indictment, setting forth the Act of Supremacy, etc. and finding that John Fisher, late of Rochester, clerk, otherwise late bishop of Rochester, did, on May 7, 1535, openly declare in English, "The king our sovereign lord is not Supreme Head in earth of the Church of England."

886 vi

June 16 (Wednesday) 1535, Westminster. The justices' precept to the constable of the Tower to bring up John Fisher, late bishop of Rochester, at Westminster, on the Thursday after the feast of St Barnabas (June 17).

886 vii

June 17 (Thursday) 1535, Westminster. The justices' precept to the sheriff of Middlesex for the return of a jury of inhabitants of the Tower for the trial of Fisher on Thursday after St Barnabas (June 17).

886 viii

June 17 (Thursday) 1535. Record of the second session held before the above justices. Fisher is brought to the bar on the Thursday after the feast of St Barnabas (June 17), by Sir William Kingston, constable of the Tower. Pleads not guilty. *Venire* awarded same day (June 17). Judgment as usual in high treason.

(June 22, 1535: Execution at Tyburn by beheading.)

Document 13

Cromwell's Remembrances, *c.* June 18, 1535

A list of 39 memos by Secretary Thomas Cromwell, titled "Remembraunces at my next goyng to the Courte," in the hand of a clerk (doubtless taken down by dictation), except for occasional interlinear additions in Cromwell's own hand. On a single sheet, front and back, London, British Library MS Titus B.1, fol. 475rv. Most of the top page is reproduced in the exhibition catalogue edited by Trapp and Schulte Herbrüggen, *"The King's Good Servant,* on the inside front cover, with an explanation on p. 126 (item no. 245); for a full illustration of the top page, see Starkey, *Henry VIII,* p. 159 no. 157, with a description by Guy, "What To Do about Sir Thomas More?"

Summary[15]

[1] For redress of the riots in the north.
[2] Letters to be written to Sir John Wallop.
[3] To declare Irish matters to the king, and desire what shall be done there.
[4] To send letters and money into Ireland, and advise the deputy of the king's pleasure.
[5] To advertise the king of the ordering of Master Fisher, and to show him the indenture which I have delivered to the solicitor (see below).
[6] To know his pleasure touching Master More, and declare the opinion of the judges (see below).
[7] To declare to him the proceedings in his cause of uses and wills.
[8] To declare the effect of Master Pate's letters.
[9] To remember specially Master Shelley
[10] and Brothers for his concealment.
[11] To remember Sir Walter Hungerford in his well-doings.
[12] When Master Fisher shall go to execution, and also the other (see below).
[13] What shall be done further touching Master More (see below).
[14] The conclusion for my lord of Suffolk.
[15] To send to the king by Raffe the behaviour of Master Fisher (see below).
[16] The sermons made in London on Sunday last, and how well Symonds behaved himself.
[17] The rich jewel brought out of Almayne.
[18] Special letters to the justices of assize to be drawn up, touching the unity of the people.
[19] To deliver the commission for the first-fruits in Surrey to Danester.
[20] To take an end with the vicar of Halifax for his fine.
[21] To remember Morette's reward at his departing.

---

[15] This list follows the entry in *LP* 8, no. 892 (pp. 353–4), with numbers added to each item.

[22] To remember the sending into Almayn and Dr Barnes.
[23] To show the king what answer shall be given to the citizens of London if they sue him for the mesurage. [Added by Cromwell at the bottom of p. 1]

[p. 2]
[24] Repairs to be done at Berwick and Carlisle.
[25] Lord Powes.
[26] Antony Bonvise and Antony Vivalde.
[27] The end between the abbot of Westminster and Antony Deny.
[28] The despatch of Master Pate's servant.
[29] A commission to be sent into the north for the examination of the riots.
[30] My lord of Northumberland.
[31] Lord Bray, who is contented to pay.
[32] My lord of Cumberland and lord Dacre.
[33] My lord of Chester and Master Inglefeld.
[34] The vacation of Bissam and the demeanor of certain canons there.
[35] Master Norys for Beaumarys.
[36] To show the king of the conclusion with Ric. Southwell, if it shall stand with his pleasure.
[37] The finishing of the matters of Calais.
[38] The establishment of a Council in the north.
[39] To remember Rokes, the traitor of Ireland, and Talbot of Ireland.

Original Text

Remembraunces at my next goyng to the Courte

...

[5] Item to aduertyse the kyng of the ordering of Maister Fissher, and to shewe hym of the Indenture whiche I haue delyueryd to the Solicitour.
[6] Item to know his pleasure touching Maister More.
 and to declare the oppynyon of the Jugges theron, & what shalbe the kynge plesure. [*insertion in Cromwell's hand*]

...

[12] Item when maister Fissher shall go to execucion with also the other.
[13] Item what shalbe done farther touching maister More.

...

[15] Item to send vnto the king by Raffe the behaviour of Maister Fissher.

Document 14

Henry VIII's Order to Publicize the Guilt of Fisher and More, June 25, 1535[16]

A circular setting forth the measures taken for the abolition of the bishop of Rome's authority, the king's assumption of the title of Supreme Head of the Church, and the instructions sent to the bishops to cause the clergy to preach accordingly, and to erase the bishop of Rome's name from mass-books, etc., used in churches.

The person addressed is to see to the execution of the premises in the parts about him, and make diligent search whether the bishops and clergy do sincerely preach to the people as above-mentioned, and is also to declare the same to the people at the assizes.

He is also to set forth the treasons of the late bishop of Rochester and Sir Thomas More.

The mutilated copy in the PRO is addressed thus: "To our trusty and right well-beloved Councillor."

The following text is taken from another copy, London, British Library MS Cotton Cleopatra E vi, fol. 214; printed in Gilbert Burnet, *The History of the Reformation of the Church of England*, ed. Nicholas Pocock, 7 vols (Oxford 1865), 6:106–9. (Certain words are put in bold for ease of parsing the syntax.)

Much of the substance of the text is taken from a circular letter of the previous year, dated June 9, 1534, printed in John Foxe, *Acts and Monuments*, 4th edn, ed. Josiah Pratt (London, 1877), 4:69–71. It does not mention letters sent to justices of the peace or to the treasons of Fisher and More; it was clearly designed to be sent to sheriffs, and the same is doubtless true of the present letter. James Gairdner, however, *LP* 8, preface, p. xxxix, says it seems to be addressed to the JPs themselves.

HENRY REX

Trusty and right well-beloved, we greet you well.

And **whereas** heretofore, as ye know, both upon most just and virtuous foundations, grounded upon the laws of Almighty God and Holy Scripture, and also by the deliberate advice, consultation, consent, and agreement as well of the Bishops and Clergy as by the Nobles and Commons Temporal of this our Realm assembled in our High Court of Parliament, and by authority of the same, the abuses of the Bishop of Rome's authority and jurisdiction, of long time usurped against us, have been not only utterly extirped, abolished, and secluded, but also the same our Nobles and Commons, both of the Clergy and Temporalty, by another several Act[s] and upon like foundation for the public weal of this our Realm, have united, knit, and **annexed to us** and the Crown Imperial of this our Realm **the title**, dignity, and style **of Supreme Head** in Earth Immediately under God of the Church of England, as undoubtedly evermore we have been; which things also the said Bishops and Clergy, particularly in their Convocations, have wholly and entirely consented, recognized, ratified, confirmed, and approved authentically in writing, both by their special oaths, profession, and writing, under their signs and seals, so utterly renouncing all

---

[16] Calendared entry in *LP*8, no. 921.

their other oaths, obedience, and jurisdiction, either of the said Bishop of Rome or of any other Potentate,

we let you wit that, perpending and considering the charge and commission in this behalf given unto us by Almighty God, together with the great quietness, rest, and tranquility that hereby may ensue to our faithful subjects both in their consciences and otherwise, to the pleasure of Almighty God, in case [= if] the said Bishops and Clergy of this our Realm should sincerely, truly, and faithfully set forth, declare, and preach unto our said subjects the very true word of God and (without all manner color, dissimulation, hypocrisy) manifest, publish, and declare the great and innumerable enormities and abuses which the said Bishop of Rome, as well in title and style, as also in authority and jurisdiction, of long time unlawfully and unjustly hath usurped upon us, our progenitors, and all other Christian Princes,

[**we**] **have not only addressed** our letters general to all and every the same **Bishops**, straitly charging and commanding them, not only in their proper persons, to declare, teach, and preach unto the people the true, mere, and sincere word of God, and how the said title, style, and jurisdiction of Supreme Head appertaineth unto us, our Crown, and dignity royal; and to give like warning, monition, and charge to all abbots, priors, deans, archdeacons, provosts, parsons, vicars, curates, schoolmasters and all other ecclesiastical persons within their diocese to do the semblable in their churches every Sunday and solemn feast, and also in their schools, and to cause all manner prayers, orisons, rubrics, and canons, in mass-books and all other books used in churches, wherein the said Bishop is named, utterly to be abolished, eradicate, and razed out in such wise as the said Bishop of Rome, his name, and memory forevermore (except to his contumely and reproach) may be extinct, suppressed, and obscured,

but also to the **Justices of our Peace**, that they in every place within the precinct[s] of their commissions do make and cause to be made diligent search, wait, and espial whether the said Bishops and Clergy do truly and sincerely, without any manner cloak or dissimulation, execute and accomplish their said charge to them committed in this behalf, and to certify us and our Council of such of them that should omit or leave undone any part of the premises, or else in the execution thereof should coldly or feignedly use any manner sinister addition, interpretation, or cloak, as more plainly is expressed in our said letters.

[**Therefore**] **we** (considering the great good and furtherance that ye may do in these matters in the parts about you, and specially at your being at [as]sizes and sessions, in the declaration of the premises, have thought it good, necessary, and expedient to write these our letters unto you, whom we esteem to be of such singular zeal and affection towards the glory of Almighty God, and of so faithful and loving heart towards us, as ye will not only with all your wisdoms, diligences, and labors accomplish all such things as might be to the preferment and setting forwards of God's word and the amplification, defense, and maintenance of our said interest, right, title, style, jurisdiction, and authority appertaining unto us, our dignity, prerogative, and Crown Imperial of this our Realm)

will and desire you, and nevertheless straitly **charge and command you, that**, laying apart all vain affections, respects, and carnal considerations, and setting before you eyes the mirror of truth, the glory of God, the right and dignity of your Sovereign Lord, thus sounding to the inestimable unity and commodity both of yourselves and all other our living and faithful subjects,

ye do not only make diligent search within the precincts of your commission and authority whether the said **Bishops** and Clergy do truly and **sincerely as before preach**, teach, and declare to the people the premises, according to their duties, **but also** at your said **sitting in [as]sizes and sessions ye do persuade**, show, and declare unto the same **people** the very tenor, effect, and purpose of the premises in such wise as the said Bishops and Clergy may the better not only do thereby and execute their said duties, but that also the parents and rulers of families may declare, teach, and inform their children and servants in the specialties of the same, to the utter extirpation of the said Bishop's usurped authority, name, and jurisdiction forever;

showing and **declaring also** to the people at your said sessions **the treasons traitorously committed against us and our laws by the late Bishop of Rochester and Sir Thomas More, Knight**, who thereby and by divers secret practices of their malicious minds against us intended to seminate, engender, and breed amongst our people and subjects a most mischievous and seditious opinion, not only to their own confusion but also of divers others who lately have condignly suffered execution according to their demerits; and in such wise dilating the same with persuasions to the same our people as they may be the better fixed, established, and satisfied in the truth; and consequently that all our faithful and true subjects may thereby detest and abhor in their hearts and deeds the most recreant and traitorous abuses and behaviors of the said malicious malefactors as they be most worthy;

and, finding any default, negligence, or dissimulation in any manner of person or persons not doing his duty in this part, ye immediately do advertise us and our Council of the default, manner, and fashion of the same;

letting you wit that, considering the great moment, weight, and importance of this matter, as whereupon dependeth the unity, rest, and quietness of this our Realm, if you should, contrary to your duties and our expectations and trust, neglect, be slack, or omit to do diligently your duties in the true performance and execution of our mind, pleasure, and commandment as before, or would halt or stumble at any part or specialty of the same, be ye assured that we, like a Prince of justice, will so punish and correct your default and negligence therein as it shall be an example to all other how, contrary to their allegiance, oaths, and duties, they do frustrate, deceive, and disobey the just and lawful commandment of their Sovereign Lord, in such things as by the true, hearty, and faithful execution whereof they shall not only prefer the honor and glory of God and set forth the majesty and imperial dignity of their Sovereign Lord, but also import and bring an inestimable unity, concord, and tranquility of the public and common state of this Realm, whereunto both by the law of God and Nature and man they be utterly obliged and bounden.

And therefore fail ye not most effectually, earnestly, and entirely to see the premises done and executed, upon pain of your allegiance, and as ye will avoid our high indignation and displeasure, at your uttermost perils.

Given under our signet at our manor besides Westminster, the 25th day of June.

Document 15

More's Trial, June 26 to July 1, 1535 (Bag of Secrets)[17]

974 i

June 26 (Saturday) 1535, Westminster. Special commission of oyer and terminer for Middlesex, to Sir Thomas Audley, chancellor; Thomas, duke of Norfolk; Charles, duke of Suffolk; Henry, earl of Cumberland; Thomas, earl of Wiltshire; George, earl of Huntingdon; Henry, lord Montague; George, lord Rochford; Andrew, lord Windsor; Thomas Cromwell, secretary; Sir William FitzWilliam; Sir William Paulet; Sir John FitzJames; Sir John Baldwin; Sir Richard Lister; Sir John Porte; Sir John Spelman; Sir Walter Luke; and Sir Anthony FitzHerbert.

There are 19 justices appointed, but they are counted as 18. As few as six are allowed to serve, of whom at least four should be Audley, Cromwell, FitzJames, Baldwin, Lister, Porte, Spelman, Luke, or FitzHerbert

974 ii

June 26 (Saturday) 1535, Westminster. Precept of Audley to the sheriff for the return of the grand jury at Westminster on Monday next after the feast of St John the Baptist (June 28).

974 iii

June 28 (Monday) 1535: The grand jury is convened by Justices Fitz-James, Baldwin, Lister, Porte, Spelman, Luke, and FitzHerbert. The sheriff's list of 30 potential jurors has 23 ticked (the tick of a twenty-fourth may be erased), of which 16 are chosen (for the names, see the indictment, **Doc. 16**)

The jury finds the indictment of Sir Thomas More to be a true bill.

974 iv

June 30 (Wednesday) 1535, Westminster. The justices' precept to the constable of the Tower, commanding him to bring up the body of Sir Thomas More, late of Chelsea, Middlesex, at Westminster, on Thursday next after the morrow of St John the Baptist (July 1).

974 v

July 1 (Thursday) 1535, Westminster. The justices' precept to the sheriff of Middlesex for the return of the petty jury this Thursday after the morrow of St John the Baptist (July 1).

---

[17] Summary of pertinent sections of PRO KB 8/7 part 3 in The National Archives, Kew. Adapted from the calendared entry in *LP* 8, no. 974 (pp. 384–5). Translation of the Latin text by H. A. Kelly.

974 vi

July 1 (Thursday) 1535. Record of the sessions held before the special commissioners, citing the above documents. Sir Thomas brought to the bar by Sir Edmund Walsingham, lieutenant of Sir William Kingston, constable of the Tower. Pleads not guilty; v*enire* awarded, returnable same day. Prisoner again brought to the bar. Verdict, guilty. Judgment as usual in high treason, with execution to be at Tyburn.

Of the 19 commissioned justices, 17 are present (missing are Montague and FitzWilliam). On the sheriff's list of 31 potential jurors, 16 are ticked, and of those 12 are chosen, namely: the knights Thomas Palmer and Thomas Spert; the esquires Gregory Lovell, Thomas Burbage, William Brown, Jasper Leyke, and Thomas Billington; and the gentlemen John Parnell, Geoffrey Chamber, Edward Stokwod, Richard Bellamy, and George Stokis.

The full text of the trial is as follows:

Et modo, scilicet, die Jovis proximo post dictam festam sancti Johannis Baptiste, anno regni domini regis nunc vicesimo septimo, coram prefatis Thoma Audeley, milite, cancellario Anglie, Thoma, duce Norffolk, Carolo, duce Suffolk, Henrico, comite Cumbrie, Thoma, comite Wilteshire, Georgio, comite Huntingdon, Georgio, duce Rocheford, Andrea, domino Windesore, Thoma Crumwell, armigero, primario secretario suo, Willielmo Paulett, milite, Johanne FitzJames, milite, Johanne Baldewin, milite, Ricardo Lister, milite, Johanne Porte, milite, Johanne Spelman, milite, Walter Luke, milite, et Antonio FitzHerbert, milite, venit predictus Thomas More per Edmundum Walsingham militem, locumtenentem Willielmi Kingston militis, constabularii Turris domini regis Londoniensis, in cujus custodiam preantea ex causis predictis per dictum dominum regem commissus fuit, et per mandatum ipsius domini regis ad barram hic ductus in propria persona.

And now, that is, the day of Jupiter next after the said feast of St John the Baptist, in the twenty-seventh year of the reign of the now king, before the aforesaid Thomas Audley, knight, chancellor of England, Thomas, duke of Norfolk, Charles, duke of Suffolk, Henry, earl of Cumberland, Thomas, earl of Wiltshire, George, earl of Huntingdon, George, duke of Rocheford, Andrew, lord Windsor, Thomas Cromwell, esquire, his first secretary, William Paulet knight, John FitzJames, knight, John Baldwin, knight, Richard Lister, knight, John Port, knight, John Spelman, knight, Walter Luke, knight, and Anthony FitzHerbert, knight, there comes the aforesaid Thomas More, by Edmund Walsingham, knight, lieutenant of William Kingston, knight, Constable of the lord king's Tower of London, into whose custody beforehand he had been committed by the said lord king for the aforesaid causes, and by mandate of the same lord king led here to the bar in his own person.

Et statim de premissis sibi superius impositis allocutus, qualiter se velit inde acquietare, dicit quod ipse in nullo est inde culpabilis, et inde de bono et malo ponit se [super] patriam, etc.

Ideo venienda inde jurata coram prefatis justiciariis apud Westmonasteriensem predictum hac instante die Jovis proxima post dictum festum sancti Johannis Baptiste. Et qui, etc. Ad recogn. etc. Quia etc. Idem dies datus est prefato Thome More in custodia prefati constabularii.

Ad quos diem et locum coram prefatis justiciariis, etc., venit predictus Thomas More sub custodia prefati locumtenentis in propria persona sua. Et vicecomes retornavit nomina viginti quattuor juratorum, etc. Et jurati per eundem vicecomitem sic impannellati inter dictum regem et predictum Thomam More exacti, diligenter venerunt. Qui ad veritatem de premissis dicendum eliciti, triati, et jurati, dicunt super sacramentum suum quod predictus Thomas More de prodicione predicta est culpabilis. Et quod ipse nulla habet terras, tenuta, bona, neque catalla, etc.

Super quo instanter servjentes domini regis ad legem et ipsius regis attornatus juxta legis formam pecierunt versus eundem Thomam More judicium et execucionem super inde pro dicto domino rege habendum, etc.

Et super hoc visis et per curiam hic intellectis omnibus et singulis premissis, consideratus est quod predictus Thomas More ducatur per prefatum Edmundum Walsingham deputatum, etc., usque Turrim Londoniensem et inde per medium civitatis Londoniensis directe usque

And being immediately arraigned of the aforesaid matters alleged against him, and [asked] how he wishes to acquit himself theron, he states that he is in no way guilty therof, and thereupon he places himself for good and ill upon his country, etc.

Therefore a jury is to come hereon before the said justices at the aforesaid Westminster this very day of Jupiter [Thursday] next after the said feast of St John the Baptist. And who, etc. For recog., etc. Because, etc. The same day is set for the aforesaid Thomas More, in custody of the foresaid constable.

In which day and place there comes before the said justices, etc., the foresaid Thomas More in custody of the aforesaid lieutenant in his own person. And the sheriff returned the names of twenty-four jurors, etc. And the jurors, impaneled by the said sheriff, summoned to be between the said king and the aforesaid Thomas More, diligently came; and, being selected, examined, and sworn to tell the truth concerning the aforesaid matters, they say on their oath that the said Thomas More is guilty of the aforesaid treason, and that he has no lands or holdings or goods or chattels, etc.

Hereupon immediately the lord king's sergeants-at-law and the said king's attorney according to the due form of the law petitioned that judgment and execution against the said Thomas More be had on behalf of the said lord king, etc.

And upon this, with each and all of the foresaid matters seen and understood here by the court, it is decided that the foresaid Thomas More be led by the said Edmund Walsingham, deputy, etc., to the Tower of London, and thence be dragged through the midst of the city of London directly to the

ad furcas de Tyborne tragatur et super furcas illas suspendatur, et vivens ad terram prosternatur et interiora sua extra ventrum capiantur ipsoque vivente comburentur, et caput ejus amputetur, quodque corpus ejus in quatuor partes dividatur, et quod caput et quarteria sua ponantur ubi dominus rex assignare voluerit, etc.	gallows of Tyburn and hanged upon those gallows, and while alive be cast upon the earth and his entrails be taken from his belly and burned, with him still alive, and his head be struck off and his body divided into four parts, and that his head and quarters be placed where the lord king shall wish to assign them, etc.

(July 6, 1535: Execution at Tyburn by beheading.)

Document 16

More's Indictment[18]

§1 Grand jurors of Middlesex County on June 28, 1535, present as follows:

Middelsexa: Juratores presentant pro domino rege quod:	Middlesex: Jurors present for the lord king that:
[Alternate version]	[Alternate version]
Middelsexa: Inquisicio capta apud villam Westmonasteriensem, in comitatu predicto, coram prefatis Johanne FitzJames, milite, Johanne Baldewyn, milite, Ricardo Lister, milite, Johanne Porte, milite, Johanne Spelman, milite, Waltero Luke, milite, et Antonio Fitzherbert, milite, justiciariis, etc., dicto die Lunae proximo post festum Sancti Johannis Baptistae, per sacramentum Thomae Tayllour, Roberti Graunt, Willielmi Russell, Henrici Croke, Roberti Bowden, Eustacii Ripley, Cristoferi Proctour, Henrici Gaffeney, Johannis Brode, Willielmi Grimbilby, Johannis Apowell,[19] Johannis Miller, Johannis Wilkinson, Thome Colte, Willielmi Stevenson, Walteri Phelipps, juratorum. Qui dicunt super sacramentum suum:	Middlesex: Inquest taken in the town of Westminster, in the said county, before the aforesaid John FitzJames, knight, John Baldwin, knight, Richard Lister, knight, John Porte, knight, John Spelman, knight, Walter Luke, knight, and Anthony FitzHerbert, knight, justices, etc., on the said Monday next after the feast of St John the Baptist, by the oath of Thomas Taylor, Robert Grant, William Russell, Henry Croke, Robert Bowden, Eustace Ripley, Christopher Proctor, Henry Gaffeney, John Grove, William Grimbilby, John Apswell, John Miller, John Wilkinson, Thomas Colt, William Stevenson, Walter Phelipps, jurors. Who say on their oath:

---

[18] Edited by Elsie Vaughan Hitchcock, in *Harpsfield's Life of More* pp. 267–76. Translated by H. A. Kelly.
[19] Corrected from Hitchcock's "Apswell."

§2 Since, by the Act of Supremacy, 26 H8 (Nov. 1534) c. 1, the King was accepted as Supreme Head of the Church in England;

Cum per quendam actum in Parliamento domini nostri regis nunc (apud Londonium tercio die mensis Novembris, anno regni sui vicesimo primo inchoato, et abinde eodem tercio die Novembris usque ad villam Westmonasteriensem in Comitatu Middelsexae prorogato, et postea, per diversas prorogaciones, usque ad et in tercium diem Novembris, anno regni sui vicesimo sexto continuato, et tunc apud dictam villam Westmonasteriensem tento), editum, inter cetera auctoritate ejusdem Parliamenti inactitatum sit, quod idem dominus rex, heredes et successores sui, hujus regni reges accepti, acceptati, et reputati, erunt unicum Supremum Caput in terra Anglicanae Ecclesiae, habebuntque et gaudebunt, annexum et unitum imperiali coronae hujus regni tam titulum et stilum inde, quam omnia honores, dignitates, praeeminentias, jurisdicciones, privilegia, auctoritates, immunitates, commoda, et commoditates dictae dignitati Supremi Capitis ejusdem Ecclesiae incumbencia et pertinencia, prout in eodem actu, inter alia, plenius continetur;

Whereas, by an act issued in the Parliament of our present lord king held in London on November 3 at the beginning of the 21st year of his reign [1529], and thence on the same November 3 prorogued to the city of Westminster in Middlesex County, and later by successive prorogations continued up to November 3 in the 26th year of his reign [1534], and on that date, in the said city of Westminster, among other things was enacted by the authority of the same Parliament that the same lord king and his heirs and successors who are accepted, ratified, and held to be kings of this kingdom, will be the sole Supreme Head on earth of the English Church, and they will have and enjoy both the title and style of this kingdom annexed and united to the imperial crown, as well as all honors, dignities, preeminences, jurisdictions, privileges, authorities, immunities, benefits, and commodities incumbent and pertaining to the said dignity of Supreme Head of the same Church, as is more fully contained, among other things, in the same act.

§3 And since, by the Act of Treason Concerning the Supremacy, 26 H8 (Nov. 1534) c. 13, it was made high treason to deprive the king of his titles:

Cumque per quemdam alterum actum, in dicto Parliamento dicto anno vicesimo sexto tento, editum, inter cetera inactitatum sit quod si aliqua persona aut aliquae personae, post primum diem Februarii tunc proximum sequentis, maliciose optaverit, voluerit, seu desideraverit per verba vel scripta, aut arte imaginaverit, inventaverit, practicaverit, sive attemptaverit aliquod dampnum corporale fiendum aut committendum regalissimae personae domini regis, reginae, aut eorum heredibus apparentibus, vel ad deprivandos eos, aut eorum aliquem, de dignitate, titulo, seu nomine regalium statuum suorum, quod tunc quaelibet talis persona et personae sic offendentes in aliquo praemissorum post dictum primum diem Februarii, atque eorum auxiliatores, consentores, consiliarii, et abettatores, inde legittime convicti existentes, secundum leges et consuetudines hujus regni adjudicabuntur proditores; et quod quaelibet talis offensa in aliquo praemissorum quae committeretur aut fieret, post dictum primum diem Februarii, reputabitur, acceptabitur, et adjudicabitur alta prodicio; et offensores in eisdem ac eorum auxiliatores, consentores, consiliarii, et abettatores, legitime convicti existentes de aliqua tali offensa qualis praedicitur habebunt et pacientur tales poenas mortis et alias poenalitates quales limitatae sunt et consuetae in casibus altae prodicionis, prout in dicto altero actu manifeste patet;

And whereas, by another act issued by the said Parliament held in the said 26th year, among other things was enacted, that if any person or any persons after the next February 1 should maliciously choose, wish, or desire, by words or writing, or by craft imagine, invent, practice, or attempt, any corporal harm to be done or committed against the most royal person of the lord king, the queen, or their heirs apparent, or to deprive them or any of them of dignity, title or name of their royal conditions, then each such person and persons so offending in any of the aforementioned after the said February 1, and also their helpers, consenters, counselors, and abettors, who are legitimately convicted of such according to the laws and customs of this realm shall be adjudged traitors; and that each such offense in any of the aforementioned which is committed or done after the said February 1 shall be held, accepted, and adjudged high treason; and offenders in them, and their helpers, consenters, counselors, and abettors, being legitimately convicted of any such offense as is aforementioned shall have and suffer such pains of death and other penalties that are specified and accustomed in cases of high treason, as manifestly appears in the said other act;

§4 Nevertheless, Thomas More on May 7, 1535, seduced by diabolical instigation, maliciously attempted to deprive King Henry of his title of Supreme Head when, before Thomas Cromwell and others, upon being asked whether he approved of the king as Supreme Head, he maliciously remained silent and refused to give a direct answer.

Quidam tamen Thomas More, nuper de Chelchehith, in Comitatu Middelsexae, miles, Deum prae oculis non habens, set instigacione diabolica seductus, septimo die Maji, anno regni dicti domini regis vicesimo septimo, statutorum praedictorum satis sciolus, false, proditorie, et maliciose, apud Turrim Londoniensem, in comitatu praedicto, imaginans, inventans, practicans, et attemptans, atque volens et desiderans, contra legianciae suae debitum, praefatum serenissimum dominum nostrum regem de dignitate, titulo, et nomine status sui regalis, videlicet, de dignitate, titulo, et nomine suis Supremi Capitis in terra Anglicanae Ecclesiae, deprivare, dicto septimo die Maji, apud dictam Turrim Londoniensem, in comitatu praedicto, coram Thoma Crumwell, Armigero, primario secretario domini regis, Thoma Bedill, clerico, Johanne Tregonell, legum doctore, consiliariis dicti domini regis, et coram diversis aliis personis ejusdem domini regis veris subditis, per mandatum ipsius domini regis examinatus et interrogatus an ipse eundem dominum regem Supremum Caput in terra Ecclesiae Anglicanae accipiebat, acceptabat, et reputabat, et eum sic accipere, acceptare, et reputare, vellet, secundum formam et effectum statuti supradicti prius recitati, idem Thomas adtunc et ibidem maliciose penitus silebat, responsumque directum ad illud interrogatorium facere recusabat, et haec verba Anglicana sequencia dictis domini regis veris subditis

Nevertheless one Thomas More, late of Chelsea in the County of Middlesex, knight, not having God before his eyes but seduced by diabolical instigation, on May 7 of the 27th year of the reign of the said lord king, sufficiently aware of the aforesaid statutes, falsely, treasonously, and maliciously, in the Tower of London in the said county, imagining, inventing, wishing, and desiring, against the duty of his allegiance, to deprive the said serene lord our king of a dignity, title, and name of his royal condition, namely, his dignity, title, and name of Supreme Head on earth of the English Church, on the said May 7 in the said Tower of London in the aforesaid county, in the presence of Thomas Cromwell, Esquire, first secretary of the lord king, Thomas Bedill, cleric, John Tregonwell, doctor of laws, councilors of the said lord king, and before divers other persons, loyal subjects of the same lord king, being examined and interrogated by mandate of the same lord king as to whether he received, accepted, and held the same lord king to be Supreme Head on earth of the English Church, and wished to receive, accept, and hold him such, according to the form and effect of the aforesaid statute first recited, the same Thomas then and there maliciously remained completely silent and refused to give a direct response to that question, and he spoke these following English words, namely, "I will not meddle

adtunc et ibidem edicebat, videlicet, "I will not meddill with any such matters, for I am fully determined to serve God and to think uppon His Passion and my passage out of this worlde";

with any such matters, for I am fully determined to serve God and to think upon His Passion and my passage out of this world";

§5 And on May 12, More maliciously wrote to Bishop John Fisher, consenting to Fisher's denial of the supremacy, telling him of his own silence, and calling the act a two-edged sword;

Posteaque, videlicet duodecimo die dictae mensis Maji, anno vicesimo septimo supradicto, praefatus Thomas More, sciens quendam Johannem Fissher, clericum, tunc, et diu antea, in dicta Turre Londoniensi, pro diversis grandibus misprisionibus per ipsum Johannem erga dicti domini nostri regis regiam majestatem perpetratis, fore incarceratum et detentum, ac per dictos domini regis veros subditos, de ejus accepcione, acceptacione, et reputacione ejusdem domini regis in praemissis fuisse examinatum, eundemque Johannem false, proditorie, et maliciose, expresse negasse praefatum dominum regem sic accipere, acceptare, et reputare Supremum Caput in terra Ecclesiae Anglicanae fore, idemque Thomas More, existimans se ipsum et praefatum Johannem Fissher de praemissis alias ex verisimili tunc fore examinandos et interrogandos, diversas literas dicto duodecimo die Maji, apud dictam Turrim Londoniensem, in praedicto Comitatu Middelsexae, continuando maliciam suam praedictam, false, maliciose, et proditorie scripsit, easque praefato Johanni Fissher in dicta Turre Londoniense tunc existenti porrexit, et, per quendam Georgium Golde, eisdem die, anno, et loco transmisit et deliberari fecit; per quas quidem literas praedictus Thomas More false,

And afterwards, namely, on the 12th day of the said month of May in the aforesaid 27th year, the aforesaid Thomas More, knowing that one John Fisher, cleric, was then, and for a long time before, incarcerated in the said Tower of London for various misprisions perpetrated by the said John against the said lord our king's royal majesty, and had been examined by the said true subjects of the lord king concerning his reception, acceptance, and holding of the same lord king as aforesaid, and that the same John falsely, treasonously, and maliciously expressly refused to receive, accept, and hold that the foresaid lord king was Supreme Head on earth of the English Church, and the same Thomas More, thinking that he himself and the foresaid John Fisher would likely be examined and interrogated then again on the foregoing, continuing his aforesaid malice, falsely, maliciously, and treasonously wrote various letters on the said 12th day of May in the said Tower of London in the said county of Middlesex, and directed them to the foresaid John Fisher then being in the said Tower of London, and through one George Gold on the same day and year and in the same place transmitted them and had them delivered; through which letters the foresaid Thomas More falsely, maliciously, and

maliciose, et proditorie praefato Johanni Fissher in dicta ejus falsa prodicione consulebat et consenciebat, et, per easdem intimans eidem Johanni dictam silenciam quam idem Thomas More, ut praefertur, interrogatus habuisset, responsumque suum negatum in verbis Anglicanis supra scriptis expressis, verbis scriptis revelans, et, insuper, per easdem literas false, proditorie, et maliciose scribens et asserens haec verba Anglicana, videlicet, "The act of Parlement" – dictum actum posterius recitatum innuens – "is like a swerde with two edgis, for if a man answere one wey it will confounde his soule, and if he answere the other wey it will confounde his body";

treasonously counseled the aforesaid John Fisher in his said false treason, and consented to it, and, through the same letters, intimating to the same John the said silence which the same Thomas More, as stated above, maintained when questioned, and revealing to him in written words his response of refusal in the spoken English words written above, and, moreover, through the same letters falsely, treasonously, and maliciously writing and asserting these English words, namely, "The act of Parliament" – meaning the said act recited above in the second place – "is like a sword with two edges, for if a man answer one way it will confound his soul, and if he answer the other way it will confound his body";

§6 And on May 26, More wrote again to Fisher, warning him not to use these words, lest there appear to be a confederacy between them;

Postmodumque praefatus Thomas More, metuens ne contingeret praefatum Johannem Fisher in ejus responso, supraitterata examinacione ipsius Johannis fienda, praedicta verba, per ipsum Thomam eidem Johanni Fissher, ut praefertur, scripta consiliariis dicti domini regis eloqui, idem Thomas More, apud Turrim praedictam, vicesimo sexto die Maji anno vicesimo septimo supradicto, per ejus alias literas scriptas et praefato Johanni Fissher directas, et apud Turrim praedictam diliberatas, eundem Johannem Fissher false, maliciose, et proditorie desiderabat, quatenus idem Johannes responsum suum secundum ejus proprium animum faceret, et cum aliquo tali responso quale idem Thomas praefato Johanni Fissher antea scripsisset nullatenus intromitteret, ne forsan

And later, the aforesaid Thomas More, fearing lest it happen that the aforesaid John Fisher in his response, when the renewed examination of the said John was made, would say to the councilors of the said lord king the aforesaid words written to the same John by the said Thomas, as stated above, the same Thomas More on the 26th day of May in abovesaid 27th year, through other letters of his directed to the aforesaid John Fisher and delivered in the foresaid Tower, falsely, maliciously, and treasonously desired the same John Fisher that the same John make his response according to his own mind, and in no way put forth any such response as the same Thomas had before written to the aforesaid John Fisher, lest perhaps he give occasion to the said Councillors of the Lord King for thinking that there was some

dictis consiliariis domini regis occasionem putandi praeberet quod aliqualis erat inter eosdem Thomam et Johannem confoederacio;

conspiracy between the same Thomas and John;

§7 Nevertheless, on June 3 Fisher remained silent on the question and called the act a two-edged sword;

Attamen, ex dictis literis praefati Thomae More prius scriptis et dicto Johanni Fissher ut praemittitur porrectis et deliberatis, ita insecutum est, videlicet, idem Johannes Fissher, per dictas literas praefati Thomae More false, maliciose, et proditorie doctus et instructus, et exinde quodammodo animatus, postea, videlicet, tercio die Junii, anno vicesimo septimo supradicto, apud Turrim praedictam, per Thomas Audeley, militem, cancellarium Angliae, Charolum, ducem Suffolciencem, Thomam, comitem Wiltescirensem, dicti domini regis nobiles subditos et consiliarios, et alios ejusdem domini regis venerabiles subditos et consilarios, denuo de praemissis examinatus et interrogatus, penitus silebat responsumque directum ad id facere nolebat, sed haec verba Anglicana sequencia adtunc et ibidem dictis nobilibus et venerabilibus domini regis subditis et consiliariis false, proditorie, et maliciose edicebat, videlicet, "I will not meddill with that matter, for the statute is like a two-edged sworde, and, if I shuld answere one wey, I shulde offende my conscience; and if I shulde answere the other wey I shulde put my life in jeopardie; wherfore I will make no answere to that matter";

However, from the said letters of the foresaid Thomas More previously written, as stated above, and directed and delivered to the said John Fisher, it followed thus, that the same John Fisher, falsely, maliciously, and treasonously taught and instructed by the said letters of the foresaid Thomas More, and thence in a certain way animated by them, later, namely on June 3 of the foresaid 27th year, in the foresaid Tower, being examined and interrogated again on the foregoing, by Thomas Audley, knight, chancellor of England, Charles, duke of Suffolk, and Thomas, earl of Wiltshire, noble subjects and councilors of the said lord king, and other venerable subjects of the same lord king, remained completely silent and was unwilling to give a direct answer to it, but falsely, treasonously, and maliciously spoke these following English words then and there to the said noble and venerable subjects and councilors of the lord king, namely, "I will not meddle with that matter, for the statute is like a two-edged sword, and, if I should answer one way, I should offend my conscience; and if I should answer the other way I should put my life in jeopardy; wherefore I will make no answer to that matter";

§8 And likewise on June 3 More maliciously persevered in his silence;

Praefatusque Thomas More, similiter dicto tercio die Junii, anno vicesimo septimo supradicto, apud Turrim praedictam, per dictos domini regis nobiles et venerabiles subditos et consilarios iterum de praemissis interrogatus, in dicta ejus silencia perseverabat, directumque responsum ad praemissa facere nolebat;

And the aforesaid Thomas More, also on the said June 3 of the abovesaid 27th year, in the foresaid Tower, again questioned about the foregoing by the said noble and venerable subjects and councilors of the lord king, persevered in his said silence, and was unwilling to give a direct response to the foregoing;

§9 Also on June 3 More likewise called the act a two-edged sword.

Immo, false, proditorie, et maliciose, adtunc et ibidem imaginans, inventans, practicans, et attemptans, atque volens et desiderans, praefatum dominum nostrum regem de dignitate, titulo, et nomine status sui regalis supradicti deprivare, sedicionemque et malignitatem in cordibus verorum subditorum domini regis erga eundem dominum regem inserere et generare, praefatis nobilibus et venerabilibus dicti domini regis subditis et consiliariis adtunc et ibidem subsequencia verba Anglicana palam dicebat, videlicet, "The lawe and statute whereby the king is made Supreme Hed, as is aforesaid, be like a swerde with two edges; for, if a man sey that the same lawes be good, then it is dangerous to the soule; and if he say contrary to the seid statute, then it is dethe to the body. Wherfore I will make therunto noon other answere, because I will not be occasion of the shortting of my life."

Rather, falsely, treasonously, and maliciously then and there imagining, inventing, practicing, and attempting, and willing and desiring, to deprive the aforesaid lord our king of a dignity, title, and name of his royal condition, and to raise up and generate sedition and malignity in the hearts of true subjects of the lord king against the same lord king, he openly spoke to the aforesaid subjects and councilors of the said lord king then and there the following English words, namely, "The law and statute whereby the king is made Supreme Head, as is aforesaid, be like a sword with two edges; for, if a man say that the same laws be good, then it is dangerous to the soul; and if he say contrary to the said statute, then it is death to the body. Wherefore I will make thereunto none other answer, because I will not be occasion of the shorting of my life."

§10   Moreover, in order to conceal their treason, More and Fisher burned each letter as soon as it had been read.

Et insuper juratores praedicti dicunt quod praefati Thomas More et Johannes Fissher, ad eorum supradictum falsum et nephandissimum proditorium propositum celandum, omnes et omnimodas literas alterutrum scriptas et deliberatas, et eorum unus et alter, immediate post lecturas earundem, combussit.

And in addition, the foresaid jurors say that the aforesaid Thomas More and John Fisher, both the one and the other of them, to conceal their above-stated false and nefarious treasonous proposal, immediately after reading the letters written and delivered by each to the other, burned them.

§11   On June 12, More told Richard Rich that subjects could not be obligated by an act of Parliament making the king Supreme Head.

(a) Et, post haec omnia et singula praemissa, ut praemittitur, peracta et dicta, videlicet, duodecimo die Junii, anno vicesimo septimo supradicto, accessit ad praefatum Thomam More, in praedictam Turrim Londoniensem, Ricardus Riche, generalis solicitator dicti domini regis, habitoque adtunc et ibidem inter eosdem Thomam More et Ricardum Riche colloquio de diversis praemissa tangentibus, idem Ricardus Riche caritative movebat praefatum Thomam More quatenus se vellet actibus et legibus suprascriptis conformare. Ad quod idem Thomas, respondendo praefato Ricardo Riche, dicebat, "Consciencia vestra salvabit vos, et consciencia mea salvabit me."

(b) Praefatusque Ricardus Riche, adtunc et ibidem protestans quod tunc non habebat commissionem sive mandatum cum eodem Thoma More de materia illa tractare sive communicare, eundem Thomam More adtunc et ibidem interrogabat, si inactitatum fuisset auctoritate Parliamenti quod idem Richardus Riche esset rex, et quod si quis id negaret prodicio esset, qualis esset

(a) And, after each and all of these aforesaid things were done and said, as stated above, on the 12th day of June of the said 27th year, Richard Rich, the general solicitor of the said lord king, came to the foresaid Thomas More in the said Tower of London, and a conversation concerning various things touching on the aforesaid matters was held then and there between the same Thomas More and Richard Rich, whereupon the same Richard Rich charitably urged the aforesaid Thomas More that he be willing to conform himself to the above-written acts and laws. To this, the same Thomas said, responding to the aforesaid Richard Rich, "Your conscience will save you, and my conscience will save me."

(b) And the said Richard Rich, then and there protesting that he had no commission or mandate to talk or converse with the said Thomas More about this matter, asked him, if it were enacted by the authority of Parliament that he himself, that is, Richard Rich, were king, and that it would be treason if anyone denied it, what would be the offense in the said Thomas More if the same Thomas said that the said Richard

offensa in praefato Thoma More si idem Thomas diceret quod praefatus Ricardus Riche erat rex? Pro certo, ulterius dicebat idem Ricardus, in consciencia ejus quod nulla esset offensa, sed quod idem Thomas More obligatus erat sic dicere, et eundem Ricardum acceptare, pro eo quod consensus praefati Thomae More per actum Parliamenti erat obligatus. Ad quod praefatus Thomas More, adtunc et ibidem respondendo, dicebat, quod ipse offenderet si diceret non, quia obligatus esset per actum, pro eo quod consensum suum ad id praebere potuit. Sed dicebat quod idem casus erit casus levis.

(c) Quamobrem idem Thomas adtunc et ibidem praefato Ricardo Riche dicebat quod ipse alium casum sublimiorem proponere vellet, sic dicens, "Posito quod per Parliamentum inactitatum foret quod Deus non esset Deus, et quod si quis impugnare vellet actum illum, foret prodicio; si interrogaretur quaestio a vobis, Ricarde Riche, 'velitis dicere quod Deus non erat Deus,' accordante statuto, et si sic diceretis, non offenderetis?"

(d) Ad quod idem Ricardus, respondens praefato Thomae More, adtunc et ibidem dicebat, "Immo, pro certe; quia impossibile est fiendum quod Deus non esset Deus. Et quia casus vester adeo sublimis existit, proponam vobis hunc casum mediocrem, videlicet: Novistis quia dominus noster rex constitutus est Supremum Caput in eerra Ecclesiae Anglicanae; et quare non deberetis vos, Magister More, eum sic affirmare et acceptare, tam sic quam in casu praemisso quae ego praefectus eram rex? In quo casu conceditis quod obligaremini sic me affirmare et acceptare regem."

Rich was king? Certainly (the same Richard continued further), there would be no offense in his conscience, but rather the said Thomas More was obliged to say so and accept the same Richard, because the consent of the said Thomas More was obligated by the act of Parliament. The said Thomas More then and there responded and said that he would indeed commit an offense if he denied it, since he was able to give his consent to it. But he said that this case will be a trivial case.

(c) Therefore, the same Thomas then and there said to the aforesaid Richard Rich that he would propose a more lofty case, saying thus: "Let us say that it was enacted by Parliament that God was not God, and that if anyone wished to impugn that act, it would be treason; if the question were put to you, Richard Rich, 'Do you wish to say that God is not God,' in accord with the statute, and you said yes, would you not commit an offense?"

(d) To which the same Richard, responding to the aforesaid Thomas More, then and there said, "Yes, certainly, because it is impossible to bring it about that God be not God. And because your case is on such a high level, I will propose to you this middle-level case: You know that our lord king has been constituted as Supreme Head on earth of the English Church; and why should not you, Master More, affirm and accept him as such in this case, just as in the foregoing case in which I was selected to be king? In that case you concede that you would be obligated to affirm and accept me as king."

(e) Ad quod praefatus Thomas More false, proditorie, et maliciose in dictis ejus prodicione et malicia perseverans, praedictumque ejus proditorium et maliciosum propositum et appetitum praeferre et defendere volens, praefato Ricardo Riche adtunc et ibidem sic respondebat, videlicet, quod casus illi non erant consimiles, quia rex per Parliamentum fieri potest, et per Parliamentum deprivari potest, ad quem actum quilibet subditus, ad Parliamentum existens, suum praebeat consensum. Sed ad primaciae casum, subditus non potest obligari, quia consensum suum ab eo ad Parliamentum praebere non potest. Et quamquam rex sic acceptus sit in Anglia, plurimae tamen partes exterae idem non affirmant."

(e) To this the said Thomas More falsely, treasonously, and maliciously, persevering in his said treachery and malice, and desiring to put forth and defend his aforesaid treasonous and malicious proposal and appetite, responded to the aforesaid Richard Rich that those cases are not like, because a king can be made by Parliament, and can be deprived by Parliament, to which act any subject being at the Parliament may give his consent; but to the case of a primacy, the subject cannot be bound, because he cannot give his consent from him in Parliament. And although the king were generally accepted as such in England, yet most outer parts do not affirm it.

§12 Thus the jurors say that Thomas More maliciously contrived to deprive the king of his title of Supreme Head.

Sicque Juratores praedicti dicunt quod praefatus Thomas More false, proditorie, et maliciose, arte imaginavit, inventavit, practicavit, et attemptavit praefatum serenissimum dominum nostrum regem de dictis dignitate, titulo, et nomine supradicti status sui regalis, videlicet, de dignitate, titulo, et nomine suis Supremi Capitis in terra Anglicanae Ecclesiae, penitus deprivare, in ipsius domini regis contemptum manifestum et Coronae suae regiae derogacionem, contra formam et effectum statutorum praedictorum, et contra pacem ejusdem domini regis.

And thus the aforesaid jurors say that the aforesaid Thomas More falsely, traitorously, and maliciously by craft schemed, contrived, practiced, and attempted to fundamentally deprive the said serene lord our king of the said dignity, title, and name of his aforesaid royal status, namely, of his dignity, title, and name of Supreme Head on earth of the English Church, to the manifest contempt of the same lord king and derogation of his royal crown, against the form and effect of the aforesaid statutes, and against the peace of the selfsame lord king.

Document 17

Guildhall Report[20]

§1(a) More is charged

Thomas Morus, nuper regni Britannici cancellarius, post carceris detentionem quindecim mensium, Calendis Julii anno millesimo quingentesimo tricesimo quinto, ad magistratus ac judices ordinatos per regem fuit adductus. Quo praesente accusationes in ipsum publice recitatae sunt.

Thomas More, recently chancellor of the kingdom of Britain, after being confined in prison for fifteen months, on July 1, 1535, was brought before the magistrates and judges appointed by the king. When he was present, the accusations against him were publicly recited.

(b) Norfolk offers a pardon

Continuo dux Nortfordiae illum hujusmodi verbis allocutus est: "Vides, More, te quidem hac ex parte in regiam majestatem graviter deliquisse. Nichilominus tamen de ipsius clementia et benignitate confidimus, si poenitere volueris tuamque hanc temerariam opinionem, cui pertinacissime adhaesisti, in melium commutare, te delicti remissionem facile ab illo consecuturum."

Immediately, the duke of Norfolk spoke to him such words as these: "More, you see that you have gravely offended against the royal majesty in this matter. Nevertheless, we have confidence in his clemency and bounty that if you should be willing to repent and change for the better this rash opinion of yours, which you have so pertinaciously adhered to, you will easily gain forgiveness of your fault from him."

(c) More points out his physical weakness

Cui Morus: "Magnifici viri, maximas vobis gratias habeo, de perquam erga me benevolentia. Verum istud solum Deum optimum maximum oro, ut ipsius adjutus ope, in hac recta mea opinione ad mortem usque perseverare valeam. Quantum autem ad accusationes quibus oneror attinet, vereor ne vel ingenium vel

To this More replied: "Noble sirs, my very great thanks to you for your exceeding benevolence to me. But I ask only this of the great good God, that by His help I may be able to persevere in my right opinion until death. But as for what concerns the accusations with which I am charged, I fear that neither my mental ability, nor memory,

---

[20] The text of Guildhall MS 1231, pp. 4–15, is recovered from the composite Latin text constructed by Derrett, "Neglected Versions," pp. 214–23. In the notes, G = Guildhall MS; NQ = *Novitates Quaedam* (pamphlet, ?Paris 1536). Translated by H. A. Kelly

memoria vel verba ad explicationem [non] sufficiant, cum non solum impediat articulorum prolixitas et magnitudo, [verum][21] etiam diuturna in carcere detentio, necnon aegritudo debilitasque corporis quibus nunc sum affectus."

nor words will suffice to explain them, because I am impeded not only by the prolixity and extensiveness of the articles, but also by my long detention in prison and the illness and bodily weakness that now afflict me."

§2(a) More responds to the indictment, the first part concerning the king's marriage

Tum jussu magistratus allata est sella, in qua cum resedisset, hunc in modum prosecutus est: "Quantum ad priorem partem accusationis pertinet, quae habet me, quo magis animi mei contra regem malevolentiam ostenderem, in contentione de secundo ejus matrimonio perpetuo obstetisse serenissimae ejus Majestati, nichil habeo aliud respondere nisi quod antea dixi, videlicet quicquid in ea materia dixi, id me urgente conscientia dixisse. Nec enim debebam nec volebam [quidem][22] principem meum celare veritatem. Quod nisi fecissem, hostem me illi, non fidelem ministrum exhibuissem. Ob quod peccatum, si tamen peccatum dici decet, adjudicatus sum perpetuis carceribus, quibus jam totis quindecim mensibus sum detentus, bonis meis praeterea fisco addictus.

Then a chair was brought by order of one of the magistrates, and, when he had seated himself in it, More continued as follows: "As for what pertains to the first part of the accusation, which has it that, to show the greatest possible malice of my mind against the king, I was a constant opponent to his serene Majesty in the contention over his second marriage, I have nothing to say other than what I have said before; and that is, that whatever I spoke in that matter, I did it at the urging of my conscience. For it did not behoove me, nor did I wish it, to conceal the truth from my prince. If I had not acted so, I would have been an enemy to him, not a faithful servant. Now for this sin, if it is proper to call it a sin, I was adjudged to perpetual imprisonment, in which I have now been detained for fifteen months, and my goods besides confiscated.

---

[21] *NQ*; G: *unde.*
[22] *NQ.*

(b) More cites the first charge concerning silence about the king's supremacy

"Solum ad praecipuum caput accusationis respondeo. Dicitis me commeruisse poenam quam inflixit statutum in postremo procerum Conventu factum, ex quo ego in custodia fui detentus, eo quod malicioso, falso, ac infido animo laeserim Regiam Majestatem et nomen et titulos et honorem and dignitatem quae illi praedicto Conventu seu Concilio consensu omnium fuerunt attributa, quo ille receptus est post Jesum Christum in Supremum Caput Ecclesiae Anglicanae; atque ante[23] omnia quod[24] mihi objicitis me nichil aliud voluisse respondere secretario regis et regiae majestatis honorabili Consilio, quum me interrogabat quaenam esset mea de illo decreto sententia, quam, ex quo jam essem mundo mortuus, me hujusmodi rebus non occupare animum, sed tantum meditari de Passione Domini Jesu Christi.

"I reply only to the main heading of the accusation. You say that I have merited the penalty inflicted by the statute passed in the last Parliament of our leaders, for which I was now held in custody, for the reason that, with malicious, false, and faithless mind, I injured the royal majesty and name and titles and honor and dignity which they in the aforesaid Parliament or Council attributed to the king, by which he is considered to be Supreme Head after Jesus Christ of the English Church; and, above all, that you object to me that I wished to answer nothing to the secretary of the king and to the honorable Council of the royal majesty, when he asked me what my opinion was about that statute, other than that, because I was now dead to the world, I did not occupy my mind with such things but only meditated on the Passion of Our Lord Jesus Christ.

(c) More says that such silence is no offense

"Ad quod clare respondeo vobis, hujusmodi silentio me morti adjudicari non licere, quum quidem neque vestrum decretum neque quicquid[25] legum in toto orbe quemquam jure supplicio afficere potest,[26] nisi quis vel dicto vel facto crimen admiserit, cum silentio nulla poena legibus sit constituta."

"To which I clearly respond to you that it is not lawful for me to be judged to death for such silence on my part, because neither your statute nor anything in the laws of the whole world can rightly afflict anyone with punishment, unless one has committed a crime in word or deed, since laws have constituted no penalty for silence."

---

[23] *NQ*; G: *autem.*
[24] G: *quae.*
[25] G: *quicquid est.*
[26] G: *possunt.*

§3 Attorney General Hales says such silence shows disapproval

Tum regius procurator, suscipiens sermonem, "Hujusmodi," inquit, "silentium certum aliquod indicium erat, nec obscura significatio, malignae alicujus cogitationis contra ipsum decretum, propterea quod singuli subjecti, ut fideles suo principi, interrogati [in] sententiam super illo decreto, obligantur aperte et sine dissimulatione respondere ipsum esse bonum ac sanctum."

Then the royal proctor started to speak, saying, "Such silence was a sure indication and a not obscure sign of some malign thinking about the statute, because all subjects, being faithful to their prince, when interrogated on their view concerning the statute, are obliged to respond openly, and without dissimulation, that it is good and holy."

§4 More: Silence shows approval

Tum Morus, "At si," inquit, "verum est quod jus commune ait, 'Qui tacet consentire videtur,' meum istud silentium plus approbavit vestrum statutum quam infirmavit. Quousque vero fidelis quisque tenetur et obligatur respondere, et cetera: respondeo, multo magis ad officium boni viri et fidelis subditi pertinere, ut suae conscientiae ac perpetuae saluti consulat, et rectae rationis praescriptum sequatur,[27] quam ullius[28] alterius rei habeat rationem, propterea quod hujusmodi conscientia qualis est mea suo principi nullam praebet offensionem neque seditionem excitat [– illud vobis asseverans, nulli mortalium meam conscientiam fuisse apertam]."[29]

Then More replied, "But if it is true what universal law says, 'One who keeps silent seems to consent,' then that silence of mine gave approval to that statute of yours more than it weakened it. But as for all the faithful being bound and obliged to make response, etc., I answer that there is a much greater obligation on the part of a good man and faithful subject to consult his own conscience and eternal salvation, and to follow the prescriptions of reason, than to take account of any other thing, especially since the kind of conscience that I have offers no offense to its prince and stirs up no sedition [– asserting this to you, that my conscience had not been opened to any mortal]."

§5 More replies to the second accusation, concerning letters to Fisher

"Quod autem in secunda parte accusor contravenisse decreto et in ejus abolitionem esse machinatus, scriptis ad episcopum Roffensem

"As for what I am accused of in the second part, that I contravened the statute and worked for its abolition in writings to the bishop of Rochester,

---

[27] *NQ*; G: *sequamur*.
[28] *NQ*; G: *illius*.
[29] The bracketed words are in *NQ*.

octonis literis quibus illum contra vestrum decretum armaverim: etiam atque etiam optarim illas literas publice fuisse recitatas. Sed quum, sicut vos dicitis, concrematae sunt per eundem episcopum, ipse vobis ultro ipsarum argumenta commemorabo. In quibusdam tractabantur res familiares, sicut nostra vetus consuetudo et amicitia postulabat. Una ex illis responsum habebat ad ipsius epistolam, qua scire desiderabat quonam modo respondissem in carcere quum primum examinarer super dicto decreto. Cui respondi me meam exonerasse conscientiam et rationem esse secutum, idque ut et ipse ageret admonebam. Haec fuit, ita mihi Deus sit propitius, mearum literarum sententia, nec ob illa debet per decretum vestrum quicquam morte[30] dignum censeri."

by means of eight letters in which I fortified him against your statute: again and again I wished for those letters to have been publicly recited. But since, as you tell me, they were burned by the said bishop, I myself will sum up for you their contents. Some of them dealt with familiar matters, such as our old custom and friendship called for. One of them responded to his request to know how I answered when first examined on the statute. I replied that I had exonerated my conscience and followed reason, and I urged him to do the same. This was, so help me God, the purport of my letters, and there is nothing on their account that should be judged worthy of death under your statute."

§6 More replies to the third accusation, on collusion with Fisher ("two-edged sword")

"Quod vero ad tertium articulum attinet, qui continet me quum a Senatu examinarer respondisse vestrum decretum simile esse gladio ancipiti, ut qui obtemperaret periclitaretur de salute animae, qui adversaretur amitteret vitam; ac eadem respondisse (sicut dicitis) episcopum Roffensem, ex quo appareat hoc inter nos de composito agi, utroque eodem modo respondente: ad eam partem[31] accusationis respondeo me non simpliciter sed sub conditione esse locutum, videlicet, si esset aliquod decretum simile gladio

"As for what pertains to the third article, which says that when I was interrogated by the Council I responded that your statute is like a two-edged sword, so that one who obeyed it imperiled the salvation of his soul, while one who opposed it would lose his life; and that the bishop of Rochester (you say), responded in the same way, from which it should appear that this was done by agreement between us, both of us responding in the same way: to this part of the accusation I respond that I was not speaking straightforwardly but only conditionally; that is, if there should

---

[30] G: *morti.*
[31] G: *ea parte.*

ancipiti, quonammodo quisquam hominum sibi possit cavere ne in alterutram aciem incurrat? Porro quid responderit episcopus Roffensis equidem ignoro, et fieri potest ut eodem modo responderit, sed illud non esse factum ex ulla conspiratione, sed potius ex ingenii disciplinarumque similitudine processit. Hoc autem pro certissimo creditote me numquam contra decretum vestrum maliciose vel dixisse aut fecisse. Interim tamen fieri potuit ut multa de me ad concitandum mihi odium ad regis Majestatem depravate ac maliciose sint prolata."

be some statute that was like a two-edged sword, how could any person take care against coming up against one edge or the other? But what the bishop of Rochester responded, I do not know. It may be that he responded in the same way, but it was not done through any conspiracy, but rather it occurred because of our similar minds and education. But believe me most assuredly on this point, that I never said or did anything maliciously against your statute. In the meantime, however, it could be that many things have been viciously and maliciously spoken about me to arouse hatred against me on the part of his royal Majesty."

§7 The jury is summoned and sent to deliberate, returning a guilty verdict

His dictis, continuo duodecim viri, de more gentis Britannicae, per ministrum publicum sunt vocati, quibus data sunt capita accusationis, ut dispicerent ac judicarent, an Morus maliciose contra Decretum peccasset.

Qui sedentes prope quarta horae parte, deliberatione inter se habita, ut redierunt in conspectum principum ac judicum delegatorum, rogati ecquid sentirent de reo, responderunt, "Gylthi," quod lingua Britannica sonat, "Condemnandus," aut "Dignus est morte."

This said, immediately twelve men were called by the public minister, after the custom of the British nation, to whom were given the chapters of accusation, to deliberate and judge whether More had maliciously sinned against the statute.

And they, sitting about a quarter of an hour, after deliberation was had among them, when they returned to the sight of the princes and judges delegate, on being asked what they thought about the accused party, responded, "Guilty," which in British speech means, "He is to be condemned," or, "He is deserving of death."

§8 After sentence, More reveals his mind

Mox cancellarius pronunciavit sententiam juxta formulam nuperrimi decreti. Quibus peractis, Morus sic orsus est loqui. "Quando," inquit, "morti sum adjudicatus, rectene an secus, novit Deus, ad exonerandam meam conscientiam

Soon the chancellor pronounced the sentence according to the formula of the recent statute. When all was finished, More arose to speak, saying: "Since I have been adjudged to death, whether rightly or wrongly, God knows, for the exonerating of my conscience I

libere vobis super vestro decreto verba faciam, meque totis septem annis affirmo omni studio in cognitione hujus argumenti incubuisse, nec tamen reperisse apud ullum probatum Ecclesiae doctorem aut posse aut debere quemquam hominum prophanum caput esse ordinis ecclesiastici."

would willingly say some words to you concerning your statute. I affirm that I have spent all my study during the whole of the last seven years, and I have never found an approved doctor of the Church to hold that any layman is the head of an ecclesiastical order."

§9 The Chancellor cites opinion against More

Hic cancellarius, interrupto ejus sermone, 'Num tu," inquit, "vis prudentior ac religiosior esse quam omnes episcopi, tota nobilitas, et universus populus regi et regno est subjectus?"

At this point the chancellor interrupted his speech and said, "Do you wish to be more prudent and religious than all the bishops, the whole nobility, and all of the people who are subjects of the king and his kingdom?"

§10 More cites greater opinion on his side

Cui Morus: "Pro uno episcopo qui facit vobiscum, mihi sunt facile centum, idque ex eorum numero qui relati sunt inter divos. Ac pro uno Concilio ac decreto vestro, quod quale sit Deus optimus maximo novit, mecum sunt omnia concilia generalia quae intra mille retro annos sunt celebrata. Et pro uno regno mecum sentit regnum Franciae omniaque regna orbis Christiani."

More replied to him, "For one bishop who agrees with you, I have easily a hundred, including some who are among the saints. And for your one Council [i.e., Parliament] and your statute (what it is worth the great good God knows), on my side are all the general councils celebrated during the last thousand years. And for one kingdom, the kingdom of France and all other kingdoms of the Christian world agree with me."

§11 Norfolk charges malice

Tunc dux Nortfordiae interloquens, "Nunc," inquit, "More, planam facis animi tui obstinatam maliciam." At Morus, "Quod dico," inquit, "necessitate cogente dico. Volo enim exonerare conscientiam meam, nec animam degravare. Hujus rei Deum qui est scrutator cordium, testem invoco."

Then the duke of Norfolk spoke up and said, "More, now you are plainly revealing your mind's stubborn malice." But More replied, "What I say, I say because necessity compels me, for I wish to exonerate my conscience and not weigh down my soul. I call on God, the searcher of hearts, as witness."

§12 More impugns the statute as invalid

"Praeterea illudque addo, vestrum decretum perperam esse factum, quoniam ex professo jurastis contra Ecclesiam,[32] quae in toto orbe Christiano est una sola integra et indivisa. Ac vos soli nullam habetis potestatem statuendi quicquam absque reliquorum Christianorum consensu, quod sit contra unitatem et concordiam religionis Christianae.

"Sed non ignoro cur me morti adjudicaveritis. Illa unica causa est quod nolui superioribus annis consentire in secundum regis matrimonium.

"I add this besides, that your Statute was wrongly made, because you deliberately swore your oaths against the Church, which alone is whole and undivided through the whole Christian world. And you alone have no power to enact anything, without the consent of all other Christians, which is contrary to the unity and concord of the Christian religion.

"But I am not unaware of the reason for which you have adjudged me to death. The one single cause is that I have been unwilling over the past years to consent to the second marriage of the king.

§13 More prays for his judges

"Sed tamen magna mihi spes est in divina clementia ac bonitate, quemadmodum Sanctus Paulus legitur persecutus Divum Stephanum, qui tamen nunc unanimes in coelo agunt, sic nos[33] omnes quamquam in hac vita dissentiamus, tamen in alia cum perfecta charitate consensuros. Oro itaque Deum optimum maximum ut regem tueatur, conservet, ac salvum faciat ac illi salubre consilium suppeditet."

"But still I have great hope in the divine clemency and goodness that, as we read that St Paul persecuted Blessed Stephen, but they are now together in heaven, so all of us, though we disagree in this life, will nevertheless agree in another life with perfect charity. I therefore pray the great good God to guard the king, conserve him, and make him safe, and send him salutary counsel."

§14 More's encounter with Margaret

Cum vero jam peracto judicio Morus in carcerem denuo abduceretur, priusquam ad carcerem esset perventus, una filiarum ejus nomine Margareta per medium satellitum ac stipatorum turbam ruens, flagrans immodico desiderio parentis, nulla

Now when the trial was over and More was being led back to prison, before he had arrived at the prison, one of his daughters, named Margaret, rushing through the midst of the crowd of guards and soldiers, burning with great desire for her parent, taking no care

---

[32] NQ: jurastis *numquam quicquam facere* contra Ecclesiam ("you swore *that you would do nothing* against the Church")
[33] G: *vos*.

habita ratione nec sui nec loci publici nec circumstancium, vix tandem ad patrem perrupit, ibique collum ejus amplexa miserando fletu suum extremum dolorem est testata. Cumque illum jam aliquanto temporis intervallo arctissime stringeret, dolore omnem viam vocis praecludente, pater permissu satellitum eam hoc modo est consolat[us]: "Margareta, esto animo forti, nec te excrucies amplius; ita visum est Deo. Jamdudum nosti animi mei archana omnia." Inde patre ferme decem vel duodecim passibus abducto rursus occurrit iterum collum patris amplexa. Ibi Morus, nullis emissis lachrimis, nulla vultus aut animi perturbatione, hoc tamen dixit, "Vale, et Deum pro salute animae meae deprecare."

for herself or the public place or those standing by, she barely broke through at last to her father, and there, embracing his neck with pitiable weeping she bore witness to her extreme grief. And after she held onto him tightly for some time, with sorrow completely overcoming her voice, her father with the guards' permission consoled her thus: "Margaret, be of strong spirit, and do not torment yourself further; this is God's will. You have long known all the secrets of my mind." Then, when her father had scarcely been taken away another ten or twelve steps, she again fell upon him and once more threw her arms around her father's neck. Thereupon More, shedding no tears, and showing no distress of countenance or mind, said only this: "Farewell, and pray to God for the salvation of my soul."

§15 More is beheaded

[Pri]die[34] Nonarum Julii fuit capite truncatus in magno campo qui est ante [Turrim] regiam, ac pauca priusquam obtruncaretur loquebatur, tantummodo rogans circumstantem multitudinem ut pro eo in hac vita deprecaretur, ipse vicissim in alia vita intercederet pro illis.

On the day [before] the Nones of July his head was struck off in the great field before the royal [Tower], and he spoke a few words before he was beheaded, simply asking the crowd standing around to pray for him in this life and he in turn would intercede for them in another life.

---

[34] G: *die*. The day of the Nones would be July 7; the beheading took place on the previous day.

§16 His last prayer

Postremo illos sedulo hortabatur, orabatque ut Deum pro rege deprecarentur, ut illi velit largiri rectum consilium et mentem bonam, palam protestans ac denuncians se mori ejus fidelem ministrum, in primis tamen Dei Omnipotentis.

Finally he strongly exhorted them and urged them to pray to God for the king, that He would grant him right counsel and good mind; openly protesting and declaring that he died a faithful minister to him, yet first of all to God Almighty.

Document 18

Spelman's Report[35]

Et puis *die Jovis*, le primer jour de July [1535], Sir Thomas More, chivaler (que fuit devaunt chauncelour de Engleter, et apres fuit dischargé de meme l'office), fuit arrainé devaunt le dit Sir Thomas Awdely, chauncelour, et comissionerz, de treson, de ceo que il fuit aidant, councelour, et abettour al dit evesque, et auxi que il fauxment, maliciousment, et traitorousment desirant, voilant, et imaginant, inventa, practisa, et attempta a deprive le roy de son dignité, nome, et title de Supreme Chiefe en terre de l'Esglise d'Engleter.

Et trové coupable, le dit chancelour done le jugement. Et le dit More tient fortment sur le statut de 26 Henri VIII, quar il dit que le Parlement ne point faier le roy Supreme Chiefe, etc. Et il fuit decollé al Tower Hill.

And then on Thursday, the first day of July, Sir Thomas More, knight (who had earlier been chancellor of England and was afterwards discharged from the same office) was arraigned before the said Sir Thomas Audeley, chancellor, and the [other] commissioners, for treason, in that he was an aider, counselor, and abettor to the said bishop [Fisher], and also that he falsely, maliciously, and traitorously desiring, willing, and scheming, contrived, practiced, and attempted to deprive the king of his dignity, name, and title of Supreme Head on earth of the Church of England.

[He was] found guilty, and the said chancellor gave judgment. And the said More stood firmly upon the statute of 26 Henry VIII, for he said that the Parliament could not make the king Supreme Head, etc. He was beheaded at Tower Hill.

---

[35] Baker, *Spelman's Reports*, 1:58.

Document 19

Pole's Account[36]

1 De iniquissima Domini Thomae Mori condemnatione

[89] Quodsi caetera deessent, annon vel Mori unius condemnatio luce clarius totum illud tenebrosum judicium, cui ipse profecto Tenebrarum Princeps praefuit, patefaceret? In episcopum enim et cardinalem Roffensem (*Roffensis cardinalis creatus fuit quum esset in carcere*), quamvis iniquissime etiam is condemnatus est, tamen aliquid habebant etsi injustum quod objicerent, quod speciem justitiae aliquam et judicii formam prae se ferret, quod is aperte, sicut episcopum decebat, legi ipsorum adversaretur. In Morum vero, nec justam nec injustam causam, nihil plane quod vel speciem aliquam praeberet ullius quae more saltem atque exemplo fieret damnationis, reperire poterant; cujus unica responsio audita, omnia illis praeciderat, quaecumque vel fingere contra eum possent.

1 The Shameful Condemnation of Sir Thomas More

[cf. 217] Even in the absence of these other events, would not More's condemnation alone reveal in the clearest light the total darkness of this judgment [against the monks], at which the very Prince of Darkness presided? Though the bishop and cardinal of Rochester (*the bishop of Rochester was created cardinal when he was in prison*) was condemned most wickedly, they had something against him, even though unjust, that would have some appearance of justice and form of due process, because he was openly opposed to their law, as was proper for a bishop. Against More, however, they could find neither a just nor an unjust charge, nothing at all, that would give even some appearance of any sort of condemnation justified by previous custom or example. Even things that they were able to invent against him were cut off from them when his one reply was heard.

2 Forma judicii

Sed explicemus parumper formam praeclari illius judicii quo est Morus condemnatus, ut melius intelligi ac perspici queat quis illi judicio praefuerit. Sic igitur accusatio est instituta. Citabatur ad causam capitis

2 The Form of the Trial

For a moment, however, let us explain the form of that renowned trial in which More was condemned, so that one might better understand who it was who presided over that trial [i.e., Satan]. The accusation, then, began

---

[36] Reginald Pole, *Pro ecclesiasticae unitatis defensione*, addressed to Henry VIII, written between September 4, 1535 and March 30, 1536; sent to Henry on May 27, 1536; printed in Rome, 1539: folios 89–93; translated by Joseph G. Dwyer, *Pole's Defense of the Unity of the Church*, pp. 217–27 (adapted).

eo in loco dicendam Morus in quo paulo ante judex summa cum potestate et incredibili totius regni gratulatione sederat (*Morus, summus Angliae cancellarius*).

in this manner. More was summoned to respond to a capital charge in the very place where just a short time previously he had sat as judge with the highest authority and the extraordinary good wishes of all the realm (*More was the high chancellor of England*).

[There follows an account of the high esteem in which he was held when functioning as chancellor.]

[...]

Hic vero talis vir cum esset reus eo in loco, apud qualem judicem causam dicebat? Age dum non mea ulla oratio, sed acta ipsa ejus judicii declarent.

[cf. 218] Now such a man as this, when he appeared in this place as defendant, before what sort of judge did he plead his cause? Attend now while not my words but the very acts of his trial make this clear.

3 Accusatio longa et perplexa intenditur in Morum

3 A Long and Intricate Accusation Is Laid Against More

Recitabatur contra reum longa et perplexa accusatio, in qua quaecumque contra sceleratissimum hominem dici possent, quaecunque in proditorem patriae et legum omnium eversorem, conferebantur in eum, qui et ipse semper innocentissime vixerat et leges sanctissime ab omnibus observandas curaverat. Laesae majestatis crimine [89v] accusabatur is qui et regis et regni ipsius majestatem minui solus ex suo ordine passus non erat. Sed ne videlicet ad omnia quae proponebantur respondere posset, ut ita suspitio aliqua criminis in eo constitueretur, iccirco longis verborum et sententiarum ambagibus accusatio contexta erat, quasi hoc plane consilii habuissent ut si eum ferire non possent, saltem ut tanquam feram retibus, sic hominem innocentissimum longissimo criminum ambitu, ne qua elabi posset, circunveniret.

A long and intricate accusation was read aloud against the defendant. In this accusation, whatever might be said against a most criminal man, whatever might be said against a traitor to his native land and against a man who had overthrown all laws, was charged against him, though he had always lived most innocently and had taken constant care that the laws were most religiously observed by all. He who alone of all his rank would not permit the majesty of the king or his realm to be diminished, was accused of the crime of lese majesty. But, in order that he might not reply to all the things that were presented, that thus some suspicion of crime might be established against him, this accusation was woven into lengthy and ambiguous words and sentences. They thus clearly had a scheme whereby, if they were not able to strike him down, as with a wild beast they would use nets: they

Itaque talis et tam prolixa oratio fuit, ut Morus ipse, quo nemo memoria magis valuit, attentissime cum audisset, palam testaretur se vix tertiam partem eorum quae sibi objicerentur memoria comprehendere potuisse. Se tamen ad pauca, vel potius ad illud unum quod caput totius accusationis esset, de novo Consilii decreto, quod argueretur non approbare, responsurum. Illud enim demum Senatus decretum illis erat ex quo sibi posse viderentur crimen in eum laesae majestatis comparare; neque quicquam praeterea habebant quod probabiliter ei objicerent.

would surround this innocent man with their lengthy circumlocution of crimes, to prevent him from escaping.

Thus the language was such, and of so great a length, that More himself, whose memory surpassed all others, even though he listened most attentively, openly testified that he was scarcely able to remember a third of the things that were objected against him. He said, nevertheless, that he would reply to a few of them, or rather to that one thing that was the chief point of the whole accusation, namely, that he was charged with not approving the new decree of the Council. It was, finally, this decree of Parliament that seemed to them to make it possible to charge him with the crime of lese majesty. For they had nothing else with which to charge him with any degree of probability.

4 Responsio Mori

4 More's Response

Ad hoc vero ille ita respondit, ut diceret eam legem, qualiscunque esset, postea esse latam quam ipse perpetui carceris, in quo reliquum vitae degeret, poena, et fortunarum omnium proscriptione, affectus esset. Itaque, sive illa justa, sive injusta lex esset, primum, nihil eam ad se pertinere, qui et occidisse civiliter, ut jura dicerent, videretur, nec jam respondere de legibus deberet quibus ipse amplius non uteretur. Deinde, ut maxime etiam ad se pertineret, se tamen nec facto ullo nec dicto suo commisisse, ut illam improbare videretur; breviter, jure condemnari ea lege non posse, contra quam nihil a se factum dictumve objici posset.

To this, however, More replied thus. He said that the law, whatever it might be, was passed after he had been committed to the punishment of perpetual prison, where he would spend the rest of his life, and after all his possessions had been confiscated [cf. 219]. Therefore, first of all, whether the law were just or unjust, it did not seem to pertain to him, who was "civilly dead," as the laws would say, nor should he make any reply concerning legislation that he himself would no longer use. Second – and this pertained to him especially – he had never committed anything, by any deed or spoken word of his, to indicate that he disapproved of that law. In brief, he could not justly be condemned by that law, against which nothing done or said by him could be charged against him.

Ad hanc responsionem cum illi egregii judices primum silerent (nihil enim in promptu habebant quod opponerent, neque enim sane Morus, quid ea de re sentiret, cuiquam exposuerat), tum alter alterum respicere, omnes haerere, aestuare omnes coeperunt. Longa enim illa et tot perplexa nodis accusatio nihil profecerat. Videbatur homo innocens, quem tanquam feram undique conclusisse se putaverant, retia effugisse. Tandem vero, omnes in advocatum regis oculos convertere. Ad eum enim praecipue pertinere censebant, ut curaret, ne tam opima praeda e manibus elaberetur.

To this response those eminent judges first remained silent. They had nothing ready to oppose to his words in reply, for More had never explained to anyone what his thinking was on the matter. Then one looked at another, all remaining fixedly where they were, and finally they all grew enraged. For that long and intricate accusation, with all its perplexities, had accomplished nothing. The innocent man whom they thought they had surrounded like a wild beast seemed to have escaped from their net. But at last they all turned their eyes toward the king's advocate. They thought it was his special business to take care lest this precious prey should escape from their hands.

5 Silentium Moro objicitur criminis loco

5 Silence Is Charged Against More as a Crime

Atque hic aliquando, cum se nonnihil collegisset, plenus illo Spiritu quo instigante tota haec fabula agebatur: "Verum," inquit, "si nullum neque dictum neque factum habemus quod tibi objiciamus, at silentium certe habemus." Et simul referebat tempus fuisse, cum Morus in carcere interrogatus quid sentiret de lege, [90] recusasset respondere, quod diceret se perpetuo carceri addictum, de legibus humanis non amplius cogitare debere; magis enim ad se pertinere ut ad divinas leges, Dei misericordiam, et Christi Redemptoris pro nobis toleratam mortem, a qua sola et sua et omnium salus penderet totum animum et omnem cogitationem converteret, quam de legibus humanis, quarum usu sibi reliquo vitae tempore interdictum esset, aut cogitaret ipse, aut alii sciscitanti responderet.

Thereupon the Royal Advocate, after he had collected himself somewhat, being filled with that Spirit at whose instigation this whole fiction was being staged, eventually said this: "Well, then, if we have neither word nor deed that we can charge you with, we assuredly do have your silence." He went on to refer to the time when More was interrogated in prison as to what he thought about the law, he refused to answer, saying that, being delivered to perpetual prison, he should not think any more about human laws, for it was now more his business to turn all his mind and thought toward the divine laws, toward the mercy of God and the death that Christ our Redeemer endured for us and upon which alone his salvation and that of all men depended, rather than concerning himself about human laws which he was prevented from using for the rest

Ita tum cum reo agebatur, cum verba et facta dessent, criminis loco silentium objiciebatur.

of his life, either to think about them himself, or to reply to another who inquired about them.

Therefore, in this action against him as a defendant, since words and deeds were lacking, silence was charged against him as a crime.

6 Silentium Mori habetur pro indicio maliciosae mentis

6 More's silence is held against him as proof of a malicious mind

Atque hoc etiam ab ingenioso advocato addebatur, silentium illud malae mentis signum fuisse. Quod verbum sic a reliquo judicum consessu exceptum est, ut eo uno judicium quod pene concidisse videbatur, constitutum putarent. Cum nemo haberet quod objiceret, omnes tamen conclamabant, "Malitia, malitia!" Argumentum autem malitiae, non factum dictumve aliquod, sed silentium ponebant. Et hoc modo jam iterum, tanquam fera pene e plagis elapsa, homo innocentissimus in accusationis laqueos conjectus videbatur.

And this too was added by the ingenious advocate, that that silence was sign of an evil mind. This word was received in such a way by the other seated judges that they believed that this judicial process, which seemed almost to have collapsed, could be reconstituted by this word alone. Even though no one had any [cf. 220] charge to make, they nevertheless all cried out together, "Malice, malice!" They proposed no deed or speech as proof of malice, but only silence. And in this way once again, like a wild beast almost escaped from the snares, the innocent man seemed to be entrapped in the accusation.

Cum autem ad haec Morus diceret neminem posse ob silentium, quod indicium esset assentientis potius legi quam adversantis animi, condemnari de legis improbatione, idque pervulgat[o] jurisperitorum verbo confirmaret, quo dici solet, "Qui taceat, eum videri consentire," hoc tum minime audiebatur.

But More replied to this by saying that no one could be condemned for impugning a law by being silent, for silence was an indication of a mind that assented to a law rather than of one that opposed it, and he confirmed it by citing the widespread adage of legal scholars, commonly expressed thus, "One who remains silent is seen to consent." However, he was paid no heed.

Sed jam duodecim viri qui patriae more vitae ac necis potestatem in judicando habent advocabantur. Qui cum vocem malitiae quae per totum judicium personuerat defixam in auribus animisque haberent, nulla interposita mora, ut mirum esset

But now the twelve men, who according to the custom of our country have the power of life and death in trials, were called forward. And these men, since they had the word "Malice," which had sounded throughout the whole courtroom,

tam cito convenire potuisse, statim pronuntiarunt, vocabulo Anglico, "Gyltie" – quod perinde valet ut si dicas Hebraeo loquendi more, "Filius est mortis."³⁷ "Crucifige, crucifige!"

fixed in their ears and minds, made no delay – in fact, it was a wonder that they could so quickly come to agreement. They immediately made their pronouncement, in English, "Guilty." This has the same effect as if one were to say in the Jewish manner of speaking, "He is a child of death." "Crucify him, crucify him!"

7 Apostrophe ad Angliam, complectens laudem Mori ... [90–92v]

7 Apostrophe to England, Containing a Eulogy of More ... [220–6]

8 Morus postquam condemnatus esset sententiam suam de nova lege protulit

8 After Being Condemned to Death, More Revealed His Opinion of the New Law

[92v] Tunc enim primum sententiam suam patefecit de lege qua rex fuerat Ecclesiae Caput constitutus, id quod nunquam ante fecerat, ea scilicet mente ne, cum nihil proficere posset, occasionem adversariis suis (tuis vero hostibus, [O Anglia]) ulterius in se saeviendi daret. Tum autem tui curam gerens, ne imprudens atque ignara pestiferae contra te ipsam legi suffragareris, ita locutus est, ut cum legibus eam et divinis et humanis omnibus pugnare diceret, magisque perniciosam iis qui ipsi assentirentur [93] fore denuntiaret, quam sibi fuisset, qui quia dissensisse argueretur, capitali sententia affectus esset.

[cf. 226] Then he first revealed his opinion concerning the law by which the king had been appointed Head of the Church. He had not done this previously, for the purpose of not giving his [cf. 227] adversaries – who were also your enemies, [O England] – an opportunity for further lashing out against him, since it could not aid his defense. But then, at that point, being mindful of your care, lest you should imprudently and ignorantly favor this pestiferous law that was against your own self, he spoke out. He declared this law to be in contradiction to all human and divine laws. He asserted that it would be more pernicious to those who assented to it than it had been to himself, who was condemned to capital punishment because he was being convicted of dissenting from it.

---

37 As in 2 Samuel 12.5: "Filius mortis est vir qui fecit hoc" ("The man that hath done this is a child of death"). See Germain Marc'hadour's review of Dwyer, *Moreana* 14 (May 1967), 99–102.

9 Morus condemnatus orat pro inimicis suis

Quo exposito, ad suos se adversarios convertit. Sed quo impetu verborum in eos est usus? Eodem quo ille qui tanquam agnus ad occisionem est ductus (Is. 53); eodem quo ipse Dei Filius, qui accepta nostrae carnis infirmitate, pro mundi salute tanquam salutarem victimam se offerri est passus (Luc. 23), cum etiam pro iis oravit qui atrocissimae pariter et injustissimae mortis sibi authores fuerant. Sic enim Morus pro tua, O Patria, salute moriens, inimicis haud tristiora quam amicis precabatur, cum diceret, nunc quidem esse locum discordiarum, dissensionis, atque tumultus; se vero nunc in ea loca pergere ubi sublata omni contentionis et dissensionis radice, amor, pax, concordia, et tranquillitas in omnibus viverent. Quo ipse illos quoque mutata in melius mente venturos esse speraret, ex animoque ut ita esset precaretur. O mitem animum, O mansuetudinem semper celebrandam! Quaenam majora aequitatis animi signa dedit [Stephanus], qui pro lapidantibus se orabat (Acta 7)?

9 More, Condemned, Prays for His Enemies

When he had made this explanation, he turned to his adversaries. But what attack of words did he employ against them? He spoke in the same way as the one who was led as a lamb to the slaughter. He spoke in the same way as the very Son of God who accepted the infirmity of our flesh and suffered Himself to be offered as a saving victim for the salvation of the world, since he prayed for those who were in like manner the authors of his most terrible and unjust death. For thus More, dying for your salvation, O Native Land, did not pray for disasters upon his enemies any more than he would upon his friends. He said that here indeed was a place of discord, dissension, and tumult, but that he was now going to where the root of all strife and dissension had been removed, where love, peace, concord and tranquillity would live in all. To which place he hoped that they too, with minds changed for the better, would come. He prayed from his heart that this might come to pass. Oh, kind heart! Oh, gentleness always to be praised! What greater sign of equanimity did he [Stephen] give, who prayed for those who were casting stones at him?

Document 20

Roper's Account[38]

[1] Account of the encounter with Richard Rich (narrated as happening before the trial, but later characterized as based on Rich's testimony at the trial)

Shortly hereupon [after two official interrogations in the Tower], Master Rich, afterwards Lord Rich, then newly made the king's solicitor, Sir Richard Southwell, and one Master Palmer, servant to the secretary, were sent to Sir Thomas More into the Tower, to fetch away his books from him. And while Sir Richard Southwell and Master Palmer were busy in the trussing up of his books, Master Rich, pretending friendly talk with him, among other things, of a set course, as it seemed, said thus unto him:

"Forasmuch as it is well known, Master More, that you are a man both wise and well learned as well in the laws of the realm as otherwise, I pray you therefore, sir, let me be so bold as of good will to put unto you this case. Admit there were, sir," quoth he, "an act of Parliament that all the realm should take me for king. Would not you, Master More, take me for king?"

"Yes, sir," quoth Sir Thomas More, "that would I."

"I put case further," quoth Master Rich, "that there were an act of Parliament that all the realm should take me for pope. Would not you then, Master More, take me for pope?"

"For answer, sir," quoth Sir Thomas More, "to your first case: the Parliament may well, Master Rich, meddle with the state of temporal princes. But to make answer to your other case, I will put you this case: suppose the Parliament would make a law that God should not be God. Would you then, Master Rich, say that God were not God?"

"No, sir," quoth he, "that would I not, sith no Parliament may make any such law."

"No more," said Sir Thomas More, as Master Rich reported of him, "could the Parliament make the king Supreme Head of the Church."

[2] Indictment

Upon whose only report was Sir Thomas More indicted of treason upon the statute whereby it was made treason to deny the king to be Supreme Head of the Church. Into which indictment were put these heinous words, "maliciously, traitorously, and diabolically."

---

[38] Roper, *Lyfe of More*, ed. Hitchcock, pp. 84–97.

[3] Answer to the indictment

When Sir Thomas More was brought from the Tower to Westminster Hall to answer the indictment, and at the King's Bench bar before the judges thereupon arraigned, he openly told them that he would upon that indictment have abidden in law, but that he thereby should have been driven to confess of himself the matter indeed, [which] was, the denial of the king's Supremacy, which, he protested, was untrue. Wherefore he thereto pleaded not guilty; and so reserved unto himself advantage to be taken of the body of the matter, after verdict, to a-void that Indictment. And moreover added that if those only odious terms, "maliciously, traitorously, and diabolically" were put out of the indictment, he saw therein nothing justly to charge him.

[4] Trial: Testimony of Rich

And for proof to the jury that Sir Thomas More was guilty of this treason, Master Rich was called forth to give evidence unto them upon his oath, as he did.

[5] More addresses the judges (lords) as a man who takes oaths seriously

Against whom thus sworn, Sir Thomas More began in this wise to say: "If I were a man, my Lords, that did not regard an oath, I needed not, as it is well known, in this place, at this time, nor in this case, to stand here as an accused person."

[6] More tells Rich his oath is not true

"And if this oath of yours, Master Rich, be true, then pray I that I never see God in the face; which I would not say, were it otherwise, to win the whole world."

[7] More gives his own account of his conversation with Rich to the court (judges and jury)

Then recited he to the court the discourse of all their communication in the Tower, according to the truth.

[8] More addresses Rich on his bad character

And said: "In good faith, Master Rich, I am sorrier for your perjury than for my own peril. And you shall understand that neither I nor no man else to my knowledge ever took you to be a man of such credit as in any matter of importance, aye, or any other,[39] would at any time vouchsafe to communicate with you. And I, as you know, for no small while have been acquainted with

---

[39] "I, or any other": this could mean, "[that] I or any other [man] ..."

you and your conversation, who have known you from your youth hitherto. For we long dwelled both in one parish together, where, as yourself can tell (I am sorry you compel me so to say), you were esteemed very light of your tongue, a great dicer, and of no commendable fame. And so in your house at the Temple, where hath been your chief bringing up, were you likewise accounted.

[9] More addresses the judges (honorable lordships) on the unlikelihood of his revealing his mind to Rich

"Can it therefore seem likely unto your honorable lordships that I would, in so weighty a cause, so unadvisedly overshoot myself as to trust Master Rich, a man of me always reputed for one of so little truth, as your lordships have heard, so far above my sovereign lord the king, or any of his noble councilors, that I would unto him utter the secrets of my conscience touching the king's supremacy, the special point and only mark at my hands so long sought for? A thing which I never did, nor never would, after the statute thereof made, reveal, either to the king's Highness himself, or to any of his honorable councilors, as it is not unknown to your honors at sundry several times sent from his Grace's own person unto the Tower unto me for none other purpose. Can this in your judgments, my lords, seem likely to be true?

[10] More pleads his lack of malice, in any case

"And yet, if I had so done in deed, my lords, as Master Rich hath sworn, seeing it was spoken but in familiar secret talk, nothing affirming, and only in putting of cases, without other displeasant circumstances, it cannot justly be taken to be spoken maliciously. And where there is no malice, there can be no offense. And over this I can never think, my lords, that so many worthy bishops, so many honorable personages, and so many other worshipful, virtuous, wise, and well-learned men as at the making of that law were in the Parliament assembled, ever meant to have any man punished by death in whom there could be found no malice, taking *malitia* for *malevolentia*. For if *malitia* be generally taken for 'sin,' no man is there then that can thereof excuse himself; *quia*, 'Si dixerimus quod peccatum non habemus, nosmetipsos seducimus, et veritas in nobis non est' [1 John 1.8: 'If we should say that we do not have sin, we deceive ourselves, and the truth is not in us']. And only this word 'maliciously' is in the statute material, as this term 'forcible' is in the Statute of Forcible Entries. By which statute, if a man enter peaceably and put not his adversary out forcibly, it is no offense. But if he put him out forcibly, then by the statute it is an offense, and so shall he be punished by this term 'forcibly.'

[11] More cites his previous relations with the king as showing lack of grounds for malice

"Besides this, the manifold goodness of the king's Highness himself, that hath been so many ways my singular good lord and gracious sovereign, that hath so dearly loved and trusted me, even at my very first coming into his noble service with the dignity of his honorable Privy Council vouchsafing to admit me, and to offices of great credit and worship most liberally advance me, and finally with that weighty room of his Grace's high chancellor – the like whereof he never did to temporal man before – next to his own royal person the highest officer in this noble realm, so far above my merits or qualities able and meet therefore, of his incomparable benignity honored and exalted me, by the space of twenty years and more showing his continual favor towards me, and (until at my own poor suit, it pleased his Highness, giving me license, with his Majesty's favor, to bestow the residue of my life for the provision of my soul in the service of God, of his especial goodness thereof to discharge and unburden me), most benignly heaped honors continually more and more upon me. All this his Highness's goodness, I say, so long thus bountifully extended towards me, were, in my mind, my lords, matter sufficient to convince this slanderous surmise by this man so wrongfully imagined against me."

[12] Rich has Southwell and Palmer testify on his behalf

Master Rich, seeing himself so disproved, and his credit so foully defaced, caused Sir Richard Southwell and Master Palmer, that at the time of their communication were in the chamber, to be sworn what words had passed between them. Whereupon Master Palmer, upon his deposition, said that he was so busy about the trussing up of Sir Thomas More's books in a sack, that he took no heed to their talk. Sir Richard Southwell likewise, upon his deposition, said that because he was appointed only to look unto the conveyance of his books, he gave no ear unto them.

[13] The jury finds More guilty

After this were there many other reasons, not now in my remembrance, by Sir Thomas More in his own defense alleged, to the discredit of Master Rich's aforesaid evidence, and proof of the clearness of his own conscience. All which notwithstanding, the jury found him guilty.

[14] More interrupts the sentence

And incontinent upon their verdict, the lord chancellor, for that matter chief commissioner, beginning to proceed in Judgment against him, Sir Thomas More said to him, "My lord, when I was toward the law, the manner in such case was to ask the prisoner before judgment why judgment should not be given against him." Whereupon the lord chancellor, staying his judgment wherein he had partly proceeded, demanded of him what he was able to say to the contrary.

[15] More speaks against the statute upon which the indictment was grounded

Who then in this sort most humbly made answer: "Forasmuch as, my lord," quoth he, "this indictment is grounded upon an act of Parliament directly repugnant to the laws of God and His holy Church, the supreme government of which, or of any part whereof, may no temporal prince presume by any law to take upon him, as rightfully belonging to the see of Rome, a spiritual pre-eminence by the mouth of Our Savior Himself, personally present upon the earth, only to St Peter and his successors, bishops of the same see, by special prerogative granted; it is therefore in law amongst Christian men insufficient to charge any Christian man." And for proof thereof, like as, among divers other reasons and authorities, he declared that this realm, being but one member and small part of the Church, might not make a particular law disagreeable with the general law of Christ's Universal Catholic Church, no more than the city of London, being but one poor member in respect of the whole realm, might make a law against an act of Parliament to bind the whole realm. So farther showed he that it was contrary both to the laws and statutes of our own land yet unrepealed, as they might evidently perceive in Magna Carta: "Quod Ecclesia Anglicana libera sit et habeat omnia jura sua integra et libertates suas illaesas"; and also contrary to that sacred oath which the king's Highness himself and every other Christian prince always with great solemnity received at their coronations; alleging moreover that no more might this realm of England refuse obedience to the see of Rome than might the child refuse obedience to his own natural father. For, as St Paul said of the Corinthians, "I have regenerated you, my children in Christ." So might St Gregory, pope of Rome, of whom, by St Austin, his messenger, we first received the Christian faith, of us Englishmen truly say: "You are my children, because I have given to you everlasting salvation, a far higher and better inheritance than any carnal father can leave to his child, and by regeneration made you my spiritual children in Christ."

[16] Chancellor Audley cites the English bishops and scholars against More

There was it by the lord chancellor thereunto answered, that, seeing all the bishops, universities, and best learned of this realm had to this act agreed, it was much marveled that he alone against them all would so stiffly stick thereat, and so vehemently argue thereagainst.

[17] More claims greater support

To that Sir Thomas More replied, saying, "If the number of bishops and universities be so material as your lordship seemeth to take it, then see I little cause, My Lord, why that thing in my conscience should make any change. For I nothing doubt but that, though not in this realm, yet in Christendom about, of these well learned bishops and virtuous men that are yet alive, they be not the fewer part that be of my mind therein. But if I should speak of those which already be dead, of whom many be now holy saints in heaven, I am very sure it is the far greater part of them that, all the while they lived, thought in this case that way that I think now. And therefore am I not bound, my lord, to conform my conscience to the counsel of one realm against the general counsel of Christendom."

[18] Audley consults with Chief Justice FitzJames on More's exceptions to quash the indictment

Now when Sir Thomas More, for the a-voiding of the indictment, had taken as many exceptions as he thought meet, and many more reasons than I can now remember alleged, the lord chancellor, loath to have the burden of that judgment wholly to depend upon himself, there openly asked the advice of the lord FitzJames, then lord chief justice of the King's Bench, and joined in commission with him, whether this Indictment were sufficient or not. Who, like a wise man, answered: "My lords all, by St Julian" – that was ever his oath – "I must needs confess that, if the act of Parliament be not unlawful, then is not the indictment, in my conscience, insufficient."

[19] More is sentenced

Whereupon the lord chancellor said to the rest of the lords, "Lo, my lords, lo, you hear what my lord chief justice saith," and immediately gave he judgment against him.

[20] More declines to make further defense, and prays for his Judges

After which ended, the commissioners yet further courteously offered him, if he had anything else to allege for his defense, to grant him favorable audience. Who answered: "More have I not to say, my lords, but that, like as the Blessed Apostle St Paul, as we read in the Acts of the Apostles, was present and consented to the death of St Stephen, and kept their clothes that stoned him to death, and yet be they now both twain holy saints in heaven, and shall continue there friends for ever, so I verily trust and shall therefor right heartily pray, that though your lordships have now here in earth been judges to my condemnation, we may yet hereafter in heaven merrily all meet together, to our everlasting salvation."

[21] Roper cites his sources

Thus much touching Sir Thomas More's arraignment, being not thereat present myself, have I by the credible report, partly of the right worshipful Sir Anthony Seint-Leger, knight, and partly of Richard Heywood and John Webb, gentlemen, with others of good credit, at the hearing thereof present themselves, as far as my poor wit and memory would serve me, here truly rehearsed unto you.

[22] More is led away from the bar

Now after this arraignment, departed he from the bar to the Tower again, led by Sir William Kingston, a tall, strong, and comely knight, constable of the Tower, and his very dear friend, who, when he had brought him from Westminster to the Old Swan towards the Tower, there, with an heavy heart, the tears running down by his cheeks, bade him farewell. Sir Thomas More, seeing him so sorrowful, comforted him with as good words as he could, saying, "Good Master Kingston, trouble not yourself, but be of good cheer; for I will pray for you, and my good lady, your wife, that we may meet in heaven together, where we shall be merry forever and ever."

Appendix 2

Thomas More's Trial: Docudrama

This dramatic presentation is intended to suggest a plausible way in which the trial of Thomas More was conducted, on the basis of the documents in Appendix 1. When the text is an exact quotation of the source (except for changes entailed by converting indirect to direct discourse), it is given in quotation marks. Numbers in brackets identify the document being drawn upon.

Speakers

Narrator
Sir Thomas More
Lord Chancellor Audley
The Duke of Norfolk
Chief Justice of the King's Bench
   FitzJames
Justice of the King's Bench Spelman
Other commission judges

Attorney general Hales
Richard Rich, king's general solicitor
Sir Richard Southwell
Master Palmer
Spokesman of the jury
Sergeants-at-law
Constable of the Tower Sir William
   Kingston

Narrator: On Saturday June 26, 1535, a special commission of oyer and terminer met at Westminster and summoned a grand jury to meet on Monday, June 28; on that day the justices among the commission judges presented the jury with an indictment against Sir Thomas More. The jury found it a true bill. [15]

    The indictment charged More with high treason under the Act of Treasons concerning the king's supremacy of the English Church, in that he sought to deprive the king of this title in the following ways:

  1 by maliciously remaining silent when asked to affirm it;
  2 by maliciously conspiring with Bishop Fisher to deny the title; and
  3 by maliciously asserting to Richard Rich that Parliament did not have power to grant the king this title. [16]

On Wednesday, June 30, Audley ordered the constable of the Tower to present Sir Thomas More before them at Westminster on the following day. On that day, Thursday, July 1, Audley ordered the sheriff of Middlesex to have a petty jury before them that very day. Sir Thomas More was brought to the bar by Sir Edmund Walsingham, lieutenant of Sir William Kingston, constable of the Tower. [15]

    Thereupon Sir Thomas More, recently chancellor of the kingdom of England, after being confined in prison for 15 months, stands before the judges appointed by the king. In his presence, the accusations against him are publicly recited. [17.1a]

Duke of Norfolk: "More, you see that you have gravely offended against the royal Majesty in this matter. Nevertheless, we have confidence in his clemency and bounty that if you should be willing to repent and change for the better this rash opinion of yours, which you have so pertinaciously adhered to, you will easily gain forgiveness of your fault from him." [17.1b]

More: "Noble sirs, my very great thanks to you for your exceeding benevolence to me. But I ask only this of the great good God, that by His help I may be able to persevere in my right opinion until death. But as for what concerns the accusations with which I am charged, I fear that neither my mental ability, nor memory, nor words will suffice to explain them, because I am impeded not only by the prolixity and extensiveness of the articles, but also by my long detention in prison and the illness and bodily weakness that now afflict me." [17.1c]

One of the judges: The prisoner requires a chair for his feebleness. [17.2a]

Audley (*when other judges nod in agreement*): Let the prisoner have a chair!

More (*after being seated*): "As for what pertains to the first part of the accusation, which has it that, to show the greatest possible malice of my mind against the king, I was a constant opponent in the contention over his second marriage, I have nothing to say other than what I have said before; and that is, that whatever I spoke in that matter, I did it at the urging of my conscience. For it did not behoove me, nor did I wish it, to conceal the truth from my prince. If I had not acted so, I would have been an enemy to him, not a faithful servant. Now for this sin, if it is proper to call it a sin, I was adjudged to perpetual imprisonment, in which I have now been detained for fifteen months, and my goods besides confiscated." [17.2a]

In regard to the indictment, I openly declare that I would abide upon it in law, were it not that I would thereby be driven to confess of myself the very matter, which is, the denial of the king's supremacy, which is untrue. Wherefore I plead thereto not guilty. [20.3]

I place myself for good or ill upon my country. [15]

And I reserve unto myself advantage to be taken of the body of the matter, after verdict, to a-void this indictment. But here I say that if only those odious terms, "maliciously, traitorously, and diabolically" were put out of the indictment, I see therein nothing justly wherewith to charge me. [20.3]

Narrator: The judges assign the same day for More's trial and remand him to Walsingham's custody until the petty jury is assembled and sworn. [15]

"Immediately twelve men are called by the public minister, after the custom of the British nation, to whom are given the chapters of accusation." [17.7]

Narrator: More is called again to the bar. [15]

Attorney General Hales: Sir Thomas More, I challenge you to reply to the charges in the indictment.

More: "I reply only to the main heading of the first accusation. You say that I have merited the penalty inflicted by the statute passed in the last Parliament of our leaders, for which I was now held in custody, for the reason that, with malicious, false, and faithless mind, I injured the royal Majesty and name and titles and honor and dignity which they in the aforesaid Parliament or Council attributed to the king, by which he is considered to be Supreme Head after Jesus Christ of the English Church; and, above all, that you object to me that I wished to answer nothing to the secretary of the king and to the honorable Council of the royal Majesty, when he asked me what my opinion was about that Statute, other than that, because I was now dead to the world, I did not occupy myself with such things but only meditated on the Passion of Our Lord Jesus Christ." [17.2b]

"To which I clearly respond to you that it is not lawful for me to be judged to death for such silence on my part, because neither your statute nor anything in the laws of the whole world can rightly afflict anyone with punishment, unless one has committed a crime in word or deed, since laws have constituted no penalty for silence." [17.2c]

Attorney General Hales: "Such silence was a sure indication and a not obscure sign of some malign thinking about the statute, because all subjects, being faithful to their prince, when interrogated on their view concerning the statute, are obliged to respond openly, and without dissimulation, that it is good and holy." [17.3]

Narrator: Then the judges consult one another and all agree that such silence is malicious. [19.6]

Judges: "Malice, malice!" [19.6]

More: "But if it is true what universal law says, 'One who keeps silent seems to consent,' then that silence of mine gave approval to that statute of yours more than it weakened it. But as for all the faithful being bound and obliged to make response, etc., I answer that there is a much greater obligation on the part of a good man and faithful subject to consult his own conscience and eternal salvation, and to follow the prescriptions of reason, than to take account of any other thing, especially since the kind of conscience that I have offers no offense to its prince and stirs up no sedition—asserting this to you, that my conscience had not been opened to any mortal." [17.4]

"As for what I am accused of in the second part, that I contravened the statute and worked for its abolition in writings to the bishop of Rochester, by means of eight letters in which I fortified him against your statute: again and again I wished for those letters to have been publicly recited. But since, as you tell me, they were burned by the said bishop, I myself will sum up for you their contents. Some of them dealt with familiar matters, such as our old custom and friendship called for. One of them responded to his request to know how

I answered when first examined on the statute. I replied that I had exonerated my conscience and followed reason, and I urged him to do the same. This was, so help me God, the purport of my letters, and there is nothing on their account that should be judged worthy of death under your statute." [17.5]

"As for what pertains to the third article, which says that when I was interrogated by the Council I responded that your statute is like a two-edged sword, so that one who obeyed it imperiled the salvation of his soul, while one who opposed it would lose his life; and that the bishop of Rochester (you say) responded in the same way, from which it should appear that this was done by agreement between us, both of us responding in the same way: to this part of the accusation I respond that I was not speaking straightforwardly but only conditionally; that is, if there should be some statute that was like a two-edged sword, how could any person take care against coming up against one edge or the other? But what the Bishop of Rochester responded, I do not know. It may be that he responded in the same way, but it was not done through any conspiracy, but rather it occurred because of our similar minds and education. But believe me most assuredly on this point, that I never said or did anything maliciously against your Statute. In the meantime, however, it could be that many things have been viciously and maliciously spoken about me to arouse hatred against me on the part of his royal Majesty." [17.6]

Judges: Malice!
Narrator: "And for further proof to the jury that Sir Thomas More is guilty of this treason, Master Solicitor Rich is called forth to give evidence unto them upon his oath, as he does." [20.4]
Rich: My Lords, I, being sent to Sir Thomas More into the Tower, along with Sir Richard Southwell and Master Palmer, servant to Secretary Cromwell, to fetch away his books from him, while Sir Richard and Master Palmer were busy in the trussing up of his books, spoke with him thus. [20.1]

I asked him, if it were enacted by the authority of Parliament that if I myself, that is, Richard Rich, were king, and that it would be treason if anyone denied it, what would be the offense in the said Thomas More if the same Thomas said that the said Richard Rich was king? Certainly (I continued further), there would be no offense in his conscience, but rather the said Thomas More was obliged to say so and accept the same Richard, because the consent of the said Thomas More was obligated by the Act of Parliament. The said Thomas More then and there responded and said that he would indeed commit an offense if he denied it, since he was able to give his consent to it. But he said that this case will be a trivial case. [16.11b]

"Therefore, the same Thomas then and there said to [me] that he would propose a more lofty case, saying thus: 'Let us say that it was enacted by Parliament that God was not God, and that if anyone wished to impugn that act, it would be treason; if the question were put to you, Richard Rich, "Do you wish to say that God is not God," in accord with the statute, and you said yes, would you not commit an offense?'" [16.11c]

"To which [I said], 'Yes, certainly, because it is impossible to bring it about that God be not God. And because your case is on such a high level, I will propose to you this middle case: You know that our Lord King has been constituted as Supreme Head on Earth of the English Church; and why should not you, Master More, affirm and accept him as such in this case, just as in the foregoing case in which I was selected to be king? In that case you concede that you would be obligated to affirm and accept me as king.'" [16.11d]

"To this the said Thomas More [responded to me], 'Those cases are not like, because a king can be made by Parliament, and can be deprived by Parliament, to which act any subject being at the Parliament may give his consent; but to the case of a primacy, the subject cannot be bound, because he cannot give his consent from him in Parliament. And although the king were generally accepted as such in England, yet most outer parts do not affirm it.'" [16.11e]

Judges: Malice!

Audley: Let the prisoner be sworn to answer concerning the witness's testimony.

More (*after being sworn specifically to respond to Rich's allegations*): "If I were a man, My Lords, that did not regard an oath, I needed not, as it is well known, in this place, at this time, nor in this case, to stand here as an accused person." [20.5]

"And if this oath of yours, Master Rich, be true, then pray I that I never see God in the face; which I would not say, were it otherwise, to win the whole world." [20.6]

My Lords, I will here recite to you the discourse of all our communication in the Tower, according to the truth. [20.7]

Master Rich said unto me, "Forasmuch as it is well known, Master More, that you are a man both wise and well learned as well in the laws of the realm as otherwise, I pray you therefore, sir, let me be so bold as of good will to put unto you this case. Admit there were, sir, an Act of Parliament that all the realm should take me for king. Would not you, Master More, take me for king?" To which I replied: "Yes, sir, that would I." "I put case further," quoth he, "that there were an Act of Parliament that all the realm should take me for pope. Would not you, then, Master More, take me for pope?" "For answer, sir," quoth I, "to your first case: the Parliament may well, Master Rich, meddle with the state of temporal princes. But to make answer to your other case, I will put you this case: suppose the Parliament would make a law that God should not be God. Would you then, Master Rich, say that God were not God?" "No, sir," quoth he, "that would I not, sith no Parliament may make any such law." "No more," said I, "could the Parliament make the king Supreme Head of the Church, that is to say, pope." [20.1]

Narrator: Thus, having shown how Master Rich changed cases, from speaking about Rich being declared pope to speaking about King Henry being declared Head of the English Church, More addresses Master Rich directly:

More: "In good faith, Master Rich, I am sorrier for your perjury than for my own peril. And you shall understand that neither I nor no man else to my knowledge ever took you to be a man of such credit as in any matter of importance, aye, or any other, would at any time vouchsafe to communicate with you. And I, as you know, for no small while have been acquainted with you and your conversation, who have known you from your youth hitherto. For we long dwelled both in one parish together, where, as yourself can tell (I am sorry you compel me so to say), you were esteemed very light of your tongue, a great dicer, and of no commendable fame. And so in your house at the Temple, where hath been your chief bringing up, were you likewise accounted." [20.8]

Narrator: Sir Thomas More then addresses the judges:

More: "Can it therefore seem likely unto your honorable lordships that I would, in so weighty a cause, so unadvisedly overshoot myself as to trust Master Rich, a man of me always reputed for one of so little truth, as your lordships have heard, so far above my sovereign lord the king, or any of his noble councillors, that I would unto him utter the secrets of my conscience touching the king's supremacy, the special point and only mark at my hands so long sought for? A thing which I never did, nor never would, after the statute thereof made, reveal, either to the king's Highness himself, or to any of his honorable councillors, as it is not unknown to your honors at sundry several times sent from his Grace's own person unto the Tower unto me for none other purpose. Can this in your judgments, my lords, seem likely to be true?" [20.9]

"And yet, if I had so done in deed, my lords, as Master Rich hath sworn, seeing it was spoken but in familiar secret talk, nothing affirming, and only in putting of cases, without other displeasant circumstances, it cannot justly be taken to be spoken maliciously. And where there is no malice, there can be no offense. And over this I can never think, my lords, that so many worthy bishops, so many honorable personages, and so many other worshipful, virtuous, wise, and well-learned men as at the making of that law were in the Parliament assembled, ever meant to have any man punished by death in whom there could be found no malice, taking *malitia* for *malevolentia*. For if *malitia* be generally taken for 'sin,' no man is there then that can thereof excuse himself; *quia*, 'Si dixerimus quod peccatum non habemus, nosmetipsos seducimus, et veritas in nobis non est' – that is, as St John says in his First Epistle, 'If we should say that we do not have sin, we deceive ourselves, and the truth is not in us.' And only this word 'maliciously' is in the statute material, as this term 'forcible' is in the Statute of Forcible Entries. By which statute, if a man enter peaceably and put not his adversary out forcibly, it is no offense. But if he put him out forcibly, then by the statute it is an offense, and so shall he be punished by this term 'forcibly.'" [20.10]

"Besides this, the manifold goodness of the king's Highness himself, that hath been so many ways my singular good lord and gracious sovereign, that hath so dearly loved and trusted me, even at my very first coming into his noble service with the dignity of his honorable Privy Council vouchsafing to admit me, and to offices of great credit and worship most liberally advance me, and finally with that weighty room of his Grace's high chancellor – the like whereof he never did to temporal man before – next to his own royal person the highest officer in this noble realm, so far above my merits or qualities able and meet therefore, of his incomparable benignity honored and exalted me, by the space of twenty years and more showing his continual favor towards me, and (until at my own poor suit, it pleased his Highness, giving me license, with his Majesty's favor, to bestow the residue of my life for the provision of my soul in the service of God, of his especial goodness thereof to discharge and unburden me), most benignly heaped honors continually more and more upon me. All this his Highness's goodness, I say, so long thus bountifully extended towards me, were, in my mind, my lords, matter sufficient to convince this slanderous surmise by this man so wrongfully imagined against me." [20.11]

Narrator: "Master Rich, seeing himself so disproved, and his credit so foully defaced, causes Sir Richard Southwell and Master Palmer, that at the time of their communication were in the chamber, to be sworn what words had passed between them." [20.12]

Palmer: My lords, I "was so busy about the trussing up of Sir Thomas More's books in a sack, that I took no heed to their talk." [20.12]

Southwell: My lords, I "was appointed only to look unto the conveyance of his books, [and therefore I] gave no ear unto them." [20.12]

Narrator: "After this are there many other reasons Sir Thomas More in his own defense alleged, to the discredit of Master Rich's aforesaid evidence, and proof of the clearness of his own conscience." [20.13]

Audley: Let the jury now make deliberation over the accusations laid against the prisoner.

Narrator: "Now the twelve men, who according to the custom of our country have the power of life and death in trials, are called forward. And these men, since they had the word 'Malice,' which had sounded throughout the whole courtroom, fixed in their ears and minds, make no delay – in fact, it is a wonder that they could so quickly come to agreement." [19.6]

The jury, "sitting about a quarter of an hour, after deliberation [having been] had among them ... return to the sight of the princes and judges delegate." [17.7]

Audley: How does the jury find? Is the prisoner guilty or not guilty of sinning maliciously against the statute? [17.7]

Spokesman of the jury: We find upon our oath that Thomas More is guilty of the treason imputed to him; and we find also that he possesses no lands or holdings or goods or chattels. [15]

Attorney-General Hales and Sergeants-at-law: We demand that judgment and execution be given against Thomas More according to the form of law. [15]

Audley: We, the commissioned justices, having seen and understood all and singular of what has gone before, are ready to pronounce judgment of high treason against Thomas More. [15]

More (*interrupting*): "My lord, when I was toward the law, the manner in such case was to ask the prisoner before judgment why judgment should not be given against him." [20.14]

Audley: What are you able to say to the contrary of such judgment?

More: "Forasmuch as, my lord, this indictment is grounded upon an act of Parliament directly repugnant to the laws of God and His holy Church, the supreme government of which, or of any part whereof, may no temporal prince presume by any law to take upon him, as rightfully belonging to the see of Rome, a spiritual preeminence by the mouth of Our Savior Himself, personally present upon the earth, only to St Peter and his successors, bishops of the same see, by special prerogative granted; it is therefore in law amongst Christian men insufficient to charge any Christian man.

"This realm, being but one member and small part of the Church, may not make a particular law disagreeable with the general law of Christ's Universal Catholic Church, no more than the city of London, being but one poor member in respect of the whole realm, may make a law against an act of Parliament to bind the whole realm. It is contrary both to the laws and statutes of our own land yet unrepealed, as you may evidently perceive in Magna Carta: 'Quod Ecclesia Anglicana libera sit et habeat omnia jura sua integra et libertates suas illaesas' ['That the English Church be free and have all of its rights whole and its liberties uninjured']; and also contrary to that sacred oath which the king's Highness himself and every other Christian prince always with great solemnity receive at their coronations. No more might this realm of England refuse obedience to the see of Rome than might the child refuse obedience to his own natural father. For, as St Paul said of the Corinthians, 'I have regenerated you, my children in Christ.' So might St Gregory, pope of Rome, of whom, by St Austin, his messenger, we first received the Christian faith, of us Englishmen truly say: 'You are my children, because I have given to you everlasting salvation, a far higher and better inheritance than any carnal father can leave to his child, and by regeneration made you my spiritual children in Christ.'" [20.15]

Audley: But seeing that "all the bishops, universities, and best learned of this realm had to this act agreed," I much marvel that "you alone against

	them all do so stiffly stick thereat, and so vehemently argue thereagainst." [20.16]
More:	"If the number of bishops and universities be so material as your lordship seemeth to take it, then see I little cause, my lord, why that thing in my conscience should make any change. For I nothing doubt but that, though not in this realm, yet in Christendom about, of these well learned bishops and virtuous men that are yet alive, they be not the fewer part that be of my mind therein. But if I should speak of those which already be dead, of whom many be now holy saints in heaven, I am very sure it is the far greater part of them that, all the while they lived, thought in this case that way that I think now. And therefore am I not bound, my lord, to conform my conscience to the counsel of one realm against the general counsel of Christendom." [20.17]
Narrator:	Sir Thomas More adds thereto many other exceptions, objections, and reasons for the voiding of the indictment. Then "the lord chancellor, loath to have the burden of that judgment wholly to depend upon himself, there openly asks the advice of the lord FitzJames, then lord chief justice of the King's Bench, and joined in commission with him." [20.18]
Audley:	My lord chief justice, I put it to you, is "this indictment sufficient" in law? [20.18]
Lord Chief Justice FitzJames:	"My lords all, by St Julian, I must needs confess that, if the act of Parliament be not unlawful, then is not the indictment, in my conscience, insufficient." [20.18]
Lord Chancellor Audley:	"Lo, my lords, lo, you hear what my lord chief justice says." I therefore give judgment against him. [20.19]
	In accord with the Statute of Treasons, therefore, we adjudge you, Thomas More, lawfully convict of high treason, to be led by Deputy Constable Sir Edmund Walsingham to the Tower of London, and thence dragged through the midst of the city of London directly to the gallows of Tyburn and hanged upon those gallows, and while alive to be cast upon the earth and your entrails be taken from your belly and burned, you being still alive, and your head to be cut off and your body divided into four parts, and that your head and quarters be placed where the lord king shall wish to assign. [15]
Sir John Spelman (*aside to his fellow judges*):	I sum up the case thus for my reports: Sir Thomas More, knight, one-time chancellor of England, having been "arraigned before the now chancellor, Sir Thomas Audley, and other commissioners, for treason, in that he was an aider, counselor, and abettor to the bishop of Rochester, and also for that he falsely, maliciously, and traitorously desiring, willing, and scheming, contrived, practiced, and attempted to deprive the king of his dignity, name, and title of Supreme Head on earth of the Church of England, is found guilty, and the said chancellor has given judgment." [18]

Other judges: Sir Thomas, have you anything else to add in your defense? We will be favorably attentive to whatever you have to say. [20.20]

More: My lords, "since I have been adjudged to death, whether rightly or wrongly, God knows, for the exonerating of my conscience I would willingly say some words to you concerning your statute. I affirm that I have spent all my study during the whole of the last seven years, and I have never found an approved doctor of the Church to hold that any layman is the head of an ecclesiastical order." [17.8]

Spelman (*aside*): He stands firmly against the statute, holding that "Parliament could not make the king Supreme Head" of the English Church. [18]

Audley (*interrupting More's statement*): "Do you wish to be more prudent and religious than all the bishops, the whole nobility, and all of the people who are subjects of the king and his kingdom?" [17.9]

More: "For one bishop who agrees with you, I have easily a hundred, including some who are among the saints. And for your one council, Parliament, and your statute – what it is worth the great good God knows, on my side are all the general councils celebrated during the last thousand years. And for one kingdom, the kingdom of France and all other kingdoms of the Christian world agree with me." [17.10]

Norfolk: "More, now you are plainly revealing your mind's stubborn malice." [17.11]

More: "What I say, I say because necessity compels me, for I wish to exonerate my conscience and not weigh down my soul. I call on God, the searcher of hearts, as witness." [17.11]

"I add this besides, that your statute was wrongly made, because you deliberately swore your oaths against the Church, which alone is whole and undivided through the whole Christian world. And you alone have no power to enact anything, without the consent of all other Christians, which is contrary to the unity and concord of the Christian religion." [17.12]

I am now for the first time revealing my opinion concerning this law by which the king has been appointed Head of the Church in England. I have not done so before this, to avoid giving my enemies further opportunity of lashing out against me, and it would have hindered my defense here today. But I speak out now, "being mindful of my care for England, lest any person therein should imprudently and ignorantly favor this pestiferous law. This law is in contradiction to all human and divine laws. It will be more pernicious to anyone who assents to it than it has been to me, who stand condemned to capital punishment for having dissented from it." [19.8]

One final word, my lords: "I am not unaware of the reason for which you have adjudged me to death. The one single cause is that I have been unwilling over the past years to consent to the second marriage of the king." [17.12]

Narrator: Now More addresses all present.

More:	"Here indeed is a place of discord, dissension, and tumult, but I go now to where the root of all strife and dissension is removed, where love, peace, concord, and tranquility will live in all." [19.9]
	"But still I have great hope in the divine clemency and goodness that, as we read that St Paul persecuted Blessed Stephen, but they are now together in heaven, so all of us, though we disagree in this life, will nevertheless agree in another life with perfect charity. I therefore pray the great good God to guard the king, conserve him, and make him safe, and send him salutary counsel." [16.13; 20.20]
Narrator:	More turns back to the judges.
More:	"More have I not to say, my lords, but that … I verily trust, and shall for that right heartily pray, that though your lordships have now here in earth been judges to my condemnation, we may yet hereafter in heaven merrily all meet together, to our everlasting salvation." [20.20]
Narrator:	"Now after this arraignment, departs he from the bar to the Tower again, led by Sir William Kingston, a tall, strong, and comely knight, constable of the Tower, and his very dear friend, who, when he has brought him from Westminster to the Old Swan Wharf in Tower Ward, with a heavy heart, the tears running down his cheeks," speaks to him: [20.22]
Sir William Kingston:	My old friend, I here bid you farewell. [20.22]
More:	"Good Master Kingston, trouble not yourself, but be of good cheer; for I will pray for you, and my good lady, your wife, that we may meet in heaven together, where we shall be merry forever and ever." [20.22]
Narrator:	Then, "before he arrived at the prison, one of his daughters, named Margaret, rushing through the midst of the crowd of guards and soldiers, burning with great desire for her father, taking no care for herself or the public place or those standing by, barely breaks through at last to her father, and there, embracing his neck with pitiable weeping she bears witness to her extreme grief. And after she holds onto him tightly for some time, with sorrow completely overcoming her voice, her father with the guards' permission consoles her thus:" [17.14]
More:	"Margaret, be of strong spirit, and do not torment yourself further; this is God's will. You have long known all the secrets of my mind." [17.14]
Narrator:	"Then, when her father has scarcely been taken away another ten or twelve steps, she again falls upon him and once more throws her arms around her father's neck. Thereupon More, shedding no tears, and showing no distress of countenance or mind, says only this:" [17.14]
More:	"Farewell, and pray to God for the salvation of my soul." [17.14]
Narrator:	"On the day before the Nones of July, his head is struck off in the great field before the royal Tower, and he speaks a few words to the crowd standing around before he is beheaded." [17.15]

More: I beg you simply "to pray for me in this life, and I in turn will intercede for you in another life." "And I strongly exhort and urge you to pray to God for the king, that He will grant him right counsel and good mind. I openly protest and declare that I die a faithful minister to him, yet first of all to God Almighty." [17.15–16]

Bibliography

Unprinted Primary Sources

Ipswich, Suffolk Record Office
MS. E 14/11/10: Dickins, Francis (d. 1755). "Summary of judicial proceedings."

Lincoln, Lincolnshire Archives Office
Act Book Cj/3: *Ex officio c. Agnes Harvey* (Diocese of Lincoln 1526).

Kew, The National Archives
PRO KB 8/7, part 1 (Bag of Secrets): Trial of Charterhouse Priors Houghton, Webster, and Lawrence and the Bridgettine monk Reynolds, April 23–29, 1535 (cf. *LP* 8, no. 609); trial of Charterhouse monks Middlemore, Exmew, and Newdigate, 1–June 11, 1535, and John Fisher, June 1–17, 1535 (cf. *LP* 8, no. 886).
PRO KB 8/7, part 3 (Bag of Secrets): Trial of Thomas More, June 26–July 1, 1535 (cf. *LP* 8, no. 974).
PRO SP 1/93 fols 52–62: Interrogations of Tower servants, June 7–11, 1535 (cf. *LP* 8, no. 856).
PRO SP 2/R, fols 21–2: Report of the conversation between Sir Thomas More and Richard Rich (cf. *LP* 8 no. 814, 2, ii).
PRO SP 2/R, fols 24–5: Tower interrogation of Thomas More, June 3, 1535 (cf. *LP* 8, no. 814).
PRO SP 6/7, fols 5–9: Tower interrogations of John Fisher and Thomas More, June 14, 1535 (cf. *LP* 8, no. 867).

London, British Library
MS Cotton Titus B 1, fol. 475rv: Cromwell's Remembrances.

Printed Primary Sources

Andrew, John. *Additiones*. In William de Durantis, *Speculum judiciale*. Basel, 1574. Repr. Aalen, 1975.
Angelus de Clavasio. *Summa Angelica*. Venice, 1569.
Calendar of Entries in the Papal Registers Relating to Great Britain and Ireland: Papal Letters. Vol. 7: AD 1417–1431. Ed. J. A. Twemlow. London, 1905.
California Civil Code. St Paul, MN, 2009.
Church of the Lukumi Babalu Aye, Inc. v. City of Hialeah. United States Reports 508 (1993), 520.
Clarus, Julius. *Sententiarum receptarum liber [seu] Practica criminalis*. Venice, 1595.
Coke, Edward. *Institutes*. Part 3. London, 1644.

Concilia Magnae Britanniae et Hiberniae. Ed. David Wilkins. 4 vols. London, 1737. Repr. Brussels, 1964.
Constitution of the United States. United States Code. 2006 edn. Washington, DC, 2008, 1:lix–lxxii.
Corpus Iuris Canonici. 2 vols. Ed. Emil Friedberg. Leipzig, 1879–81.
Corpus Juris Canonici. 3 vols. Rome, 1582. With ordinary gloss. Available online at http://digital.library.ucla.edu/canonlaw
Corpus Juris Civilis. 3 vols. Ed. Paul Krueger *et al*. Berlin 1872–95. Repr. Berlin, 1970–72.
Covarruvias, Didacus. *Variarum resolutionum libri quatuor*. Geneva, 1723.
Cummings v. Missouri. United States Reports 71 (1867), 277, 323 (4 Wall.).
Decisiones Antiquae Rotae Romanae. Turin, 1579.
Derrett, J. Duncan M., ed. "Neglected Versions of the Contemporary Account of the Trial of Sir Thomas More." *Bulletin of the Institute of Historical Research* 33 (1960), 202–23.
Durantis, William de. *Speculum judiciale*. Basel, 1574. Repr. Aalen, 1975.
The English Reports. 178 vols. Edinburgh, 1900–32.
Expositio fidelis. In *Opus epistolarum Des. Erasmi Roterdami*, vol. 11. Ed. H. M. Allen and H. W. Garrod. Oxford, 1948, Appendix 27, pp. 368–78.
Fortescue, John. *De laudibus legum Angliae*. Ed. and trans. S. B. Chrimes. Cambridge, 1942, repr. 1949.
Gigas, Hieronymus. *Tractatus de crimine laesae maiestatis*. Lyons, 1557.
Hall's Chronicle: Containing the History of England During the Reign of Henry the Fourth ... to the End of the Reign of Henry Eighth. Ed. Henry Ellis. London, 1809.
Harpsfield, Nicholas. *Harpsfield's Life of More. The Life and Death of Sir Thomas Moore, Knight, Sometymes Lord High Chancellor of England*. Ed. Elsie Vaughan Hitchcock with historical notes by R. W. Chambers. Early English Text Society original series, 186. London, 1932.
Hartley, L. P. *The Go-Between*. London, 1953.
Hitchcock, Elsie Vaughan, ed. "Sir Thomas More's Indictment." In *Harpsfield's Life of More*, ed. Hitchcock, pp. 267–76.
Innocent IV. *Apparatus in quinque libros Decretalium*. Frankfurt, 1570.
Johannes Petrus de Ferrariis. *Aurea practica*. Venice, 1690.
Judicial Council of California Criminal Jury Instructions. CALCRIM. Eagan, MN, 2006–7.
Letters and Papers, Foreign and Domestic, of the Reign of Henry VIII. 23 vols. in 38. Vols. 1–4 ed. J. S. Brewer; vols. 5–13 ed. James Gairdner; vols. 14–21 ed. James Gairdner and R. H. Brodie. Emended repr. Vaduz, 1965.
Lyndwood, William. *Provinciale*. Oxford, 1679. Repr. Farnborough, 1968.
Mascardus, Josephus. *Conclusiones probationum omnium quae in utroque foro quotidie versantur*. Frankfurt, 1587.
More, Thomas. *The Apology*. Ed. J. B. Trapp. In *Complete Works*, vol. 9. 1979.
—— *Complete Works of St Thomas More*. 15 vols. New Haven, CT, 1963–97.
—— *Conscience Decides: Letters and Prayers from Prison Written by Sir Thomas More*. Ed. Dame Bede Foord. London, 1971.
—— *The Correspondence of Sir Thomas More*. Ed. Elizabeth Frances Rogers. Princeton, NJ, 1947.
—— *The Debellation of Salem and Bizance*. Ed. John Guy, Ralph Keen, Clarence H. Miller, and Ruth McGugan. In *Complete Works*, vol. 10. 1987.
—— *A Dialogue Concerning Heresies*. Ed. Thomas M. C. Lawler, Germain Marc'hadour, and Richard C. Marius. In *Complete Works*, vol. 6. 1981.
—— *English Poems, Life of Pico, Last Things*. Ed. Anthony S. G. Edwards, Katherine Rodgers, and Clarence H. Miller. In *Complete Works*, vol. 1. 1997.

—— *The History of King Richard the Third: A Reading Edition*. Ed. George M. Logan. Bloomington, IN, 2005.
—— *The Last Letters of Thomas More*. Ed. Alvaro de Silva. Grand Rapids, MI, 2000.
—— *St Thomas More: Selected Letters*. Ed. Elizabeth Frances Rogers. New Haven, CT, 1961.
—— *The Workes of Sir Thomas More 1557*. 2 vols. Facsimile edition. Introduction K. J. Wilson. London, 1978.
Parsons, Robert. *The Jesuit's Memorial for the Intended Reformation of England under Their First Popish Prince*. Ed. Edward Gee. London, 1690.
People v. Cook. California Reports, 4th series, 39 (2006), 566, 597; West's Pacific Reporter, 3rd series, 139 (Cal. 2006), 492, 515–16.
Pole, Reginald. *The Correspondence of Reginald Pole: A Calendar*. 3 vols. Ed. Thomas F. Mayer. Aldershot, 2002–4.
—— *Pro ecclesiasticae unitatis defensione*. Rome [1539]. Repr. Farnborough, 1965.
"R. v. Ponting." Criminal Law Review (August 1986), 491–510.
Rastell, William. *The Rastell Fragments, Being "Certen Breef Notes Apperteyning to Bushope Fisher, Collected out of Sir Thomas Moores Life, Writt by Master Justice Restall*. In *Harpsfield's Life of More*, ed.Hitchcock, Appendix 1, pp. 219–52, 359–70.
Reports of Cases by John Caryll. 2 vols. Ed. J. H. Baker. Publications of the Selden Society, 115–16. London, 1999–2000.
Reports of Cases from the Time of King Henry VIII. 2 vols. Ed. J. H. Baker. Publications of the Selden Society, 120–1. London, 2003–4.
The Reports of Sir John Spelman. 2 vols. Ed. J. H. Baker. Publications of the Selden Society, 93–4. London, 1977–78.
Ro. Ba. *The Lyfe of Syr Thomas More, Sometymes Lord Chancellor of England*. Ed. Elsie Vaughan Hitchcock and P. E. Hallett, with additional notes by A. W. Reed. Early English Text Society, original series, 222. London, 1950.
Roper, William. *The Lyfe of Sir Thomas Moore, Knight, Written by William Roper, Esquire, Which Married Margreat, Daughter of the Sayed Thomas Moore*. Ed. Elsie Vaughan Hitchcock with historical notes by R. W. Chambers. Early English Text Society original series, 197. London 1935.
—— *The Life of Sir Thomas More*. Ed. Richard S. Sylvester. In *Two Early Tudor Lives: The Life and Death of Cardinal Wolsey, by George Cavendish, and The Life of Sir Thomas More, by William Roper*. Ed. Richard S. Sylvester and Davis P. Harding. New Haven, CT, 1962.
Rymer, Thomas. *Foedera*. 2nd edn, 17 vols. London 1726–35.
St German, Christopher. *A Dialogue Betwixt Salem and Byzance*. In More, *Debellation*, Appendix B, pp. 323–92.
—— *Christopher St German on Chancery and Statute*. Ed. John Guy. Publications of the Selden Society, supplementary series 6. London, 1985, pp. 106–26.
—— *Little Treatise Concerning Writs of Subpoena*. In *A Collection of Tracts Relative to the Law of England*. Ed. Francis Hargrave. London, 1787, pp. 332–55.
—— *Treatise Concerning the Division Between the Spiritualty and Temporalty*. In More, *Apology*, Appendix A, pp. 173–212.
Smith, Thomas. *De Republica Anglorum*. Ed. Mary Dewar. Cambridge, 1982.
Stapleton, Thomas. *The Life and Illustrious Martyrdom of Sir Thomas More*. Trans. Philip E. Hallett. Ed. E. E. Reynolds. New York, 1962.
State Trials. 33 vols. Ed. T. B. Howell and T. J. Howell. London, 1816–26.
The Statutes of the Realm. 12 vols. London, 1810–28. Repr. London, 1963; Buffalo, NY, 1993.

Stubbs' Select Charters from the Beginning to 1307. 9th edn. Ed. H. W. C. Davis. Oxford, 1921.
Tomoya Kawakita v. United States. United States Reports 343 (1952), 717, 736.
United States v. Brown. United States Reports 381 (1965), 437, 447.
Yearbooks of Henry VIII: 1520–1523. Ed. J. H. Baker. Publications of the Selden Society, 119. London, 2002.
Young, John (?). *A Treatise Containing the Life and Manner of Death of That Most Holy Prelate and Constant Martyr of Christ John Fisher, Bishop of Rochester and Cardinal of the Holy Church of Rome*. Ed. François Van Ortroy. In "Vie du bienheureux martyr Jean Fisher, cardinal, evêque de Rochester (†1535)." *Analecta Bollandiana* 10 (1891), 121–365; 12 (1893), 97–247.
—— *De schismate, sive de ecclesiasticae unitatis divisione*. 8 vols. Louvain, 1573.

Secondary Sources

Ackroyd, Peter. *The Life of Thomas More*. London, 1998.
Apple, R. W., Jr. "Gallery in London Presents an Exhibition for All Seasons." *New York Times*. December 4, 1977.
Arkes, Hadley. "The Natural Law, the Laws of Reason, and the Distractions of History." *Journal of Law, Philosophy and Culture* 3 (2009), 203–20.
Baker, J. H. "Criminal Courts and Procedure at Common Law, 1550–1800." 1977. Repr. in *The Legal Profession and the Common Law*, by J. H. Baker. London, 1986, pp. 259–301.
—— "Hales, Sir Christopher (d. 1541)." *ODNB*.
—— *An Introduction to English Legal History*. 4th edn. London, 2002.
—— *Manual of Law French*. 2nd edn. Aldershot, 1990.
—— *The Oxford History of the Laws of England*. Vol. 6: *1483–1558*. Oxford, 2003.
—— "Rastell, William (1508–1565)." *ODNB*.
Bellamy, John G. *The Tudor Law of Treason*. London, 1979.
Benedict XIV, Pope. *Opus de servorum Dei beatificatione et beatorum canonizatione*. 7 vols. Prato, 1839–42.
Black's Law Dictionary. 9th edn. St Paul, MN, 2009.
Bolt, Robert. *A Man for All Seasons: A Play in Two Acts*. London, 1960.
Bowen, Catherine Drinker. *The Lion and the Throne*. London, 1957.
Bridgett, T. E. *Life and Writings of Blessed Thomas More, Lord Chancellor of England and Martyr under Henry VIII*. London, 1904.
Brundage, James A. "The Ethics of Advocacy: Confidentiality and Conflict of Interest in Medieval Canon Law." In *Grundlagen des Rechts: Festschrift für Peter Landau*. Ed. Jörg Müller *et al.* Paderborn, 2000, pp. 454–66.
Burnet, Gilbert. *The History of the Reformation of the Church of England*. 7 vols. Ed. Nicholas Pocock. Oxford, 1865.
Byron, Brian. "The Fourth Count of More's Indictment." *Moreana* 10 (May 1966): 33–46. Repr. in *Loyalty in the Spirituality of St Thomas More*, by Brian Byron. Nieuwkoop, 1974, pp. 157–65.
Carbasse, Jean-Marie. "Le juge entre la loi et la justice: approches médiévales." In *La conscience du juge dans la tradition juridique européenne*. Ed. Jean-Marie Carbasse and Laurence Depambour-Tarride. Paris, 1999, pp. 67–94.
Chambers, R. W. "The Continuity of English Prose from Alfred to More and His School." In *Harpsfield's Life of More*, ed. Hitchcock, pp. xlv–clxxiv.
—— *Thomas More*. London 1935. Ann Arbor, MI, 1958.

Chrimes, S. B. *English Constitutional Ideas in the Fifteenth Century*. Cambridge, 1936.
Clarke, Anthony. "Constitutional Justice: Lessons from Magna Carta." Lecture given at Royal Holloway, University of London, Surrey. June 16, 2008. Available online at http://www.runnymede.gov.uk/portal/site/magnacarta/menuitem.d12521181aaae4b-dc534227c9f8ca028/
Cockburn, J. S. "Twelve Silly Men? The Trial Jury at Assizes, 1560–1670." In *Twelve Good Men and True: The Criminal Trial Jury in England, 1200–1800*. Ed. J. S. Cockburn and Thomas A. Green. Princeton, NJ, 1988, pp. 158–81.
Cormack, Brian. *A Power To Do Justice: Jurisdiction, English Literature and the Rise of Common Law, 1509–1625*. Chicago, 2007.
Cross, Claire. "Hastings, George, First Earl of Huntingdon (1486/7–1544)." *ODNB*.
Davies, R. G. "Martin V and the English Episcopate." *English Historical Review* 92 (1977), 309–44.
Derrett, J. Duncan M. "The Affairs of Richard Hunne and Friar Standish." In More, *Apology*, Appendix B, pp. 215–46.
—— "*Juramentum in Legem*: St Thomas More's Crisis of Conscience and the 'Good Roman.'" *The Downside Review* 91 (1973), 111–16.
—— "More and How to Choose a Wife." *Moreana* 168–70 (Dec. 2006, March–June 2007), 222–4.
—— "More's Attainder and Dame Alice's Predicament." *Moreana* 6 (May 1965), 9–26.
—— "More's Conveyance of His Lands and the Law of 'Fraud.'" *Moreana* 5 (Feb. 1965), 19–26.
—— "More's Silence and His Trial." *Moreana* 87–8 (Nov. 1985), 25–7.
—— "The 'New' Document on Thomas More's Trial." *Moreana* 3 (1964), 5–19.
—— *An Oriental Lawyer Looks at the Trial of Jesus and the Doctrine of the Redemption: An Inaugural Lecture Delivered on 21 October 1965*. London, 1966.
—— "Sir Thomas More and the Nun of Kent." *Moreana* 15–16 (Sept.–Nov. 1967), 267–84.
—— "Thomas More and the Legislation of the Corporation of London." *The Guildhall Miscellany* 2.5 (1963), 175–80. Reprinted in *Essential Articles for the Study of Thomas More*. Ed. Sylvester and Marc'hadour, pp. 49–54, 589–91.
—— "The Trial of Sir Thomas More." In *Essential Articles for the Study of Thomas More*. Ed. Sylvester and Marc'hadour, pp. 55–78, 591–6. (Revised version of article first published in *English Historical Review* 79 (1964), 449–77.)
Dictionary of Medieval Latin from British Sources. Ed. R. E. Latham et al. 13 fascs. to date. 1975–.
Doe, Norman. *Fundamental Authority in Late Medieval English Law*. Cambridge, 1990.
Dohar, William J. "*Sufficienter litteratus*: Clerical Examination and Instruction for the Cure of Souls." In *A Distinct Voice: Medieval Studies in Honor of Leonard E. Boyle, OP*. Ed. Jacqueline Brown and William Stoneman. Notre Dame, IN, 1997, pp. 305–21.
Dowling, Maria. *Fisher of Men: A Life of John Fisher, 1469–1535*. Basingstoke, 1999.
Dwyer, Joseph G. *Pole's Defense of the Unity of the Church*. Westminster, MD, 1965.
Elton, G. R. *Policy and Police*. Cambridge, 1972.
—— "Sir Thomas More and the Opposition to Henry VIII." *Bulletin of the Institute of Historical Research* 41 (1968), 19–34. Reprinted in *Essential Articles for the Study of Thomas More*. Ed. Sylvester and Marc'hadour, pp. 55–78, 591–6.
—— *The Tudor Constitution: Documents and Commentary*. Cambridge, 1962.
Emden, A. B. *A Biographical Register of the University of Oxford, AD 1501 to 1540*. 3 vols. continuous pagination. Oxford, 1974.
Fears, J. Rufus. "Natural Law: The Legacy of Greece and Rome." In *Common Truths:*

New Perspectives on Natural Law. Ed. Edward B. McLean. Wilmington, DE, 2000, pp. 19–56.

Fleisher, Martin. *Radical Reform and Political Power in the Life and Writings of Thomas More.* Geneva, 1973.

Ford, Judith. "Young, John (1514–1581/2)." *ODNB.*

Foriers, Paul. "La conception de la preuve dans l'école de droit naturel." In *La Preuve.* Recueils de la Société Jean Bodin, 17:2. Brussels, 1965, pp. 169–92.

Foxe, John. *Acts and Monuments.* 4th edn. Ed. Josiah Pratt. London, 1877.

Fraher, Richard. "Conviction According to Conscience: The Medieval Jurists' Debate Concerning Judicial Discretion and the Law of Proof." *Law and History Review* 7 (1989), 23–88.

—— "The Theoretical Justification for the New Criminal Law of the High Middle Ages: *Rei Publicae interest, Ne crimina remaneant impunita.*" *University of Illinois Law Review* (1984), 577–95.

—— "*Ut nullus describatur reus prius quam convincatur*: Presumption of Innocence in Medieval Canon Law." In *Proceedings of the Sixth International Congress of Medieval Canon Law.* Ed. Stephan Kuttner and Kenneth Pennington. Vatican City, 1985, pp. 493–506.

Gairdner, James. "Reynolds, Richard (*d.* 1535)." *DNB.*

Glöckner, Hans Peter. *Cogitationis poenam nemo patitur (D. 48. 19. 18): Zu den Anfängen einer Versuchslehre in der Jurisprudenz der Glossatoren.* Frankfurt, 1989.

Guy, John. *A Daughter's Love: Thomas and Margaret More.* London, 2008. Published in the US as *A Daughter's Love: Thomas More and His Dearest Meg.* Boston, 2009.

—— *The Public Career of Sir Thomas More.* New Haven, CT, 1980.

—— *Thomas More.* London, 2000.

—— "What to Do about Sir Thomas More?" In Starkey, *Henry VIII: Man and Monarch,* p. 159.

Hatt, Cecilia A. "The Two-Edged Sword as Image of Civil Power for Fisher and More." *Moreana* 175 (2008), 67–86.

Helmholz, R. H. "Bonham's Case, Judicial Review, and the Law of Nature." *Journal of Legal Analysis* 1 (2009), 325–54.

—— "Natural Law and Human Rights in English Law: From Bracton to Blackstone." *Ave Maria Law Review* 3 (2005), 1–22.

—— *The Oxford History of the Laws of England.* Vol 1: *The Canon Law and Ecclesiastical Jurisdiction from 597 to the 1640s.* Oxford, 2004.

—-, ed. *The Privilege against Self-Incrimination: Its Origins and Development.* Chicago, 1997.

Hexter, J. H. *More's Utopia: The Biography of an Idea.* Princeton, NJ, 1952.

Hobbins, Daniel. *The Trial of Joan of Arc.* Cambridge, MA, 2005.

Holweck, F. J. *A Biographical Dictionary of the Saints.* St Louis, MO, 1924.

House, Seymour Baker. "More, Sir Thomas." *ODNB.*

Ibbetson, D. J. "Natural Law and Common Law." *Edinburgh Law Review* 5 (2001), 4–20.

Jacob, E. F. *The Fifteenth Century, 1399–1485.* Oxford History of England 6. Oxford, 1961.

Jonakait, Randolf N. "The Origins of the Confrontation Clause: An Alternative History." *Rutgers Law Journal* 27 (1995), 77–168.

Kelly, Henry Ansgar. *Inquisitions and Other Trial Procedures in the Medieval West.* Variorum Collected Studies. Aldershot, 2001.

—— "Inquisitorial Due Process and the Status of Secret Crimes." In *Proceedings of the Eighth International Congress of Medieval Canon Law.* Ed. Stanley Chodorow. Vatican City, 1992, pp. 407–27. Repr. in Kelly, *Inquisitions,* as chapter 2.

—— "Joan of Arc's Last Trial: The Attack of the Devil's Advocates." In *Fresh Verdicts on Joan of Arc*. Ed. Bonnie Wheeler and Charles T. Wood. New York 1996, pp. 205–38. Repr. in Kelly, *Inquisitions*, as chapter 4.

—— *Law and Religion in Chaucer's England*. Variorum Collected Studies. Farnham, 2010.

—— "Lollard Inquisitions: Due and Undue Process." In *The Devil, Heresy and Witchcraft in the Middle Ages: Essays in Honor of Jeffrey B. Russell*. Ed. Alberto Ferreiro. Leiden, 1998, pp. 279–303. Repr. in Kelly, *Inquisitions*, as chapter 6.

—— *The Matrimonial Trials of Henry VIII*. Stanford, CA, 1976.

—— "Medieval *Jus commune* versus/uersus Modern *Ius commune*; or, Old 'Juice' and New 'Use.'" In *Proceedings of the Twelfth International Congress of Medieval Canon Law (Washington, DC, August 1–7, 2004)*. Ed. Kenneth Pennington and Uta-Renate Blumenthal. Vatican City, 2008, pp. 377–416.

—— "Penitential Theology and Law at the Turn of the Fifteenth Century." In *A New History of Penance*. Ed. Abigail Firey. Leiden, 2008, pp. 239–317. Repr. in Kelly, *Law and Religion*, as chapter 6.

—— "The Right to Remain Silent: Before and After Joan of Arc." *Speculum* 68 (1993), 992–1026. Repr. in Kelly, *Inquisitions*, as chapter 3.

—— "Saint Joan and Confession: Internal and External Forum." In *Joan of Arc and Spirituality*. Ed. Ann W. Astell and Bonnie Wheeler. New York, 2003, pp. 60–84.

—— "Thomas More on Inquisitorial Due Process." *English Historical Review* 123 (2008), 847–94.

—— "Trial Procedures against Wyclif and Wycliffites in England and at the Council of Constance." *Huntington Library Quarterly* 61 (1999), 1–28. Repr. in Kelly, *Inquisitions*, as chapter 5.

Krampe, Christoph. "'Qui tacet, consentire videtur': über die Herkunft einer Rechtsregel." In *Staat, Kirche, Wissenschaft in einer pluralistischen Gesellschaft: Festschrift zum 65. Geburtstag von Paul Mikat*. Ed. Dieter Schwab *et al.* Berlin 1989, pp. 367–80.

LaFave, Wayne R. *Principles of Criminal Law*. St Paul, MN, 2003.

Langbein, John H. "The Historical Origins of the Privilege Against Self-Incrimination at Common Law," *Michigan Law Review* 92 (1994), 1047–85.

—— *Torture and the Law of Proof: Europe in the* Ancien Régime. Chicago, 2006.

LaRocca, John J. "Hall, Richard (*c*.1537–1604)." *ODNB*.

A Latin Dictionary. Ed. Charlton T. Lewis and Charles Short. Oxford, 1879. Repr. Oxford, 1969.

Lehmberg, Stanford E. *The Reformation Parliament, 1529–1536*. Cambridge, 1970.

Lemon, Rebecca. *Treason by Words: Literature, Law, and Rebellion in Shakespeare's England*. Ithaca, NY, 2006.

Lewis, Jayne Elizabeth. *The Trial of Mary Queen of Scots: A Brief History with Documents*. Boston, 1999.

Lewis, John, *The Life of Dr John Fisher, Bishop of Rochester in the Reign of King Henry VIII*. 2 vols. London, 1855.

Macnair, Mike. "Equity and Conscience." *Oxford Journal of Legal Studies* 27 (2007), 659–81.

Marc'hadour, Germain. "Raymond Wilson Chambers." *Moreana* 105 (1991), 61–80.

—— Review of *Pole's Defense of the Unity of the Church*, trans. Joseph G. Dwyer. *Moreana* 14 (1967), 99–102.

Marius, Richard. *Thomas More: A Biography*. New York, 1984.

Martz, Louis L. *Thomas More: The Search for the Inner Man*. New Haven, CT, 1977.

—— "Thomas More: The Tower Works." In *St Thomas More: Action and Contemplation*. Ed. Richard S. Sylvester. New Haven, CT, 1972, pp. 57–83.

Martyrologium Romanum. Ed. Cuthbert John and Anthony Ward. Rome, 1998. New edn, Vatican City, 2001; rev. edn, 2004.

Mayer, Thomas F. "Pole, Reginald (1500–1558)." *ODNB*.

—— *Reginald Pole, Prince and Prophet*. Cambridge, 2000.

McCutcheon, Elizabeth. "Denying the Contrary: More's Use of Litotes in *Utopia*." *Moreana* 31–2 (1971), 107–21. Reprinted in *Essential Articles for the Study of Thomas More*. Ed. Sylvester and Marc'hadour, pp. 263–74, 623–5.

—— "Margaret More Roper: The Learned Woman in Tudor England." In *Women Writers of the Renaissance and Reformation*. Ed. Katharina M. Wilson. Athens, GA, 1987, pp. 449–80.

McKechnie, W. S. *Magna Carta: A Commentary on the Great Charter of King John*. 2nd edn. Glasgow, 1914.

Mantel, Hilary. *Wolf Hall*. London, 2009.

Michael, Helen K. "The Role of Natural Law in Early American Constitutionalism: Did the Founders Contemplate Judicial Enforcement of 'Unwritten' Individual Rights?" *North Carolina Law Review* 69 (1991), 421–90.

Minnucci, Giovanni. "Diritto e processo penale nella prima trattatistica del XII secolo." In *"Ins Wasser geworfen und Ozeane durchquert": Festshcrift für Knut Wolfgang Nörr*. Ed. Mario Ascheri *et al.* Cologne, 2003, pp. 581–608.

Moskos, Charles and J. W. Chambers, II, eds. *The New Conscientious Objection: From Sacred to Secular Resistance*. Oxford, 1993.

Noonan, John T., Jr. *The Lustre of Our Country: The American Experience of Religious Freedom*. Cambridge, MA, 1998.

Nörr, K. W. *Zur Stellung des Richters im gelehrten Prozeß der Frühzeit: Iudex secundum allegata non secundum conscientiam iudicat*. Munich, 1967.

O'Connell, Marvin. "*A Man for All Seasons*: An Historian's Demur." *Catholic Dossier* 8 no. 2 (March–April 2002), 16–19.

Oldham, James. *Trial by Jury: The Seventh Amendment and Anglo-American Special Juries*. New York, 2006.

Padoa-Schioppa, Antonio. "Sulla conscienze del giudice nel diritto comune." In *Iuris Vincula: Studi in onore di Mario Talamanca*. Naples, 2001, pp. 119–62.

Parmiter, Geoffrey de C. "The Indictment of St Thomas More." *The Downside Review* 75 (1957), 149–66.

—— *The King's Great Matter: A Study of Anglo-Papal Relations 1527–1534*. London, 1967.

—— "Tudor Indictments, Illustrated by the Indictment of St Thomas More." *Recusant History* 6 (1961–62), 141–56.

Pennington, Kenneth. "'Innocent until Proven Guilty': The Origins of a Legal Maxim." In *A Ennio Cortese*. Ed. Domenico Maffei and Italo Barocchi. 3 vols. Rome, 2001, vol. 3, pp. 59–73.

Rex, Richard. *Henry VIII and the English Reformation*. 2nd edn. London, 2006.

Reynolds, E. E. Comments on "The 'New' Document on Thomas More's Trial," by J. Duncan M. Derrett. *Moreana* 3 (1964), 20–2.

—— *The Field Is Won: The Life and Death of Saint Thomas More*. London, 1968.

—— *Margaret Roper: Eldest Daughter of Sir Thomas More*. New York, 1960.

—— *Saint John Fisher*. Rev. edn. Wheathamstead, 1972.

—— *The Trial of St Thomas More*. Montreal, 1964. Published in Italian as *Il processo di Tommaso Moro*. Trans. Marialisa Bertagnoni. Rome, 1985.

—— "An Unnoticed Document." *Moreana* 1 (Sept. 1963), 12–17.

Salmond, John. *Jurisprudence*. 10th edn. Ed. Glanville L. Williams. London, 1947.

Scarisbrick, J. J. *Henry VIII*. Berkeley, CA, 1968.

Schoeck, Richard J. "Sir Thomas More, Humanist and Lawyer." *University of Toronto Quarterly* 34 (1964), 1–14.
Schulte Herbrüggen, Hubertus. "The Process Against Sir Thomas More." *Law Quarterly Review* 99 (1983), 113–36.
Shapiro, Barbara J. *Beyond Reasonable Doubt and Probable Cause.* Berkeley, CA, 1991.
Simpson, A. W. B. *History of the Common Law of Contract.* Oxford, 1975.
Starkey, David, guest curator. *Henry VIII: Man and Monarch.* Ed. Susan Doran. Catalogue for the exhibition held at the British Library, April 23 to September 6, 2009. London, 2009.
Stephen, James Fitzjames. *History of the Criminal Law of England.* Vol. 3. London, 1883.
Sylvester, R. S., and G. P. Marc'hadour, eds. *Essential Articles for the Study of Thomas More.* Hamden, CT, 1977.
Tierney, Brian. "Religious Rights: An Historical Perspective." In *Religious Human Rights in Global Perspective.* Ed. John Witte, Jr. and Johan D. van der Vyver. The Hague, 1996, pp. 17–45.
Trapp, J. B. and Hubertus Schulte Herbrüggen, eds. *"The King's Good Servant": Sir Thomas More: 1477/8–1535.* Catalogue for the exhibition held at the National Portrait Gallery from November 25, 1977 to March 12, 1978. London, 1978.
Trevor-Roper, Hugh. "Roper, William (1495x8–1578)." *ODNB.*
Trusen, Winfried. "Rechtliche Grundlagen der Hexenprozesse und ihrer Beendigung." In *Gelehrtes Recht im Mittelalter und in der frühen Neuzeit.* By Winfried Trusen. Goldbach, 1997, pp. 297–320.
Ullmann, Walter. "A Decision of the Rota Romana on the Benefit of Clergy in England." *Studia Gratiana* 13 (1967), 455–89.
Van Ortroy, François. "Vie du bienheureux martyr Jean Fisher, cardinal, evêque de Rochester (†1535)." *Analecta Bollandiana* 10 (1891), 121–365; 12 (1893), 97–247.
Warner, J. Christopher. *Henry VIII's Divorce: Literature and the Politics of the Printing Press.* Woodbridge, 1998.
Wegemer, Gerard. *Thomas More: A Portrait of Courage.* Princeton, NJ, 1995.
——— *Thomas More on Statesmanship.* Washington, DC, 1996.
Wegemer, Gerard and Stephen Smith, eds. *A Thomas More Source Book.* Washington, DC, 2004.
Whitman, James Q. *The Origins of Reasonable Doubt: Theological Roots of the Criminal Trial.* New Haven, CT, 2008.
Whittick, Christopher. "Shelley, Sir William (1478/9–1549)." *ODNB.*
Wigmore, John Henry. *Evidence in Trials at Common Law.* Vol. 7. Rev. edn. ed. James H. Chadbourn. St Paul, MN, 2003.
Williams, Glanville. *Criminal Law: The General Part.* 2nd edn. London, 1961.

Index

abortion, conscientious objection to, 64
Ackroyd, Peter, 92 n101, 98, 107 n85
acts (statutes) of Parliament:
acts of attainder, 72–73, 76; act against More (Nov.–Dec. 1534), xiv, 13, 73, 76, 78, 90, 100
Act of Ecclesiastical Appointments (Jan.–Mar. 1534), 85
Act of Forcible Entry (1429), 38, 76, 133, 205
Act on Human Rights (1998), 117
Act Against Maiming (1404), 112
Act of Oath of Succession (Nov.–Dec. 1534), 13, 26–27, 74 n14, 76, 91–92
Act of Papal Dispensations and Peter's Pence (Jan.–Mar. 1534), 85
Act of Praemunire (1393), 67
Act of Provisors (1390), 67
Act of the Six Articles (1543), 24 n103
Act of Submission of the Clergy and Restraint of Appeals (Jan.–Mar. 1534), 85
Act of Succession (Jan.–Mar. 1534), xiv, 11–13, 34 n152, 73–74, 76–78, 91–92, 160, 163; Cromwell and, 11–12; Fisher and, 28; malice and, 12, 73–78; mandatory oath of, xiv, 13, 26–28, 98; rejected by More, 97–98; punishment of life in prison for refusing oath (misprision of treason), xiv, 100; trial of More and, xiv
Act of Supremacy (Nov.–Dec. 1534), xiv–xv, 7–8, 13, 34, 43, 50, 52, 73, 77, 79, 89, 91, 100–1, 110, 121, 131;176; Church law and, xvi, 26–27, 42, 89, 106; Cromwell and, 49; Fisher and, 9; indictment of More and, 7–8, 36; invalidity of, 65, 66–69, 89, 192; judges and, 84; natural law and, 66–69; no oath required, xiv, 26–28, 91; Parliament and, 49; pope and, 69; text of, 137–38; trial of More and, xv
Act of Treasons (Nov.–Dec. 1534), xiv–xv, 7–8, 12, 13, 48, 51, 71, 73–80, 84, 90, 93, 100, 110, 121, 131, 177, see treason; Carthusian priors and, 12; divine law and, 55; Fisher and, 12, 28; House of Commons and, 12; malice and, 12, 73–74, 80–81; natural law and, 55; penalty specified by, 33; text of, 138–40
Act of Treasons and Felonies (1547), 24, 75

Act of Treasons (1552), 86 n73
Act of Treasons (1696), 86 n73
actus reus, 118
adultery, 60–61
American Bar Association, 87–88
anarchy, and conscience, 65
Andrew, John (Johannes Andreae), 29
Apology (More), xiii, 47–48, 68 n74
Aquinas, St Thomas, 25
arrest (stopping), 45, *see* motion
attainder, 72–63, *see* acts; Bill of Attainder Clause in the US Constitution, 73
Audley, Thomas, chancellor, 3, 4, 15, 26, 30, 31–32, 41, 42–43, 72, 84, 89, 96, 98, 101 n45, 102, 103, 104, 109, 110, 141, 145, 148, 172, 173, 181, 207, 208
Austin, St (Augustine of Canterbury), 207

Bag of Secrets, xv, 3, 14, 85, 140, 148, 165, 172
Baker, Herschel, xii
Baker, John, 2, 5 n20, 6, 47, 48, 53 n1, 71, 72, 75; Act of Supremacy (1534) and, 49; on Church trials, 47; on evidence in More's trial, 10–11, 39–41; on fairness in More's trial, 47–51, 81–82; jury system and, 46, 113, 118; on malice, 111–12; on silence, 50; treason trials and, 10–11, 82, 86 n74
Becket, Thomas, archbishop of Canterbury (d. 1170), 66, 135
Bedill, Thomas, 100, 109, 110, 142, 150, 159, 163
Bellamy, John, 12, 17, 38–39, 71, 72, 75, 76, 77, 84, 86, 89
Benedict XIV, pope (1740–58), xii
Benson, William, abbot of Westminster, 98, 109
Bill of Rights, US, 129, 135
bishops, English, xiii, 25 n119, 29–30, 41–43, 67, 83, 90, 101, 107, 121, 147, 169–71, 191, 205, 207, 215; *see* clergy
Boleyn, Anne, 3–4, 27, 28 n119, 72, 91, 102, 125, 134; Act of Succession (1534) and, xiv, 73–74; Henry VIII, marriage to, xiii n11, 18, 34, 92 n102, 110, 133, annulment trial of, xiii n11; treason trial of, xiii n11, 1

Boleyn, George, lord (viscount) Rochford, 4, 23, 72
Boleyn, Thomas, earl of Wiltshire, 3, 72, 102, 110, cf. 6 n21, 82
Bolt, Robert, *A Man for All Seasons* (play, 1960; film, 1966), xi, xvi, 4, 5, 119
Bonham's Case, 116–17
Boniface VIII, pope (1294–1303), 22, 29
Bridgettine monk, *see* Reynolds, Richard
Bushell's Case, 113
Byron, Brian, 36–37, 51–52, 157 n11

caesaro-papism, xi
California Civil Code, 131, 132
California Supreme Court, 88
Campeggio, Cardinal, xiv
canonization, xi, xii, xv
canon law, 22 n93, 24, 29, 46–48, 53–70, 79
capital punishment, xii, xii n5
Carthusian (Charterhouse) monks, trial of, xv, 4, 5, 6, 13, 52, 148–49; beatified (1886), xii; canonized (1970), xv
Carthusian (Charterhouse) priors, trial of, xv, 4, 13, 14, 43, 50, 52, 72, 113–15, 118, 125, 126, 131, 140–42; beatified (1886), xii; canonized (1970), xv
Catherine of Aragon, xiii n11, xiv, 26, 64, 133
Cauchon, Pierre, xiii–xiv
challenges to potential jurors, 6, 82, cf. 40
Chambers, R. W., 6 n21, 13 n55, 14 n60, 82 n57, 107–8
Charterhouse, *see* Carthusian
Church, Universal, contrasted with the Church in England, xvi, 29, 37, 41, 67, 89, 90, 91, 92 n102
Church courts, criminal procedure in, xiii, 25, 47, *and see* heresy
civil (Roman) law, *see* Justinian
civil rights movement, 64
civilian (expert on Roman civil law), 61, 62, 79; *see* Legh, Tregonwell
Clarus, Julius (d. 1575), 57 n18, 59 n23
clergy, benefit of, 67–68; recognizing king as Supreme Head of English Church (1531), 23; submission by (1532), xii, 84–85; submission of (enacted by Parliament, 1534), 85
coercion, 48, 60–61; of jury, 14, 48, 125–26; political, xv, 53, 70, 113, 127, 130, 131
Coke, Edward, 59, 112, 118
Columbus, Christopher, xi
commissions of oyer and terminer, xv, 3, 6, 47, 49, 72, 140
common law (English), xiii, 23–24, 40, 54–55, 56, 59, 60, 61, 63, 66 n62, 79, 85, 112, 129, 134–35

Common Pleas, justices of, 4, 46 n194, 48–49, 72, 84
Commons, House of, xiv, 12, 13, 33, 41, 43, 49, 50, 74, 75, 85, 120, 132, 134
compurgation, 24
confession, sacrament of, 24–25
conflict-of-interest doctrines, 84, cf. 17, 72, 87–88
conscience, convictions on basis of, 55; dictates of, 64–65, 77, 124; does not excuse from positive laws, 65, 69, 70, 77 n35, 114; mistaken, 64–65; natural law and, 55, 63–65; and prosecutorial discretion, 124–25; recipe for anarchy, 65, 114; as right of dissent, 128; rights of, 55, 63–65, 122–23
consciences: of judges, 70; of jurors, 14, 39, 59, 85, 113, 130–31; of Parliament, 132; Fisher's, 15, 113–14; More's, attack on, 102, 104; and the Church, 42, 127–28; clearness of, 38, 93, 103; died for it, 134; exoneration of, xvi, 31, 41, 43, 44, 46, 50, 51, 64, 90, 92; on the king's marriage, 18, 99; on the king's supremacy, 26; no offense to the king on any point, 19; as "opinion," 19, cf. 29–30, 50; his primary obligation, 19, 42–43, 63, 77, 78, 90–91, 99, 103, 104, 110, cf. 22; his theory of liberty of, 77 n35, 93; as voice to others, 125
conscientious objection, 64, 78 n35
Constitution, US, 56, 64, 66, 68, 73, 74–75, 86, 117, 122, 128, 129
constitutionality, 30, 47, 50, 51, 52, 68, 122, 134
contumacy, 25n103, 58n21
convocation of the clergy, 23, 27 n119, 28 n119, 131
Council, Church, of Constance (1414–18), 30; Fourth Lateran (1215), 29
Council, king's, 4 n14, 11, 72, 79, 100; and Fisher in the Tower, 14, 16, 32, 33–34; and More in the Tower, 26, 28, 34, 35, 90, 94–95, 96, 100, 102, 104–5, 106–7
counsel (attorneys), limited use for criminal defendants, 9, 81, 86
Court of Human Rights (Strasbourg), 117
crime, excepted (exceptional), 60 n28, 62, cf. 58
Cranmer, Thomas, archbishop of Canterbury, xiii n11, 98, 109, 110
Cromwell, Thomas, xii, 1, 4, 72, 77, 84, 92; and Act of Succession (Jan.–Mar. 1534), 11–12; and Act of Supremacy (Nov.–Dec. 1534), 49; jury of Carthusian priors and Reynolds threatened by, 14, 125–26, cf. 15; and Henry VIII's annulment, xiv; and indictment of More, 4, 32, 120, 178; his

interrogations of More, 95, 96, 98–99, 101, 109; and More's silence, 18, cf. 26, 29, 30; "remembrances" of, 4–5, 105, 167–68; present as judge at More's trial, 4, 173

Dacre of the North, lord, 24, 168
Daniel and the trial of Susanna, 59
death penalty, xii, xiii, xiv, xvi, 15, 18, 24, 30, 41–42, 43, 44, 46 n197, 54, 65, 75, 93, 95, 103, 110
Debellation of Salem and Byzance (More), xiii, 12 n49, 40, 48, 58 n21, 62n39, 67 n68, 68 n71
Decretals of Gregory IX (1234), 57–58, 70; 56–66 *passim*
defamation law, 112
demurrer, 45, 81
De occultis non judicat Ecclesia, 56, 79
Derrett, J. Duncan M., account of More's trial, xvi–xvii, 1–3, 6, 9–11, 17, 35–36, 40, 49–50, 71, 81–82, 86, 123–24; and Guildhall Report, 2, 8 n35, 107 nn84, 87, 108; and malice, 115; on motion in arrest of judgment, 9, 44–46, 51, 116; on Richard Rich, 51–52, 86; and silence, 24 n106, 25, 50; theory of dismissed charges, xvi, 6, 9–10, 35–36, 40–41, 49–50, 81–82, 85
Devil's Advocate, xi, xii
Dialogue Concerning Heresies (More), 29, 54 n3, 91, 127, 130
discretion, of judges, 46–47, 88, cf. 69–70; of jury, 39; prosecutorial, 124–25
due process, 29, 48, 71, 120, 122, 127
Durantis, William, 62

Edward VI (1548–53), 24 n104, 86
Elizabeth I (1558–1603), xii n8, 13, 132–33
Elton, G. R., 2, 12, 13, 14 n60, 57 n14, 106 n79
English common law, xiii, xvi, 1–2, 23–24, 40, 56, 59, 63, 79
equity, English courts of, 63
Erasmus, 20, 162
European Convention on Human Rights, 117
evidence, documentary, 17, 86–87; by witnesses, *see* witnesses; rules of, 86–87; best-evidence rule, 123
evolution, theory of, 65
exceptions (objections), 42, 43, 45
exceptions to laws or rules, 56 n10, 57, 58, 61–62, 64, 86
excommunication, 58 n21
Exmew, William, 4, 5, 6, 148–49; *see* Carthusian (Charterhouse) monks
Expositio fidelis, 20, 107 nn84, 87, 108
ex post facto laws, 73, 76

Falklands War, 113
Fifth Amendment, 56, 57, 79
Fisher, John, bishop of Rochester, beatified (1886), xii; canonized (1935), xv; correspondence with More in Tower, 17, 31–35, 78, 80, 94, 105; execution of, 4 n14, 5, 20, 105; inquires if oath is required for supremacy, 28; interrogations of in the Tower, 12, 14, 33–34, 37, 96, 159–65; and king's supremacy title in 1532, 23; on malice, 14–16, 49, 52, 76, 113–14, 118, 131; More accused of conspiracy with, xv–xvi, 7–9, 11, 17, 31–35, 36, 41, 50, 80, 103, 123, 131; on conviction by single witness, 39; trial of, xv, xvii, 1, 4–6, 15–16, 21, 39, 40, 43, 113–14, 165–66
Fisher, Robert (brother of Bishop Fisher), 12, 28, 33, 34, 156, 161, 162
FitzJames, John, chief justice of the King's Bench, 4, 15, 43, 72, 89, 101 n95, 122
Fitzwater, Sidney, judge, xvii, 119, 122, 124–30, 133, 134
FitzWilliam, Sir William, treasurer of the royal household, appointed to More's commission, but absent from the trial, 4, 176
Fortescue, John, *De laudibus legum Angliae* (1471), 40, 60
Fourth Lateran Council (1215), 29
Franklin, Benjamin, 133

Gairdner, James, 1, 3, 14, 20 n85, 28 nn119–21, 42 n184, 105 n73, 142 n4, 169
general law (*jus commune*), 19, 22, 22 n93
Gigas, Hieronymus (*fl.* 16th cent.), 58 n19, 60 n28
gloss, ordinary (*glossa ordinaria*), to canon law, 22 n94, 29, 57 n17, 63–64, 66 n64, 68 n73, 70
Gold, George, Tower servant, 32–34, 35, 94, 151–55, 157, 160–61, 164–65, 179
Gratian's *Decretum* (ca. 1140), 70; 54–68 *passim*
Gregory the Great, pope (590–604), 207
Guildhall Report, xv–xvii, 2, 8, 16, 20, 50, 107; charges against More, 7–11, 17–19, 31, 35–36, 81; and the jury, 35, 39; malice and, 31, 115; post-verdict events, 41, 44, 46; silence and, 9, 18–19, 76–78; on More's last words, 108; text and translation of, 186–95
Guy, John, 2, 3 n9, 5 n16, 6 n21, 55n7, 82, 96 n12, 97 n23, 99, 104, 105 n73, 106 n74, 107, 108 n92

Hales, Christopher, attorney-general, 4n14; prosecutor in More trial, 11, 16–17, 18–19, 21, 38, 100, 109, 115
heaven, More's wish to meet in, 41, 44, 69, 106, 193, 202, 208, 209
Helmholz, R. H., 53–70, 71, 72, 77, 79, 86, 112, 114, 118, 121
Henry VIII, against Luther and heresy, xi; annulment of his marriage to Catherine of Aragon and marriage to Anne Boleyn, xii, xiii n11, xiv, 18, 26, 27, 34, 64, 73–74, 92 n102, 133, *and see* Act of Succession; commissioning trial against More, 73; letter condemning More before his trial, 1, 83, 105, 169–71; and Reginald Pole, 19–20; as Supreme Head of Church in England, xii, xiv–xvi, 7, 14, 23, 25–26, 34, 36–37, 49–50, 52, 65, 73, 79–80, 84–85, 90–92, 116, 131, *and see* Act of Supremacy
heresy, heretics, 58 n21; death penalty and, xii; inquisitorial system and, 29–30; Luther and, xi; treatment of, 48; trials for, xiii, 47–48, *and see* St German
History of King Richard III (More), 99
Hitchcock, Elsie Vaughan, 6–7, 9 n36, 13 n55, 96 n14
Houghton, John, 14, 50, 72, 113, 140–42; 140–42; *see* Carthusian (Charterhouse) priors
House, Seymour Baker, xi n2, xii n5, 119, 134
Howard, Thomas, duke of Norfolk, 3–4, 41, 72, 141, 172, 173, 186, 192
Human Rights Act of 1998, 117

indictment of More, text of, xv, 3, 175–85; summarized, xv, 7–9, 79–80; divisions of, 6–9, 80; speculation on authorship of, 4–5, 10–11, 21, 24 n106, 26, 48–49, 80, 84, 120; presented to grand jury by the justices, 5; presented to More, 6; his plea of not guilty, with comments, 11, 81; parts of it allegedly dismissed by the judges (Derrett theory), xvi, 6, 9–10, 35–36, 40–41, 49–50, 81–82, 85; More's responses to the charges, 17–38, 87, 103–4; meaning of malice in, 11, 37, 71–72, 76, 80–81, 111, 123; attempt to void after verdict, 11, 42–43, 44–46, 51, 66–67, 71, 89, 122
indictments: of Bishop Fisher, 14n60, 16; of Carthusian priors and Richard Reynolds, 14; and Cromwell, 4; required plea in, 23–24; in treason trials, 10–11
Innocent III, pope (1198–1216), 29
Innocent IV, pope (1243–54), 56 n9
inquisitorial system, xiii; due process and, 48; fairness of, xiii; examining heretics in, 29; jury system vs., 46–48; silence and, 24, 25, 29–30
interpretation, rules of, 117
ius commune (body of canon law and Roman civil law), 22 n93, 55–56, 59–62, 70 n78, 79; *see jus commune*

Jackson, Robert, justice (d. 1954), 128
Joan of Arc, xi, xii–xiv
Jones, Edith, judge, xvii, 119–20, 121, 123, 127, 128, 130, 132–33
judicial review, 46–47, 72, 84, 90, 116, 128, 129
judges: independence of, 71, 85, 122, 128; jury system and, 46–47; obligations of, 46–47, 49–52, 63, 67, 68, 69, 84–85, 88, 118–19, 121; no power of nullifying verdict, 37, 89, 116; no power to strike down laws, 47, 68, 69, 116–17, 122
judges, of the Carthusian priors, 4, 14, 113, 118, 131; of the Carthusian monks, 4; of Bishop Fisher, 4, 15–16, 39, 43, 113–14, 118; of Thomas More, 3–5, 72; consultation with Cromwell, 4–5, 100; included some of his interrogators in the Tower, 30–31, 100; theory that they dismissed some charges, xvi, 6, 9–10, 35–36, 40–41, 49–50, 81–82, 85; as concluding to malice in More's silence 20–21, 31, 39, 50, 115, 118, 121–22; as discounting requirement of malice, 13–16, 76, 83, 85, 90, 93, 113, 117–18, 129, 131; response to his post-verdict challenge, 43–44, 47, 49–52, 69–70
judgment notwithstanding verdict, 59–60, 89
jury, grand, 3–7, 59, 79–81, 105
jury, petty: anonymity of, 127; charges of judges to, 115, 118–19, 121; fear of retribution, 127; jurors as witnesses, 39–40, cf. 59; in More's fable of "Company," 130–31; selection and duties of, 82–83, 85; verdicts of, 89, 113, 127, 131–32; verdicts nullified, 116; directed verdicts, 118
jury, of Bishop Fisher, 6, 43; of the Carthusian priors and Richard Reynolds, 14, 43, 113, 125, 126; of More, names of: 6 n21, 82, 173; indictment explained to, 10, 17, 35; addressed by More, 38; verdict of, 35–36, 38–39, 41, 48–51. 60, 64, 96 n15, 115–16, 121, 124, 126
jury system vs. inquisitorial system, xiii, 46–48, cf. 61
jus commune, as used by More (general law on a specific point), 19, 22, 22 n93, 207; modern meaning of the body of canon and civil law, *see ius commune*

Justinian, collections of Roman law (*Code, Digest, Institutes, Novels*), 70; 22 n95, 24 n106, 54–68 *passim*

Karlin, Louis, xvii, 71–93, 119, 122–23, 125–26, 127, 128, 130–31
Kelly, Henry Ansgar, xi–xiv nn, xvi, xvii, 1–52, 53, 71, 72, 75, 77, 83, 85, 114, 116, 119, 121, 131–32
King's Bench, justices of, 4, 9 n38, 10 n40, 11, 43, 48–49, 72, 84, 85, 89
Kingston, Sir William, 3, 149, 166, 173, 208–210, 220

Lambert, John, 30
Lambeth Palace, 94, 95, 97–98, 109
Latimer, Hugh, 99
Latta, Jennie, judge, 119, 120, 121–22, 125, 126–27, 127–28, 130, 131, 133, 134
Lawrence, Robert, 140–42; *see* Carthusian (Charterhouse) priors
Legatine trial of Henry VIII and Catherine of Aragon (1529), xiii and n11, xiv
Legh, Thomas, doctor of civil law, examiner of Tower servants, 17–18, 150, 155
legal death, More's argument of, 21
lenity, rule of, 132
Liber Sextus (Boniface VIII), 22, 29, 57, 58 n21
Life of Fisher (Young), 15, 39
Life of More (Rastell), 13, 14, 39, 52
Life of Pico (More), 92 n103
lieutenant, *see* Walsingham
litotes (understatement by negating contrary), 101–2
Locke, John, 120
Luther, Martin, xi, 133, cf., 6 n21
Lyndwood, William, 25 n107, 29

Magna Carta, xvi, 42, 66, 89, 117, 129, 207, 217
malice, modern and earlier legal meanings of, 52, 111–16, 117–19, 123, 129–34; refusing to plead interpreted as malice, 24, 26, 115; requirement and meaning of in Act of Succession (March 1534), 11, 73, 74; in Act of Treasons (Nov. 1534) and in More's indictment, xv–xvi, 7–8, 11–12, 25–26, 73–75, 80, 100, 111–16, 120, 123, 124, 129, 131, 134; as "surcharge," 49; Parliament's intention, 11–13, 33–34, 49, 50, 52, 75, 78, 80, 85, 93, 120, 132; defense against malice by Fisher, 16, 32–34, 43, 49, 113–14, 131; declared meaningless by judges in trials of Carthusian priors and Bishop Fisher, 14, 16, 43, 52, 113, 114, 131; defense against malice by More, xvii, 9 n37, 11, 31, 38, 41, 49–50, 71,76, 79, 81, 102–4, 106–7, 115, 133–34; prosecutor alleging malice in More's silence, 18–19, 21; the judges' agreement, 21, 31, 39, 41, 50–52, 88, 115, 117, 121–22, or judges' rejection of need to prove malice, 50–52, 83, 85, 117–18
A Man for All Seasons (Bolt), xi, xvi, 4, 5, 119
Mantel, Hilary, xii
Marius, Richard, 96, 98, 99–100, 107 n85
Martin V, pope (1417–31), 30
martyrdom, xii–xiv
Mary Queen of Scots, xii
Mary Tudor, queen of England (1553–58), xvi, 13
McCutcheon, Elizabeth, xvii, 94–110, 95 n5, 101 n45
Middlemore, Humphrey, 4, 5, 6, 148–49; *see* Carthusian (Charterhouse) monks
Miranda ruling (1966), 29
misprision of treason, offense for speaking against the succession or refusing oath (Act of Succession, Jan.–Mar. 1534) with penalty of life imprisonment, xiv, 11–12, 73–74; More and, 13, 73, 76, 78, 90, 100; in modern law, 75
Model Rules of Professional Conduct, 87–88
Montague, Henry, lord, *see* Pole
More, Sir John, xiv
More, Thomas, early career, xiv; chancellor (1529), xiv; resigned upon submission of clergy (1532), xiv, 92; and heretics, xii, defended bishops' treatment of heresy suspects against St German (1533), xiii, 13 n49, 30, 40, 47–48, 67–68; refused oath of succession, sent to Tower (April 1534), xiv, 28, 90, 91–92, 98–99, 100; convicted of misprision of treason by act of attainder (Nov.–Dec. 1534), xiv, 13, 73, 76; interrogated in Tower on king's title of Supreme Head of English Church (April–June 1535), xvii, 7–8, 21, 28–30, 31–32, 34–35; letters to Margaret Roper, 26, 32, 90, 92, 94–110; letters to and from Bishop Fisher, 7–8, 31–35; conversation with Richard Rich (12 June 1535), xv–xvi, 8, 35–38, 157–59, *see* Rich; tried and found guilty of impugning the king's supremacy (1 July 1535), *see* trial of Thomas More; words before death by beheading (6 July 1535), 107–8; beatified (1886), xii; canonized (1935), xv; modern reputation, xi–xiv
"motion," 18th-century term, 9; motion in arrest of judgment, xvi–xvii, 9, 44–46, 51, 53, 70, 81, 89, 116

natural law, Act of Supremacy and, 66–69; Act of Treasons and, 55; canon law and, 64; conscience and, 55, 63–65; positive law and, 54; in practice, 55; proof, necessity of and, 59–65; silence and, 55, 56–59; two-witness requirement and, 55, 86; US Constitution and, 68

Nemo tenetur prodere seipsum, 56, 79

Newdigate, Sebastian, 4, 5, 6, 148–49; *see* Carthusian (Charterhouse) monks

Norfolk, *see* Howard, Thomas

notoriety in court, 30, 54, cf. 25

Novitates quaedam, 18

Oakley, David, xvii, 71–93, 119, 134

oath, coronation, 89; required for pleading in inquisitions, but not in common-law trials, 24, 58 n21; self-incriminating, 56 n9; taken by witnesses in trials, 38, 85; of jurors, 40, 85; obligation to respond to required oaths, 78, cf. 58; no oaths allowed for defendant and defense witnesses, 86 n75; oaths of members of Parliament as sworn against the Church, 90

oaths under Henry VIII: required by Act of Succession (Jan.–Mar. 1534), xiv, 13, 74, 91; oath of succession imposed on More rejected by him as not conforming to Act of Succession, xiv, 26–27, 73, 74n14, 76–78, 90, 92, 97–100, 106, 129, 130; new oath formulated in Act of Oath of Succession (Nov.–Dec. 1534), 13, 26–27, 74 n14, 76, 77, 91–92; oath affirming king's supremacy imposed on friars and new bishops (April 1534), 27–28; oath not required by Act of Supremacy (Nov.–Dec. 1534) or Act of Treasons (Nov.–Dec. 1534), xiv, 26–28, 74; Fisher's concern about, 28; discussed by More's interrogators, 28; More invited to take oath on king's supremacy, but he declines all oaths (3 June 1535), 28, 97, 104; More's oath after verdict (takes God as witness), 41

Palmer, Master, Cromwell's servant, 38, 157–58, 203

Palmer, Sir Thomas, juror, 6 n21, 173

Paris News Letter, xv, 2 n5, 20, 107, 108

Parliament, *see* acts

Parmiter, Geoffrey de C., 7, 47, 81, 87, 89

Parnell, John, gentleman, member of More's petty jury, 6 n21, 173; perhaps More's Lutheran opponent, 6 n21, 82

Parsons, Robert, SJ (d. 1610), 60

Paul, St, at stoning of St Stephen, 41, 44, 69; 1 Corinthians, 91, 207; Romans, 104–5

peine forte et dure, 58 n21, cf. 24

Penn, William, 113, 126

perjury, xvi, 17, 24, 36. 38, 119, 120, 122, 123

Pole, Henry, lord (baron) Montague, 4, 20; not present at trial, 4, 20; dismay at Reginald's opposition, 20

Pole, Reginald, brother of Lord Montague, 4; cousin of Henry VIII, future cardinal and archbishop of Canterbury, xvi, 19n83; shocked reaction to deaths of Fisher and More, 20; his account of More's trial (1536), xvi, 16, 20–21, 35–36, 196–202; based on eyewitness report, xvi, 8; addressed to Henry VIII, 8n34; on the charge of silence, 8, 10, 19–21, 31, 50, 52, 77 n33, 88; on the judges' finding of malice, 8, 21, 31, 39, 50, 52, 77 n33, 88, 115, 117, 121; on the verdict, 39; on More's statement after the verdict, xvi, 41–42, 44, 46

pope, primacy of, xii, 23, 29, 30, 68–69, 91, 92–93, 104

presumption, legal, 22 n94, 59, 60, 62, 74, 77, 83, 89–90, 112, 117; of innocence, 59, 83

Queen's Bench, William Rastell as justice of, 13, 119

Qui tacet consentire videtur, in Boniface VIII's *Liber Sextus* (1298), 22, 57; cited by Archbishop Warham (1531), 23; cited by More in his trial, 19 n80, 21, 22, 57, 189, 200

Rastell, William, 12–13, 14–15, 43, 52, 97, 98, 109, 113, 114, 131

Reformation, 77, 91

Reynolds, E. E., 3, 10, 51–52, 65

Reynolds, Richard, Bridgettine monk, trial of with Carthusian priors, xv, 4, 6–7, 14, 42, 72, 77, 113, 131, 140–42; executed by hanging, drawing, and quartering, May 4, 1535, 142; beatified (1886), xii; canonized (1970), xv

Rich, Richard, as solicitor-general, 17; one of the Council visitors to More in Tower, 2–3 May 1535, 100, 109; alleged interlocutor of Fisher in Tower, 15–16; conversation with More in Tower on 12 June 1535: his (distorted) report of in PRO, xvi, 36–37, 49, 52; More's report of it to Fisher, 34, 37–38, 107; More's version in Roper, xvi, 36, 37–38, 50, 51; indictment's charge that More spoke to him against king's supremacy, 8, 10, 35–38, 40–41, 50, 80, 85, 97; charge reported only by Roper, 9, 35–36; Derrett's theory that it was the only charge prosecuted, *see* indictment; as possible prosecutor in More's trial, 17, 87; as witness in More's trial, 17–18, 38, 39, 60, 78, 86, 119–24, 126; More's denial and defense, xvi, 38, 51–52, 60, 76, 115, 131, 133

Roman (civil) law, *see* Justinian

Roman Martyrology, xiii

Roper, Margaret, daughter of Thomas, wife of William Roper, 34, 76–77, 160, 164; correspondence with More, 26, 32, 92, 94–110, 142–44, 193–94

Roper, William, More's son-in-law, xv; his *Life of More*, 9 n36, 10 n40, 35, 46, 97, 108; on the oath of succession, 92; the account of More's trial, xv; written 20 years later, xv, 9; his informers, 9, 44; reports only the Richard Rich charge, xvi, 9–10, 35, 81–82, 86, 124; More's response to the charge, 11, 44n188; gives More's version of his conversation with Rich, xvi, 36, 37; on Rich's testimony, 38; on More's defense against Rich, 17, 38, 39; on More's argument about malice, 76, 113; on More's post-verdict comments, xvi–xvii, 42, 44–45, 46, 49, 50, 69, 106; on the responses of the judges, 43–44, 89, 101 n45, 122

Rota (papal tribunal), 67

R. v. Ponting, 113

R. v. Throckmorton, 113

St German, Christopher, on common-law trials, 46; dispute with More on heresy proceedings, xiii, 12 n49, 30, 40, 46, 47–48, 67–68

Scroggs, Sir William, lord chief justice (d. 1683), 63, 64

separation-of-powers doctrine, 84

Sext (Boniface VIII), 22, 29, 57, 58 n21

silence, in general:
as affirmation, 19 n80, 22, 23, 29, 57; ambiguous, 116, 124; and conscientious objection, 78 n35; as crime or sin, 23–25, 57–59; danger of, 107; multiple meanings of, 22 n94; as opposition (Rich), 29–30, 107

right to remain silent before arraignment, in American law, 29; in inquisitorial procedure, 25, 29–30; no such right in early common-law trials, 77, 87; right to silence to avoid self-incrimination, 24–25, 29–30, 55, 56–59, cf. 47, 87, 104; as response to unlawful questioning, 25

obligations to break silence, 18–19, 23–30, 57–59, 69, 78, 79; Pole breaks silence, 20

silence and acts of Parliament: silence (refusal to take oath) punished as misprision of treason, 74, 77; no punishment stated for silence with regard to supremacy, 74

silence in trial of Thomas More:
in indictment: charged with malicious silence, xv–xvi, 7–10, 18, 80; Derrett's theory of dismissal, 11, 50, 123–24; Fisher's silence, 7, 80

More's response: confesses silence, 30–31, 55, 131; asserts that it falls outside statute, 18, 49, 52, 55, 76, 85, 88, 116, 122, 123–24, 131, 134; signifies assent, 19, 21–23, 57–58, 77, 89–90; obligation to break silence superseded by conscience, 19, 77, 92, cf. 122–23; his silence as speaking volumes, 125, 130; says he broke silence to no one, especially Rich, 38; breaks silence after verdict, 43

prosecutor: signifies malice, 18–19, 21, 77, 115; shows opposition (Rich), 34

judges: signifies malice (Pole's account), 20–21, 31, 39, 50, 115, 118, 121–22

jury: perhaps takes silence as corroborating evidence, 78, 81, 124, cf. 116; perhaps convicts on, 39, 40–41 122

Southwell, Sir Richard, 38, 158, 168, 203, 206

Spelman, John, justice of the King's Bench, judge at trials of Carthusians, Fisher, and More, 4, 15; on allegations of arrest of judgment, 45; report on More's trial, xvi, xvii, 2, 8, 10, 11, 24, 36, 44, 45–46, 49, 50, 85, 195

Star Chamber, 28, 134, 147

statute, *see* act

statutory interpretation by judges, 139–40

submission of the clergy (1532), xiv, 84–85, 92

Submission of the Clergy and Restraint of Appeals, Act of (Jan.–Mar. 1534), 85

Supreme Court, California, 88; United States, 117, 122, 128

Susanna and the Elders (in Catholic Bibles, Daniel 13; in Protestant Bibles, in the Apocrypha), 60

torture, 60, 61, 79

Tower servants, interrogations of, 12, 16, 17–18, 32–33, 150–57

treason (= high treason), death penalty and, xiv; malice and, 74, 93; misprision of, xiv, 73, 74; modern law and, 74–75; silence and, 10; trials for, 10–11, 17, 39, 85–86 *and see* trial of Thomas More, trials; US Constitution and, 74–75, 86. *See also* Act of Treasons (Nov.–Dec. 1534)

A Treatise Concerning the Difference Between the Spiritualty and Temporalty (St German), 47–48
Tregonwell, John, doctor of civil law, 100, 109, 110, 142
Trevor-Roper, Hugh, xi, 10 n40
trial of Thomas More, differing accounts of, xv, xv–xvi, xvi; docudrama of, xvii, 210–21; evidence in, 17–18, 39–40, 86–87, 116–18; judicial commentary on, 111–35; as miscarriage of justice, xv, 1, 51, 72, 119–22, 128, 129; modern assessments of, xvi–xvii, 46–52; and modern law, 71–93; and natural law, 53–70
trial of Thomas More, events of:
  commissioned (Saturday, June 26, 1535), 3; names of judges, 3–4; the seven justices on the panel present indictment to grand jury (Monday, June 28), 4–5; contents of indictment, *see* indictment; grand jury finds it a true bill (Monday, June 28); More charged, pleads not guilty (Wednesday, July 1), 4; More reserves right to a-void indictment after verdict, 11; petty jury selected and impaneled (Wednesday, July 1), 4, 16, 82; names of jurors, 6 n21, 82, 173; indictment presumably explained to them by the prosecutor, Attorney-General Sir Christopher Hales, 16–17; charge of malicious silence, and More's defense, 18–31; judges' alleged intervention, 20–21, 31, 39, 50, 115, 118, 121–22, *see also* malice, silence; charges of collusion with Bishop Fisher, and More's defense, 31–35; Richard Rich's testimony and More's defense, 35–38; the jury's verdict of guilty, 38–41; More's comments after the verdict, 41–46; judges' reactions, 43–44; sentence of death by hanging, drawing, and quartering, 41, 42, 43–44, 174–75
trials, of Anne Boleyn, annulment of marriage to Henry VIII (1536), xiii n11; for treason (1536), xiii n11, 1; of Carthusian (Charterhouse) monks (June 1–11, 1535), xv, 4, 5, 13, 52, 148–49; of Carthusian priors and Bridgettine monk Reynolds (Apr. 23–29, 1535), xv, 4, 13, 14, 43, 50, 52, 72, 113–15, 118, 125, 131, 140–42; of Lord Dacre of the North (1534), 24; of Bishop John Fisher (June 1–17, 1535), *see* Fisher; of heretics, xiii, 46–47, *see also* St German; of Joan of Arc (1431), xiii–xiv, canonization of (1892ff), xi, xii; Legatine, of marriage of Henry VIII and Catherine of Aragon (1529), xiii and n12, xiv; of Mary Queen of Scots (1586), xii; of Thomas More (June 26–July 1, 1535), *see* trial of Thomas More
Tugendhat, Sir Michael, xvii, 111–19, 120–21, 121, 123–24, 124–25, 126, 129–30, 132, 134–35
two-edged sword analogy, 7–8, 31–32, 35, 51, 103–4, 123

United States v. Brown, 73
Utopia (More), xi

verdict, directed, 48, 59; judgment notwithstanding verdict, 59–60, 89; nullification of, 116–18, *see* motion in arrest of judgment; *and see* jury, petty; trial of Thomas More
Vives, Juan Luis, 107

Walsingham, Sir Edmund, lieutenant to the constable of the Tower (Sir William Kingston), 3, 33–35, 96, 141–42, 144, 149–65, 173–74
Warham, William, archbishop of Canterbury, 23
Webster, Augustine, 140–42; *see* Carthusian (Charterhouse) priors
Wegemer, Gerard, xvii, 63 n45, 69 n76, 85 n65, 107 n87
Wigmore, John Henry (d. 1943), 61
Wilson, Nicholas, former king's chaplain, 98 n24, 99, 108
Wilson, Richard, Bishop Fisher's servant in the Tower, 12, 16, 32–33, 34, 150, 151, 152, 154, 156, 162–63
witnesses, eyewitnesses of More's trial, xv–xvii, 2, 5, 8–9, 13, 20 n97, 41, 44; defense witnesses, little used, 86; judge as (constituting notoriety), 25, 30; jurors as, 39–40, 60–61, 126, More on, 40; prosecution witnesses, 6 n20, modern law on, 87–88; More's indictment based on, 80; in Fisher's trial, 15, 39, 43; in More's trial, 17, 38, 60, 86, 87, potential others, including some of his judges, 17–18, 30–31, 123; single-witness conviction, 60–62, 86, Fisher on, 39; two-witness requirement, 48, 55, 60–63, 74, 75, 86, 90
Wolf Hall (Mantel), xii
Wolsey, Thomas, cardinal, xiv, xvii, 85
Wood, John, More's servant in the Tower, 33, 35, 95, 151, 155, 156
Wycliffites, 30

Young, John, supposed author of *Life of Fisher*, 15

www.ingramcontent.com/pod-product-compliance
Lightning Source LLC
Chambersburg PA
CBHW051609230426
43668CB00013B/2039